THE ZONDERVAN 2023 PASTOR'S ANNUAL

For a *FREE* downloadable copy of the book,
please visit Zondervan.com/p/zpa2023/.

THE ZONDERVAN PASTOR'S ANNUAL 2023

An Idea and Resource Book

T. T. Crabtree

ZONDERVAN REFLECTIVE

ZONDERVAN REFLECTIVE

The Zondervan 2023 Pastor's Annual

Requests for information should be addressed to:
Zondervan, *3900 Sparks Dr. SE, Grand Rapids, Michigan 49546*

Zondervan titles may be purchased in bulk for educational, business, fundraising, or sales promotional use. For information, please email SpecialMarkets@Zondervan.com.

Much of the contents of this book was previously published in *The Zondervan 1983 Pastor's Annual.*

ISBN 978-0-310-13593-7 (softcover)

ISBN 978-0-310-13594-4 (ebook)

Cover design: Angela Grit
Cover photo: © Jenny Sturm / Shutterstock
Interior design: Sue Vandenberg Koppenol

Printed in the United States of America

22 23 24 25 26 27 28 29 30 31 32 /TRM/ 15 14 13 12 11 10 9 8 7 6 5 4 3 2 1

Contents

PREFACE

Favorable comments from ministers who serve in several different types of churches suggest that the *Pastor's Annual* provides valuable assistance to many busy pastors as they seek to improve the quality, freshness, and variety of their pulpit ministry. To be of service to fellow pastors in their continuing quest to obey our Lord's command to Peter, "Feed my sheep," is a calling to which I respond with gratitude.

I pray that this issue of the *Pastor's Annual* will be blessed by our Lord in helping each pastor to plan and produce a preaching program that will better meet the spiritual needs of his or her congregation.

This issue contains series of sermons by several contributing authors who have been effective contemporary preachers and successful pastors. Each author is listed with his sermons by date in the section titled "Contributing Authors." I accept responsibility for those sermons not listed there.

This issue of the *Pastor's Annual* is dedicated to the Lord with a prayer that he will bless these efforts to let the Holy Spirit lead us in preparing a planned preaching program for the year.

Contributing Authors

Tom S. Brandon	AM	January 1, 8, 15, 22, 29
		February 5, 19, 26
		April 23
Harold T. Bryson	PM	March 5, 12, 19, 26
		September 6, 13, 20, 27
		October 4, 11, 18, 25
		November 1, 8, 15, 22, 29
		December 6, 13, 20, 27, 31
Robert G. Campbell	AM	July 9, 16, 23, 30
		August 6, 13, 20, 27
James E. Carter	AM	June 7, 14, 21, 28
	PM	December 3, 10, 17, 24
Bennie Cole Crabtree		Sentence Sermonettes
T. T. Crabtree		All messages except those indicated otherwise
W. T. Holland	PM	April 2, 9, 16, 23, 30
		July 2, 9, 16, 23, 30
		August 6, 13, 20, 27
		October 29
		November 5, 12, 26, 29
David L. Jenkins	PM	January 4, 11, 18, 25
		February 1, 8, 15, 22
		March 1, 8, 15, 22, 29
		Miscellaneous Helps
D. L. Lowrie	PM	May 7, 14, 21, 28
		June 4, 11, 18, 25
		September 3, 10, 17, 24
		October 1, 8, 15, 22
Jerold R. McBride	PM	January 1, 8, 15, 22, 29
Charles R. Wade	AM	May 7, 14, 21, 28
		June 4, 11, 18
Bill Whittaker	AM	February 12
		March 5, 12, 19, 26
		April 2, 9, 16, 30
Fred M. Wood	AM	November 5, 12, 19, 26
	PM	April 5, 12, 19, 26
		May 3, 10, 17, 24, 31

SUGGESTED PREACHING PROGRAM FOR THE MONTH OF JANUARY

■ Sunday Mornings

January is a time of new beginnings, and an appropriate response is one of celebration and praise for life with all of its opportunities. The theme for the January Sunday morning sermons is "Celebrating the Life That Christ Makes Possible."

■ Sunday Evenings

The four gospels contain the written testimony of inspired writers who report not only the events in Jesus' life but also the significance of those events. Paul's letters were written to exalt Jesus Christ and to explain the meaning of his life and teachings. They were also written to meet the great needs of the early disciples. "The Central Theme of the Great Apostle" is the theme for a series of sermons based on five of Paul's major letters.

■ Wednesday Evenings

Every believer needs to know what the Bible says about spiritual issues. For the next three months, "What the Bible Says" will be the theme of the Wednesday evening sermons.

SUNDAY MORNING, JANUARY 1

Title: Finding the Lost Book

Text: "Hilkiah the high priest said unto Shaphan the scribe, I have found the book of the law in the house of the LORD" **(2 Kings 22:8)**.

Scripture Reading: 2 Kings 22

Hymns: "O Worship the King," Grant
"Word of God, across the Ages," Blanchard
"Break Thou the Bread of Life," Lathbury and Gross

Offertory Prayer: Heavenly Father, your Holy Word tells us to bring our whole tithe into your storehouse so that your work may be accomplished on earth. We humbly and gratefully offer to you our tithes and offerings this day. Thank you for the privilege. May your name be honored through Christ, our Savior and Lord. Amen.

Introduction

During the reign of King Josiah a great discovery was made. Hilkiah the priest announced to Shaphan the scribe, during the time that the temple was being repaired, "I have found the book of the law in the house of the LORD" (2 Kings 22:8).

From that simple statement occurs one of the most interesting happenings in the Old Testament. Not only did this discovery have significance then, but it has a message for now. Finding the lost book, or rediscovering the Bible, is an especially appropriate message for the beginning of a new year. We can consider this great discovery in two ways.

I. Rediscovering the Bible historically.

A. *The discovery of the lost book.*

1. The times. Josiah was the grandson of Manasseh, one of the wickedest kings of Judah. During his reign, the nation was flooded with idolatry and immorality. The worship of Baal was restored in a land that was filled with sorcerers, mediums, and star worshipers. Violence reigned; the temple of God was neglected. The king and the people had heard the prophets' words, but they rebelled against the God of their fathers.
2. The king. Then along came Josiah. He was eight years old when he was crowned king, and he reigned thirty-one years. He was righteous before the Lord, loyal to his heritage, and dedicated to God throughout his reign. The influence of godly people prompted him to seek the Lord and repair the temple. While this was happening, the lost book was found.
3. The book. The book that Hilkiah found was called "the book of the law" and was either part or all of the book of Deuteronomy. It was God's Word discovered anew! It had been lost for some time under a pile of stones in the temple or in one of the chambers, where it had remained unnoticed for years. Wherever it was, it is quite evident that the people of God had not been reading the Scriptures as they should have been.

B. *The dynamic response to its discovery.* Josiah's response is described in four ways.

1. Josiah heard it read (2 Kings 22:11). The first step toward a personal discovery of God's Word is a willingness to read it or hear it read. Josiah's heart was tender, and he humbled himself before the Lord.
2. Josiah responded to the message of the book (2 Kings 22:11). He was so moved by what he heard that he tore his clothes in grief and repentance.
3. Josiah read the book to all the people (2 Kings 23:1–2). God spoke to their hearts as he did to Josiah's. They were convicted of forgotten vows, and they renewed the covenant of the nation to the Lord.
4. Revival came in response to finding the book. The temple was cleansed of heathen worship, and the land was cleansed of idolatry.

Immorality was stamped out. The observance of the Passover was renewed. Rediscovering God's book brought new leadership, new purpose, and a new spirit of worship to the people.

May we remember that the Word of God is powerful! It kindles fire in our hearts. It leads to life and creates light by which to live. It is God's Word to us!

Many people seem to have lost their Bibles today. Christians can lose their Bibles not just physically but spiritually. If you are not reading your Bible with meaning, it is as lost to you as was the Word of God to the people of Judah. You may "lose your Bible" by turning aside to wealth, pleasure, ambition, or success. But you can rediscover God's Word! Open your Bible and begin to read it, and a new spiritual day will be yours.

II. Rediscovering the Bible presently.

You can rediscover the Bible in three ways.

A. *Rediscover the Bible authoritatively*. The Bible is not an authority on science or history; it is an authority on spiritual things. It is not just a book of religion; it is divine revelation. It is the book of redemption, the book of divine inspiration. It reveals God to us!

The Bible is our final authority in life, the authoritative basis of our faith. Johann Wolfgang von Goethe said, "When I go to hear a preacher preach, I may not agree with what he says, but I want him to believe it." We need something to stand on for our faith and practice. The Bible is the answer.

B. *Rediscover the Bible personally*. It has the power to speak to us personally. The Holy Spirit will open the Word to our hearts as we open our hearts to the Word. Jesus did this for the disciples on the road to Emmaus as he explained the Scriptures about his coming. When their eyes were opened, they recognized him and said, "Did not our heart burn within us, while he talked with us by the way?" (Luke 24:32). Jesus still does that today in our hearts through the Spirit.

C. *Rediscover the Bible practically*. One goal for our lives should be a renewed emphasis on the Bible.

1. Hear it. Proverbs 1:5 says, "A wise man will hear, and will increase learning."
2. Read it. We forget 90 to 95 percent of what we hear. So read the Bible for yourself. Read it with a searching spirit. Read it in faith. Read it for fellowship with the heavenly Father. Read it prayerfully.
3. Study it. We forget 70 percent of what we read. So study the Scriptures personally using a notebook to take notes on what you discover. Study it in Sunday school. Study it whenever you have an opportunity.
4. Memorize it. Hide it in your heart. Memorize verses, chapters, whole sections of Scripture. Set a goal to commit it to memory.

5. Meditate on it. The psalmist said that the person who meditates on the Word day and night is blessed (Ps. 1:2). Get up in the morning thinking about it. Go to bed at night meditating on it.

Conclusion

The Bible becomes a living book to us when we experience its truth and life for ourselves. Bishop E. Berggrav of the Lutheran Church in Norway spent most of World War II in a Nazi concentration camp. It was there that he found Christ in the pages of the Bible. His reading it aloud brought the reality of Christ to his life so that his faith was restored and his spirit renewed.

Discover the Bible for yourself. Commit yourself to God's Word this year. It brings new life!

Sunday Evening, January 1

Title: Believe and Behave

Text: "And be not conformed to this world: but be ye transformed by the renewing of your mind, that ye may prove what is that good, and acceptable, and perfect will of God" **(Rom. 12:2)**.

Scripture Reading: Romans 1:16; 12:2

Introduction

"Believe and behave" is the central theme of the book of Romans. Paul contends that what we believe has everything to do with how we behave. If our belief is wrong, our behavior will be wrong. And if our behavior is wrong, our belief cannot be right. Our behavior says more about our beliefs than does our verbal testimony or written creed.

We often tend to emphasize either belief or behavior to the exclusion of the other, which makes for a partial and imbalanced Christianity. Paul, a man of balanced faith, assigned equal importance to each. The first eleven chapters of Romans deal with belief and the last five with behavior.

In the winter of AD 57–58, Paul was in Corinth at the close of his third missionary journey. He was soon to return to Jerusalem with an offering for the poor. A woman named Phoebe, who lived in a suburb of Corinth, was soon to sail to Rome. Paul saw an opportunity to send this letter to the church of Rome with her.

Because there was no postal service in the Roman Empire except for government business, personal letters had to be carried by friends. Paul was not sure he would get away from Jerusalem alive. Desiring to leave a written explanation of the gospel of salvation in the hands of the Christians at Rome, he wrote this letter, which Phoebe delivered safely to the church.

Realizing that this may be his only communication with the church so strategically located in the capital of the world, he stressed what he must have felt to be the two cardinal truths of the Christian faith—the belief that results *in* salvation and the behavior that results *from* salvation.

I. The belief that results in salvation (Rom. 1:16).

After a few brief words of introduction, Paul proclaimed, "For I am not ashamed of the gospel of Christ" (Rom. 1:16). What kind of belief enables us to receive salvation?

A. *Belief in the unlimited power of salvation.* Paul said that he was proud of the gospel of salvation. He considered himself privileged to preach it. What a strange statement in light of all that had recently happened to him! At Philippi he had been jailed, at Thessalonica he had been expelled, at Berea he had been smuggled out, and at Athens he had been scorned.

   The gospel Paul preached in Corinth was considered "foolishness" by the Greeks and a "stumblingblock" by the Jews (1 Cor. 1:23). In spite of the opposition, Paul said the gospel is "the power of God unto salvation" (Rom. 1:16). The unlimited power of the gospel made Paul victorious over every obstacle in his path.

   When Paul spoke of "the power of God unto salvation," he spoke from personal experience. At first he hated the Christian faith; his heart was calloused against the call of God. He even planned a journey to Damascus to arrest and persecute those who were followers of Christ.

   If ever a man was unbending in his conviction, Paul was that man. Nothing could change him—until he encountered the person of Jesus Christ. It was then he discovered the unlimited power of God that can change any person anywhere in any condition! The belief that results in salvation is a belief in the unlimited power of salvation.

B. *Belief in the unrestricted availability of salvation.* Paul proclaimed that this salvation is available to all who believe. Why did Paul say, "To the Jew first"? Because they were in the immediate proximity and had the best religious background for accepting the gospel. Then he said, "And also to the Greek." The gospel reached Greeks as well as Jews.

   The Greeks were the intellectuals of the first century and were often cynical. Stoicism and Epicureanism were four hundred years old, and in each the excitement had almost gone out of the movements and decay had set in. Greek-Roman religion in the first century was confused and chaotic, with so many gods and deities that cities even maintained "catch-all" shrines to provide for deities that might have been overlooked.

   What caused Greeks to become Christians? The answer is revealed in the opening of Paul's address on Mars Hill: "The God who made the world and everything in it is the Lord of heaven and earth and does not live in temples built by human hands" (Acts 17:24 NIV). In place of the randomness that Athens offered, Paul told of a God who can speak for himself and who is not contained in human thought. Jesus provides an unrestricted, universally available salvation.

In his letter to the church at Rome, Paul said that salvation is available without restriction because of several factors.

1. The *need* that requires it. "For all have sinned, and come short of the glory of God" (3:23). Since all have sinned, salvation is available to all. It is available without restriction because people have sinned without exception.
2. The *grace* that provides it. "For the wages of sin is death; but the gift of God is eternal life through Jesus Christ our Lord" (6:23). Salvation is available without restriction, not because of human goodness but because of God's grace. If salvation were available on the basis of our goodness, it could not be available without restriction.
3. The *price* that purchased it. "But God commendeth his love toward us, in that, while we were yet sinners, Christ died for us" (5:8). How could God "prove his love to us" through the death of Christ? Because "God was in Christ reconciling the world unto himself" (2 Cor. 5:19). Christ died *for us.* He died on our behalf—voluntarily. He said, "I lay down my life . . . no man takes it from me" (John 10:17–18).

   A little boy made a toy boat, but soon he lost it in the street gutter in front of his home. It was swept down a sewer. Later he saw it in a window of a pawn shop. He saved his pennies and paid one dollar for his boat. As he left the shop, he said, " 'Little boat, you're mine twice—I made you and I bought you."

   We are God's twice. He made us and he purchased us.
4. The *love* that ensures it. Robert Bruce, a disciple of John Knox, died on July 27, 1631. That morning he had come to breakfast and his younger daughter sat by his side.

> As he mused in silence, suddenly he cried: "Hold, daughter, hold; my Master calleth me." He asked that the Bible should be brought, but his sight failed him and he could not read. "Cast me up the eighth of Romans," cried he, and he repeated much of the latter portion of this Scripture till he came to the last two verses: "'I am persuaded that neither death, nor life, nor angels, nor principalities, nor powers, nor things present, nor things to come, nor height, nor depth, nor any other creature, shall be able to separate us from the love of God which is

> in Christ Jesus our Lord.' Set my finger on these words," said the blind, dying man; "God be with you, my children. I have breakfasted with you, and shall sup with my Lord Jesus this night. I die believing in these words" (Marcus Loane, *The Hope of Glory* [Waco: Word, 1969], 160).

For belief to be valid, it must accompany the right behavior.

II. The behavior that results from salvation (Rom. 12:1–2; 13:1–5; 14:21; 15:1–3).

Belief results *in* salvation—behavior results *from* salvation. In other words, belief saves us and behavior proves that we are saved. Paul pointed out that our belief in the gospel will affect three areas of our behavior.

A. *Our conduct (Rom. 12:1–2).* "I beseech you therefore. . . ." Whenever we see the word *therefore* in Scripture, we should ask, "What is it 'there for'?" It always looks back on what has been said. Paul was saying, "In light of the belief that results *in* salvation, I now set forth the behavior that results *from* salvation. You have believed; therefore, you should behave!" He did not say, "I command you!" He said, "I beseech you." After all, he was writing to those who had already believed in Christ and thus should of their own volition have been behaving as believers.

There may be many things we cannot do and much we cannot give, but by the grace of God we can behave!

1. Our conduct should be voluntary—"present your bodies" (v. 1).
2. Our conduct should refuse to be molded by others. "Be not conformed" (v. 2). Christians don't take on the color of their social environment. Like their Savior, Christians are distinctively different from those about them.
3. Our conduct should come from within. "But be ye transformed by the renewing of your mind" (v. 2). Until we have genuine belief that results in salvation, we lack the power within to behave. But when Christ comes into our lives, we become new creatures. Christ becomes the center of our lives.

B. *Our citizenship (Rom. 13:1–5).* Our citizenship—the way we relate to the guidelines set forth by our forefathers in our country's Constitution—may be the greatest testimony we have. In God's economy there is no place for the destructive spirit of rebellion and anarchy.

C. *Our concern (Rom. 14:21; 15:1–3).* In chapter 14 Paul wrote that salvation enables Christians to place the concerns of others above their own selfish interests. When we reach this level of behavior, the criteria is no longer merely "Is it right or wrong?" but rather "Will it cause my brother to stumble?"

If our belief in Christ is genuine, we will behave as Christ would. We won't be out to please ourselves, to prove our point, or to insist on our own way. Rather, our lives will be characterized by the Christian love of which Paul spoke in 1 Corinthians 13: "Love is patient, love is kind. . . . It does not dishonor others, it is not self-seeking, it is not easily angered, it keeps no record of wrongs" (vv. 4–5 NIV).

Conclusion

Believe and behave! That's the message of the book of Romans. "Believe *and* behave"—not "Believe *or* behave." When we grasp *both* of these truths so that they are translated into our everyday lives, then Paul's letter to the church at Rome has accomplished its purpose both in the church in centuries past and in our time.

WEDNESDAY EVENING, JANUARY 4

Title: What the Bible Says about Itself

Text: "For the word of God is quick, and powerful, and sharper than any twoedged sword, . . . and is a discerner of the thoughts and intents of the heart" **(Heb. 4:12)**.

Scripture Reading: Hebrews 4:12

Introduction

In recent years there has been considerable division among Christians of all persuasions in regard to the Bible and its contents. Some claim that only parts of it are inspired. Others declare that its thoughts are inspired but not its language. Theological terminology has been used to describe certain concepts regarding the Bible and its contents, such as *verbal inspiration, plenary inspiration, inerrancy*, and so forth.

Perhaps the safest course to pursue is to let the Bible speak for itself. We should always be wary of those persuasions that lead toward bibliolatry, or the worship of the Bible as though it were a good-luck charm. The important thing about the Scriptures is that they reveal to humans what God is like and how we can be reconciled to God through his Son Jesus Christ.

I. What the Scriptures are called.

A. *The Word of God (Heb. 4:12).* As the Word of God, the Scriptures are an extension of God's being (John 1:1). They are more than just what God "said." They are the essence of his nature.

B. *The Word of truth (James 1:18).* Jesus said, "I am the way, the truth, and the life." God's Word does not merely contain truth; it *is* absolute truth. Jesus said, "Ye shall know the truth, and the truth shall make you free" (John 8:32).

C. *The oracles of God (Rom. 3:2).* Pagans referred to messages from their gods as "oracles." Paul was writing to Roman Christians (many of whom were only recently out of paganism), explaining to them that the messages of the *true* God (which he called "oracles") were first given to the Jews.

D. *The Word (James 1:21–23).* The "engrafted word" suggests the personification of Jesus Christ, who is "in you" in the person of the Holy Spirit.
E. *Holy Scriptures (Rom. 1:2).* They are holy because they are uniquely God's words.
F. *Sword of the Spirit (Eph. 6:17).* As the "sword," the Word of God serves as the Christian's defense against Satan. The Holy Spirit makes the Word powerful in the heart of believers. He "activates" it.

II. How the Scriptures are described.

A. *They are authoritative (Ps. 19:7–8).* Because they are the words of God, they contain absolute authority.
B. *They are inspired (2 Tim. 3:16–17).* They are God-breathed, and thus they communicate to us the very personality of God.
C. *They are "sharp" (Heb. 4:12).* "For the word of God is quick, and powerful, and sharper than any twoedged sword, piercing even to the dividing asunder of soul and spirit" (Heb. 4:12). This means that God's Word is incisive like a surgeon's scalpel. It does not mangle, but opens the heart to reveal its contents.
D. *They are pure (Prov. 30:5).* "Every word of God is pure." When people try to add to God's Word, they destroy its purity. One of Satan's ploys is to tamper with God's Word, to make people doubt it and twist its truth.

III. How the inspiration of the Scriptures is proved (Heb. 2:1–4).

A. *They were first spoken by the Lord (thundered from Mount Sinai).*
B. *They were confirmed by those who heard them.*
C. *They were accompanied by signs and wonders.*
D. *They were corroborated by the gifts of the Holy Spirit and by the coming of the Spirit in power on the day of Pentecost.*

IV. How the Scriptures are understood.

A. *By illumination provided through the indwelling ministry of the Holy Spirit (1 Cor. 2:10–14).*
B. *By examination.* "Study to shew thyself approved unto God, a workman that needeth not to be ashamed, rightly dividing the word of truth" (2 Tim. 2:15).
C. *By reasoning (Acts 17:2).* Paul reasoned with the Jews in the synagogues. Through the prophet Isaiah, the LORD God challenged, "Come now, and let us reason together, saith the LORD: though your sins be as scarlet, they shall be as white as snow; though they be red like crimson, they shall be as wool" (Isa. 1:18).

D. *By human help (Acts 8:27–35).* With his limited understanding, the Ethiopian was searching the Scriptures. God provided human help through Philip, who came and interpreted the meaning of the Scriptures to the Ethiopian.

V. How the Scriptures should be received.

A. *Let them dwell in us richly (Col. 3:16).* In other words, let them be alive and effective in our lives.

B. *Search and study them daily (Acts 17:11).* Daily reading and studying God's Word is an excellent habit to form.

C. *Hide them in our hearts (Ps. 119:11).* They provide a "reserve power" that can help us combat sin and temptation. Furthermore, when we hide the Scriptures in our hearts, God will bring them to our remembrance in our time of need.

D. *Delight in them (Ps. 1:2).*

E. *Teach them to our children (Deut. 11:19).* This means not just in church or Sunday school but in our homes as well.

Conclusion

Through the Word of God we learn of our sinful nature and our need for salvation. Because the Word of God is alive and powerful, it is used by the Spirit to probe relentlessly into our hearts. The spiritual nourishment it provides brings about spiritual growth and releases within us a marvelous defense mechanism against sin.

SUNDAY MORNING, JANUARY 8

Title: Celebrating Supernatural Living

Text: "Enlarge the place of your tent, stretch your tent curtains wide, do not hold back; lengthen your cords, strengthen your stakes" **(Isa. 54:2 NIV)**.

Scripture Reading: Isaiah 54

Hymns: "I Stand Amazed in the Presence," Gabriel
"Faith Is the Victory," Yates
"Blessed Assurance, Jesus Is Mine," Crosby

Offertory Prayer: Thank you, Father, for the privilege of giving to you for the glory of your name and cause. The words of Jesus are so true, "It is more blessed to give than to receive." Thank you for this heavenly blessing! Amen.

Introduction

The Christian life is a supernatural life, an exciting adventure that begins with a life-changing, spiritual birth. It begins with faith and continues as a work of faith. Living the Christian life this year can be a celebration!

In Isaiah 54:2 the Lord called for Israel to expand their vision, "Enlarge the place of your tent, stretch your tent curtains wide, do not hold back; lengthen your cords, strengthen your stakes" (NIV). This was to be done in preparation for the Lord's restoration of Israel.

The prayer of our hearts should be for the Lord to stretch our vision, enlarge our faith, and expand our goals. A faith vision is one in which we visualize what God intends to do and act in harmony with it. Hebrews 11 records men and women who had a faith vision. They saw by faith and obeyed God's call. If we are to experience the adventure of believing God, we must do four things.

I. Learn to think supernaturally.

Isaiah 55:9 says, "As the heavens are higher than the earth, so are my ways higher than your ways and my thoughts than your thoughts" (NIV). We must strive to have the mind of Christ, and we can control our thoughts as an act of the will.

How can we change our thought life? First we can saturate our minds with God's Word. Then we can follow the words of Colossians 3:1–2: "Seek those things which are above. . . . Set your minds on things above." Think worthy thoughts, faith thoughts, and thoughts of praise, worship, and thanksgiving. Finally, think about the attributes of God—his goodness, greatness, generosity, and glory.

Think supernaturally! Think about who you are spiritually. No longer a servant, but a son or daughter of God. No longer lost, but found. No longer an alien, but a citizen of the kingdom.

Think of your spiritual heritage—the hope of your calling, the riches of Christ's glorious heritage, and the abundant greatness of his power for believers.

Think like children of the King! When we begin to think these thoughts, we stretch our vision. Knowing God for who he is will change our lives.

II. Learn to plan supernaturally.

Supernatural planning includes our personal lives, our families, the church, our business, or whatever pertains to our need for planning.

A. *There is nothing wrong with planning.* Proverbs 16:9 says, "In their hearts humans plan their course, but the Lord establishes their steps" (NIV). God himself is a planner. He has a well-thought-out plan for the world from the first day until the last. Psalm 139:16 indicates divinely detailed planning for our lives.
B. *Let God reveal his vision to you.* This becomes the basis of our faith. Then we set our goals so that they become his goals for us.
C. *Prepare for the fulfillment of his goals.* Our faith will be tested, but God is faithful when we trust and obey him. He will confirm his direction for us and assure us through prayer of his will (1 John 5:14–15).

Our obedience to God requires supernatural planning—planning by faith, following God's plans.

D. *Have big plans, God-sized plans.* The plans and goals God gives to people have two consistent elements: a wide scope of influence and a lasting impact.

God's goal for Adam and Eve was to "be fruitful and multiply and fill the earth and subdue it" (Gen. 1:28). God's goal for Abraham was not just to have a son, but to start a nation and to be a blessing to all people on earth (Gen. 12:1–13). Jesus' goal for the disciples was for them to be witnesses in the power of the Holy Spirit from Jerusalem to the ends of the earth (Acts 1:8).

God-sized plans are big plans, supernatural plans. If they are so small that we can fulfill them ourselves, they aren't God-sized, and God will not bless them. Our plans are big enough when they need God's intervention.

Dr. Joon Gon Kim, evangelist and founder of Korea Campus Crusade for Christ, received a vision from the Lord to have a gathering for Christian training in Korea. His goal was 300,000 delegates, but more than 323,000 came from seventy-eight countries, including 15,000 pastors and evangelists. The largest evening service was attended by 1.5 million. More than a million registered salvation decisions in one evening. This happened because the Lord touched the heart of one man to believe God for great things.

III. Learn to pray supernaturally.

Supernatural praying is found in John 14:12–14: "Greater works than these shall ye do." God gives us the faith to pray for something, and as we pray, he causes our faith to grow and to pray even greater things for him. "According to your faith, be it unto you" (Matt. 9:29).

We can never ask God for too much if our hearts and motives are pure and if we pray according to the Word and will of God. Someone has said, "Whatever we vividly envision, ardently desire, sincerely believe, and enthusiastically act upon will come to pass if there is a scriptural authority for it."

A while back a Christian organization was praying for the Lord's miraculous provision of a certain sum of money. Within a few days a man announced that he would give the ministry a gift of $1.1 million. This was unquestionably a supernatural provision!

IV. Learn to claim supernatural resources.

We are not ordinary people. Our lives are joined with the one who spoke the world into existence. We belong to him who has been given all authority in heaven and on earth. He dwells in us in all his resurrection power. We can claim Philippians 4:13 for our lives: "I can do all things in him who strengthens me" (RSV).

Our faith may be small, but like a muscle it will grow with exercise. If you are struggling to trust God for some physical need, for someone's salvation, or for financial help, then pause to meditate on whatever barrier to your faith you are facing right now. Remind yourself of God's power available to you to accomplish the supernatural. If you are not trusting God, that is sin. Confess your unbelief to him and claim by faith his supernatural resources.

Conclusion

We have seen what it means to celebrate supernatural living. This is God's will for our lives and for the church!

SUNDAY EVENING, JANUARY 8

Title: The Most Excellent Way

Text: "Now eagerly desire the greater gifts. And yet I will show you the most excellent way" **(1 Cor. 12:31 NIV)**.

Scripture Reading: 1 Corinthians 12:29–31; 13:13

Introduction

You can live any way you want to live. You are the only person who has the power to determine how you will live. You can be agreeable or disagreeable, a help or a hindrance, an asset or a liability to yourself, your family, your coworkers, and the kingdom of God. But Paul said, "Yet I will show you the most excellent way." The Christian life was never meant to be a good way or even a better way, but rather the most excellent way!

Paul had just received a letter from the church at Corinth listing all kinds of problems that had arisen in their fellowship for one reason: they were not following the most excellent way. Paul was saying, "In light of your varied lifestyles and the difficulties and heartaches they have brought upon the church, it is high time you recognize your need to follow the most excellent way!"

In his first letter to the church at Corinth, Paul gave four reasons why love is the most excellent way.

I. Its ministry of healing (1 Cor. 1:10–17).

The church at Corinth had written a long letter to Paul listing several of their problems. But one problem that was not listed was divisions in the church. Paul learned of this problem from the relatives of Chloe, a well-known member of the congregation. He was not secretive; he named the source of his information and then dealt directly with the problem.

The fact that he chose to deal first with divisions in the church proves that of all the problems mentioned, he considered this one to be the most critical. It is to this problem that he applied the healing ministry of love.

A. *The healing ministry of love is realized when Christ is honored (1:12–16).* In 1 Corinthians 1:12 we can see what Paul had to say about each group that wanted to rally around some human personality. Some said, "I follow Paul." Paul did not take this as a compliment, nor does any preacher. In claiming to follow Paul the theologian, they were claiming to be "great theologues." Others said, "I follow Apollos." These were the "cultured vultures" who worshiped oratory, since Apollos was a prince of preachers. Still others said, "I follow Cephas [Peter]," the fiery evangelist. This is the "tell-it-like-it-is" crowd. And the "super Christians" said, "I follow Christ."

In light of these childish divisions, Paul turned to some wholesome humor. He had fun with the situation as he singled out himself as an example. In verse 13 he asked a series of questions: "Is Christ fragmented? Tell me about it." "Was Paul crucified for you? I haven't noticed any nail prints in my hands." "Did Christ say in the Great Commission to baptize in the name of the Father and of the Son and of Paul the apostle?" In verses 14–16 Paul expressed relief that he baptized but a few, lest that make them into his followers.

B. *The healing ministry of love is realized when the gospel is preached (1:17).* The gospel is the good news about the healing ministry of Christ's love. Christ is the focal point of the gospel—not Paul or Apollos or Peter or any other man.

II. Its simplicity of language (1 Cor. 2:1–2).

Love is never concerned with impressing others with our importance, our knowledge, our intelligence, or our "eloquence or human wisdom" (2:1 NIV). Love of self is vitally concerned about these things, but not the love that is the most excellent way. This kind of love is concerned with clearly proclaiming the gospel of Jesus Christ and his power to save.

If any man could have complicated the simple with multisyllabic verbiage, Paul could have. He certainly had the vocabulary and the intellect to do it. But Paul had been down the empty halls of academia as a Pharisee and found nothing until he encountered the most excellent way of God's redemptive love.

Someone has said, "It is nice to be important, but it is more important to be nice." Paul was nice enough to speak in love's simplicity of language so that all could understand. No wonder Paul said, "My message and my preaching were not with wise and persuasive words, but with a demonstration of the Spirit's power, so that your faith might not rest on human wisdom, but on God's power" (2:4–5 NIV).

As long as our faith is based on "men's wisdom," it can fall. There will always be someone wiser than us who can undermine that faith. But when our faith rests on God's power, no one on earth and no power of Satan can cause that faith to fall!

III. Its competency for problem-solving (1 Corinthians 5–12).

In these eight chapters, Paul addressed that long list of problems the Christians of Corinth had written. The problems included lawsuits, sexual immorality, marriage, food sacrificed to idols, the place of women in the church, abuses of the Lord's Supper, and false piety. In all fairness, Paul dealt with one problem at a time. He did not rush through these problems as though they were not serious. Rather, his discussion of them amounted to eight chapters. But at the end of his discussion, he informed the Corinthians that there was not one problem they had shared that love couldn't solve. Especially in the face of life's problems, Paul saw love as the most excellent way because of its competency for problem-solving.

A. *The problem of sexual immorality (5:1–2).* Paul was saying that when our Christian friends fall into sin, we must confront them in love and ask them to turn from their sin. If they refuse, we must cut off all association with them. Because we love the church, we cannot allow the continuation of this problem to infect it. Love is the most excellent way to handle any form of sexual impurity. When we love others, we won't use them to satisfy our own desires. We won't inflict on them the guilt and hurt of sexual immorality.

B. *The problem of lawsuits (6:1–8).* Love is the most excellent way to resolve differences. Paul said it is unchristian for fellow believers to take their differences to heathen courts—to rely on those who know nothing of the grace of God to settle their problems. Paul noted that any problem between Christians can and ought to be solved in the spirit of Christian love.

C. *The problem of abusing our Christian liberty (chap. 8).* Paul contended that souls are more important than steak. People are more valuable than meat. Lives are more important than our liberty. When we are tempted to say, "It is my right to do this, or to say that," we must remember the words of Paul, who advocated the most excellent way: "'I have the right to do anything,' you say—but not everything is beneficial" (6:12 NIV).

   There are certain times when we have every right to do a certain thing. But the most excellent way of love reminds us that if exercising our liberty causes even one brother or sister to stumble, we should renounce that liberty.

D. *The problem of placing our piety on parade (chap. 12).* When the more excellent way of love binds us together as the body of Christ, nothing can sever that unity. We care for one another—we rejoice with one another. Love is the most excellent way because it removes any competitive or jealous spirit among God's people. It takes piety off parade and puts Jesus Christ on parade!

IV. Its superiority of value (1 Cor. 12:31–13:13).

Paul concluded chapter 12 by saying, "And yet I will show you the most excellent way" (NIV). Then he set forth the beautiful love chapter of 1 Corinthians 13. "And now these three remain: faith, hope and love. But the greatest of these is love" (v. 13 NIV). Why is love "the greatest of these"? Why is it the most excellent way? Because of its superiority of value.

A. *The superiority of love's value is seen in the worth it imparts to the gifts of the Spirit (13:5–13).* These gifts have no intrinsic value. The only value they have is the value love imparts to them.

B. *The superiority of love's value is seen in the words used to describe it (13:5–13).*

Conclusion

Paul ended his letter with this exhortation: "Do everything in love" (16:14 NIV). Then he closed with, "My love to all of you in Christ Jesus" (16:24 NIV). Love is the most excellent way because of its ministry of healing, simplicity of language, competency for problem-solving, and superiority of value.

WEDNESDAY EVENING, JANUARY 11

Title: What the Bible Says about God

Text: "The LORD is righteous in all his ways, and holy in all his works. The LORD is nigh unto all them that call upon him, to all that call upon him in truth" **(Ps. 145:17–18)**.

Scripture Reading: Psalm 145

Introduction

It is impossible to define God. To do so is to limit him. It is possible, however, to describe God. And the sourcebook from which we arrive at a description is the Bible. Thus it is appropriate to title this study "What the Bible Says about God"—for that is all that matters.

I. The nature of God.

A. *God is a Spirit (John 4:24).* People tend to depend on some tangible evidence for the existence of God. But the Holy Spirit is the one who enables people to grow in their understanding and concept of God as "Spirit."

B. *God is one (Deut. 6:4).* Monotheism was the great distinctive of Judaism. Polytheism was the curse of the ancient world. Even though God has expressed himself to humans in a multiplicity of ways, he is still one God.

C. *God is personal (John 17:1–3).* People can't "know" (experience) an "impersonal force" or an "absolute power," but they can know a God who has personality and identity with humans.

D. *God is Trinitarian.* Though God is one person, he reveals himself to people as bearing three relationships (Gen. 1:1–3, 26; Matt. 3:16–17). As the *Father* he is infinite in love, power, and wisdom. He is the Creator who has divine purpose in all that he does. As the *Son* he is the revealer of God, the key to humankind's knowledge of God and history. As the *Holy Spirit,* he manifests himself spiritually to humans. The Holy Spirit "came upon" people in the Old Testament, enabling them to prophesy and perform mighty works. He was the agent in Jesus' conception and was present at his baptism and during his temptation in the wilderness. In the church age, he empowers and indwells believers and convicts both the saved and the unsaved of sin.

II. God's natural attributes.

A. *God is infinite (1 Kings 8:27).* There is no limit to his being.

B. *God is omnipotent.* He has all power and can do anything in keeping with his nature and purpose. The only limits to his power are self-imposed. He cannot lie or act contrary to his own laws, character, and purpose.

C. *God is omnipresent.* He is always present—in all parts of his creation and universe. He is limited by neither time nor space, but is a free, personal Spirit.

D. *God is omniscient.* He has all knowledge and knows all things simultaneously. His knowledge is immediate without processes of thought or reason. God's foreknowledge is a part of his omniscience.

E. *God is changeless (immutable).* He is the one in whom there "is no variableness, neither shadow of turning" (James 1:17).

III. God's moral attributes.

A. *God is capable of hatred of evil and of those things that oppose and seek to interrupt his divine purposes.*

B. *God is impartial (1 Peter 1:17).* He does not show "respect of persons."

C. *He is longsuffering (Ex. 34:6).* God's longsuffering attitude toward sinful humans is one of his most amazing characteristics.

D. *He is love (1 John 4:8, 16).* God does not possess love; he is love. Love *is* the essence of his nature and character.

E. *God is capable of showing vengeance (Deut. 32:35; Rom. 12:19).* God's vengeance, unlike human vengeance, is not a calculated retaliation because of personal hurt. Our refusal to respond to God's loving invitation ultimately releases his judgment.

IV. The roles of God.

A. *He is Creator (Gen. 1:1).* He is the one who conceived and created all things.
B. *He is Judge.* God judges us through his Word, by his Spirit, by his perfect and holy nature.
C. *He is our Shepherd (Gen. 49:24; Ps. 23; John 10:11, 14).* One of the most beautiful descriptions of Jesus' relationship to and concern for people is that of Shepherd.

Conclusion

Human intellectual limitations make it impossible for us to exhaust our descriptions of God. Every day lived as a member of his family produces new insights and discoveries concerning him. We can say with Paul, "O the depth of the riches both of the wisdom and knowledge of God! how unsearchable are his judgments, and his ways past finding out!" (Rom. 11:33).

SUNDAY MORNING, JANUARY 15

Title: Christ—the Only Hope

Text: "We have heard of your faith in Christ Jesus and of the love you have for all God's people—the faith and love that spring from the hope that is stored up for you in heaven and about which you have already heard in the true message of the gospel that has come to you" **(Col. 1:4–6 NIV)**.

Scripture Reading: Colossians 1:3–8

Hymns: "Crown Him with Many Crowns," Bridges
"The Solid Rock," Mote
"Victory in Jesus," Bartlett

Offertory Prayer: Heavenly Father, thank you for giving us the opportunity to bring our tithes and offerings to you this day. May you be pleased with the gifts we bring. Amen.

Introduction

The key word in today's message is *hope*, and the conviction of truth that is as deep as life and eternity is that Christ is the only hope! This year, 2023, is a year to acknowledge this truth.

The claim that Christ is the only hope is a bold claim because it eliminates all other claims to hope. It is a timeless claim because it has been believed for centuries. It is also a very serious claim because to believe it is to accept certain responsibilities.

I. Christ is the only hope for salvation.

A mine shaft collapsed and a rescue team was immediately organized to dig out the entombed men before their air supply was exhausted. As the rescue team approached the doomed miners, they thought they heard a tapping on the rocks. As they paused to listen, in Morse code came the question repeatedly: "Is there any hope? Is there any hope?" People living under the weight of sin may ask, "Is there any hope for salvation?"

A. *Christ is the only hope for a salvation desperately needed.* The Bible says that without Christ people have "no hope" and are "without God in the world" (Eph. 2:12). They are spiritually lost, "condemned already" (John 3:18). Not tomorrow, not next year, not at age twenty-one, not at death, but now, already condemned! People are spiritually trapped in sin.

   "The heart is deceitful . . . and desperately wicked: who can know it?" (Jer. 17:9). Out of the human heart proceeds all types of sin (Matt. 15:19). The nature of the human heart is to sin and rebel against God and spiritual authority.

   People are also trapped in the agonizing results of sin. "The wages of sin is death" (Rom. 6:23). People are trapped in human weakness and despair. The cry of the apostle Paul was, "Who shall deliver me from the body of this death?" (Rom. 7:24). Christ is the only hope!

B. *Christ is the only hope for salvation divinely provided.* In answer to a seeking heart, "What must I do to be saved?" is the reply, "Believe on the Lord Jesus Christ, and thou shalt be saved" (Acts 16:30–31).

   The Lord Jesus Christ is the Savior. There is much confusion at this point. Salvation is not in a parent's faith, in religious principles, in a church, in culture, in outward symbols, or in a good life. Salvation is in a person, Jesus Christ!

   Jesus Christ is God's provision (1 Tim. 1:15), God's deed (1 Cor. 15:3), and God's gift (Rom. 6:23). He is the living Savior and Lord.

C. *Christ is the only hope for salvation personally received.* What are we to do? How are we to respond? Upon hearing "the hope of the gospel," which is Christ, we are to believe him. We are to acknowledge the truth of Christ; accept the facts of his life, death, and resurrection, then trust ourselves to him in personal surrender. John 1:12 says, "But as many as received him, to them gave he power to become the sons of God, even to them that believe on his name."

   Several years ago an air force sergeant moved to Sherman, Texas. He and his family were saved before they were transferred to another base. He said, "We came to Sherman so poor; we are leaving so rich." Christ is the only hope!

II. Christ is the only hope for life's needs.

Paul spoke of the hope of the gospel "that has come to you . . . [and] is bearing fruit and growing . . . among you" (Col. 1:6 NIV). Christ touches lives now and transforms them. He gives power to live now, not just for heaven. Many testify to what Christ is doing in their lives today.

J. B. Phillips's book *God Our Contemporary* has a chapter titled "The Inadequacy of Humanism," in which Phillips described secular humanism as a bleak and cruel creed. It denies the Christian faith and the need for any moral or spiritual authority outside humanity. Humanism restricts life to this earth; it denies God and says there is no life beyond this one. So it offers no hope to the severely handicapped, no power to guide and strengthen someone defeated by emotional conflicts. It has nothing to offer for the crises of life.

Secular humanism would have been useless some time ago, when in one week's time I ministered to two families who lost teenage sons, to a man whose mother died in her sleep, to the family of a five-year-old girl who died of a brain tumor, and to a wife whose husband was killed in military service. Secular humanism had nothing to say. It was cold and cruelly silent. But Christ was not!

Matthew 11:28 says, "Come unto me, all ye that labor and are heavy laden." John 10:10 says, "I am come that they might have life; and . . . have it more abundantly." And Philippians 4:13 says, "I can do all things through Christ who strengtheneth me." Christ is the only hope!

III. Christ is the only hope for eternity.

The hope of Christ is an eternal certainty by pointing beyond life now to life forever. Colossians 1:5 speaks of "the hope stored up for you in heaven" (NIV).

A. *The hope of Christ is the hope of his return.* He personally promised it (John 14:3), the angels divinely announced it (Acts 1:11), and Paul the apostle victoriously described it (1 Thess. 4:16). Jesus is personally, powerfully, and suddenly coming again. This is hope!

B. *The hope of Christ is the hope of the resurrection.* Christ has abolished death (2 Tim. 1:9–10), and resurrection is promised in 1 Corinthians 15. Death is not the end for the believer because Christ is our hope.

C. *The hope of Christ is the hope of deliverance from judgment.* Hebrews 9:27 says, "People are destined to die once and after that to face judgment" (NIV). Christ bore our judgment on the cross. Though judgment is certain, in Christ we need not fear for we have passed from death unto life.

Conclusion

Christ is the only hope. What an audacious yet wonderful claim! Do we believe it? Then we must proclaim it, share it, and testify to it everywhere we go.

Sunday Evening, January 15

Title: When You Have Been Wronged

Text: "We are hard pressed on every side, but not crushed; perplexed, but not in despair; persecuted, but not abandoned; struck down, but not destroyed" **(2 Cor. 4:8–9 NIV)**.

Scripture Reading: 2 Corinthians 4:8–10

Introduction

Some people at Corinth did not like Paul. They were infuriated by his insistence on Christian morality and his daring to correct those whose lives proved to be a contradiction to their profession. These worldly church members and the Judaizers joined forces against him. The man who seemed to be the ringleader was the same man Paul reprimanded in 1 Corinthians (5:1–5) for having an affair with his stepmother. Apparently this man was influential. He persisted in his sin, leading an open revolt against Paul and taking some of the leaders with him.

Because of Paul's second letter, the church came back into line. They recognized the evil of this man and disciplined him. But in the process, Paul was grievously wronged, both by this man and others in the church. They said Paul had no authority to advise them, that he bore no letters of commendation from leaders in Jerusalem as they did, and that he had a weak and unimpressive personal appearance. They also accused him of going back on his word by not visiting Corinth when he said he would. If ever a man was wronged, Paul was. But because of his strong Christian witness even under fire, he has provided us with three basic truths that we can apply to our own lives when we have been wronged.

I. Lessons to learn (2 Cor. 2:14).

Anytime we are wronged, we can learn a lesson from the experience and emerge stronger and wiser. When Paul was wronged, he learned three worthy lessons from his experience.

A. *How to triumph over wrong (2:14).* To triumph over wrong does not mean to overcome it or defeat it. Rather, it means to refuse to be overcome or defeated by the wrong done to us. We may not be able to control what others do, but we can control how we respond to the wrong done. This victory has both a human and a divine side. If we do our part, God will be faithful to do his part.

1. Human endurance. "If we are distressed, it is for your comfort and salvation; if we are comforted, it is for your comfort, which produces in you patient endurance of the same sufferings we suffer" (2 Cor. 1:6 NIV).

   An old mule, thought to be of no further use, was put in a deep ditch, and shovelful after shovelful of dirt was thrown down to bury him. The old mule refused to be buried. He would shake the dirt off his back, pack it down with his feet, and gradually but surely stand higher and higher until after enough dirt had been thrown on him, he simply stepped out of the ditch and galloped away!

2. Divine comfort. "For just as we share abundantly in the sufferings of Christ, so also our comfort abounds through Christ" (2 Cor. 1:5 NIV). We are not left to face our trials with sheer human endurance alone. The comfort of God sustains us. Between verses 3 and 7, the word *comfort* appears nine times. "The God of all comfort" (v. 3) upholds us with his compassion and care.

B. *How to comfort others who are wronged.* Our God is the one "who comforts us in all our troubles, so that we can comfort those in any trouble with the comfort we ourselves receive from God" (2 Cor. 1:4 NIV). Once we have endured suffering and sorrow, we are better able to help others who are struggling with the hardships of life.

C. *How dependent we are on God.* "We were under great pressure, far beyond our ability to endure, so that we despaired of life itself. Indeed, we felt we had received the sentence of death. But this happened that we might not rely on ourselves but on God, who raises the dead" (2 Cor. 1:8–9 NIV).

We have no information about the terrible experience Paul went through at Ephesus. But he recognized that the experience had been beneficial—it had driven him back to God. It had proved to him his utter dependence on God.

II. Attitudes to display (2 Cor. 1:13; 2:5–11; 3:1–2).

Anytime we are wronged, we must realize that the real injury is not the wrong itself but the attitude it invokes. Seldom does being wronged cripple us. But we can cripple ourselves by having an unforgiving attitude toward those who have wronged us. Paul portrayed the kind of attitude we must display whenever we suffer an injustice.

A. *An attitude of openness.* "Our conscience testifies that we have conducted ourselves in the world, and especially in our relations with you, with integrity and godly sincerity. . . . For we do not write you anything you cannot read or understand" (2 Cor. 1:12–13 NIV).

Some claimed that Paul in his letters did not quite mean what he said. Paul replied that there were no hidden meanings in his words. He had maintained an attitude of absolute openness during this entire experience. He had told nothing but the truth, being honest with all involved. In the language of today, he had "called an ace an ace and a spade a spade."

What are we supposed to say when we have been wronged? We just need to tell the truth. We are not to be vindictive or accusative; we are to be open. And an attitude of openness is always the right attitude in trying times.

B. *An attitude of forgiveness (2 Cor. 2:5–11).* When Paul came to Corinth, he encountered the ringleader of the opposition. Paul's short visit had been poisoned by the efforts of one man. This man had insulted Paul. Although the man had been disciplined, some church members felt that it had not been severe enough and wanted to impose a still greater punishment. It was then that Paul's greatness shone through. Paul said that enough had been done. The man was now penitent, and to exercise further discipline would do more harm than good. It might even drive the man to despair.

Our job is not to render sinners harmless by beating them into submission. Instead, our job is to gather them back into the kingdom of God.

C. *An attitude of innate integrity (2 Cor. 3:1–2).* There are two kinds of integrity. Infused integrity is the reputation we hope to gain by what others say about us. *Innate* integrity is the character that is ours because of the persons we are. One is counterfeit, the other is genuine. One is assumed, the other is inherent.

When we have been wronged, we should display the attitude of innate integrity. We don't have to answer every charge leveled at us. Our lives and character are answer enough.

III. Ministries to fulfill (2 Cor. 4:1).

Paul said, "Therefore, since through God's mercy we have this ministry, we do not lose heart" (2 Cor. 4:1 NIV). In essence, Paul was saying, "In spite of the terrible wrong that has been done to me, I will not be discouraged and I will not quit—I have a ministry to fulfill!"

Too many people give up when they are wronged. If Paul had been easily discouraged, he would have quit the ministry long before he reached Corinth. We cannot allow the criticisms and ill will of others to distract us from our calling—we have ministries to fulfill. And the more quickly we begin to fulfill our ministry, the more quickly we will recover from the wrong done to us.

A. *The ministry of proclaiming Jesus Christ (2 Cor. 4:5, 7–11; 5:18–20).*

B. *The ministry of separating ourselves from the world (2 Cor. 6:17).* Even when we are wronged by professing Christians, we have a ministry to fulfill. We must not allow offenses to cause us to give up our faith and return to the world. We are called to separate ourselves from the world.

C. *The ministry of dedicating our possessions (2 Cor. 9:7).* Even if we have been wronged by others in the church, we are still called to dedicate our possessions to God. Our Christian stewardship is not unto people but unto God.

D. *The ministry of celebrating our sufferings (2 Cor. 12:7–10).* Paul said, "Therefore I will boast all the more gladly about my weaknesses, so that Christ's power may rest on me. That is why, for Christ's sake,

I delight in weaknesses, in insults, in hardships, in persecutions, in difficulties. For when I am weak, then I am strong" (12:9–10 NIV).

Paul was saying, "If it is God's will that this suffering stay with me, I will turn my suffering into celebration. It will become a ministry of celebration because my suffering is a living demonstration of Christ's power to sustain."

Conclusion

When we have been wronged, we have (1) lessons to learn, (2) attitudes to display, and (3) ministries to fulfill. Whatever wrongs we may have faced, we can say with Paul, "Thanks be to God, who always leads us as captives in Christ's triumphal procession" (2 Cor. 2:14 NIV).

Wednesday Evening, January 18

Title: What the Bible Says about the Trinity

Text: "For there are three that bear record in heaven, the Father, the Word, and the Holy Ghost: and these three are one" **(1 John 5:7)**.

Scripture Reading: 1 John 5:7

Introduction

The doctrine of the Trinity is a distinctive mark of Christianity. Though there are triads of divinities in many of the world religions and philosophies, none of these carries any similarity to the Christian teaching concerning the Trinity. It must be understood, however, that it is not possible to "prove" the Trinity from the standpoint of human reason. The Trinitarian nature of God comes to humans by divine revelation. It is interwoven throughout the Old and New Testaments. Thus the Bible presents God as a rational Spirit being who is infinite in his attributes of love, holiness, wisdom, power, majesty, justice, truth, and goodness. It also presents him as one who exists externally in three persons yet is still one in substance and in purpose.

I. There is one God.

A. *In the Old Testament, God is revealed in the Shema (Deut. 6:4–5), with which every Jewish synagogue service is opened; in the Decalogue (Ex. 20:3); and by the prophets (Isa. 45:5–6).*

B. *In the New Testament, God is revealed in the words of Jesus (John 10:30), the words of James (James 2:19), and the words of Paul (1 Cor. 8:4–6).* He is described as the Father "of whom are all things" (v. 6) and in whom "we live, and move, and have our being" (Acts 17:28).

C. *Adam and Eve believed in one God, but sin gave birth to polytheism, because in their guilt, humans manufactured gods whom they could appease.* Sinful humans feared demonstrations of natural power, so they worshiped the wind, the sun, fire, and so on. Today material things often become gods in people's lives.

II. The one God exists as three persons.

A. *The first inference of the Trinity is discovered in Genesis 1:1, when Moses used the plural form of the divine name: "In the beginning God (Elohim) created the heavens and the earth."* Our God is so great in his being and in his attributes that to limit him to one expression or manifestation of himself is to ignore his majesty and power.

B. *Several passages use more than one Hebrew word for God, making a distinction between God the Father and God the Son (see Pss. 45:6–7; 110:1 [messianic references]; Hos. 1:7).* Other remarkable passages refer to the Angel of Jehovah (Gen. 16:7–14; 22:11–16; Ex. 3:2–5; Judg. 13:20–22).

C. *The amazing fact of the New Testament is the way in which it presents the doctrine of the Trinity without any struggle or controversy.* The teaching of Jesus is Trinitarian throughout. He speaks *to* the Father and *of* the Holy Spirit, and he does so without apology and without explanation (see John 14:16–17; 15:26).

D. *Paul gives an apostolic benediction in 2 Corinthians 13:14, which is a prayer directed to Christ for his grace, to the Father for his love, and to the Holy Spirit for his fellowship.* Here the deity and equality of each person of the Godhead are taken for granted. God exists as three persons, and each of the three is equal in power and glory, being one in substance.

E. *It is also important to note that in the Great Commission (Matt. 28:19–20) Jesus instructed his followers to go into all the world "baptizing them in the name [not "names"] of the Father, and of the Son, and of the Holy Spirit."* This is another indication of the unity and oneness of the Trinity.

Conclusion

The Father is God. On many occasions, Jesus prayed to God the Father (Mark 14:36; John 11:41; 17:11; et al.). In 1 Corinthians 8:6 Paul declared, "To us there is but one God, the Father, of whom are all things." Again Paul identified himself as "an apostle—sent . . . by Jesus Christ and God the Father" (Gal. 1:1 NIV).

The Son is God. John wrote, "In the beginning was the Word, and the Word was with God, and the Word was God. . . . The Word became flesh and made his dwelling among us" (John 1:1, 14 NIV). Paul wrote, "For in him [Christ] dwelleth all the fulness of the Godhead bodily" (Col. 2:9). Hebrews 1:3 is one of the strongest statements in the New Testament that declares the deity of Jesus. He is said to be the exact expression of the substance of God. What is substance? It is whatever is necessary to be God. The Son is declared to be the exact expression of that substance. Also, the attributes of Deity ascribed to God alone are also ascribed to the Son: holiness (John 6:69; Heb. 7:26), immutability (Heb. 1:11–12; 13:8), omnipotence (Matt. 28:18), omniscience

(Matt. 9:4; John 16:30), life (John 1:4; 11:25; 14:6), eternity (John 1:1; 8:58; 17:5; Heb. 1:8), omnipresence (Matt. 28:20), judgment (Matt. 25:31–46), and creation (John 1:3, 10; Col. 1:16–17).

The Holy Spirit is God. Peter declared in his words to Ananias that the Holy Spirit is God (Acts 5:3–4). Paul also declared it (1 Cor. 2:11). And Jesus implied in the Great Commission (Matt. 28:19–20) that the Holy Spirit is equal with the Father and the Son as Deity.

SUNDAY MORNING, JANUARY 22

Title: The Secret of Facing Need

Text: "My God shall supply all your need according to his riches in glory by Christ Jesus" **(Phil. 4:19)**.

Scripture Reading: Philippians 4:4–20

Hymns: "Come Thou Fount of Every Blessing," Robinson
"All That Thrills My Soul," Harris
"God Will Take Care of You," Martin

Offertory Prayer: Praise the Lord for the joy of giving! As the Lord Jesus Christ gave himself for us, so we also give ourselves to you. We bring to your altar our hearts and possessions. Use them for your sake and for the salvation of souls. Amen.

Introduction

When you are confronted with special needs for yourself, your family, your job, or your church, what do you do? Paul wrote his letter to the Philippians with some great needs himself. As a servant of Christ, he was a prisoner in Rome. He acknowledged that he was afflicted (4:12) and that he was under pressure (4:14); he referred to his necessity and to their need (4:15–19).

Paul had learned the secret to facing need. This is a key to celebrated Christian living. Today we are going to look at some specific ways to deal with our needs.

I. Be enthusiastic (4:4).

When we have a need, we are not to hide it, deny it, or disregard it; we are to rejoice in the Lord. The word *rejoice* is an imperative, a command. It is present tense, urging continual action. It is an attitude of life, "always." It is given double emphasis in the light of the Philippians' difficulties. Our focus is to be on the Lord, not on our need.

It was one of those never-should-have-gotten-out-of-bed days for a certain preacher. He cut his face while shaving. Then he burned his toast for breakfast. After he rushed out the door so he wouldn't be late for an appointment, one of his tires blew out a few miles down the road.

He finally got his car back on the road and was going a few miles over the speed limit when a police officer stopped him and gave him a ticket for speeding. By that time, he was extremely upset, and he made a rather sorry picture as he complained bitterly to the policeman about the kind of day he was experiencing. "I know what you mean," said the officer. "It used to happen to me that way—before I became a Christian!"

II. Be gentle (4:5).

Christians' enthusiasm is not without reason. The word *moderation* means a readiness to listen to reason. It is the attitude of yielding one's rights, thus showing consideration and gentleness to others.

The tendency of the world is to become hard and tough, to demand one's rights, but this is not the Christian response. We are to be gentle toward all people.

III. Be peaceful (4:6–7).

The natural tendency in the time of need is to worry. Every night Americans take millions of sleeping pills. Worry is not the answer! We can either worry or pray.

God's Word says we are to worry about nothing—not even one thing. When we worry, we are sinning by showing a lack of trust in God. Instead, we are instructed to commit our requests to God in prayer and allow him to be Lord in our lives.

Peace comes through prayer as an act of worship, through supplication for our personal needs, and through thankfulness for what is happening in our lives. Peace beyond human understanding keeps guarding our inner life. This is the way to respond to need.

IV. Be positive (4:8).

Think positively, not negatively. Think spiritual thoughts. Think high thoughts, honest thoughts, just thoughts, thoughts worthy of respect, living by God's standards. Think agreeable, loving, and pure thoughts. Carefully reflect on these thoughts and keep practicing them. This is the way the God of peace will bless.

V. Be teachable (4:9, 11).

"Whatever you have learned or received or heard from me, or seen in me—put it into practice" (v. 9 NIV). The Lord has a purpose for the need in your life.

A. *The Lord uses a need to develop us.* What happens to us is not as important as how we respond to what happens. The Lord is developing spiritual qualities in our lives. In this chapter, we discover several strong qualities: gratefulness (v. 6), joyfulness (v. 10), contentment (v. 11), flexibility (v. 12), and faith (v. 13). What quality is he developing in you?

B. *The Lord uses a need to reprove us.* Having a need causes us to search our hearts and ask him, "What's wrong?"

C. *The Lord uses a need to test us.* When we have a need and the funds for it are not available, the Lord may be testing us. Whatever our need and whatever God's purpose, we are to thank him.

VI. Be content (4:10–12).

Contentment is an attitude that none of us possesses naturally. It is something we have to learn. Paul learned it; he had not always known it. Our natural inclination is not to learn to be content. Rather, it is to complain of our circumstances or to covet what we do not have. Contentment is realizing that God has provided everything we need for our present happiness. The opposite is covetousness, lusting for more and more.

VII. Be expectant (4:13).

"I can do all things through Christ which strengtheneth me." There is no greater verse in all the Bible. When we have the right attitude, there is nothing we cannot do! This verse is positive: "I *can*." It is personal: "*I* can." It is powerful: "do *all* things." In the face of your need, you can be defeated or you can be expectant of the victory Jesus gives.

VIII. Be generous (4:14–18).

The Philippian church was a generous church; consequently, Paul's needs were met (vv. 14, 16, 18).

In the time of our need, we tend to be stingy, but the key to qualifying for verse 19 is the attitude of generosity within us. If we are in "need," this means we should begin giving.

IX. Be fulfilled (4:19).

All our need is supplied and satisfied. God's treatment of the Philippians would correspond to their treatment of Paul. This is the divine principle of reciprocity—giving and receiving.

Conclusion

What about your needs? How are you responding to them? What are you doing with them? We need to take our eyes off the financial page and put them on God. Paul wrote, "My God shall supply all your need according to his riches in glory by Christ Jesus" (Phil. 4:19).

SUNDAY EVENING, JANUARY 22

Title: Christian Unity

Text: "As a prisoner for the Lord, then, I urge you to live a life worthy of the calling you have received. Be completely humble and gentle; be patient, bearing with one another in love. Make every effort to keep the unity of the Spirit through the bond of peace" **(Eph. 4:1–3 NIV)**.

Scripture Reading: Ephesians 4:1–6, 28–32

Introduction

Paul didn't deal with any problems in his letter to the Ephesians. All news was good news from the people at Ephesus, and Paul had the joyous privilege of writing a positive letter to encourage them. The theme of his letter is "Christian unity." Paul had established many churches and watched them grow, so he realized that without unity nothing else really matters. And with unity nothing can defeat the church.

In his first three chapters, Paul laid the foundation for Christian unity. In his last two chapters, he described the practical results of unity. And in chapter 4, he dealt with the heart and soul of Christian unity. Today we are going to focus our attention on this fourth chapter. Here Paul spoke of (1) the behavior of Christian unity, (2) the basis of Christian unity, and (3) the benefits of Christian unity.

I. The behavior of Christian unity (Eph. 4:1–3).

Paul began with behavior because it has everything to do with Christian unity. Often it appears that *behavior* is more important than *beliefs* in maintaining unity in the church. For example, in the church there are many different beliefs concerning prophecy, the return of Christ, and social practices, and yet there is unity. But we can absolutely destroy this unity by misbehavior.

Few church splits can be traced to bad theology. But many can be traced to bad behavior. Therefore, Paul quickly and directly dealt with behavior as a matter of priority. "I urge you to live a life worthy of the calling you have received" (v. 1 NIV). In case the church at Ephesus didn't understand what kind of behavior Paul was talking about, he spelled it out. He listed seven characteristics of the kind of behavior that builds Christian unity.

A. *It is compatible with our calling.* If we are to help bring Christian unity, we must conduct ourselves in a manner that doesn't reflect poorly on our calling as Christians. Since we bear the name of Christ, we must never bring that name into disrepute.

B. *It is humble (v. 2).* We must not be conceited, egotistical, or proud. A very wise person said, "Egotism is the sedative that nature provides to deaden the pain of being a fool."

But how does humility come about? It comes from two things:

1. Self-knowledge. Humility depends on honesty. It depends on having the courage to look at ourselves without the rose-tinted spectacles of self-admiration and self-love.
2. God-knowledge. Humility comes from comparing our lives with the life of Christ. As long as we compare ourselves with others, we may come out of the comparison well. It is when we compare ourselves with Christ that we see our own failure. God knowledge plus self-knowledge equals humility.

C. *It is gentle (v.2).* Those who are gentle are so God-controlled that they are continually kind and gracious toward others. They are people in whom self has died and through whom Christ in all of his humility lives. Paul said, "I have been crucified with Christ and I no longer live, but Christ lives in me" (Gal. 2:20 NIV).

D. *It is patient (v. 2).* Chrysostom defined patience as the spirit that has the power to take revenge but never does so. Patience is the spirit that bears insult without bitterness or complaint.

E. *It is magnanimous (v. 2).* As Christians we must make allowances for one another; we must be magnanimous toward others and their faults as God has been magnanimous toward us.

F. *It is loving (v. 2).* We should bear with one another not through sheer grit and determination but through Christian love. There are four Greek words for love, but the word used here is the highest. It means that we must love others so much that nothing they do or say will keep us from loving them and seeking their highest good. Even though they mistreat and hurt us, we will feel only kindness toward them.

G. *It is peaceable (v. 3).* Peace doesn't happen on its own; we must make it happen.

II. The basis of Christian unity (Eph. 4:4–6).

Behavior is important to Christian unity. But a sound basis is absolutely indispensable. What is the basis, the foundation, on which Christian unity is built? Paul laid seven foundation stones: one body, one Spirit, one hope, one Lord, one faith, one baptism, and one God.

A. *One body (v. 4).* Christ is the head and the church is the body. The unity of the church is essential for the work of Christ.

B. *One Spirit (v. 4).*

C. *One hope (v. 4).* This is the hope of the ultimate consummation of our salvation in heaven.

D. *Our Lord (v. 5).*

E. *One faith (v. 5).* Paul was not talking about a set of beliefs that may characterize a particular denomination. There is "one faith" by which people come into a saving relationship with Christ as Lord. There may be many "faiths" (denominations), but there is only one faith by which we are saved—faith in Jesus Christ as Savior.

F. *One baptism (v. 5).* Just as there is one faith through which we come into a saving relationship with Christ, there is "one baptism" through which we make outward demonstration of that inward experience.

G. *One God (v. 6).* There is one God—and one God unites us into one family of God. Paul said four things about the one God.
   1. He is Father of all—that is, he created all.
   2. He is above all—that is, he controls all.
   3. He is through all—that is, he sustains all.
   4. He is in all—that is, he is present everywhere.

III. The benefits of Christian unity (Eph. 4:28–32).

Quite predictably someone may ask, "Why all the fuss about unity? Does it really make that much difference? What are the benefits of Christian unity?"

The last five verses of this chapter list those benefits. Here we learn that unity in the church does make a difference—a big difference! Let's look at what happens when unity prevails.

A. *Conduct is changed (v. 28).* When there is Christian unity, there is a change in conduct. No longer do we ask, "What can I get?" but rather, "What can I share?" When we are united in allowing the Holy Spirit to fill us, the hope of heaven to challenge us, and the Lord Jesus Christ to guide us, our conduct is changed.

B. *Conversation is clean (v. 29).* "Do not let any unwholesome talk come out of your mouths" (NIV). It is difficult, if not impossible, to be in unity with God and his people and still have a filthy mouth. An ancient proverb says, "The heart of man is a well, and the mouth of man is a bucket, and that which is in the well of the heart can be determined by what is in the bucket of the mouth."

C. *Commitment is deepened (v. 30).* When we live each moment aware that there is but one Holy Spirit by whom we have been born again, we desire to do nothing to grieve him. One of the benefits of Christian unity is that we reach a level of commitment beyond which we will not grieve the Holy Spirit.

D. *Conflict is eliminated (v. 31).* Unity gets rid of conflict. Conflict comes from "the sins of the spirit." Paul had dealt with the sins of the flesh (stealing, foul language, etc.). Now he dealt with the sins of the spirit—or "Christian sins." These are identified as "bitterness, rage and anger, brawling and slander, along with every form of malice" (NIV). When we are one in Christ, we are free from all such disruptive and divisive conflicts.

E. *Kindness is practiced (v. 32).* To be kind means to exercise thoughtful consideration.

Conclusion

When the Roman soldiers on guard at Jesus' crucifixion were dividing the prisoner's clothes, they came to Jesus' coat and discovered that it was seamless. To tear it would ruin it. For this reason, they decided to keep it intact and cast lots for it.

The seamless robe of Christ has become a metaphor for the unity of the church. Henry Ward Beecher prayed that the church might be one again, like the seamless robe of its Lord. The metaphor is one of great beauty and appropriateness. Strife and divisions within the church have been ugly efforts to tear into pieces the sacred garment of the truth.

The Crucified One must look down sadly at the miserable conflict between those he died to redeem. His look of love and sorrow is reminiscent of his prayer "that they may be brought to complete unity. Then the world will know that you sent me and have loved them even as you have loved me" (John 17:23 NIV).

WEDNESDAY EVENING, JANUARY 25

Title: What the Bible Says about the Three Stages of Man

Text: "But now, by dying to what once bound us, we have been released from the law so that we serve in the new way of the Spirit, and not in the old way of the written code" **(Rom. 7:6 NIV)**.

Scripture Reading: Romans 7

Introduction

In Romans 7 Paul described humans as being either natural, carnal, or spiritual. The *natural man* is the unsaved person who can rise no higher than his intellectual, moral, or volitional powers can lift him. The *carnal man* is a saved man who is still dominated at least partially by the power of sin and lives under the control of the old nature of Adam within him. The *spiritual man* is the believer whose life is controlled by the Holy Spirit.

I. The spiritual man (Rom. 7:1–6).

A. *Paul said first that the spiritual man shows that he is delivered from the law.* Paul illustrated this with the marriage relationship, showing the validity of the claims of the law until the time of death.

B. *How is this fact—that the power of the law ends at death—revealed in the life of the spiritual man?* He is no longer "trying" for victory any more than he is "trying" to be saved. The spiritual Christian has discovered a more thrilling way to victory in his life. Because of his identification with Christ in his death, the claims of the law are broken (v. 4).

C. *The spiritual man has also discovered a more thorough way to victory.* The failure of the flesh no longer overpowers him (v. 5). Paul explained that when we were "natural" beings, the law ignited our sinful passions. It told us what sin is without giving us the power to overcome it.

D. *Note the* Living Bible*'s paraphrase of verse 6:* "And now you can really serve God; not in the old way, mechanically obeying a set of rules, but in the new way, with all of your hearts and minds."

II. The natural man (Rom. 7:7–13).

A. *In these verses Paul explained that if the spiritual man is delivered from the law, the natural man is doomed by the law.* As a "natural man," Paul discovered that the law of God exposed the hidden nature of sin in his life. The law did this in two ways. First, it showed him his sinful nature (v. 7). He saw, because of the law, a hideous caricature of what he was without God in his life. Second, the law activated his sinful nature (vv. 8–9). Paul was saying that before the law was instituted, there was freedom from an accusing conscience, a kind of "false peace" brought about by his ignorance of sin. The coming of the law changed all of that. Its straight edge revealed the crookedness in his human nature.

B. *The law of God also shows us the seriousness of sin.* All sin is against God; thus it demands eternal damnation and condemnation. There are at least fifteen Hebrew words in the Old Testament for sin, and they cover the entire spectrum of all possible kinds of wrong attitudes toward and actions against God and others. And the Greek New Testament has almost as many words to cover the various kinds of sin. When you consider all of these words for sin, you have an idea of what God thinks about sin in all of its forms.

C. *The law cannot save.* Salvation alone is the glorious prerogative of God's incomparable grace. Paul, as a sinner, found that even his best efforts to win salvation were to no avail. The law that stood before him was holy, just, and good. It was an uncrossable barrier. The best moral efforts he could muster shriveled up and died under the unrelenting searchlight of God's perfect law.

III. The carnal man (Rom. 7:14–18).

A. *If the spiritual man is delivered from the law by the grace of God, and the natural man is doomed by the law, by the same token, the carnal man is defeated by the law.* Between what the law demands and what the flesh can produce, there is "a great gulf fixed." The temptation of the carnal man (the saved but defeated Christian) is continually to revert to human effort and good works as a means of meriting God's approval.

B. *The word* carnal *describes, then, a Christian who, though saved, is still in bondage to the power of the flesh.* In verses 15–17 Paul shows us the conflict in potentialities that exists in the carnal Christian. There is a clash within the carnal man because of the old, Adamic nature and the new Christlike nature existing side by side.

C. *The* Living Bible *paraphrases verse 18:* "I know I am rotten through and through so far as my old sinful nature is concerned. No matter which way I turn I can't make myself do right. I want to but I can't." Paul described a conflict within himself so intense that he was almost pulled apart at times. The answer lies only in daily submission to the Holy Spirit.

Conclusion

In the last verses of Romans 7, Paul asked, "Who will rescue me from this body that is subject to death? Thanks be to God, who delivers me through Jesus Christ our Lord!" (vv. 24–25 NIV).

SUNDAY MORNING, JANUARY 29

Title: Christian Rewards

Text: "They will each be rewarded according to their own labor. . . . If what has been built survives, the builder will receive a reward" **(1 Cor. 3:8, 14 NIV)**.

Scripture Reading: 1 Corinthians 3:8–15

Hymns: "Lead On, O King Eternal," Shurtleff
"Face to Face with Christ My Savior," Breck
"O That Will Be Glory," Gabriel

Offertory Prayer: Heavenly Father, cultivate in us the grace of giving. Cause us to know the joy and celebration of giving to you. And teach us to be generous for your glory. Amen.

Introduction

Living the supernatural life is a blessing not only now but also in the future. There is a great difference in the doctrine of salvation for the lost and the doctrine of rewards for the saved. Salvation is by grace, not by works, but rewards are according to the works of the believer. Salvation is a gift; rewards are earned.

First Corinthians 3:8–15 reveals several truths about rewards: (1) Every believer will be rewarded according to his or her own labor (v. 8). (2) We are laborers together with God, not for salvation but for his service (v. 9). (3) We are to build on Christ as our foundation (v. 11). (4) We have a choice of two kinds of building materials: gold, silver, and costly stones or wood, hay, and straw. The first kind represents eternal materials; the second represents temporal materials. Building with eternal materials results in rewards. Building with temporal materials results in loss at the judgment seat of Christ.

A minister sat at the bedside of a dying friend. As the friend talked of going home, tears filled his eyes. Knowing the man was young in the Lord, the minister thought he was afraid to die and tried to speak words of encouragement to him. The friend said, "I'm not afraid; I'm just ashamed to die." Christ was his Savior, but he had to meet him empty-handed. His life was like "wood, hay, and straw."

It doesn't have to be that way. Christians can live and die crowned with victory. Sometimes the Christian's reward is called a prize, but several times it is called a crown. Five crowns are mentioned in the New Testament.

I. The crown of life (James 1:12).

The crown of life is sometimes called "the lover's crown." We find strength to overcome temptation and endure trials through the love of God. Without his love in our hearts, trials can cause us to become bitter and critical and lose the crown of life.

This is also the crown that is received for being "faithful unto death" (Rev. 2:10). All believers have eternal life, but not all believers will be rewarded the crown of life. To receive it, we must love the Lord more than our lives (Mark 8:35). We must live for Christ and endure temptations and trials in the power of the love of God.

II. The crown of rejoicing (1 Thess. 2:19–20).

The crown of rejoicing is called the soul-winner's crown. The greatest work we are privileged to do for the Lord is to bring others to a knowledge of Christ as personal Savior.

A. *Why win souls?*
   1. It is wise to win the lost (Prov. 11:30).
   2. It is a work against sin (James 5:20).
   3. It is a cause for joy in heaven (Luke 15:10).
   4. Every soul-winner will shine as the stars forever (Dan. 12:3).

B. *How do we win souls?*
   1. We can win souls by the example we set. Others see Christ in us as we respond properly in life situations (2 Cor. 3:2).
   2. We can lead others to Christ with our mouths. We need to witness verbally for Christ, trusting the Holy Spirit to give us power (Acts 1:8).
   3. We can win souls through our giving. We should give tithes and offerings to support others who are preaching Christ and so have fruit abound to our account (Phil. 4:15–17).

There is much rejoicing when the lost are saved. Heaven rejoices (Luke 15:10); the new believer rejoices (Acts 8:39); the sower and reaper rejoice together (John 4:36); and the whole family of God rejoices.

III. The crown of righteousness (2 Tim. 4:8).

The crown of righteousness is the crown earned by believers who eagerly anticipate the second coming of Christ. In light of that, Paul could say, "I have fought a good fight" (2 Tim. 4:7). In the realm of spiritual warfare, Paul won the battle. He could also say, "I have finished my course" (v. 7). In the course of travel, there was no detour around hard places. There was no looking back (Luke 9:61–62). Instead, Paul kept his eyes on Christ (Phil. 1:6). Finally, he could say, "I have kept the faith" (2 Tim. 4:7). He preached all the counsel of God (Acts 20:24–31).

IV. The crown of glory (1 Peter 5:4).

The crown of glory is a special reward for the faithful, obedient, God-called pastor. The Chief Shepherd himself gives it. It is eternal; it "fadeth not away." Yet every believer may share in the pastor's "crown of glory" (Matt. 10:41). God will reward those who support his chosen servant through prayer and encouragement and giving freely of self and possessions.

The pastor earns this reward by:

A. *Feeding the church (1 Peter 5:2).*
B. *Taking the spiritual oversight of the church (v. 2).*
C. *Being an example to the church (v. 3).* Pastors are to walk with God by faith. They are to be spiritual leaders.

V. The incorruptible crown (1 Cor. 9:24–25).

This is the crown for victorious living. In the Greek games, the competitors ran for a corruptible crown; in the Christian race, we run for an incorruptible one.

The key to victory is a disciplined life, whether in the Olympic games or in the Christian life. Athletes deny themselves many things their bodies crave. Likewise, Christians must subdue their bodies or else be disqualified for the prize. The New Testament contains guidelines for us to win the crown of victory.

A. *We must deny self of anything that would weigh us down and hinder us (Heb. 12:1).*
B. *We must keep our eyes fixed on Christ (Heb. 12:2).*
C. *We must find our strength in the Lord (Eph. 6:10–18).*
D. *We must place our all on the altar of the Lord (Rom. 12:1–2).*
E. *We must, by faith, refuse anything that would impede spiritual progress (Heb. 11:24–29).*

There is no way to win this crown and be a spectator in the Christian life. We must enter the race and run to win!

Conclusion

In an old legend, an angel was talking with an aged Christian. Going into a great vault, he brought out a beautiful crown with shining jewels of rare value. He said, "This is the crown I designed for you when you were a youth, but you refused to surrender yourself completely to the Lord; now it is gone."

From the vault he brought another crown. It was beautiful but not nearly as beautiful as the first one. He said, "This is the crown I designed for your middle age, but you gave those years to indolent discipleship; now it is gone."

The angel brought a third crown from the vault. It was just a plain gold crown with no jewels in it. He said, "Here is the crown of your old age. This is yours for all eternity."

Every one of us will receive a reward according to our labor. What will be your reward?

SUNDAY EVENING, JANUARY 29

Title: Free at Last!

Text: "It is for freedom that Christ has set us free. Stand firm, then, and do not let yourselves be burdened again by a yoke of slavery" **(Gal. 5:1 NIV)**.

Scripture Reading: Galatians 5:1

Introduction

The Magna Carta of spiritual emancipation, the Declaration of Independence from salvation by works, and the Manifesto of Gospel Liberty are but a few of the phrases that we could use to describe the main theme of Paul's letter to the Galatians. If we were to reduce the 149 verses of this letter to three words, they would be "Free at last!"

Freedom is generally assumed to be the birthright of all people, yet people are anything but free. Bondage is more likely to be their lot. For some the cause is psychological, for others economic, and for still others political. But Paul, with his profound insight into people's most basic need, made clear that only in Christ Jesus are people truly free.

For this very reason, Paul was determined that every obstacle should be removed between people and God. Nothing—not legalism, not moralism, not ritualism—will be allowed to prevent people from experiencing the freedom that comes only from Christ. Like the Galatians, ours is the happy experience of knowing that because of Jesus Christ and him alone, we are free at last!

I. Free to be saved by faith (Gal. 2:16).

In this verse Paul was saying, "We are free at last from all bondage to the law and to works." For the first time in this letter, the word *justify* occurs. Yet it is one of the most significant terms in Paul's theology. It means "to pronounce righteous." That righteousness, by which a person is accepted by God, comes not from the fulfillment of any legal enactments, but by faith.

A. *Faith liberates us from bondage to the law.* If the law cannot save, then what is its purpose? "Clearly no one who relies on the law is justified before God, because 'the righteous will live by faith.' . . . Christ redeemed us from the curse of the law by becoming a curse for us" (Gal. 3:11, 13 NIV). The law tells us what sin is, but most important, the law drives us to the grace of God. It shows us our own weakness and makes us see that we can do nothing but throw ourselves on the mercy and love of God.

"Before the coming of this faith, we were held in custody under the law, locked up until the faith that was to come would be revealed. So the law was our guardian until Christ came that we might be justified by faith. Now that this faith has come, we are no longer under a guardian" (Gal. 3:23–25 NIV). The law system was God's method of preparing the world for Jesus' coming.

B. *Faith appropriates the saving grace of Christ.* "For it was through reading the Scripture that I came to realize that I could never find God's favor by trying—and failing—to obey the laws. I came to realize that acceptance with God comes by believing in Christ" (Gal. 2:19 TLB). Paul was certain that, through faith, Jesus Christ had done for him what he never could have done for himself. Only when we give up our struggle can the saving grace of Christ be ours.

II. Free to grow in grace (Gal. 5:1).

"It is for freedom that Christ has set us free. Stand firm, then, and do not let yourselves be burdened again by a yoke of slavery" (5:1 NIV). No longer do we serve God as slaves to laws and ceremonies. Rather, we serve him as people free to grow in grace.

Unfortunately, some people today have reverted to the error of the Galatians. They teach that we are initially "saved by grace" but that we remain saved and thus grow by works. In other words, Christ makes the "down payment," but we must make the "monthly installments" or suffer a divine foreclosure and repossession of our salvation.

Here Paul declared that nothing could be further from the truth. In Philippians 1:6 he speaks with certainty: "Being confident of this, that he who began a good work in you will carry it on to completion until the day of Christ Jesus" (NIV).

We are free to grow in grace for several reasons.

A. *Because of the continuing work of the Holy Spirit.* Paul asked the Galatians, "Are you so foolish? After beginning by means of the Spirit, are you now trying to finish by means of the flesh?" (Gal. 3:3 NIV).

"Not by might, nor by power, but by my spirit, saith the Lord of hosts" (Zech. 4:6). Our rate of growth in grace is in direct proportion to the degree to which we allow the Holy Spirit to fill us. Often we leave areas of our lives off-limits to the Holy Spirit, thereby choking our growth in grace. This is why Paul said to born-again believers, "Be filled with the Spirit" (Eph. 5:18).

B. *Because of the indwelling presence of Christ (Gal. 2:20).* Paul was dead; his old self was in the bonds of sin, vainly striving for righteousness by observing the law. Elsewhere the change is called the new birth or regeneration; here Paul said, "Christ lives in me." Christ, the Life, lived in Paul.

Yielding our lives to the indwelling presence of Christ is not a once-in-a-lifetime experience. It is something we must do each day. Paul said, "I die daily" (1 Cor. 15:31), and here (Gal. 2:20) he said, "I am crucified with Christ."

When Christ is in control of our lives, we will naturally want to read our Bible, pray, witness to others, and fellowship with other Christians, and we will grow in grace.

III. Free to live as members of God's family (Gal. 3:26–29).

"So in Christ Jesus you are all children of God through faith, for all of you who were baptized into Christ have clothed yourselves with Christ. There is neither Jew nor Gentile, neither slave nor free, nor is there male and female, for you are all one in Christ Jesus. If you belong to Christ, then you are Abraham's seed, and heirs according to the promise" (Gal. 3:26–29 NIV).

Let's consider five characteristics of God's family.

A. *We are equal (Gal. 3:28).* What does this mean to the church today? It means that none of us has vested rights—no one is above or better than others. It means that the opinion of each person is of great value but of no more value than any other person's opinion. It means that the congregation is to be the church. It means that as members of the family of God, we are more concerned about our responsibilities to other members than our own individual rights.

It means that because we are members of God's family, we are "devoted to one another in love," and we "honor one another above [ourselves]" (Rom. 12:10 NIV). It means that as we reach out to others, as we witness to them and lead them to Christ, we do so regardless of their past, their culture, or their social status. It means that when they become members of God's family, we accept them as our equals.

B. *We are heirs (Gal. 4:7).* Every member of a family is an heir to the father's wealth. We are not servants, laboriously striving to keep the law. We are sons and daughters of God, born into his family by grace through faith and thus full heirs to all of his riches.

My Father is rich in houses and lands,
He holdeth the wealth of the world in his hands!
Of rubies and diamonds, of silver and gold,
His coffers are full; He has riches untold.

I once was an outcast stranger on earth,
A sinner by choice, and an alien by birth.

But I've been adopted, my name's written down,
An heir to a mansion, a robe, and a crown.

I'm a child of the King, a child of the King:
With Jesus my Saviour, I'm a child of the King.
—*Harriet E. Buell, "A Child of the King"*

C. *We care for and encourage one another (Gal. 6:1–3).* "If anyone thinks they are something when they are not, they deceive themselves" (Gal. 6:3 NIV). Paul said that when our fellow Christians slip, we are responsible for helping them get back on their feet again.
D. *We bear the fruit of the Spirit (Gal. 5:22–23).*
E. *We are productive (Gal. 6:9).* "Let us not become weary in doing good, for at the proper time we will reap a harvest if we do not give up" (Gal. 6:9 NIV). Salvation by grace does not mean freedom from service but rather freedom to serve.

The more we realize that we are members of God's family not through any merit of our own but solely through the grace and love of God, the harder we will work and the more productive we will become—not to remain a member of God's family but because of the thrill of being a member of his family.

Conclusion

An old African American spiritual captures the spirit of Paul's letter to the church at Galatia.

Way down yonder in the graveyard walk,
Me and my Jesus goin' to meet and talk.

On my knees when the light passed by,
Thought my soul would rise and fly.

One of these mornin's bright and fair,
Gonna meet King Jesus in the air.

Free at last, free at last,
Thank God, I'm free at last!

SUGGESTED PREACHING PROGRAM FOR THE MONTH OF
FEBRUARY

■ Sunday Mornings

The theme for Sunday mornings in February and continuing through the first Sunday in March is "The New Life That Is Possible through Christ."

■ Sunday Evenings

In every congregation there is at least one person with a broken heart. One function of the pastor-shepherd is to help bind up the brokenhearted. The theme for the Sunday evening sermons is "Is There Any Good News for Those Who Suffer?"

■ Wednesday Evenings

Continue with the theme "What the Bible Says."

WEDNESDAY EVENING, FEBRUARY 1

Title: What the Bible Says about Things That Accompany Salvation

Text: "Even though we speak like this, dear friends, we are convinced of better things in your case—the things that have to do with salvation" **(Heb. 6:9 NIV).**

Scripture Reading: Hebrews 6:7–12

Introduction

One fallacy that has stopped the spiritual growth of countless Christians is the concept of salvation as a termination point rather than a starting point. It is almost as though some people, when they are saved, look back on that experience and say, "Whew! I took care of that; now I can settle down to the business of living!" And they build a fence around their Christianity and pay periodic visits to it, but by and large they live their lives as they want to.

In this Hebrews passage, the author is talking not about what constitutes salvation; rather, he is recalling what manifests or demonstrates a genuine salvation experience—both in believers themselves and to those who observe. In the letter to the Hebrews, we discover four major gifts that accompany our salvation.

I. First, we have the gift of assurance (Heb. 6:17–20).

A. *Quite often a pastor hears someone say, "Pastor, there are times when I seriously doubt that I have ever been saved."* And the look on the person's face indicates that those are not idle words, because the distress and uncertainty are plainly seen. Often the person will add, "I just don't feel the way I used to feel about my faith and my relationship with God." What people who doubt their salvation fail to realize is that few things in the world are more undependable than feelings. And because of the inconsistency of our feelings, Satan delights in attacking us at this point.

B. *In Hebrews 6:17–20 we are taught that the security of our salvation rests exclusively on the faithfulness of God, not of ourselves.* Two things are underscored in this passage that form the basis for the assurance of our salvation. First, the Word of God (v. 18). Our confidence in fellow believers may be shattered because of their human weakness. But God's Word never changes. It is alive with the breath of God. Jesus said, "Heaven and earth shall pass away, but my words shall not pass away" (Matt. 24:35). Second, Jesus' mission in heaven for Christians right now is further assurance that we are eternally secure in the grace of God. Jesus functions now as our High Priest (v. 20). He is there to intercede for us, to represent us before the Father in heaven.

II. Second, we have the awakening of spiritual appetite (Heb. 5:12–14).

A. *In this passage, the writer tells us that milk is important for children.* Milk contains certain elements that are necessary to the development of young bodies. It contributes to the growth and development of the bone structure, enabling one to stand upright and walk. But there comes a time in the growth development when there must be a supplement to the milk diet. The body needs the strength that comes from meat. The milk supplied the calcium for the child's teeth, and now the child is equipped to chew meat. The "meat" represents all the solid foods that a child can eat after passing through infancy.

B. *The spiritual analogy is obvious.* During the first stage in our spiritual development, we must have the "milk" of God's Word. We would choke on the strong "meat" of the Word in the early days of our Christian life. Before long the "milk" of the Word provides the bone structure and the teeth, and we are ready for the "strong meat" of God's Word.

III. Third, we have a longing for association with God's people (Heb. 10:25; 13:7, 17).

A. *"Association" is referred to three times in the Hebrews letter.* First, the writer appealed to the Hebrews to "not [give] up meeting together" (NIV). Then he reminded them to remember those who first spoke the Word of God to them. Finally, he instructed them to obey their leaders and submit to their authority. He was saying that we are not to stop coming together in Jesus' name. We are to follow the admonishments and exhortations of those whom God has set over us as teachers and shepherds, and we are to show appreciation and thanksgiving for those whom God uses to speak his Word to us.

B. *Then, in Hebrews 13:1, we are told to "let brotherly love continue."* This cannot be done effectively or consistently unless we assemble together with our brothers and sisters in Christ. This is why the Lord's Day in the Lord's house should be meaningful to the people of God. Not only do we receive strength, but we have the opportunity to share strength in Christ with each other.

C. *Third, we are told to strive for peace and avoid bitterness (12:14–5).* The way some Christians act when they come to God's house is disgraceful; they sow discord and are hurtful and snobbish. But when Christ is Lord in our lives, we act as magnets and draw those who are lonely and confused. Gathering with other genuine Christians makes us eager for the Lord's Day to come so that we can be in the Lord's house and fellowship with the people of God forever. On the other hand, failing to meet together on a regular basis is a symptom of spiritual regression.

IV. Fourth, we have a determination to adhere to that which is essential for spiritual growth (Heb. 4:14; 12:3).

A. *Throughout the letter to the Hebrews, the clearest emphasis falls on faith—not faith simply as "trust," but rather as a steadfast loyalty to what has been known, heard, seen, and experienced of God. It is a quality of faith that holds fast (4:14).* How tragic that some Christians are like clouds in the sky, driven by the wind first this way and then the other. There is no stability in their faith.

B. *Then there is a quality of faith that persists (12:3).* There come those trying times in all of our lives when we feel like "throwing in the towel." But true faith persists; it "keeps on keeping on" even in the face of overwhelming difficulties. Believers may indeed be "down" occasionally, but they must rise again, tenaciously and perseveringly. God gives us the strength to do this.

Conclusion

Many other things accompany our salvation as well. But these are basic: assurance, appetite, association, and adherence or perseverance. Are these things present and operative in your life? What is the state of your spiritual health? Are you failing to grow in the faith because these "accompaniments" to your great and free salvation are dormant and inoperative in your life?

SUNDAY MORNING, FEBRUARY 5

Title: Where Is Jesus?

Text: "So then after the Lord had spoken unto them, he was received up into heaven, and sat on the right hand of God" **(Mark 16:19)**.

Scripture Reading: Mark 16:14–20

Hymns: "How Great Thou Art," Hine
"Glorious Is Thy Name," McKinney
"Jesus Shall Reign Where'er the Sun," Watts

Offertory Prayer: "Bless the Lord, O my soul: and all that is within me, bless his holy name. Bless the Lord, O my soul, and forget not all his benefits." This is our prayer of recognition of your many blessings and our prayer of release to you of our gifts of self and money. To your name be all glory! Amen.

Introduction

Today's church desperately needs new life. The hope of the church is Christ himself. The basic question is, Where is Jesus? The answer to this question enables us to praise Jesus Christ for his position now in God's eternal plan. Mark 16:19 says, "He was received up into heaven, and sat on the right hand of God." Luke 24:50–51 says, "He led them out as far as to Bethany, and he lifted up his hands, and blessed them. And it came to pass, while he blessed them, he was parted from them, and carried up into heaven."

Acts 1:9–11 describes this scene again: "When he had spoken these things, while they beheld, he was taken up; and a cloud received him out of their sight. And while they looked steadfastly toward heaven as he went up, behold, two men stood by them in white apparel; which also said, Ye men of Galilee, why stand ye gazing up into heaven? this same Jesus, which is taken up from you into heaven, shall so come in like manner as ye have seen him go into heaven." We need to answer two questions today.

I. Where is Jesus?

A. *Jesus' ascension was his homecoming.* He was coming home to his Father in heaven. His ascension was the restoration of the glory he possessed before the creation of the world. As John 17:5 says, "And now, Father, glorify me in your presence with the glory I had with you before the world began" (NIV).

Jesus longed to be there. In a parable, he compared himself with a landowner who traveled to a far country and later returned to reward his servants (Matt. 21:33). He talked about being "lifted up" (John 12:32); he talked about preparing a place for us (John 14:3); and he announced, "I go unto my Father" (John 14:12, 28; see also 16:5, 7).

B. *Jesus is exalted to the Father's right hand.* Mark 16:19 says that Jesus "sat at the right hand of God" (NIV). In Acts 2:33 Peter proclaimed that Jesus is "by the right hand of God exalted." In Philippians 2:9–11 Paul concluded, "Wherefore God also hath highly exalted him." These are powerful Scriptures. However, Ephesians 1:19–23 even more fully describes where Jesus is and what that means. He is at the Father's right hand, "far above all principality, and power, and might, and dominion, and every name that is named."

This passage describes Jesus' victory. His work on earth is finished. He has done all the Father told him to do. He triumphed over Satan, sin, the world, the flesh, and death. Jesus' position at the Father's right hand demonstrates his authority and sovereignty. He is Lord of heaven and earth, the highest authority of all.

II. What is Jesus doing?

The second question is, what kind of ministry is Jesus doing today?

A. *Jesus is drawing people.* According to John 12:32 Jesus is drawing all people to himself. This is his saving ministry (Acts 4:12). He is not dragging people but magnetically drawing them. He is doing this right now in the world through his Spirit, through his love, through his Word, and through his people. From heaven he is drawing people on earth!

B. *Jesus is interceding for people.* He stands between us and the Father. Romans 8:34 says, "Christ Jesus who died—more than that, who was raised to life—is at the right hand of God and is also interceding for us" (NIV). First John 2:1–2 teaches that Jesus Christ is our Advocate, our heavenly lawyer, our Counselor. He represents us before the Father. Satan accuses us to the Father and the Father to us, but Jesus represents our case before the Father. What hope and encouragement this is!

C. *Jesus is directing the church.* Ephesians 1:22–23 indicates that God "hath put all things under his feet, and gave him to be the head over all things to the church, which is his body, the fulness of him that filleth all in all." Jesus is the head of the body. As the head leads the body, so Christ leads the church. He is directing the ministry of the church.

   As the head, Jesus is doing two things for the church.

   1. Jesus is pouring out the gift of the Holy Spirit (Acts 2:33, 38).
   2. Jesus is imparting spiritual gifts to believers (Rom. 12:6). We are empowered by the Spirit to exercise our spiritual gifts in relation to other members of the church—all under Christ's direction.

D. *Jesus is building the church.* Jesus said in Matthew 16:18, "I will build my church." Acts 2:47 describes saved people being added to the church. And Acts 6:7 reveals that the Lord is not satisfied with just adding to his church; he wants to multiply it. That is his desire for the church today!

E. *Jesus is preparing believers.* He is doing something in heaven. John 14:2 says he is preparing a place for us, a heavenly home. When our home is ready, he will call us to heaven. In fact, he will come and escort us to heaven.

F. *Jesus is sharing his power with us.* His desire for us is expressed in John 17:24: "Father, I want those you have given me to be with me where I am, and to see my glory, the glory you have given me because you loved me before the creation of the world" (NIV). The reality of this desire is expressed in Ephesians 2:5–6, where we are seated with him in heaven, and in Romans 8:28–30, where we are glorified in his likeness! And in Ephesians 1:19–22, not only does Jesus have authority, but we also are given authority. His victory is our victory! "As he is, so are we in this world" (1 John 4:17). All that Jesus has, we share with him. All that he does, we do with him. His new position and ministry in heaven are our new position and ministry on earth!

Conclusion

Christ's position in the heavenly realms is the basis of knowing victory in our Christian life. We are in him. We are identified with him. This means victory over the world and every circumstance.

Sunday Evening, February 5

Title: How Do You Face Trouble?

Text: "At this, Job got up and tore his robe and shaved his head. Then he fell to the ground in worship and said: 'Naked I came from my mother's womb, and naked I will depart. The Lord gave and the Lord has taken away; may the name of the Lord be praised'" **(Job 1:20–21 NIV).**

Scripture Reading: Job 1:13–22

Introduction

Is there any good news for those who suffer? In times when trouble strikes, we need to take an inventory to see if there is any good news that can cheer our hearts and help us bear the burden of pain.

Trouble and suffering are facts of life that all of us must cope with sooner or later. An incurable disease may afflict someone we love or even us personally. A financial disaster may wipe out our fortunes. A domestic tragedy may tear apart our home. Fatal accidents occur on life's highways, and there are dead-end streets where all hopeful expectations are brought to a stop.

How should Christians cope with suffering and trouble?

When trouble comes, some people turn to religion, hoping it will deepen and strengthen their faith. Others turn away from religion in disappointment and despair. Still others turn against religion in hate and cynicism.

How do people cope with pain and trouble? Some bluster and bluff and cuss. Some develop a headache and take an aspirin. Some drink or take drugs that enable them to escape the pain of reality temporarily. Some pray and trust God.

What will you do when trouble comes? Will you turn to God? Will you run from God? Will you turn against God?

Let's take a look at Job, the ultimate example of a man who struggled with suffering in the times before Christ.

I. Job's character (Job 1:1, 8).

Job is a dramatic illustration of one who experienced undeserved suffering. He is a striking example of how the innocent can suffer.

A. *Job was a blameless man.* He was blameless in the eyes of God, in the eyes of others, and in his own eyes.
B. *Job was upright.* He was straight and genuine and right in his relationships.
C. *Job feared God.* He was a reverent worshiper of God as he understood him.
D. *Job was a man who turned away from evil.* There was no compromise in his life.

II. Job's position.

Job lived in a time when people commonly believed that anyone who was good and did good would be happy and prosperous. Job was a good man, and he was also happy and prosperous.

A. *Job was the best of the best; there was none other like him.*
B. *Job enjoyed great wealth.*
C. *Job had a wonderful family.*
D. *Job was a priest in his own household (1:5).*
E. *Job was the epitome of success and happiness.*

III. Job's calamity and suffering.

Suddenly Job experienced great suffering and catastrophe that was both undeserved and unexplained.

A. *Job suffered the loss of his property (1:14–17).*
B. *Job suffered the tragic death of his children (1:18–19).*
C. *Job experienced the loss of his health (2:7–8).*
D. *Job experienced bad counsel and advice from his wife (2:9).*
E. *Job endured the frustration of sincere friends who blundered in their efforts to comfort and counsel him.*

    Nonetheless, we should recognize that Job was fortunate in some respects.

    1. His friends did come to him. This required great effort on their part.
    2. They sat in silence with him for seven days. Sometimes silence is the best way to support someone who is suffering.

3. They gave the best advice they knew to give. Basically they said to him, "Job, acknowledge your sinfulness. Admit your hypocrisy. Confess your secret sins." Job's friends were philosophers and thinkers, and they offered him the best solutions they knew for the complex problems he faced.

Job and his friends believed that suffering was the result of sin and that people who suffered must have sinned. In the midst of his pain, Job held on to his conviction regarding his personal integrity. He was convinced that he did not deserve the suffering he was experiencing. His suffering was totally out of proportion to any sin of which he might have been guilty.

We learn from the book of Job as we study it in its entirety that suffering is not always the result of sin. We also learn from the book of Job that God is often blamed for tragedies and catastrophes and hurts for which he is not responsible.

Job's friends came to him with the suggestion that his sufferings were the unavoidable consequence of some great flaw in his character and in his beliefs and conduct. Job was patient in the sense that he held on to his integrity and denied that his sufferings were due to some great sin in his life.

When suffering comes to us, we must hold on to the conviction that God is love and that God is good. We must believe that God always acts in conformity with his good character.

Conclusion

How will we handle trouble? Will it bring us closer to Christ? Will it turn us away from Christ? Will it turn us against Christ?

Several suggestions may be helpful to us as we consider the possibility of suffering in the future. First, let's get acquainted with Christ as Savior, Teacher, Friend, and Helper. Let's study the example of Jesus Christ as he dealt with the pain and suffering of others. And let's be assured that he is the same yesterday, today, and forever.

Before suffering comes, we need to develop some resources to assist us in times of trouble. In the same way that we take out liability or accident insurance, let's take out some spiritual insurance.

1. We must develop the daily habit of a quiet time in which we let God speak to us from his Word.
2. We must let prayer be a conversation with God in which we not only speak to him but let him speak to us.
3. We need to participate regularly in public worship and allow God to use this time to draw us closer to him.
4. We need to develop genuine Christian friendships with other members of the family of God so they can be the medium of God's ministry to us when trouble comes.

5. We must expect the angels of God to come in our time of need. In the meantime, we must not be anxious about trouble that may come in the future. Let's determine to live now for the highest and best under the leadership of the risen Christ and in the power of the Holy Spirit.

Wednesday Evening, February 8

Title: What the Bible Says about Prayer

Text: "'And when you pray . . .'" **(Matt. 6:5 NIV)**.

Scripture Reading: Matthew 6:5–13

Introduction

What is prayer? To say that prayer is "communication with God" is an oversimplification. Prayer is the sincere desire of our souls expressed to God. Prayer is what allows us to establish intimacy with the Creator. Prayer creates an awareness of God's constant nearness to his people.

Prayer is also how unbelievers, recognizing their sinful nature and need for salvation, reach out by faith to receive God's gift of eternal life. Prayer is the expression of praise to God as well as the medium through which petitions are made on behalf of human need.

Prayer is described, explained, and illustrated throughout the Bible. The greatest and most profound demonstration of prayer is illustrated in the earthly life of Jesus, who is often recorded praying to his heavenly Father.

I. General requirements for effective prayer.

A. *A forgiving spirit (Matt. 6:14).* Why is forgiveness so difficult for us? Our nature thrives on retaliation, on seeking vengeance. To truly forgive as Christ taught us means to relinquish all tendencies to "get even" with those who have wronged us. An unforgiving spirit can overwhelm us and create a barrier between us and God. Actually, *our* forgiveness toward others is but the *outgoing* of God's forgiveness expressed toward us—like the ebb tide!

B. *Simplicity (Matt. 6:5–6).* To the Pharisees, prayer was a performance for the sake of those around them. These words of Jesus do not constitute an indictment against one of God's children leading as each heart silently joins in the prayer, affirming and enforcing the spoken prayer. "Entering the closet" may be more symbolism than a literal act, suggesting the closing out of the interfering world while we communicate one-on-one with God. People can pray like this anywhere, even in the busy marketplace.

C. *Humility and repentance (Luke 18:10–14).* Both the Pharisee and the publican (or tax collector) in this story could represent lost men.

The publican expressed the only prayer that God can hear from the sinner—a prayer of confession, admission of sin, a cry for mercy. The prayer of the Pharisee describes the person who considers himself "good" and therefore a credit to God and his kingdom. This person considers his good works the price of admission into the kingdom of God.

D. *Unity of believers (Matt. 18:19–20).* The explanation of this apparent "blank check" from God is in verse 20. The realization and recognition of God's presence with us will position our prayer requests within his will. Prayer is never like rubbing a magic lamp in order to bring forth some divine genie to do our bidding. Prayer, in its petitionary nature, is primarily seeking the will of our heavenly Father.
E. *Intensity (Matt. 7:7–11).* Again, the thrust of this prayer promise relates to the finding of God's will. Never do we need to beg or cajole God. It is because of our slowness of heart and spiritual immaturity that we spend so much time searching for his will but so little time doing it. But as we "ask, seek, and knock," the very exercise of faith has a cleansing effect on us, preparing us to receive the answer in accord with God's will and not our own wishes.
F. *Unceasingly (1 Thess. 5:17).* "Pray without ceasing." We must keep the communication lines between us and God open constantly. Our very attitude on life should be an expression of prayer to God. This unceasing communication with the Father God will foster a beautiful and cherished "naturalness" in our prayer life.

II. Personal requirements for effective prayer.

A. *Purity of heart (Pss. 24:3–5; 66:18–19).* God, through the ministry of the indwelling Holy Spirit, reveals sin when it exists in the lives of his people. If, after that, we don't deal with our sin, our prayers are aborted. "The hill of the Lord" and "his holy place" describe the experience of personal confrontation with God. "Clean hands" indicate that our actions are open for God to see, and "a pure heart" indicates that any sin in our lives is confessed.
B. *Faith (Matt. 21:22).* Sadly, not every Christian who prays believes that God has the power to answer prayer. To truly believe with intensity of faith requires us to cultivate the gift of faith that God gives to each believer in embryonic form.
C. *In Christ's name (John 14:13).* "And whatsoever ye shall ask in my name, that will I do." This is not just a religious formula we use to close our prayers. It is a recognition that the source of all good things is Christ. His "name" represents all that he is.
D. *According to God's will (1 John 5:14).* "And this is the confidence that we have in him, that, if we ask anything according to his will, he heareth us." This, indeed, is the ultimate secret to effective prayer.

III. The constituent parts of prayer.

A. *Adoration (Ps. 103).* Adoration of God diminishes self and exalts God.

B. *Confession (1 John 1:9).* Confession of sin is the key that opens the door to continuing, unbroken fellowship with God.

C. *Thanksgiving (Phil. 4:6).* The sin of ungratefulness is perhaps the most common sin among Christians. Too often we take God for granted.

D. *Supplication (1 Tim. 2:1–3).* "Supplication" describes a humble and earnest request before God.

E. *Intercession (James 5:15).* We must intercede for those who are sick, because people can be so far from God that they cannot pray for themselves.

Conclusion

Prayer must be an integral part of every Christian's life. We should engage in secret (private) prayer (Matt. 6:6), in family prayer (Acts 10:2, 30), in group prayer (Matt. 18:20), and in public prayer (1 Cor. 14:14–17).

SUNDAY MORNING, FEBRUARY 12

Title: What the World Needs Now Is Love

Text: "What great love the Father has lavished on us" **(1 John 3:1 NIV)**.

Scripture Reading: 1 John 3:1, 11–18; 4:7–12

Hymns: "Love Is the Theme," Fisher
"I Love Thee," Anonymous
"The King of Love My Shepherd Is," Baker

Offertory Prayer: Our heavenly Father, we praise you for loving us while we were yet sinners. We realize the extent of your love by the gift of Jesus and his death on the cross. We praise you for your continuing love, active in temptation and trial, forgiving and fortifying us. Remind us that to whom much is given much is required. We ask you to impart comfort to the bereaved and healing to the ill, power to the spiritually weak and joy to the downcast. We present our gifts in the hope that they will be used to help your church minister to people in need. We give in order to share your love, which we have so generously received. We pray this in Jesus' name. Amen.

Introduction

One of our most basic needs is to be loved. The lyrics of a classic song reflect this worldwide longing—"What the world needs now is love." God has met this need in Christ. Because of Jesus, a new kind of love is possible and is at work in our world.

I. See the Father's love.

A. *God loves us (1 John 3:1).* When Martin Luther's translation of the Bible was being printed, a piece of type fell to the floor. The printer's daughter later found the section, which said, "For God so loved the world that he gave." Excitedly, she showed it to her mother.

Her mother said it didn't make any sense. "Gave what?"

The girl responded, "Oh, Mama, it doesn't matter. If God loves me enough to give me anything, I don't have to be afraid of him."

Many think of God as harsh, judgmental, or indifferent toward the world. The truth is, he loves us. "God is love" (4:8).

B. *The gift of love (1 John 4:9–10).* How do we know God loves us? "This is how God showed his love among us: He sent his one and only Son into the world that we might live through him" (v. 9 NIV). The cross is God's bold demonstration of love. Because he loved us, he sent his only beloved Son to suffer the shame and agony of crucifixion. Because he loved us, he made a bridge across the gulf of sin that separated us from him.

Bennett Cerf told of an eight-year-old girl in a Pennsylvania orphanage. She was painfully shy, unattractive, and generally shunned by the other children. The orphanage directors regarded her as a problem child. A rule of the home required the directors' approval of any written communication prior to mailing. One afternoon the girl was seen hiding a letter in the branches of a tree that hung over the wall. The letter was seized and opened. It read: "To anybody who finds this: I love you." Likewise, our Lord Jesus was driven by a loveless world outside the city wall. He hung on a cross, a message from God to the world—*I love you!*

II. The example of Christ.

A. *Inclusive and active (1 John 3:16–18).* We are to live out the pattern of Christ's love. "This is how we know what love is" (v. 16 NIV). How do we know? By considering the example of Christ—the perfect pattern of love. The way to respond to others is to walk in his steps. His love included all people and was active in their lives.

Jesus faced many "untouchables" in his day. No one wanted to touch the lepers. When they went out in public, they cried out "unclean" so that people could avoid them. But Jesus went out of his way to touch the lepers; they needed his love. The Samaritans also were considered social untouchables. Jesus ministered to the Samaritan woman and honored every Samaritan in his parable of the good Samaritan. Jesus had fellowship with the religious untouchables, people who did not scrupulously keep the law and were regarded as ceremonially unclean. Jesus saw each person as valuable and full of potential. That kind of love is the pattern for every Christian. "Dear friends, since God so loved us, we also ought to love one another" (4:11 NIV). Can his love be seen in us?

We ask, "Who is our brother?" When in love we seek people in need, we discover our brother. We naturally tend to love those who love us or share our values. Too often we demand change before we show love. But *agape* love includes everyone and actively seeks to share Christ's love with them.

B. *Exclusive and eternal (2:15–17).* The love of Christ is not gullible nor naive. If we love God, who is holy, we cannot love the things that are against Christ. We love sinners but do not love the sin. "Do not love the world or anything in the world. . . . For everything in the world—the lust of the flesh, the lust of the eyes, and the pride of life—comes not from the Father but from the world" (vv. 15–16 NIV). Christ's love is exclusive.

Christ's love is also eternal: "Whoever does the will of God lives forever" (v. 17 NIV). Those who receive Christ by repentance and faith begin to do God's will and become united with his love. Paul affirmed that nothing could "separate us from the love of God that is in Christ Jesus our Lord" (Rom. 8:39 NIV).

> God's boundless love! As arching sky
> Above us when we wake and sleep,
> Above us when we smile and weep,
> Above us when we live and die. . . .
>
> God's endless love! What will it be
> When earthly shadows flee away,
> For all eternity's bright day
> Th'unfolding of that love to see!
>
> —*Maltbie D. Babcock, "God's Boundless Love"*

Conclusion

Probably no word in our vocabulary is as misunderstood as *love.* We apply it to food and clothing tastes, to romantic relationships, and to religious experiences. My four-year-old asked me one day, "Daddy, how do you spell *love*?" I told her the four letters, which she proudly printed on a special note to those she loved. The spelling of love in our lives is infinitely more complex. In Christ the true meaning is available, and the world desperately needs this love now. Can they see it in us?

SUNDAY EVENING, FEBRUARY 12

Title: Is There a Connection between Sin and Suffering?

Text: "[Job's] wife said to him, 'Are you still holding on to your integrity? Curse God and die!'

"He replied, 'You are talking like a foolish woman. Shall we accept good from God, and not trouble?'

"In all this, Job did not sin in what he said" **(Job 2:9–10 NIV)**.

Scripture Reading: Job 2:11–13

Introduction

When calamity struck the house of Job, his friends came at great trouble and inconvenience to comfort and counsel him.

Job's friends held to the traditional thoughts of their day, which in many respects are still the thoughts of our day. They believed that God always rewards righteousness. They believed that God always punishes wickedness. They perceived that righteousness always pays off with peace, prosperity, popularity, plenty, and permanence.

Job's friends saw God as a judge. They understood him somewhat in terms of his being a prosecuting attorney or a policeman. They believed God to be an executioner. They believed that God's law was self-operating and self-executing, and that if you found yourself in great pain and suffering, it was proof that you were a great sinner.

The writer of the book of Job challenges all of our simple solutions to the complex questions that plague us when we are faced with pain and trouble. The easy answer is usually the incorrect answer.

While recognizing that sin ultimately results in suffering, when you study the book of Job, you cannot help but conclude that not all suffering is the direct result of sin. Job is an excellent illustration of this truth.

I. Job was a very good man who did not deserve to suffer as he was suffering.

A. *He suffered the loss of all his worldly property.*

B. *He suffered the tragic death of his children.*

C. *He suffered the absence of an empathetic wife.* We should recognize that when she came to Job and advised him to commit suicide, she was suffering from deep depression from the losses their family had sustained.

D. *He suffered the misunderstanding of his sincere friends.*

E. *He suffered indescribable pain.* Is there a connection between sin and suffering? The answer could be yes, and the answer could just as well be no.

II. Job's suffering is ascribed to Satan (Job 2:7–8).

Job did not know that his pain and suffering had been brought on him by the activity of Satan. Nor did Job's friends realize that Satan was responsible for Job's suffering. Both Job and his friends believed that sin always produces suffering. Consequently, his friends concluded that because Job was suffering, he must be a great sinner. Job knew in the deepest part of his being that he had not sinned in a manner that would provoke God to pour out such suffering on him.

In the midst of his agony, Job gave voice to some very painful and pointed questions:

A. *How can a man be just before God?*
B. *How can I stand before God?*
C. *Why does God not come to me in my time of pain?*
D. *Why will God not listen to my pleas?*
E. *Why does God let things like this happen?*

Job was plagued with the agony that many experience when undeserved suffering threatens their very existence. If God is all-powerful, why do these things happen? If he is love, why does he permit bad things to happen?

The traditional answer during Job's day was that God does good for the good and bad for the bad. And many people today hold to these ancient ideas. The other side of the coin is that many of us expect favored treatment by God because of our virtues and our high self-esteem. Many become indignant with God because of suffering and want to know what they have done to deserve such.

To the problem of why the innocent suffer, the book of Job gives no complete and satisfactory answer.

III. The painful problem of undeserved suffering.

From before the days of Job up to the present, men and women have grappled with the painful problem of suffering. We have come to recognize that while sin will produce suffering, not all suffering is due to sin.

Pain and suffering assault us from all directions. Natural disasters produce suffering. Many suffer because of historical decisions made by the different countries of the world. Ancestral choices bring pain on descendants.

The Hindus and Buddhists have built their whole philosophy on the question of the responsibility for pain and suffering. They believe in reincarnation and say that pain is inevitable because of evil deeds and conduct in a previous existence. They encourage kind and benevolent behavior to improve one's lot in a future existence.

Medical science can shed much light on the problem of pain. One physician has said, "We differentiate between pain that serves a useful purpose and pain that serves no useful purpose. Examples of pain that serve a useful purpose are pain in the side that indicates appendicitis, pain in the back indicting a herniated disc, or difficulty in chewing indicating an abscessed tooth. Some pain serves no useful purpose, for instance, a muscle-tension headache. It is a job for the doctor to differentiate between pain that serves a useful purpose and pain that is useless."

We have several choices when faced with the problem of pain.

A. *We can ignore it.* This could cause further damage because pain is often a warning of a serious physical problem.
B. *We can investigate the causes of the pain.*
C. *We can do something about the pain.*

Dr. Norman L. Geisler wrote a book dealing with the problem of pain and the results of evil (*The Roots of Evil* [Grand Rapids: Zondervan, 1978]). He explained that much pain comes directly from our own free choices. It also comes on us indirectly from the exercise of our freedom. We also experience pain because of the free choice of others. We experience some pain because of the good choices that other people make, but in which accidents are involved. Geisler also called attention to the fact that some suffering occurs because of the activity of evil spirits (Job 1:6; Matt. 17:14–19; Mark 5:1–13).

Some physical pains or evils may be God-given warnings of greater physical harms. Not all pain is bad. Some physical suffering may be used by God to warn us against moral evils. C. S. Lewis said, "God whispers to us in our pleasures, speaks in our conscience, but shouts in our pain; it is His megaphone to rouse a deaf world."*

Some pain and suffering may be permitted as a condition of producing spiritual refinement in our hearts and lives (Rom. 8:28).

Conclusion

We have no satisfactory solution to the problem of pain and suffering. Our great hope and our steadfast faith must be in God, who throughout all the record of his self-revelation in the Scriptures reveals himself as the God who is for life and health and relief from pain. In heaven "he will wipe every tear from their eyes. There will be no more death or mourning or crying or pain, for the old order of things has passed away" (Rev. 21:4 NIV). We should think of heaven not only as a destination but as a way of life. God is at work in the world to bring heaven into the present for those who will trust Christ and obey him.

We can trust God to help us with the problem of pain and suffering. We can believe that he hurts when we hurt. We can believe that he weeps with us when we weep. And we can look forward by faith to the day when pain will be no more.

Wednesday Evening, February 15

Title: What the Bible Says about Vengeance

Text: "'Not seven times, but seventy-seven times'" **(Matt. 18:22 NIV)**.

Scripture Reading: Matthew 18:21–22

* C. S. Lewis, *The Problem of Pain* (New York: HarperOne, 2001), 91.

Introduction

Peter's question, "How many times shall I forgive my brother when he sins against me? Up to seven times?" and our Lord's answer, "Not seven times, but seventy-seven times," reflect our struggle with the problem of vengeance. Because of our fallen nature, our instinctive reaction is to fight back, to lash out at those who infringe on our "rights."

Jesus, of course, had a great deal to say about this in his Sermon on the Mount, radiating from his basic and startling command, "Love your enemies." That kind of attitude was totally unheard of, even among the most religious in Judaism. In fact, the exhortation of the rabbis was, "Love your friends and hate your enemies."

The apostle Paul expanded on Jesus' theme in Romans 12:14–21. In rapid-fire succession, he provided a list of exhortations that deal both directly and indirectly with a Christian's attitude toward vengeance.

I. First, "Bless them which persecute you: bless, and curse not" (Rom. 12:14).

A. *The* Living Bible *paraphrases this verse, "If someone mistreats you . . . don't curse him; pray that God will bless him."* This is the true spirit of Christianity. On the cross, Jesus prayed for those who were crucifying him. In so doing, he demonstrated the proper attitude of a Christian toward his enemies.

B. *To retaliate against those who mistreat us is to push them further away from God.* We will more likely win them to faith in Christ—or if they are Christians, to repentance of their wrongdoing—if we disarm them with our love rather than castigate them with our vengeance.

II. Second, "Rejoice with them that do rejoice, and weep with them that weep" (v. 15).

A. *What is the principle demonstrated in this exhortation?* Whenever something good happens to our fellow Christians, we need to share their joy rather than sulk in jealousy.

B. *Weep with those who weep.* We may be inclined to criticize those who suffer, thinking, *Well, they got what they deserved!* Instead, we should feel deeply and meaningfully with others in their sorrow. To weep with those who weep means to enter into their sorrow, to empathize with them. Jesus was a prime example of this principle at the graveside of Lazarus, even though he would soon turn that scene of sorrow into joy.

III. Third, "Be of the same mind one toward another. . . . condescend to men of low estate" (v. 16).

A. *Paul does not mean that we must agree with others in every respect.* Rather, he means that we must make allowances for one another. We are not to sacrifice the harmony and good spirit of the body of Christ merely to win a point. This kind of stubbornness is most often the result of pride.

B. *"Condescend" in this verse does not mean to patronize or talk down to, as it means in modern usage.* Rather, it suggests that we are to deliberately seek out the lowly and the meek. In so doing, we deal a death blow to sinful pride in our lives.

IV. In verses 17–21 Paul lists four distinct methods by which we can triumph over vengeance.

A. *First, "Recompense to no man evil for evil" (v. 17).* In other words, never repay evil with evil. Retaliation is part of our unregenerate human nature, but turning the other cheek is divine.

B. *Second, "Provide things honest in the sight of all men" (v. 17).* The New International Version translates, "Be careful to do what is right in the eyes of everyone." Christians are to be above reproach in all of their dealings with others. Nothing provides more ammunition for unbelievers in their attacks against the Christian faith than inconsistency or questionable principles in the lives of Christians whom they observe.

C. *Third, "If it be possible, as much as lieth in you, live peaceably with all men" (v. 18).* Paul was a realist; he knew from personal experience that the gospel would be resisted with great violence wherever it was preached with power. Although it is not always possible to live at peace with everyone, we should always strive to be peacemakers.

D. *Finally, in verses 19–21 Paul sets out his fourth principle: repay hatred, opposition, and persecution with good.* One of human nature's greatest temptations is to pay back—to get even with the person who has wronged us. This is contrary to what Christ taught his followers.

Conclusion

We belong to God, so we never need to avenge ourselves. God always protects his property! Instead, we are to love our enemies—not just with words, but with our deeds. We are to actively express the Christian attitude of concern and agape love toward them.

Nowhere did Jesus promise us that the world would be kind to us. Rather, he said, "In the world ye shall have tribulation." But he also added, "Be of good cheer; I have overcome the world" (John 16:33). Only in his strength can we overcome unchristian attitudes that issue forth in acts of vengeance.

SUNDAY MORNING, FEBRUARY 19

Title: The Living Christ in the Church

Text: "'Silver or gold I do not have, but what I do have I give you. In the name of Jesus Christ of Nazareth, walk. . . . It is Jesus' name and the faith that comes through him that has completely healed him, as you can all see'" **(Acts 3:6, 16 NIV).**

Scripture Reading: Acts 3:1–18

Hymns: "There Is a Name I Love to Hear," Whitfield
"Because He Lives," Gaither
"The Church's One Foundation," Stone

Offertory Prayer: Heavenly Father, praise be to your name for your bountiful gifts. We acknowledge them with thanksgiving, and we present our gifts to you in joy and praise. Thank you for the privilege of giving. In Jesus' name. Amen.

Introduction

Lenin's embalmed remains lie in a crystal casket in a tomb in Red Square in Moscow. An inscription on the casket reads: "He was the greatest leader of all peoples, of all countries, of all times. He was the lord of the new humanity. He was the savior of the world." All that Lenin did is in the past tense. We have the true Savior of the world, the living Christ.

How do we know that Jesus Christ is living in power among us? For the Jerusalem church, the healing of the lame man signified the power of the living Christ and that he was present among them. How about us? Do we see lives being changed miraculously? Are things happening among us that amaze us and fill us with wonder? The book of Acts emphasizes the reality of the living Christ in the church. Let's consider three lessons from Acts 3.

I. The lesson of a crippled society and what can be done about it.

Peter and John had an encounter with a lame man who had been crippled from birth. Each day someone carried him to the gate Beautiful. He begged from the crowds of worshipers who passed this prominent place. This is where the man's healing took place.

The lame man saw Peter and John approaching the gate, so he begged them for money. Why Peter and John? Only God can answer that. But Peter's words changed the man's life: "Silver or gold I do not have, but what I do have I give you. In the name of Jesus Christ of Nazareth, walk" (Acts 3:6 NIV). Peter took the man by the hand and helped him up. The man was healed instantly. He jumped to his feet and walked around the temple courts praising God. This crippled man had been made whole.

The truth is that all of us are crippled, and all of us need healing. All of us have sinned (Rom. 3:23); we are like sheep who have gone astray (Isa. 53:6), and we are dead spiritually (Luke 13:3). Like the lame man at the gate, we are helpless and powerless, spiritually crippled without Christ. Salvation is our most basic need.

Our society is crippled too, with its crippled morals, marriages, and relationships. Our society is crippled by perversion. Abortion continues to claim innocent lives. Pornography continues to destroy homes. The sin of homosexuality is a way of life for millions. People are crippled by alcohol and drug abuse. People are crippled with negative attitudes, anger, hate, resentment, bitterness, and unforgiveness. Only Jesus Christ can bring us the healing we need.

II. The lesson of divine authority and how to appropriate it.

Acts 3:6 says that Peter healed "in the name of Jesus Christ of Nazareth." Jesus promised his disciples, "Whatsoever ye shall ask in my name, that will I do, that the Father may be glorified in the Son" (John 14:13). So Peter spoke in the name of Jesus Christ.

There is power and authority in Jesus' name! The answer to our crippled generation is the name of Jesus Christ, not silver or gold or self-help or positive thinking. And Peter claimed this authority of Jesus' name.

Jesus was given all authority in heaven and earth (Matt. 28:18). He shared his power with the apostles, and according to Ephesians 1:19–23, all believers share the privilege of this authority. All that we do should be done in the awareness of spiritual authority. We have the authority to call people to salvation. We have the authority to pray victoriously. We have the authority to resist the devil and make him flee. We have the authority to enforce Christ's victory in life and home and church and nation.

This spiritual authority is not to be taken lightly; it is to be exercised by believers who are filled with the Spirit, living cleansed lives, and walking by faith. There is power in the church when believers appropriate this authority.

III. The lesson of a living message and its relevance for our times.

Peter explains that the miraculous healing of the crippled man was God's work. It was the living Christ at work. What makes this first-century message relevant to twenty-first-century times?

A. *The message of the responsibility for Christ's death (Acts 3:13–14).* The apostles declared that the crucifixion was the greatest crime in human history. The fact is, all of us are responsible for Christ's death.
B. *The message of the resurrection of Christ from the dead (Acts 3:15).* Without the resurrection there is no hope, no salvation, no church, and no living Christ.
C. *The message of the power of Christ's presence (Acts 3:16).* This is the secret of the Christian life and the source of power in the church.
D. *The message of repentance and new life (Acts 3:19).* Repentance is a forgotten message in our generation, but there is no new life without it.
E. *The message of revival from the Lord's presence (Acts 3:19).*
F. *The message of the return of the Lord (Acts 3:21).* The message of the early church was the second coming of Jesus Christ. His coming was always in the consciousness of the first believers.

G. *The message of response to God's message (Acts 3:22–26).* It is a simple message: hear and be blessed (v. 22), or refuse to hear and be destroyed. Responding to Christ brings untold joy; rejecting him brings spiritual ruin.

Conclusion

Whenever the message of salvation is preached, something happens. The book of Acts is living proof of the living Christ in the church. The living Christ means hope for a crippled society, authority for the people of God, and a message for all times. Apply his power and authority to your life by faith, and let his Word be living and active in you.

SUNDAY EVENING, FEBRUARY 19

Title: The Management of Pain

Text: "To keep me from becoming conceited, I was given a thorn in my flesh, a messenger of Satan, to torment me" **(2 Cor. 12:7 NIV)**.

Scripture Reading: 2 Corinthians 12:7–10

Introduction

From cradle to grave, we spend much of our existence trying to avoid pain.

If you watch television commercials, you have probably noticed that many of them offer advice about how to manage pain. Such solutions are temporary. Some people try to escape pain through drugs and alcohol, but they find that their pain increases rather than disappears. Still others stoically just "grin and bear" their pain. How do you manage pain?

I. Paul experienced great pain (2 Cor. 12:7–9; Gal. 4:12–13).

Paul was no stranger to pain. There are several theories about the nature of his "thorn in the flesh."

A. *Some people have speculated that it was a form of recurring malaria that produced serious headaches.*

B. *Others have speculated that it was a form of epilepsy that resulted from his temporary blindness during his conversion experience.*

C. *Still others have proposed that it was a painful eye problem (cf. Gal. 4:15; 6:11).* In any case, Paul experienced great suffering because of it.

II. Paul recognized that Satan uses pain to hurt and to hinder.

A. *Paul speaks of his thorn in the flesh as "a messenger of Satan."*

B. *Satan uses pain to make people doubt God's goodness.* Satan wants to inject doubt into our minds until we distrust the character and behavior of our Father God.

C. *Satan seeks to foster bitterness and hate because of pain.* We must beware of the strategies of the evil one; he is out to destroy us because he is the enemy of God and our enemy as well (1 Peter 5:8–9). If Satan can make us angry at God and react with bitterness and hostility toward either God or others, he is leading us down a path of self-destruction.

III. Paul perceived that God would use his pain for good.

Paul believed that God would use his "thorn in the flesh" to strengthen his character.

A. *Paul's thorn in the flesh was not punishment for sin.*
B. *Paul's thorn kept him from becoming proud, arrogant, and self-sufficient.*

IV. Paul prayed for the removal of the thorn.

A. *Paul was a man of great faith and prayer.* He believed in bringing every problem before God's throne of grace for help and mercy.
B. *Three times Paul prayed for relief from the agony of this painful thorn.* Remember that Jesus prayed three times for the removal of the cup of suffering in the garden of Gethsemane as he faced the agony of crucifixion on the following day. The Scriptures say that the angels came and ministered to him, but the cup was not removed.
C. *Paul's persistent prayer for the removal of the thorn was not granted.* When you pray for relief from the pain that plagues your body and seemingly there is no answer, what will you do? You will not be able to ignore pain, because pain is no illusion.

V. Paul used all possible proper resources for the management of his pain.

A. *Luke was a physician and was Paul's traveling missionary partner through Asia Minor and on many of his journeys from then until he suffered martyrdom in Rome.*
B. *Paul accepted pain as something that was permitted by the will of God even when he could not understand it.*
C. *Paul offered thanksgiving to God in the midst of his suffering.* This does not mean that he thanked God for his suffering; rather, in the midst of his pain he found things for which he could be thankful. His words to the Thessalonian believers are appropriate at this point: "Rejoice always, pray continually, give thanks in all circumstances; for this is God's will for you in Christ Jesus" (1 Thess. 5:16–18 NIV). Searching for something to be thankful for in the midst of great pain creates a positive way of thinking and an open mind and heart through which God can minister to us in our times of need.
D. *Paul made the most and best of each day.* He tried not to let yesterday distress him in the present. He tried not to worry about tomorrow.

E. *Paul did not let bitterness rule and ruin him when pain throbbed through his body.* A dramatic illustration of the manner in which he dealt with pain is revealed in his experience in the Philippian jail when, following a cruel beating, he and Silas "were praying and singing hymns to God, and the other prisoners were listening to them" (Acts 16:25 NIV).

F. *Paul believed that through Jesus Christ he could overcome the painful circumstances of life (Phil. 4:13).* Many people have this false impression that if they try to be good and try to do right that God will exempt them from pain and suffering and trouble. This way of thinking is unrealistic and unbiblical. It is contrary to the experience of the great saints.

Conclusion

Jesus came to help people cope with pain. We have no record in the Scriptures of Jesus turning away from those who were in pain. He healed the sick. He gave sight to the blind and hearing to the deaf. He enabled the lame to walk. With faith in his love and kindness, we can face the pain that comes our way.

We can be assured that God's blessings will rest on our doctors and modern medical facilities, and we should not hesitate to seek these services as we cope with pain.

Jesus also came to help us cope with the pain of being fallen creatures, mistake makers, sinners who are lost and do not know the way home. Jesus came to help us cope with our incompleteness and our spiritual deadness toward God. Jesus came to help us avoid the agony of missing heaven when this life is over. He died on a cross and conquered death and the grave in order to prepare for us a home in heaven.

Let us trust Jesus to help us overcome all of the pain associated with being human beings, and let us rejoice in the fact that there will come a day when there will be no more pain.

Wednesday Evening, February 22

Title: What the Bible Says about Stewardship

Text: "Give an account of your management, because you cannot be manager any longer" **(Luke 16:2 NIV).**

Scripture Reading: Luke 12:13–34

Introduction

Perhaps no area in life is more sensitive than our finances. We may be open about every other part of our lives, but the moment someone questions us about our money or possessions, we become very defensive. Nonetheless, some of Jesus' most pertinent parables and teachings are about the stewardship of our possessions. Jesus knows the joy that awaits believers when they attain the level of commitment where they completely surrender all they have to God, including the stewardship of their possessions.

Luke 12:13–34 contains one of Jesus' clearest commentaries on stewardship. He began by using a parable to illustrate the truth he wanted to drive home. This particular story was precipitated by an incident that arose between two brothers. Evidently their father had died, and one brother was not pleased with the way the estate had been divided. He asked Jesus, "Master, speak to my brother, that he divide the inheritance with me."

Then note verse 15: "He said unto *them*" (emphasis added). No doubt the disciples and the crowd listened carefully to Jesus, but he likely directed his remarks specifically to these brothers. First, he stated a principle: "Take heed, and beware of covetousness: for a man's life consisteth not in the abundance of the things which he possesseth." Then, after he had the attention of the brothers, he began to relate a story about a rich man. Traditionally we have assumed that this man was an unbeliever who worshiped the god of materialism. He may have been. Or he may have been a believer, but an immature, egocentric, materialistic believer.

I. The first lesson in this parable is the danger of a false sense of security in one's possessions.

A. *Here we see a man who had become a success in his work.* He may have been an affluent farmer with a palatial home, fine barns and outbuildings, and impeccable fields symmetrically tilled and planted. And we say, "What a fortunate man! Ah, to have one year's income from that man's possessions! It would remove the pressure, and I could breathe again!" All too often we think of security in terms of relief from financial strain. And we rationalize that it is good to be rich.

B. *Yet Jesus said that one of the hardest things in life is for a rich man to keep his riches and God in proper perspective.* In Matthew 13:22 Jesus spoke of "the deceitfulness of riches." Wealth can give us a false sense of security. It can mislead us and make us think more highly of ourselves than we ought. We start to rely on our riches and our status in life rather than on God. Therefore, anything that gives us a sense of security other than God is false and hopelessly unreliable.

II. The second lesson in Jesus' parable is the foolishness of planning without God.

A. *In the midst of his false security, this rich farmer, who had pushed God aside, made some clever and even admirable plans.* In spite of his wealth, he was a prudent and practical-minded man. He insured against every contingency. His plans included not just the present but the distant future as well. He did not intend to play the miser and drive himself to acquire more and more. He was going to retire and enjoy life! So he made detailed plans to enjoy the wealth he had accumulated.

B. *But he failed to recognize that a sovereign God might have other plans for him.* In short, this man had not consulted God, and his plans exploded because he had considered himself, and himself only. In our human nature, we try to master our circumstances and be the lord of our own destinies. In so doing, we presume upon God, treating him as though he were a genie in a magic lamp.

C. *God said to this clever schemer, "You fool!"* Caesar Borgia of Italy was a great schemer and a successful diplomat. He made shrewd plans to achieve upon the death of his father, Alexander, a sudden overthrow of the government that would crown him ruler of Italy. He told his confidant Machiavelli that he had prepared for every possible contingency on his father's death. But all his planning was in vain. When his father passed away, Caesar Borgia was ill and not one of his plans could be put into action. His conspiracy had been very clever, but God said, "You fool!" God had other plans.

III. The third lesson in Jesus' parable is the tragedy of an impoverished soul.

A. *The rich farmer was not rich toward God on the night that God demanded his life.* Jesus said, "This is how it will be with whoever stores up things for themselves but is not rich toward God" (Luke 12:21 NIV). God searches for riches in our hearts and souls. From the world's perspective, the rich man had been a success, but his life was pathetic viewed in the light of eternity.

B. *When Jesus finished the parable, he turned to his disciples and gave the deeper interpretation.* He spoke of the folly in worrying about material things. He reminded them of the ravens who never go hungry and the lilies adorned with beauty. Yet ravens are such small creatures, and lilies flourish one day and wither the next. Then Jesus asked his disciples, "How much more will he clothe you, O ye of little faith?" (Luke 12:28).

Conclusion

Jesus hit the nerve center of this whole matter of stewardship when he said, "Seek ye the kingdom of God; and all these things shall be added unto you. Fear not, little flock; for it is your Father's good pleasure to give you the kingdom.... For where your treasure is, there will your heart be also" (Luke 12:31–32, 34).

SUNDAY MORNING, FEBRUARY 26

Title: Heart Cry for Revival

Text: "Why hast thou then broken down her hedges, so that all they which pass by the way do pluck her? . . . Return, we beseech thee, O God of hosts: look down from heaven, and behold, and visit this vine" **(Ps. 80:12, 14)**.

Scripture Reading: Psalm 80

Hymns: "God of Grace and God of Glory," Fosdick
"Lord, Send a Revival," McKinney
"Rise Up, O Men of God," Merrill

Offertory Prayer: Lord, we worship your holy name and give you all the glory for your blessing to us. We offer ourselves, our time, our hearts, and our gifts of money to you. Cause your work to grow and your church to glow, as we give in Jesus' name. Amen.

Introduction

Psalm 80 contains a truth that is urgently important to all of us. It is a word from God that will help us understand the events in our times. It will lead to a heart cry for revival, which in turn will lead to new life in the church. Let's consider three words that pinpoint this truth.

I. Hedges.

Verse 12 says, "Why hast thou then broken down her hedges . . . ?"

A. *The purpose of "hedges."* At the heart of this truth is a biblical understanding of hedges. In the Bible we find hedges around three things: a nation (Ps. 80:12; Ezek. 13:5), a family (Job 1:10), and a person (Hos. 2:6).

   God's hedge is his invisible wall of protection that he builds around a nation, a family, a person, a church, or even our possessions when we are obedient to him. In our Scripture reading today, the hedge was protection for a vineyard and a property marker for the owners.

   In the New Testament, Jesus prayed for Peter, essentially building a hedge of protection around him (Luke 22:31–32). Jesus also prayed for protection for his disciples (John 17:11, 15). Paul prayed for those under his spiritual care. Second Corinthians 10:4–5 provides powerful insight into this kind of protection.

B. *The problem with "hedges."* Verse 12 mentions "broken-down hedges." Somehow the hedge around Israel was demolished, and the nation was ravaged by enemies like a wild boar ravages a vineyard (v. 13).

   Today enemies like "wild boars" are running rampant throughout the world, the nation, and even our own area. The United States has been suffering a critical moral crisis for many years. We have been confronted with terrorism, street crime, domestic violence, alcohol and drug abuse, sexual immorality, and the decay of marriage and the family. But there is more. Spiritual illiteracy, apathy, irreverence, greed, pride—all these threaten America. Something has been happening in America. Our hedges are almost broken down.

   Who has broken down the hedges? Verse 12 says that God is the one who has done this. But why? For three reasons:

   1. To bring judgment on his people (Isa. 5:5).

2. To awaken us to spiritual vigilance.
3. To bring us to confession and repentance. A holy God demands a holy life.

II. Hope.

The second word is *hope.* Is there any hope that God will rebuild the hedges? Yes, if we understand the ways that God builds a hedge.

A. *God builds a "hedge" through godly people.* Ezekiel 22:30 says, "I sought for a man among them, that should make up the hedge." Job was a godly man (Job 1:5). He was "perfect," not without sin but wholeheartedly devoted to pleasing God. He was "upright"; that is, all his relationships were right—with God, with self, and with others. He "feared God," honored him, and "eschewed evil," hated evil and turned away from it. His outward walk was like his inward relationships.

B. *God builds a "hedge" through his Word.* Ezekiel 13 teaches this truth. Ezekiel was speaking against the prophets of Israel, who had not retained the hedge. They followed their own minds and saw nothing (v. 3). They did not have the vision the Lord gives to his true prophets. This example from Scripture teaches us that God builds a hedge through prophets who preach his Word. As these servants of God proclaim his standard, God can build a hedge of protection around a person, family, church, city, or nation.

C. *God builds a "hedge" through prayer.* Ezekiel 22:30 says, "And I sought for a man among them, that should make up the hedge, and stand in the gap before me for the land, that I should not destroy it: but I found none." God builds a hedge when his people engage in intercessory prayer.

Soon after the colonists came to America, many of them turned away from God and the nation experienced a moral slump. The people were poisoned by greed, the churches were almost empty, and European atheism filled the vacuum.

In New England some people began to pray for revival. In 1734 in Northampton, Massachusetts, Jonathan Edwards preached his famous sermon "Sinners in the Hands of an Angry God," and in one service hundreds of people repented of their sins and turned to the Lord. Unbelief was diverted, righteous living returned, and in a short time one-sixth of the population was won to Christ. Churches were filled with worshipers.

In 1849 revival again came in answer to prayer. The Lord always works in response to prayer. God builds the hedges of protection when we pray.

III. Heart cry.

When the psalmist Asaph realized what was happening to the hedges of protection, he wrote this heart cry for revival: "Return, we beseech thee,

O God of hosts: look down from heaven, and behold, and visit this vine" (v. 14). Lord, visit this nation! You have broken down the hedge that guarded our country, but we know you want to bless us again. Turn us to you! This is our heart cry!

Lord, visit your church! You birthed it. You are building it. It belongs to you. It exists for your purpose. This is our heart cry for revival and for souls.

Lord, visit our families! Many are suffering. We need help. Restore the hedge around our families. Visit our homes with revival!

Lord, visit our lives! Get our attention. We are being overcome with evil. We have sinned. Protection is gone. Lord, visit our lives!

Conclusion

A while back, a young seminary student was preparing to preach the evening service at a church one Sunday. The elderly pastor had witnessed some glorious outpourings of the Spirit in his early years. He longingly told the seminary student that he and his wife had prayed every morning for ten years to see one more mighty move of the Spirit.

The young student had hardly started his sermon when a woman began to weep, and then another and another. Soon the entire congregation was on its knees. In the midst of prayer and weeping, people were accepting Christ as Savior, old animosities were being healed, broken families were being united, and new spiritual commitments were being made. The pastor walked slowly down the aisles and whispered, "He did it one more time." Lord, visit this vine!

SUNDAY EVENING, FEBRUARY 26

Title: The Mystery of Pain and Suffering

Text: "'Do you think that these Galileans were worse sinners than all the other Galileans because they suffered this way?'" **(Luke 13:2 NIV)**.

Scripture Reading: Luke 13:1–5

Introduction

Some people see no mystery about the problem of suffering. They believe that suffering is the result of an inevitable law that every cause produces an effect. They would reason that suffering is due to some great sin the sufferer has committed.

Christians have a problem with suffering that non-Christians do not have. Christianity proclaims that God is love and that he loves the whole world. If this is true, why does he permit undeserved suffering? If God loves and if he has all power, then he should protect us from pain and suffering. Some have sought to solve this problem by saying that those who suffer have been guilty of some sin and have brought God's judgment on themselves. This simplistic solution to a complex question is unsatisfactory and incorrect.

Between our entrance into life and our exit from life, we experience many kinds of pain and suffering: physical, mental, emotional, spiritual, visible, invisible, recognized, and unrecognized. Many suffer because of natural disasters. Many suffer because of historical events and decisions that were made in the past. Many suffer because of choices made by their ancestors. We must also recognize that much suffering comes to us because of our personal choices and the choices of others.

What does Jesus teach about pain and suffering? Does Jesus have any good news for those who suffer?

I. Jesus rejected the thought that all suffering comes from God.

Jesus lived in a time when people were making false diagnoses of the problems they confronted in daily life. Because they believed that sin resulted in suffering and that God was a just God who would punish the wicked, they reasoned that all suffering was due to God's anger. The end result of this incorrect way of thinking served to deprive believers of the comfort and encouragement they needed in times of weakness, pain, and insecurity.

John 11 records that Jesus wept in sorrow when Mary and Martha were grief stricken over the death of their brother, Lazarus. We must have faith to believe that the Lord weeps with us when we experience the pain of sorrow. The fact that our Lord ministered to those whose bodies were racked with pain and whose minds were tormented with insecurity should encourage us to believe that he comes to us as well in the midst of our sufferings. The prophet Isaiah had proclaimed in regard to the suffering of God's people that God responded to their plight with empathy and compassion: "In all their distress he too was distressed, and the angel of his presence saved them. In his love and mercy he redeemed them; he lifted them up and carried them all the days of old" (Isa. 63:9 NIV). We must reject every proposed solution to the mystery of suffering that deprives us of the benevolent presence and grace of our loving God.

II. Jesus rejected the doctrine that all suffering was due to sin committed by the sufferer.

Jesus lived in a time when people had a very simple solution to the problem of suffering. They believed that people suffered because either they or their parents had sinned. They were concerned about fixing responsibility for suffering. But Jesus categorically denied that suffering can be traced directly to some sin in the life of the sufferer.

Many of us have responded to unexpected and undeserved pain with the question, "What have I done to deserve this?" Often when we witness the undeserved suffering of others, we ask the question, "Why does a good person have to suffer while others are spared?"

To explain the problem of pain as always being the result of some sin that has been committed by the sufferer is inaccurate and contradicts the teachings of Jesus Christ.

In Luke 13:1–5 Jesus called attention to the fact that some suffering is due to the cruelty of others, while some suffering may be due to the faulty construction of a tower that collapsed.

III. Jesus would have us reject the idea that pain is an illusion.

Some people believe there is no such thing as pain, that it is a mere illusion; and they suggest that we use our minds to eliminate the negative thoughts that produce pain.

A. *It is true that many of our ills are in our minds.* Psychosomatic illness afflicts many people. Much suffering could be eliminated if we would think correctly and eliminate negative and destructive ways of thinking, and instead fill our minds and hearts with positive and affirmative thoughts.

B. *To make pain an illusion is a form of escape from reality that will ultimately disappoint and lead to tragedy.* Many have suffered indescribable pain and anguish because they accepted this inadequate and inaccurate solution to the mystery of pain and suffering.

IV. Jesus would have us reject the idea that present suffering is due to evil done in a previous existence.

In many parts of the world, people believe they have no personal responsibility for the suffering they endure in this life. Rather, they believe that pain in the present is due to a life of cruelty and evil and selfishness in a previous existence. This belief leads to an attitude of fatalism and helplessness. Those who agree with this philosophy know nothing about the joy that can be experienced as a result of God's forgiveness.

Conclusion

There is no one simple solution that is always satisfactory regarding the mystery of pain and suffering. But we can be assured that our Father God will not permit any pain to enter our lives that he will not help us bear.

Our Father God is no stranger to suffering. His heart has hurt with the hurt of all humankind. Our Savior is no stranger to suffering. He suffered the pain of misunderstanding, loneliness, criticism, rejection, humiliation, and crucifixion. Because our Savior has experienced pain and suffering, he is able to empathize with us in whatever life may bring to us (Heb. 2:18).

How can we cope with the mystery of pain and undeserved suffering? Let us recognize and grasp the truth that God loves us and that he cares and wants to help us. Let us remember that our Lord himself has suffered. Let us respond to his precious promise to be with us until the end of the age. Let us secure medical services, and let us pray for our doctors and for all of those who give themselves to the healing ministry. Let us make the best of each day as we live one day at a time.

SUGGESTED PREACHING PROGRAM FOR THE MONTH OF MARCH

■ Sunday Mornings

Complete the series "The New Life That Is Possible through Christ" on the first Sunday of the month. Then on the second Sunday of the month, begin a series titled "Going to Jerusalem" as a prelude to Easter.

■ Sunday Evenings

"The Past Speaks to the Present" is the theme for a four-part series of messages based on the lives of the patriarchs.

■ Wednesday Evenings

Complete the series "What the Bible Says."

WEDNESDAY EVENING, MARCH 1

Title: What the Bible Says about Death

Text: "'You must not eat from the tree of the knowledge of good and evil, for when you eat of it you will certainly die'" **(Gen. 2:17 NIV)**.

Scripture Reading: Revelation 21:1–4

Introduction

The fact that there are so many different theories about what happens to our souls when we die indicates our desire to understand the phenomenon of death. We hear and use such expressions as "life in the next world," "life after death," and "life on the other side." Does the Bible speak conclusively about this question? Yes! And the scriptural answer provides abiding hope for Christians, particularly as we deal with the death of a loved one or prepare to face death ourselves.

I. What is death?

A. *Death is the consequence of sin (Rom. 5:12).* When Adam and Eve broke God's command in the garden of Eden, death became their companion. They died spiritually because they broke their relationship with God. The vital fellowship they had enjoyed with God in the garden was gone, dead. The principle of death became operative in their physical lives as well: they began to die physically. The inevitable deterioration of the physical body is a result of sin.

B. *Death is the lot of all people (Heb. 9:27).* Death is inescapable. We are dying (progressively), and we will die (terminally).

C. *Death terminates earthly life (Eccl. 9:10).* Death proves the temporal nature of physical existence.

D. *Death is described as a return to dust (Gen. 3:19), the absence of breath (Gen. 25:8), and a "departure" (Phil. 1:23).* Students of the Bible will discover an amazing difference in the attitudes of various Old and New Testament saints in regard to death. The coming of Christ and his teachings clarified the death experience for Christians in an extraordinary way.

E. *The physically dead have been recognized by the living (Matt. 17:1–8).* Peter, James, and John spiritually recognized Moses and Elijah during the transfiguration. We will have a greater knowledge of all things in heaven (1 Cor. 13:12). All the mysteries and perplexities of this earthly life will be clear to us in heaven.

II. The state of the dead.

A. *Before the resurrection of Christ, the dead apparently went to "Sheol."* In the story about the rich man and the beggar named Lazarus in Luke 16, the rich man suffered in a place of torment but was able to look across a great chasm and see Lazarus by Abraham's side in paradise. Also, as Jesus was dying on the cross, he told the thief on his right, "Today shalt thou be with me in paradise" (Luke 23:43).

B. *After the resurrection of Christ, believers who die are said to be "absent from the body, and . . . present with the Lord"* (2 Cor. 5:8). Death is also referred to as "sleep" in the New Testament, while the soul immediately goes to be "with the Lord." John, in Revelation, described believers who die as being "happy" because they are able to "rest from their labours," knowing that "their works do follow them" (Rev. 14:13).

C. *Paul considered death for believers to be an experience of "gain" (Phil. 1:21) instead of loss.* To Paul death meant the final victory over self and temptation.

D. *Paul anticipated "the crown of righteousness" that awaited him and all those who "love his [Christ's] appearing" (2 Tim. 4:8).* Paul's attitude toward death was not a morbid desire to escape from life; rather, he knew the joys that awaited him after this life were far and beyond anything he could imagine.

III. The Christian attitude toward death.

A. *Paul said, "I am torn between the two: I desire to depart and be with Christ, which is better by far; but it is more necessary for you that I remain in the body" (Phil. 1:23–24 NIV).* Again, this was not "escapism" on Paul's part. He lived in such constant and close communion with his Lord that he longed to be with Jesus. At the same time, he felt the pressing responsibility of establishing these churches and strengthening these new Christians in the faith. He was "needed" in this life and would find joy fulfilling the purpose God had for him.

B. *Paul also described for the Thessalonian believers (and us) the Christian attitude toward the death of loved ones (1 Thess. 4:13–14).* He attached the certainty of the resurrection of the dead to the belief and assurance that Christ had been raised from the dead.

Conclusion

While physical death is not something we normally look forward to, God regards death as the glorious homecoming of his children. Jesus said to his disciples, "In my Father's house are many mansions" (John 14:2). He has gone to prepare a place for us, and he will come again to receive us (vv. 3–4). Death is no longer an enemy to believers in the Lord Jesus Christ. It is simply a blessed transition from an earthly life of imperfection and incompletion to one of perfection and eternal joy.

SUNDAY MORNING, MARCH 5

Title: Living at a New Address

Text: "But you know that he appeared so that he might take away our sins. And in him is no sin. No one who lives in him keeps on sinning" **(1 John 3:5–6 NIV).**

Scripture Reading: 1 John 1:5–9; 3:5–10

Hymns: "Power in the Blood," Jones
"I Need Thee, Precious Jesus," Whitfield
"Grace Greater Than Our Sin," Johnston

Offertory Prayer: Heavenly Father, we are grateful for this new week. May our worship today be in the right spirit and consistent with the truth revealed in Jesus. We ask your forgiveness for doing those things we should not have done this past week as well as for our failure to do the good things we knew to do. We desire power over sin, so lead us into the relationship in which that power is possible. Motivate us to give with the assurance that Paul had: "My God will supply every need of yours according to his riches in glory in Christ Jesus." In Jesus' name we pray. Amen.

Introduction

Being a Christian is like living at a new address. A Christian is someone who has moved from the house of sin and death into a new home with Christ. This new relationship to sin is the second gift made possible by Christ's victory over death.

I. The living Christ brings death to sin.

A. *A remedy for sin (1 John 3:5).* Humankind has always sought relief from the crushing weight of wrong. Sin brings guilt, death, and shame.

How can the sin problem be handled? One approach is to place the blame on someone or something else. Even Adam and Eve played this ancient game called "pass the buck." Some people attempt to handle sin by doing good works in an effort to balance the scale, but new sins keep upsetting the balance. Presenting a sacrifice to appease the offended individual is another futile effort. John declared the absolute remedy for sin: "He [Jesus] appeared so that he might take away our sins" (NIV). The angel prophesied about Jesus' work: "He will save his people from their sins" (Matt. 1:21 NIV). John the Baptist introduced Jesus as "the Lamb of God, who takes away the sin of the world!" (John 1:29 NIV). "God made him who had no sin to be sin for us, so that in him we might become the righteousness of God" (2 Cor. 5:21 NIV). Jesus' critics were right when they said that only God can forgive sin (Mark 2:7). His death and resurrection are the only adequate remedy for sin.

Jesus' resurrection assures us of this. Since death is the wages of sin, a dead Christ would be powerless over sin. "If Christ has not been raised, your faith is futile; you are still in your sins" (1 Cor. 15:17 NIV). His resurrection means victory over sin and death.

B. *The defeat of the devil.* Sin is a work of the devil, "because the devil has been sinning from the beginning" (1 John 3:8 NIV). Jesus came to defeat the work of this prince of darkness. When the Seventy returned from their successful evangelistic assignments, Jesus exclaimed, "I saw Satan fall like lightning from heaven. I have given you authority . . . to overcome all the power of the enemy" (Luke 10:18–19 NIV). Christians have power to resist and defeat the devil's temptations. Satan continues his work of deception, but King Jesus is more powerful than the prince of evil.

II. Sin in a Christian's life.

A. *Christians are not perfect (1 John 1:8).* The assurance of victory over sin and Satan is quickly countered by the evidence of sin in the life of professing Christians. How are we to reconcile this reality with the truth that "no one who lives in him keeps on sinning"? Power over sin does not mean sinless perfection, and the Christian who claims to have reached such a state is guilty of self-deception. "If we claim to be without sin, we deceive ourselves and the truth is not in us. . . . If we claim we have not sinned, we make him out to be a liar and his word is not in us" (1 John 1:8, 10 NIV).

B. *A different pattern of life (1 John 3:6–10).* On the surface, it appears that John contradicted himself. In chapter 1 he admitted sin in the Christian life; in chapter 3 he declared, "No one who lives in [Christ] keeps on sinning" (v. 6 NIV). The verbs in this section are in the perfect tense and refer to continuous, habitual action. Genuine Christians exhibit a new pattern in their lives. New desires, direction, and destiny are clearly evident. They live at a new address (2 Cor. 5:17).

III. Victory over sin.

A. *Walk in the light (1 John 1:7).* The way to daily victory over the pull of the old life is to "walk in the light." The closer we are to the Lord, the further we will be from sin.

B. *Continual confession and cleansing (1 John 1:9).* Whenever we sin, we need to confess it to the Lord and accept his cleansing. His grace is greater than our sin. He will forgive us and purify our hearts.

Conclusion

The apostle Paul expressed well what every Christian has experienced: "If anyone is in Christ, the new creation has come: The old has gone, the new is here! All this is from God, who reconciled us to himself through Christ." Note that Paul then added, "And gave us the ministry of reconciliation" (2 Cor. 5:17–18 NIV). What a great gift we have been given, as well as a great responsibility to bring others to Christ.

Sunday Evening, March 5

Title: Getting Guidance from God

Text: "Isaac brought her into his mother Sarah's tent, and took Rebekah, and she became his wife; and he loved her: and Isaac was comforted after his mother's death" **(Gen. 24:67).**

Scripture Reading: Genesis 24:1–67

Introduction

Each day thousands of airplanes fill the skies all around the world. Guiding them so that they avoid accidents is a serious responsibility shared by air traffic controllers and pilots. Each plane has an intricate guidance system as well, on which the pilots depend.

In the book of Genesis, we can read the story of how Abraham received intricate guidance from God to obtain a wife for his son of promise, Isaac. We can examine this story to learn what steps Abraham, his servant, and Isaac took to obtain God's guidance.

I. Determine to follow God's will.

A. *Isaac was confident that God wanted a wife for him.* She would share his faith and be like-minded in purpose. He knew the marriage would work best if she was from a similar family background. Consequently, Abraham sent a servant back to his home in Mesopotamia to find a woman who fit the profile.

B. *If we want to receive God's guidance, we must be willing to do his will.* We cannot follow God's will when we have determined within ourselves to do what we please. If we refuse to yield our will to the will of God, we cannot find the guidance we are seeking. Isaac was willing to do God's will.

II. Use your rational powers.

A. *The servant used his rational powers to find a wife.* With Abraham's instruction, the servant took ten camels and all kinds of choice gifts and set out. He reached the city of Nahor late in the afternoon when the women came to the well for water. The servant then reasoned, "Behold, I stand here by the well of water; and the daughters of the men of the city come out to draw water: And let it come to pass, that the damsel to whom I shall say, Let down thy pitcher, I pray thee, that I may drink; and she shall say, Drink, and I will give thy camels drink also: let the same be she that thou hast appointed for thy servant Isaac; and thereby shall I know that thou hast shewed kindness unto my master" (Gen. 24:13–14). The servant understood that Isaac needed a self-reliant and outgoing woman for his wife. Locating the right woman was not a matter of mere chance. It was the deliberate use of rational powers.

B. *God wants people to use the rational powers of the mind in seeking God's will.* Some people think they can discover God's will by chance, much like flipping a coin and calling "heads" or "tails." Others expect some miraculous intervention from heaven. They expect God himself to appear, speak audibly, and tell them exactly what he wishes them to do. Still others rely on strong emotional feelings to discover God's will.

God wants us to use our heads in seeking his will. We should examine both the pros and cons of the issue in a rational manner. We should think of every possible angle of the decision. This will help us clarify our thinking.

III. Pray about the matter.

A. *Isaac's servant prayed for the right woman for his master.* "And he said, O Lord God of my master Abraham, I pray thee, send me good speed this day, and shew kindness unto my master Abraham" (Gen. 24:12). The servant believed in the power of prayer. If he wanted light from the Lord, he had to look in that direction.

B. *Prayer is one of the best means of receiving God's guidance.* Jesus continually searched for God's will through prayer. One example is Jesus' prayer in the garden of Gethsemane. He was honest with God and told him he wanted to find some way other than crucifixion. Three times he asked God to remove the cup, yet he was reaching the place of submission. Finally, he said, "O my Father, if this cup may not pass away from me, except I drink it, thy will be done" (Matt. 26:42). Thus Jesus used prayer to arrive at the right decision.

IV. Wait on the Lord!

A. *The servant of Abraham waited on the Lord.* "And the man wondering at her held his peace, to wit whether the LORD had made his journey prosperous or not" (Gen. 24:21). Rebekah came to the well to draw water. After she had done so, she offered the servant some water. "And she said, Drink, my lord: and she hasted, and let down her pitcher upon her hand, and gave him drink. And when she had done giving him drink, she said, I will draw water for thy camels also, until they have done drinking" (Gen. 24:18–19). Rebekah offered both the servant and his camels water. Without doubt this action was an immediate answer to the servant's prayer. Yet he did not want to act hastily. While Rebekah went for more water, he waited for the feeling of certainty.

B. *In getting guidance from God, we must respond to his leadership with prudence.* God guides deliberately. He does not lead recklessly. Therefore we need to be careful not to make quick decisions. "They that wait upon the LORD shall renew their strength; they shall mount up with wings as eagles; they shall run, and not be weary; and they shall walk, and not faint" (Isa. 40:31).

Conclusion

Are you trying to go through life directing yourself? This path will lead to frustration and ultimately to disaster because you don't know where you are going. You need to follow God's guidance. Make up your mind to follow his will, use your rational powers, pray about the matter, and wait on the Lord.

WEDNESDAY EVENING, MARCH 8

Title: What the Bible Says about the Devil

Text: "Be alert and of sober mind. Your enemy the devil prowls around like a roaring lion looking for someone to devour" **(1 Peter 5:8 NIV)**.

Scripture Reading: Matthew 4:1–11

Introduction

Satan doesn't want us to study his characteristics and learn about his tactics. He would much rather work behind the scenes and keep alive the fallacy that he is a red-skinned creature with horns, a forked tail, and a pitchfork, with smoke perpetually coming out of his nostrils. This caricature of Satan gives rise to the sinister persuasion that he is not a real person at all, but a mythological or fictional character who only represents an evil influence in the world. However, the Bible clearly describes the devil and carefully outlines his strategy.

I. The origin of the devil.

A. *Satan is a created being.* The fact that all things in heaven and on earth, "visible and invisible, whether they be thrones, or dominions, or principalities, or powers," were created by Christ and for Christ is stated in Colossians 1:16.

B. *We don't know when the angelic host was created.* The Bible doesn't tell us exactly when God created the angels, but it does imply that their creation preceded all material things as we know them and were themselves preceded by the eternal existence of God (John 1:1–2).

C. *Among all the angelic host, Satan's creation alone is mentioned in particular (Ezek. 28:15).* This fact suggests the supreme place Satan held in relation to all the invisible creatures of God. (For a symbolic portrayal of Satan, read Ezekiel 28:11–19.)

II. The personality of the devil.

A. *Satan exercises all the functions of a person.* Isaiah described him as having completed his course and having been judged at the end of time, addressing him with the title "Lucifer, son of the morning," and seeing him as fallen from his primal state of glory (Isa. 14:12–17). Verses 13–14 list five ways in which he set his own will against God's.

B. *Because of his sinister and deceitful nature, Satan gained the title of "serpent" in the garden of Eden (Gen. 3:1–15).* Every word spoken there and the design of Satan's strategy revealed are evidence of his personality (cf. 2 Cor. 11:3, 13–15; Rev. 12:9; 20:2).

C. *Further indication of Satan's personality is the fact that he apparently has access to God (cf. Job 1:6–12; 2:1–13; Luke 22:31; Rev. 12:10).* He also has access to men (Eph. 6:10–12; 1 Peter 5:8); therefore he exhibits every feature of a true personality. Further insight into his personality is discovered in his temptation of Jesus (Luke 4:1–13).

III. The power of the devil.

A. *Though morally fallen and now judged in the cross (John 12:31; 16:11; Col. 2:15), Satan has not lost his position, and he has lost little of his power.*

B. *His personal strength cannot be estimated.* The writer of Hebrews said that Satan had the power of death (Heb. 2:14), but that power has been surrendered to Christ (Rev. 1:18). He had the power of sickness in the case of Job (Job 2:7) and was able to "sift [Peter] as wheat" in a sieve (Luke 22:31). He is said to have weakened the nations, shaken kingdoms, made the earth tremble, and made the earth a wilderness, destroying the cities thereof (Isa. 14:12–17).

C. *But Christians can have victory over Satan through the power of the Spirit of God and the blood of Christ (Eph. 6:10–12; 1 John 4:4; Rev. 12:11).* Satan's power and authority are exercised always and only within the permissive will of God.

IV. The work of the devil.

A. *Isaiah 14:12–17 is one of many passages bearing on the work of Satan.* This passage reveals Satan's original and supreme purpose. He would ascend into heaven, exalt his throne above the stars of God, and be like the Most High. The supreme motive of Satan was to be like the Most High, and it guided all of his activities. It was behind his approach to Adam and Eve (Gen. 3:5), and they adopted Satan's ideal, becoming self-centered, self-sufficient, and independent of God. This attitude has been transmitted to all people to the extent that they are called "children of wrath" and must be born again.

B. *Satan does all in his power to keep the unsaved from being delivered from the power of darkness and translated into the kingdom of God (Col. 1:13).* To this end Satan will even promote extensive religious systems (2 Cor. 11:13–15; 1 Tim. 4:1–3). Such satanic delusions are now in the world, and millions are deceived by them. These false systems are always to be tested by the attitude they take toward the saving grace of God through the blood of Christ (Rev. 12:11).

V. The destiny of the devil.

A. *As the Word of God is explicit in regard to the origin, personality, power, and work of Satan, it is equally clear regarding his destiny.* A perfect judgment of Satan has been secured through the cross (John 12:31; 16:11; Col. 2:14–15), but the execution of that sentence is still in the future. It was predicted in the garden of Eden (Gen. 3:15).

B. *Satan will be cast out of heaven (Rev. 12:7–12) and confined to the abyss, making it impossible for him to be active and to continue to deceive the nations.*

C. *Finally, Satan will be cast into the lake of fire to be tormented day and night forever (Rev. 20:10).*

Conclusion

Many believe that Satan does not really exist and that the supposed person of Satan is no more than an evil influence that is in people and in the world. This conception is proved to be wrong because there is the same abundant evidence that Satan is a person as there is that Christ is a person. Scripture, which alone is authoritative on these matters, treats Satan as a person as much as Christ. If the personality of Christ is accepted on the testimony of the Bible, then the personality of Satan must also be accepted on the same testimony.

SUNDAY MORNING, MARCH 12

Title: Going to Jerusalem

Text: "As the time approached for him to be taken up to heaven, Jesus resolutely set out for Jerusalem" **(Luke 9:51 NIV)**.

Scripture Reading: Luke 9:22–27, 51

Hymns: "Hail, Thou Once Despised Jesus," Bakewell
"Jesus, I My Cross Have Taken," Lyte
"Living for Jesus," Chisholm

Offertory Prayer: Our Father, we praise you for the gift of life. Your creative power brought us into being and daily sustains us. We thank you for Jesus, who paid the wages of sin and whose resurrection makes possible our victory over death. May you find us walking in his steps, obedient to your will, and willing even to die if that sacrifice should be needed. Accept our gifts as an expression of our love for the gift of Christ, our Savior and Lord. In his name we pray. Amen.

Introduction

Each year thousands of pilgrims make their way to Israel and the holy city of Jerusalem. For many it is the fulfillment of a lifetime to say, "I walked today where Jesus walked." A journey to Jerusalem can be a rewarding travel experience. Today we begin a *spiritual* journey to Jerusalem, walking with Jesus through those crucial hours surrounding his crucifixion and resurrection. Carefully observe the individuals on the journey—we will see ourselves!

In chapters 9–20 of his gospel, Luke mentions Jesus' movement toward Jerusalem several times (9:51; 13:22; 17:11; 18:31; 19:28). Luke uses this repetition to signal a decisive turn in Jesus' ministry. Jesus' journey to Jerusalem is what gives meaning to the Easter holiday.

I. An act of courage.

A. *Jerusalem—the hot spot.* Jerusalem was the center of Jewish life and religion. As such, it was the center of growing animosity to this itinerant Nazarene. Jesus' decision to "set out for Jerusalem" was a deliberate choice to enter the storm. Jesus demonstrated true courage. On an earlier occasion when Jesus announced his intention to go to Bethany to the home of Lazarus, the disciples warned him, "Rabbi, the Jews were but now seeking to stone you, and are you going there again?" Jesus replied, "If any one walks in the day, he does not stumble" (John 11:8–9). He knew what he was facing. Jesus' journey to Jerusalem was not the irresponsible action of a blind fanatic. He knew the risks but met them with courage. Christian commitment does not shrink from involvement in the hot spot.

B. *Our example.* Jesus is the continuing example and inspiration for us to face life and its difficulties with courage. "Let us run with perseverance the race marked out for us, fixing our eyes on Jesus, the pioneer and perfecter of faith. For the joy set before him he endured the cross, scorning its shame, and sat down at the right hand of the throne of God" (Heb. 12:1–2 NIV).

II. Commitment to God's will.

A. *Doing the Father's will.* The journey to Jerusalem was part of Jesus' desire to do the Father's will. At age twelve he expressed this desire: "Did you not know that I must be in my Father's house?" he said to his parents when they finally found him (Luke 2:49). His prayer in the garden summarized his entire life: "Not my will, but thine, be done" (Luke 22:42). Dwight L. Moody once heard a preacher declare the world had yet to see what God could do with a person completely dedicated to his will. Moody determined to be such a person—and the world has felt the impact. What could be done through us if we had a similar commitment to do God's will?

B. *A willing offering.* Some view the will of God as a decision forced on us. But God did not coerce Jesus to die on the cross. The content of his message and the nature of his person made it inevitable. Sin and holiness conflict; holy people have a hard time in this world. Jesus knew this but still remained willing to give himself. He said, "I lay down my life, that I might take it again. No man taketh it from me, but I lay it down of myself. I have power to lay it down, and I have power to take it again" (John 10:17–18). Christ became our sin offering. He voluntarily offered himself for our sins to free us from sin and death. The writer of Hebrews explained, "[Christ] said, 'Here I am, I have come to do your will.' . . . And by that will, we have been made holy through the sacrifice of the body of Jesus Christ once for all" (Heb. 10:9–10 NIV).

III. Lose life to find life.

A. *Take up the cross.* Christ's offering brought life. To possess that life, we must offer our lives. In a few weeks, we will celebrate the event that culminated Christ's journey to Jerusalem. Do not forget that the crucifixion preceded the resurrection. The discovery of life comes in the loss of life. We must do God's will and give our lives. Jesus said, "If any man would come after me, let him deny himself and take up his cross and follow me" (Matt. 16:24). There can be no life without that courageous decision.

B. *Lent—a journey to Jerusalem.* We are now in the midst of Lent, the forty days preceding Easter. These are days of spiritual preparation, renewal, and dedication. Lent corresponds to Christ's journey to Jerusalem. On his way to Jerusalem, Christ tried to lead the disciples into God's will and enable them to give themselves. The Master Teacher taught crucial lessons about values and motives.

Conclusion

Will you join me on a journey to know God's will and to do it? Will you make the commitment to follow him wherever he leads, even into the hottest spot? Set your face toward Jerusalem, remembering the words of him who has gone before you: "Whosoever will save his life shall lose it: and whosoever will lose his life for my sake shall find it" (Matt. 16:25).

Sunday Evening, March 12

Title: Watch Your Weak Moments

Text: "Esau said to Jacob, Feed me, I pray thee, with that same red pottage; for I am faint: therefore was his name called Edom. And Jacob said, See me this day thy birthright. And Esau said, Behold, I am at the point to die: and what profit shall this birthright do to me?" **(Gen. 25:30–32)**.

Scripture Reading: Genesis 25:19–34

Introduction

Each of us experiences weak moments when we should not make decisions. In a weak moment, a dieter may see an appetizing dessert and yield to temptation. In a weak moment, a tired driver may decide to keep driving instead of pulling over, and that decision could be dangerous, even deadly. Weak moments can cause us to lose our character.

Esau had a lot of advantages. He was the oldest son of Isaac and Rebekah and thus had the birthright. He was a rugged outdoorsman and a skillful hunter. Unfortunately, he had a flaw that cost him dearly. He had trouble handling weak moments. This flaw was especially apparent when he sold his birthright to Jacob because of sheer hunger.

The story of Esau teaches us some valuable lessons about the weak moments of life. Let's consider these lessons today and take them to heart.

I. We must tame physical desires.

The first lesson we can learn from Esau's life is that we need to tame our physical desires. Esau allowed physical impulses to dictate his actions, and he lived to regret his carelessness.

A. *Consider the occasion of Esau's weak moment.* Esau had been in the field hunting. When he returned home, Jacob was cooking some stew. Esau was hungry and tired, and that was his favorite dish. He asked Jacob to give him some of the stew, and Jacob refused. Under one condition could Esau have the stew—he would have to sell his birthright. Listen to Esau's response: "Look, I am about to die. What good is the birthright to me?" (Gen. 25:32 NIV).

B. *Weak moments are inevitable.* These are the times when our resources are depleted. Our focus shifts to the temporal, and we zero in on satisfying the particular appetite that is nagging us and give little heed to the consequences.

J. Wallace Hamilton wrote a book called *Ride the Wild Horses.* The thesis of his book is that God gave us every desire we have. No desire is bad within itself, but it must be controlled by God. So the first lesson here is to allow God to tame your physical desires. But there is another lesson.

II. We must treat privileges responsibly.

The story of Esau teaches believers a valuable lesson about treating the gifts entrusted to us responsibly.

A. *Consider the gift of Esau's birthright.* Esau was the firstborn son of Isaac and Rebekah. This was a distinguished position, because in those days the firstborn son had the privilege of ruling the other children. The family inheritance would ultimately belong to Esau as well.

Esau had a marvelous privilege that he never could have attained through human achievement. Unfortunately, he disdained his gift during a moment of weakness. Feeling the pains of hunger caused him to treat his privilege carelessly.

B. *Gifts are not to be taken lightly.* God endows all believers with one or more gifts, and he greatly desires that we acknowledge and use those gifts. We must not disregard them as Esau did. Let's learn to cherish our privileges and to treat them responsibly.

So far we have learned two valuable lessons from Esau's life. We can learn at least one more lesson.

III. We must consider decisions carefully.

Perhaps the greatest lesson Esau learned is the crucial importance of moments of decision. The decisions we make influence the rest of our lives.

A. *Consider Esau's crucial decision.* Esau's decision was a momentous one at the time. Stated simply, it was the decision to remain hungry and keep his birthright or to satisfy his appetite and lose his birthright. At the moment, the decision seemed obvious to Esau. But later he lived to regret that decision because he could never get his birthright back. That decision in a moment of weakness cast a shadow on the rest of his days on earth.

B. *The decisions of life demand great care.* Life brings all kinds of decisions, both big ones and little ones. We should be ever conscious of God's leadership in our lives. He leads us during our moments of strength and during our moments of weakness. If we look to him for guidance, he will never lead us to regret a decision.

Conclusion

Do you have a resource for the weak moments of life? All of us have those times, and we need help from someone greater than ourselves. Invite Christ into your life. He will join his life with yours.

Wednesday Evening, March 15

Title: What the Bible Says about Demons

Text: "Jesus had said to him, 'Come out of this man, you impure spirit!'" **(Mark 5:8 NIV)**.

Scripture Reading: Mark 5:1–20

Introduction

The subject of demons has run the gamut in people's thinking. Some people become obsessed with the study of demons, allowing their imaginations to run away with them. They see "demons" everywhere. Some become self-appointed exorcists and set about to rid their world of these emissaries of Satan. They tend to ascribe everything evil to demonic activity. At the other extreme are those who deny the existence of demons, relegating them to ancient mythology or to an earlier era of ignorance and superstition.

The ancient Greeks believed that demons were the souls of evil people who had died. Others have believed that demons are the disembodied spirits of a race of people who existed before Adam and Eve were created. The Scriptures, however, make no mention of such a race.

It is the general consensus of conservative theologians that demons are the angels who revolted with Satan. (Note the close relationship between Satan and angels in Matthew 12:24 and 25:41.) They are also referred to as "unclean spirits" (Mark 9:25). Whereas the King James Version of the Bible refers to them as "devils," the proper translation of the Greek word is "demons." There is one devil but many demons.

I. The nature and activity of demons.

A. *Demons do not appear to be omnipresent; each demon can be in only one place at any given moment.* The incident near Gadara when Jesus allowed the demons that had inhabited the wild man to enter the swine shows that demons can be confined and indicates their lack of omnipresence (Mark 5:1–13; see also 2 Peter 2:4). Though they possess a high degree of intelligence by virtue of their long existence and experience, they are not omniscient.

B. *They are promoters of a system of doctrine (1 Tim. 4:1–3; cf. 2 Cor. 11:13–15; 1 John 2:19; 4:3).* The doctrine of demons includes salvation through works (1 Tim. 4:1–3) and the denial of the divinity of Jesus (1 John 2:22–23).

C. *They are agents of destruction, particularly of the bodies and souls of men (Matt. 9:33; 12:22; Mark 3:10; Luke 13:11, 16; Acts 8:7).*

D. *They are promoters of delusion (Rev. 12:9).* One of Satan's basic designs is to deceive, and his emissaries, the demons, carry out that design.

Daniel 10:13 and 20 seem to relate this activity particularly to the governments of the world.

II. The phenomenon of demon possession.

A. *Demon possession is a real phenomenon.* Jesus and his disciples confronted it, as did other first-century Christian leaders. Nonetheless, not every expression of evil can be called demon possession.

B. *Because believers are not their own but are bought with a price (1 Cor. 6:19–20), they are God's property.* God is greater than Satan or his demons; therefore, neither Satan nor his demons can have ultimate victory over believers. They may, however, influence and harass believers. Satan would destroy every believer if he could.

C. *The Bible indicates that a believer may be delivered to Satan "for the destruction of the flesh," but the spirit will "be saved in the day of the Lord Jesus" (1 Cor. 5:5).* Whatever relationship Satan or his demons may have to believers during this earthly life, it cannot be permanent or eternal.

III. The defense against demon power.

A. *It is never wise for Christians to dabble in the occult, even on a superficial or entertainment level.* God warned his ancient people about this (Deut. 18:10–11; see also the account of the "book burning" in Acts 19 in regard to the Ephesians). Although astrologers and palm and tarot card readers may not be taken very seriously today, throughout the ages their satanic influence has been openly recognized and even deferred to. Today Satan worshipers and occult practitioners can be found in abundance in our country and the world. They include government officials, celebrities, and prominent businesspeople who influence many areas of life.

B. *Even more practically, Paul said, "Let not the sun go down upon your wrath: Neither give place to the devil" (Eph. 4:26–27).* While the Bible does speak of righteous anger or indignation, that is probably not what Paul was speaking of here. Paul advocated getting rid of angry feelings one may be harboring before the close of each day rather than carrying anger and bitterness into the next day. Harboring wrath gives Satan an opportunity to gain a foothold in a believer's life.

C. *Christians should always rely on the presence of the indwelling Holy Spirit, acknowledging that "greater is he that is in you, than he that is in the world" (1 John 4:4).*

Conclusion

In the light of these facts about demons, every believer in the Lord Jesus Christ should be alert (1 Peter 5:8). We should be careful to clothe ourselves with the whole armor of God (Eph. 6:13–18). We should always recognize that our bodies are the temple of the Holy Spirit, and we should strive to keep ourselves physically, mentally, and spiritually strong (Rom. 12:2; 2 Cor. 10:5; Phil. 4:8).

SUNDAY MORNING, MARCH 19

Title: Consequences of Bad Religion

Text: "Then the chief priests and the Pharisees called a meeting of the Sanhedrin.

"'What are we accomplishing?' they asked. 'Here is this man performing many signs. If we let him go on like this, everyone will believe in him. . . .'

"So from that day on they plotted to take his life" **(John 11:47–48, 53 NIV)**.

Scripture Reading: John 11:45–53

Hymns: "Great Redeemer, We Adore Thee," Harris
"I Stand Amazed in the Presence," Gabriel
"Am I a Soldier of the Cross?" Watts

Offertory Prayer: Our heavenly Father, we thank you for the promise of your presence where two or three are gathered in your name. We ask your blessing on our worship this day in the desire that a new encounter with you will empower us for greater service. Forgive us of anything that makes our worship a religious performance rather than a spiritual fellowship. Liberate us from an attachment to religious tradition so that we can be responsive to the free work of the Spirit. We are grateful for the opportunity to give in support of your mission as it is fulfilled through this fellowship. We pray that our gifts are a true indication of greater sacrifice. In Jesus' name we pray. Amen.

Introduction

Christ died during Passover week in Jerusalem. It was the high holy week of the year for the Jewish people. Jerusalem was crowded with religious pilgrims. It does not take much reading of the gospel narratives to realize that Jesus was crucified by religious people. The voices that shouted, "Crucify him!" had frequently prayed in the temple. The cross is an example of the evil that can be accomplished by bad religion.

I. Religion and the cross.

A. *Jerusalem—the Holy City.* Mark records an impressive list of religious leaders who participated in devising Christ's death. The Sadducees were the priestly party whose work and interest focused on the temple. They loved a smooth, formal worship service; they had a flair for pomp and ritual. The Pharisees were the legalists whose pride in keeping the fine points of the law separated them from "sinners."

The scribes interpreted and preserved the law. The chief priests officiated at worship and spoke the words of forgiveness. Completing the group were the elders—community leaders and various rulers. All of these leaders mingled with a crowd of zealous Jews, many of whom journeyed many miles for the annual exodus deliverance celebration.

It was not the down-and-out group who crucified Jesus. The up-and-in crowd did it—law-abiding, hardworking, religious people.

B. *The Jerusalem-Rome connection.* The ease with which these religious leaders became a party to evil was partly the result of an unhealthy connection between them and the state. The Romans controlled the Sanhedrin; the high priest was a Roman appointee who acted at the bidding of the Roman officials. One of the chief priests expressed their dilemma: "Here is this man performing many signs. If we let him go on like this, everyone will believe in him, and then the Romans will come and take away both our place and our nation" (John 11:47–48 NIV).

The equivalent of the church had bowed before the state. God was no longer acknowledged as the supreme authority. But the alliance never paid off. The power with whom they cooperated turned on them in AD 70 and destroyed Jerusalem and the temple. Only evil can result from an unhealthy connection between church and state. A free church in a free state is the ideal. Then the church can exercise its prophetic role and petition the state to use its God-given authority responsibly.

Out of self-interest Caiaphas said it was better for Jesus to die for the nation than for the entire nation to perish (v. 50). Jesus did die for the nation but for an entirely different reason. "Righteousness exalts a nation, but sin is a reproach to any people" (Prov. 14:34). Only through Christ's death can a nation have the reproach of sin replaced by the righteousness of God.

II. Lost concern for people.

A. *People or place.* Jesus' resurrection of Lazarus was the immediate experience that precipitated this religious conspiracy. Some people put their faith in Jesus, while others "went to the Pharisees and told them what Jesus had done" (John 11:46 NIV). For the Pharisees, new life for the dead was not as important as retaining their religious leadership. Stones and mortar took priority over sin and mortality. The people whom God called to be "a light to the nations" had replaced their world vision with concern solely for their own nation.

Religion is an evil force when it becomes an institutional caretaker and loses concern for people. Missionary Billie Pate said, "The church must translate its heart from the empty cavity of brick and mortar to the throbbing marketplace of human need. Too long it has lifted the cup of cold water to its own lips."

B. *Rules or right.* One Sabbath day when Jesus entered the synagogue, a man with a withered hand was among the worshipers. The religious authorities "watched [Jesus], to see whether he would heal him on the sabbath, so that they might accuse him" (Mark 3:2). The Lord is in the business of putting things right; religious rules are of secondary importance. Bad religion, on the other hand, is concerned with the status quo. The "old-time religion" that some people yearn for may be only an emotional, actionless, and archaic relationship to God that is totally foreign to the abundant life Jesus imparts.

III. Something greater than religion.

Jesus once answered the criticism of the Pharisees, saying, "I tell you, something greater than the temple is here" (Matt. 12:6). Heaven will have "no temple in the city, for its temple is the Lord God the Almighty and the Lamb" (Rev. 21:22). It has been said, "One man's religion is another man's burden." Religion had become a burden in Jesus' day. The religion of the Pharisees brought despair and futility. Christ offered joy, hope, life. He offered himself instead of a religion. He asks us to accept him rather than a creed or dead religion. Caiaphas and his religious conspirators thought they had put an end to the Nazarene. Instead, his death let life loose for all the world.

German pastor Martin Niemöller tells of "the sermon of the gallows":

> There was in front of my cell window in the Dachau concentration camp a gallows, and I often had to pray for those who were hanged on it, poor souls. This gallows put a question to me: What will happen when one day they put *you* to this test and lay the rope around *your* neck? Will you then with your last breath cry out, "You criminals, you think you are right in executing me as a criminal, but there is a living God in heaven, and he will show you!"? And then the second question followed: What do you think would have happened if Jesus had died that way, cursing his enemies and murderers? You know the answer: Then you would be rid of him; for there then would be no gospel, no good tidings of great joy, no salvation, no hope! Not for anyone, not for you! But—thank God—he, Jesus, died otherwise, differently, not cursing his murderers, but praying on their behalf: "Father, forgive them; they know not what they do!" They *could not* get rid of him, for he held on and kept them in his forgiving love; and his Father heard his prayer and was well pleased with his son. So there *was* no escape. This death worked too well—and there *is* no escape—this death marks his final victory: "I have overcome the world!" How? By overcoming hatred with love, evil with doing good! (Clyde Fant Jr. and William Pinson Jr., eds., *Twenty Centuries of Great Preaching* [Waco, TX.: Word, 1971], 10:249)

Conclusion

Look at the cross. Religious people killed Christ! The right lost out to rigid rules; self-interest prevailed over service to others; religion took the place of a relationship with God. Evil was the result, but Jesus triumphed over evil, and he lives. To all who receive him comes faith that changes the world, faith that overcomes evil with good.

SUNDAY EVENING, MARCH 19

Title: A Name Change

Text: "Then the man said, 'Your name will no longer be Jacob, but Israel, because you have struggled with God and with humans and have overcome'" **(Gen. 32:28 NIV)**.

Scripture Reading: Genesis 32:22–32

Introduction

Occasionally people become dissatisfied with the names their parents have given them. Many years ago the country singer Johnny Cash recorded a popular song called "A Boy Named Sue." You could not blame a boy named Sue for wanting to change his name!

Names were significant in the Old Testament. Often they described a person's character. The name Jacob, for example, meant "deceiver" or "supplanter." He definitely needed a name change! The story of Jacob is about a person taking on a new nature and then receiving a new name to describe that new nature. Genesis 32:28 says, "Your name will no longer be Jacob, but Israel, because you have struggled with God and with humans and have overcome" (NIV). Let's examine the insights into Jacob's story of change.

I. All of us need a name change.

The story of every human being is one of rebellion against God. Therefore, everyone needs a name change.

A. *Jacob's story underscores the sinful nature.* Jacob's character is first reflected in his name. Throughout his life the meaning of his name matched his reputation as a trickster. He cheated his brother, Esau, out of his birthright. Then he tricked his father, Isaac, into blessing him rather than Esau. When Isaac and Esau realized they had been tricked, Jacob had to flee to his uncle Laban in Haran. Nevertheless, Jacob continued in his deception.

B. *Jacob's sinful nature represents every human being's nature.* A French writer once said, "I never examined the heart of a wicked man. I once became acquainted with the heart of a good man: I was shocked."

Confronting our sinful nature causes us to conclude, "All have sinned." We desperately need a new nature.

II. All of us can have a new nature.

The story of the Bible is that every human being can have a new nature. No one needs to remain trapped in sin. Our character can be changed.

A. *Jacob's name change required submission.* Jacob was led to submission in an unusual manner. On his return to Canaan from Laban's home in Haran, he came to a stream called the Jabbok. He knew that he would encounter Esau, so he made preparations to appease his brother and sent flocks ahead as gifts.

Having sent his flocks, servants, and family ahead, he spent the night alone beside the Jabbok. During the night, he experienced a turning point in his life. "Jacob was left alone; and there wrestled a man with him until the breaking of the day" (32:24). The thought came to Jacob that his real antagonist was not Esau or Laban but the Lord. The Lord wrestled with Jacob until Jacob yielded in submission. When Jacob met God, he got a new nature and a new name.

B. *Jacob's story portrays what can happen to every human being.* Harry Emerson Fosdick, pastor for many years at Riverside Church in New York City, preached a sermon titled "No Man Need Stay the Way He Is." If we don't like ourselves the way we are, we can change. That is what happened to Jacob at Jabbok—a deceiver became a good man.

A change in nature results from submission to God's will. Instead of trying to run our own lives, we must allow God to control our lives.

III. All of us are changed to serve the Lord.

Having our nature changed is not a passive transaction. It means a change in lifestyle. When we are changed, we are led to service.

A. *Jacob's story reflects a new lifestyle.* Jacob became a new man when the Lord prevailed in his life. His name was changed from "Jacob the deceiver" to "Israel," which means "prince" or "he struggles with God." He changed his relationship with Esau, his brother. In previous years, he had cheated and exploited Esau; but after Jacob's encounter with God, he made every effort to seek reconciliation with Esau.

B. *Jacob's service indicates that every life-changing encounter should result in service.* Being saved and serving others go hand in hand. Serving others keeps us from a destructive preoccupation with ourselves.

In the 1700s a man named John Newton traveled to Africa. He got involved in the slave trade and truly made a mess of his life. But then John Newton had a life-changing encounter with the Lord and wrote the words to "Amazing Grace."

Conclusion

Jacob desperately needed a change. His change in nature came when he allowed the Lord to prevail in his life. When the Lord prevailed, Jacob became a profitable servant of the Lord. Do you acknowledge that you need a new nature? Will you allow God to change your life?

WEDNESDAY EVENING, MARCH 22

Title: What the Bible Says about Hell

Text: "'The rich man also died and was buried. In Hades, where he was in torment, he looked up and saw Abraham far away, with Lazarus by his side'" **(Luke 16:22–23 NIV).**

Scripture Reading: Matthew 25:41–46

Introduction

In common usage, hell designates the place of future punishment for the wicked. Satan hates the doctrine of an eternal hell. As a result, many groups today (some purportedly evangelical) either deny the existence of hell or make it a place of annihilation. Satan has even used mythology to discredit the existence of hell in modern minds—such as the character Mephistopheles from Faust; the River Styx; and Pluto, who is conceived to be the ruler of this region in the depths of the earth (Dante's *Inferno*); and so on.

I. Descriptions of hell.

A. *Hell is described as a place of everlasting fire (Matt. 25:41) and eternal punishment (Matt. 25:46).*

B. *Jesus also called hell a place of "outer darkness" (Matt. 8:12).* The "children of the kingdom" to whom he referred were apparently Jews who, because of natural birth, considered themselves automatically children of the kingdom of God.

C. *Paul referred to hell as a place of everlasting destruction (2 Thess. 1:9).*

D. *Perhaps the most common description of hell is found in John's revelation:* "The beast was taken, and with him the false prophet that wrought miracles before him, with which he deceived them that had received the mark of the beast, and them that worshipped his image. These both were cast alive into a lake of fire burning with brimstone" (Rev. 19:20).

II. The reason for hell's existence.

A. *Jesus clearly taught that hell was prepared "for the devil and his angels" (Matt. 25:41).* The inference is that human beings who go there must choose the philosophy and lifestyle of Satan's kingdom over the invitations of God.

B. *Hell exists for the wicked.* "But the fearful, the unbelieving, and the abominable, and murderers, and whoremongers, and sorcerers, and idolaters, and all liars, shall have their part in the lake which burneth with fire and brimstone: which is the second death" (Rev. 21:8).

C. *Hell exists for those who are disobedient.* "But unto them that are contentious, and do not obey the truth, but obey unrighteousness, indignation and wrath, tribulation and anguish, upon every soul of man that doeth evil, of the Jew first, and also of the Gentile" (Rom. 2:8–9).

D. *Hell was also prepared for the fallen angels.* "God spared not the angels that sinned, but cast them down to hell, and delivered them into chains of darkness, to be served unto judgment" (2 Peter 2:4).

E. *Hell awaits those who reject the gospel.* "Verily I say unto you, It shall be more tolerable for the land of Sodom and Gomorrah in the day of judgment, than for that city" (Matt. 10:15).

III. The punishment of hell.

A. *The punishment of hell will be eternal, everlasting.* "They will be tormented day and night for ever and ever" (Rev. 20:10 NIV).

B. *It will be a painful punishment.* "So shall it be at the end of the world: the angels shall come forth, and sever the wicked from among the just, and shall cast them into the furnace of fire: there shall be wailing and gnashing of teeth" (Matt. 13:49–50).

C. *Apparently the punishment of hell will vary in degree, according to the opportunity one had to avoid hell.* "Woe unto you, scribes and Pharisees, hypocrites! for ye devour widows' houses, and for a pretence make long prayer: therefore ye shall receive the greater damnation" (Matt. 23:14).

D. *The punishment of hell will be unchangeable, revoking the possibility of a "second chance" (see Luke 16:22–31).*

IV. The condition of the inhabitants of hell.

A. *They will be able to remember people, events, and opportunities in the earthly life (see Luke 16:23, 25).*

B. *They will cry for release (see Luke 16:24).*

C. *They will have no escape from the sovereignty of God (Ps. 139:8).*

V. Major words for hell in the Scriptures.

A. *"Sheol" occurs sixty-five times in the Old Testament and is translated thirty-one times "hell" and three times "pit."* The general idea is "the place of the dead," not the grave, but the place of those departed from this life. It is used both for the righteous and the wicked (righteous: Ps. 16:10; 30:3; Isa. 38:10; et al.; wicked: Num. 16:33; Job 24:19; Ps. 9:17; et al.).

B. *"Hades"—one of the New Testament terms rendered "hell"—is similar in significance to the Old Testament "Sheol."* It refers to the underworld, or the region of the departed. It occurs eleven times in the New Testament and is rendered "hell" every time with one exception (1 Cor. 15:55, "grave"). Jesus associated judgment and suffering with the condition of the inhabitants of "Hades" (Matt. 11:23).

C. *"Gehenna," or "the valley of Hinnom," was a place where the Jewish apostasy, the rites of Molech, were celebrated (1 Kings 11:7).* King Josiah converted the valley of Hinnom into a place of abomination where dead bodies were thrown and burned (2 Kings 23:13–14). The word occurs twelve times in the New Testament and in every case denotes the eternal state of the lost after the resurrection. Christ's descent was into "Hades" (intermediate state) and not into "Gehenna."

Conclusion

Because of the movement in the Scriptures between the literal, symbolic, and figurative in regard to the descriptions and teachings about hell, sincere students of the Bible may come to different interpretations and understandings. Of one thing we can be certain: hell is eternal and is primarily to be considered a place of separation from God. In the final analysis, everything else is incidental.

SUNDAY MORNING, MARCH 26

Title: Keeping Warm at the Enemy's Fire

Text: "Peter followed at a distance. But when some there had kindled a fire in the middle of the courtyard and had sat down together, Peter sat down with them" **(Luke 22:54–55 NIV)**.

Scripture Reading: Luke 22:31–43, 54–62

Hymns: "Stand Up, and Bless the Lord," Montgomery
"In the Hour of Trial," Montgomery
"Jesus, and Shall It Ever Be," Grigg

Offertory Prayer: Loving Father, we are thankful for every blessing of life. We thank you for health and strength. We are grateful for meaningful work. And we praise your name for the love of family and friends. We acknowledge that every good and perfect gift comes from you. Forgive us for unfaithful stewardship of our relationships and our possessions. Open our eyes to the needs of others and especially to those without Christ. We offer these gifts out of our abundance to send the gospel to others. May the glory of the Lord fill this house of worship today and send us forth with gladness. In Jesus' name we pray. Amen.

Introduction

When we see an apparently strong Christian face a spiritual defeat, we tend to think, *I would have expected that to happen to anyone but him.* Peter's denial while keeping warm at the enemy's fire creates a similar surprise. Peter was a strong individual, a great leader, and a dynamic Christian.

I. Peter: a person of strength.

A. *Strength of leadership.* Whenever the disciples are listed, Peter's name comes first, reflecting the disciples' view of his leadership. Peter was one of the inner circle of disciples privileged to share in special experiences with Jesus, such as the transfiguration. On the day of Pentecost, it was Peter who stood to preach.

B. *Strength of spirit.* Peter had no timid spirit. He was a bold spiritual adventurer. Once he tried to walk on water, and later he ran to Jesus' tomb.

C. *Strength of body.* As a fisherman, Peter had developed his muscles by rowing boats and casting heavy nets. He showed his physical strength in the garden; he was strong enough to take on the entire mob.

In spite of all these qualities, Peter denied the Lord. "If you think you are standing firm, be careful that you don't fall!" (1 Cor. 10:12 NIV). No Christian is immune from "the flaming arrows of the evil one" (Eph. 6:16 NIV).

II. Peter: vulnerable to sin.

A. *Blind to his weakness.* Peter, a typical human, had strengths and weaknesses, but he seemed to be blind to his weaknesses. Peter confidently told the Lord, "I am ready to go with you to prison and to death" (Luke 22:33 NIV). This was a noble expression and a wonderful assurance—apparently uttered in ignorance of his fleshly potential for succumbing to sin's temptation.

Victor Hugo wrote, "I feel two men struggling within me." The apostle Paul also had a realistic view of the tension between good and evil that rages in every soul: "For I do not do the good I want to do, but the evil I do not want to do—this I keep on doing. . . . I see another law at work in me, waging war against the law of my mind and making me a prisoner of the law of sin at work within me. What a wretched man I am! Who will rescue me from this body that is subject to death?" (Rom. 7:19, 23–24 NIV).

B. *Satan attacks the vulnerable spot.* Jesus warned Peter of Satan's impending attack: "Satan has asked to sift all of you as wheat" (Luke 22:31 NIV). The evil one caught the strong disciple in a vulnerable moment—surrounded by the enemy and separated from the other disciples. He will sift us until he finds the most vulnerable place at which to hurl his temptation.

"Our struggle is not against flesh and blood, but against the rulers, against the authorities, against the powers of this dark world and against the spiritual forces of evil in the heavenly realms"

(Eph. 6:12 NIV). Jesus taught us to pray for deliverance from the evil one (Matt. 6:13). We say with Paul, "Thanks be to God, who delivers me through Jesus Christ our Lord!" (Rom. 7:25 NIV).

III. Peter: the pressure to conform.

A. *The pressure of men.* What was the vulnerable spot for Peter? He let himself be guided by those around him. Is this entirely wrong? A healthy concern for what others think is an asset. But Peter went beyond this concern and allowed his actions to be molded by those around him. A dialogue between Jesus and Peter recorded in Matthew 16 illustrates this peer pressure. Jesus was talking about his coming rejection and death when Peter strongly reacted: "Never, Lord! . . . This shall never happen to you!" (v. 22 NIV). Peter's concept of the Messiah did not include Jesus as the Suffering Servant. Instead, Peter subscribed to the popular concept of the victorious Messiah conquering the Romans and reestablishing the throne of David. Jesus rebuked him: "Get behind me, Satan! You are a stumbling block to me; you do not have in mind the concerns of God, but merely human concerns" (v. 23 NIV).

Peter again exhibited a tendency to reflect the prevailing social pressure on a later occasion, which Paul described in Galatians 2. "Before certain men came from James, [Peter] used to eat with the Gentiles. But when they arrived, he began to draw back and separate himself from the Gentiles because he was afraid of those who belonged to the circumcision group" (v. 12 NIV). Peter knew the Lord was no respecter of persons, but he was afraid to resist the pressure of a strong group in the church. Peter was a strong man but not strong enough to stand against the values of immature Christians—even though they were against God.

B. *The pleasure of God.* What are we to do in the face of compromising peer pressure? Paul expresses what is pleasing to God: "Do not conform to the pattern of this world, but be transformed by the renewing of your mind. Then you will be able to test and approve what God's will is—his good, pleasing and perfect will" (Rom. 12:2 NIV).

In the mid-1800s, two distinguished statesmen delivered addresses before a British university. Benjamin Disraeli said, "If you would succeed, know the temper and spirit of the times in which you live and act accordingly." William Gladstone said, "Do not drift with the age. Have fixed principles and stand by them." At the enemy's campfire, Peter did drift with the age and lived to regret it.

Conclusion

In the days following Jesus' resurrection, some of the disciples had breakfast with the Lord beside the Sea of Galilee (John 21). Three times Jesus asked Peter if he loved him and then told Peter he would have to suffer for him.

Peter pointed to John and asked, "'Lord, what about him?' Jesus answered, 'If I want him to remain alive until I return, what is that to you? You must follow me'" (John 21:21–22 NIV). The tension was still present; it was still difficult for Peter to face God's will.

The same crucial question that confronted Peter confronts us as well: "What will you do with Christ?" You can't pass the decision off to someone else. You must decide. The pressure of others offers convenient options. The warmth of the enemy's fire is appealing. May the Lord hear us say, "Yes, I know Jesus—he is my Lord!"

SUNDAY EVENING, MARCH 26

Title: A Godly Man

Text: "So now it was not you that sent me hither, but God: and he hath made me a father to Pharaoh, and lord of all his house, and a ruler throughout all the land of Egypt" **(Gen. 45:8)**.

Scripture Reading: Genesis 45:1–15

Introduction

Thomas Mann told the story of Joseph in four lengthy volumes collectively called *Joseph and His Brothers.* Indeed, Joseph is one of the most exciting characters in the Bible. He was blessed with natural endowments that gain our admiration. His life was beset with adversity that evokes our sympathy. And he exhibited godly qualities that demand our imitation.

The biblical writer tells the story of Joseph in thirteen chapters (Gen. 37–40). The story begins in the land of Canaan. Joseph was his father's favorite son. His brothers became jealous of his privileged standing and intended to kill him. Instead, they decided to make a profit and sold Joseph to some Ishmaelite merchants, and he soon became a slave in Egypt. His story continues in a mixture of sorrow and happiness and concludes with a great reunion with his family. Tonight let's consider the godly qualities of Joseph's life.

I. A godly person forgives injustices.

A. *Joseph suffered numerous injustices.* First, his brothers mistreated him. They put him in a large pit and threatened to leave him to die. Later they sold him to some slave traders, and these traders in turn sold him to an officer in the Egyptian government. Second, Joseph was treated unfairly by Potiphar's wife. She falsely accused him of an illicit sexual affair, and he was thrown into prison. Third, while Joseph was in prison, he did a favor for the pharaoh's baker. The baker promised to help bail Joseph out of prison but later forgot him. Joseph's story contains one injustice after another.

B. *Joseph forgave each injustice.* Even when Joseph rose to a position of power in the land of Egypt, he did not seek vengeance. Instead, he forgave those who had treated him unfairly. The mercy he showed to his brothers is a prime example of how we should forgive others. "Moreover he kissed all his brethren, and wept upon them; and after that his brethren talked with him" (Gen. 45:15). The best way to deal with injustice is to overcome evil with good.

II. A godly person withstands adversity.

A. *Joseph knew adversity.* Joseph's story is filled with physical and mental hardship. Joseph knew the sting of disappointment. His ambition for the future was stifled when he was sold as a slave. His brothers betrayed him. Potiphar's wife betrayed him. The baker in prison betrayed him. Joseph easily could have grown bitter and resentful after living as a prisoner and a slave. This man knew the meaning of hardship.

Believers are not exempt from adversity. Study the Bible carefully, and you will discover many accounts of godly people who faced adversity. We must learn to withstand hardships without allowing our spirits to turn sour.

B. *Joseph saw adversity in light of God's plan.* Listen to how he viewed his hardships: "Now therefore be not grieved, nor angry with yourselves, that ye sold me hither: for God did send me before you to preserve life. . . . And God sent me before you to preserve you a posterity in the earth, and to save your lives by a great deliverance. So now it was not you that sent me hither, but God: and he hath made me a father to Pharaoh, and lord of all his house, and a ruler throughout all the land of Egypt" (Gen. 45:5, 7–8).

We need to evaluate hardships from a biblical perspective, realizing that God's plan is bigger than ours. Listen to Paul: "We know that all things work together for good to them that love God, to them who are called according to his purpose" (Rom. 8:28).

III. A godly person resists temptations.

A. *Joseph resisted Potiphar's wife.* Another reason we can consider Joseph a godly man is that he resisted temptation. As the manager of Potiphar's household, he had great authority. He was a handsome man, and Potiphar's wife was attracted to him. Several times she tried to seduce him, but he refused her appeals.

Temptation is a part of life. Satan continually seeks to lure us from the straight and narrow path. We must turn to God for strength to defend against Satan's enticement. The only way we can resist temptation is by having God's power within to say no.

B. *Joseph resisted the woman's appeal for several reasons.* First, he had respect for Potiphar. "But he refused, and said unto his master's wife, Behold, my master wotteth not what is with me in the house, and he hath committed all that he hath to my hand. There is none greater in this house than I" (Gen. 39:8–9). Second, Joseph had a great sense of responsibility to God. "How then can I do this great wickedness, and sin against God?" (v. 9). Third, Joseph had respect for himself as well as for Potiphar's wife. He knew the destructive consequences of an illicit sexual affair. He wanted to be able to live with himself. He had the resources to resist temptation.

Conclusion

Would you like someone to say about you, "He sure is a godly man" or "She sure is a godly woman"? Well, you have a good model. Joseph's life is an excellent example for you. If you seek to emulate his godly qualities, you will know how to be a good person. But greater than following Joseph's example is having a relationship with Joseph's God. If you open your life to God, you will have the resources to be a godly person!

WEDNESDAY EVENING, MARCH 29

Title: What the Bible Says about Heaven

Text: "'My Father's house has many rooms'" **(John 14:2 NIV)**.

Scripture Reading: Revelation 21:1–4; 22:1–5

Introduction

All believers look forward to spending eternity in heaven. It's natural, then, for us to have a healthy curiosity about what heaven is like. Understandably, the Scriptures are highly symbolic in their descriptions of heaven. This is true because the Bible must use "earthly" words to describe a celestial place. Most of what the Bible says about heaven must be recognized in its symbolic and figurative setting. The writers, under the inspiration of the Holy Spirit, were simply using the most exquisite language at their disposal to portray heaven. Some concentrated on those characteristics of heaven that parallel the material and physical nature of earth, such as the "streets of gold," "walls of jasper," and "gates of pearl." Heaven is a place where spirit beings dwell; material things are of no significance there. Thus the purpose of this study is to emphasize the spiritual nature of heaven and not necessarily its "physical" properties.

I. The inhabitants of heaven.

A. *God is there.* "Hear the supplication of your servant and of your people Israel when they pray toward this place. Hear from heaven, your dwelling place, and when you hear, forgive" (1 Kings 8:30 NIV).

B. *Christ is there.* "He did not enter by means of the blood of goats and calves; but he entered the Most Holy Place once for all by his own blood, thus obtaining eternal redemption. . . . For Christ did not enter a sanctuary made with human hands that was only a copy of the true one; he entered heaven itself, now to appear for us in God's presence" (Heb. 9:12, 24 NIV).

C. *The Holy Spirit is there.* "Where can I go from your Spirit? Where can I flee from your presence? If I go up to the heavens, you are there; if I make my bed in the depths, you are there" (Ps. 139:7–8 NIV).

D. *The angels are there.* "See that you do not despise one of these little ones. For I tell you that their angels in heaven always see the face of my Father in heaven" (Matt. 18:10 NIV).

E. *God's people are there.* "But you have come to Mount Zion, to the city of the living God, the heavenly Jerusalem. You have come to thousands upon thousands of angels in joyful assembly, to the church of the firstborn, whose names are written in heaven. You have come to God, the Judge of all, to the spirits of the righteous made perfect" (Heb. 12:22–23 NIV).

II. Things not in heaven.

A. *There will be no marriage, thus apparently no family unit relationships as we know them on earth (Matt. 22:30).*

B. *There will be no death, no termination of existence and relationships (Luke 20:36).*

C. *There will be no "flesh and blood" bodies (1 Cor. 15:50).*

D. *There will be no corruption; that is, nothing will deteriorate or pass away in heaven (1 Cor. 15:42, 50).*

E. *There will be no weariness.* Part of the curse connected with Adam's sin in the garden of Eden was that he would toil to make his bread, which is indicated by "the sweat of thy face" (Gen. 3:17–19). Heaven's inhabitants will not grow tired (2 Cor. 5:1–10).

F. *There will be no sorrow (Rev. 7:17), pain (21:4), night (22:5), wicked people (22:15), or end (Matt. 25:46).*

III. Characteristics of heaven.

A. *Heaven is a place of unending joy (Luke 15:7, 10), peace (Luke 16:25), and rest (Rev. 14:13).*

B. *Heaven is a place of righteousness (2 Peter 3:13), which, along with love, is the emanating nature of God.*

C. *Heaven is a place of reward (Matt. 5:11–12).* God will give proper commendation to those who have been faithful to him.

D. *Heaven offers opportunity for service (Rev. 7:15).* It is not a place of barren inactivity. Its inhabitants do not "float about on a fleecy white cloud, strumming a harp," as heaven is so often caricatured.

E. *God's people receive an inheritance in heaven (1 Peter 1:3–5), which underscores our sonship and heirship with Christ.*

Conclusion

Because the Scriptures give us this "foretaste" of heaven (Acts 7:55–56), we should earnestly anticipate our eternal state (2 Cor. 5:2, 8), realizing that it will be a state of existence far superior to any we could conceive on earth. We should "look for" the coming of the new heavens and the new earth (2 Peter 3:12–13), realizing that it will be "far better" than now (Phil. 1:23–24).

SUGGESTED PREACHING PROGRAM FOR THE MONTH OF

APRIL

■ Sunday Mornings

As Easter approaches, believers and nonbelievers alike can benefit from a series of sermons on our Lord's determination to face the crucifixion and thereby reveal God's love for sinners. Continue and complete the series "Going to Jerusalem." Following Easter, use the theme "Recognizing and Responding to the Living Lord."

■ Sunday Evenings

"Thinking about the Cross" is the theme for Sunday evenings in April. As Christians, we live with the inspiration of a crucified and risen Savior. God's gift to us on the cross motivates us to unselfish service.

■ Wednesday Evenings

We are in a continual process of being changed into the image of Jesus Christ. Jacob, originally a crook, had a life-changing experience with God. "Lessons from a Changed Man" is this month's theme.

SUNDAY MORNING, APRIL 2

Title: A Man Passing through the Crowd

Text: "A certain man from Cyrene, Simon, the father of Alexander and Rufus, was passing by on his way in from the country, and they forced him to carry the cross" **(Mark 15:21 NIV)**.

Scripture Reading: Mark 15:16–32

Hymns: "O Sacred Head, Now Wounded," Gerhardt
"At the Cross," Watts
"Lead Me to Calvary," Hussey

Offertory Prayer: Lord, you know our hearts and are aware of the motivation for our presence here today. Even as you see our sin, we pray you will bless us with a new transfusion of your love, forgiveness, and power. We know you see the amount of our gifts only as it reflects our capability and commitment. We love you and rejoice in the changes you have made in our lives. In Jesus' name. Amen.

Introduction

"Simon . . . was passing by on his way in from the country, and they forced him to carry the cross" (Mark 15:21 NIV). A man passing through the crowd was suddenly thrust to center stage of the drama of redemption. Can you imagine the shock and shame that Simon of Cyrene must have experienced? A proud Jew entangled in the ugly proceedings of a crucifixion—a site reserved for criminals and slaves. They "forced" him into service. Did Simon resist? If so, his resistance was useless because Roman authorities could exercise this selective service on the spur of the moment.

Although Simon recoiled at the demand to carry Jesus' cross, the experience led to a complete turnaround in his life. Not only did Simon bring relief to the weak and emaciated body of Jesus, his walk to "the place of the skull" (Matt. 27:33 NIV) took him to the Source of real life.

I. A Cyrenian with character.

Simon was probably a dedicated Jew. Acts 6:9 notes that the Cyrenian Jews had their own synagogue in Jerusalem. Simon's presence in Jerusalem could indicate his commitment to the faith of Abraham, Isaac, and Jacob. Simon was coming in from the country. This very likely means he was an immigrant from North Africa who lived in the farming districts near Jerusalem. Cyrene was noted for its farming. As a farmer, Simon was accustomed to hard work, and his body probably gave evidence of physical strength and endurance. The soldiers did not have time to waste to lay the cross on a man unused to toil and hardship.

Simon was "passing by"—going about his business. No doubt he had left home early that morning and had many errands to run that day. Simon was a marked contrast with the unruly mob moving from Pilate's palace to Calvary. They had been easily distracted from meaningful work and gave shouts of allegiance to anyone who could arouse their emotions. This Cyrenian with character was on his way to accomplish something.

II. Caught in the clutches of circumstance.

A. *The innocent suffer.* Simon's determined and purposeful journey was interrupted by circumstances not of his own choosing. He had another's burden thrust on him. He was caught in the clutches of circumstance. Some of our failures and disappointments come as a result of our own selfish sowing, unwise decisions, or hasty judgment. At other times we are caught in the consequences of another's sin. Simon typifies the suffering of good people throughout all time. His experience illustrates the widening circle of influence that individual decisions have on others. "No man is an island"—that is, it is not just *my* business what I do.

B. *More than conquerors.* Simon's experience is an assurance of God's special concern for those who have to bear burdens they did not choose. Jesus said, "Come to me, all you who are weary and burdened, and I will give you rest" (Matt. 11:28 NIV).

In Vietnam a grenade exploded near Max Cleland, causing the loss of both of his legs and an arm. He courageously faced this tragic circumstance and in 1977 was made head of the Veteran's Administration. Cleland testified, "There is help available from God when we need it most." He closed many of his speeches and interviews with this prayer written during the Civil War by a Confederate soldier:

> I asked God for strength, that I might achieve,
> I was made weak, that I might learn humbly to obey.
> I asked for health, that I might do greater things,
> I was given infirmity that I might do better things.
> I asked for riches, that I might be happy,
> I was given poverty, that I might be wise.
> I asked for power, that I might have the praise of men,
> I was given weakness, that I might feel the need of God.
> I asked for all things, that I might enjoy life,
> I was given life, that I might enjoy all things.
> I got nothing that I asked for—
> but everything I had hoped for.
> Almost despite myself, my unspoken prayers were answered.
> I am, among all men, most richly blessed.

With Christ we can conquer the circumstances of life (Rom. 8:37).

III. Converted at the cross.

Mark identified Simon as "the father of Alexander and Rufus." These were men known to the readers of the gospel, evidently active in the fellowship of believers. In Romans 16:13 Paul sent greetings to "Rufus chosen in the Lord." Is this the same individual—Simon's son? Is this scriptural evidence that Simon was converted and established a Christian home that nurtured two Christian boys who became leaders in the church? I think so.

Did Simon and Jesus talk as the procession made its way to Calvary? How was Simon changed by his encounter with Jesus? Bitterness turned to belief; hatred became hope; shame moved to salvation. He heard Jesus pray, "Father, forgive them, for they know not what they do." Simon saw Jesus willingly give himself, and slowly the hope of the prophets dawned into reality—"He was pierced for our transgressions, he was crushed for our iniquities; the punishment that brought us peace was upon him, and by his wounds we are healed" (Isa. 53:5 NIV).

Conclusion

Arthur Blessitt, chaplain of Sunset Strip, California, carried a ninety-pound cross across America and many countries of the world. Speaking at a national conference, he related how he had carried the cross across the newly opened border between Israel and Egypt soon after the historic Camp David peace treaty was signed. The Arab commander at the border asked for a piece of his cross.

Jesus said, "Whoever wants to be my disciple must deny themselves and take up their cross and follow me" (Mark 8:34 NIV). You may be passing by today—just a person in the crowd. Maybe a jeweled cross hangs around your neck. What does that mean to you? Have you taken up the cross? The way of the cross leads to forgiveness of sin, abundant life, and the defeat of death. Simon of Cyrene, a man passing through the crowd, found this amazing hope in the cross. So can you!

SUNDAY EVENING, APRIL 2

Title: The Necessity of the Cross

Text: "'Did not the Messiah have to suffer these things and then enter his glory?'" **(Luke 24:26 NIV)**.

Scripture Reading: Luke 24:13–35

Introduction

This message is not addressed to those who are offended by the cross, nor to unbelievers, nor to those wise in their own minds who think it foolish. Rather, it is addressed to those who might share, to some degree, the attitude of those two brokenhearted disciples to whom Jesus appeared on the road to Emmaus. They loved him. They knew he had died. But they did not see why his death was necessary. Why did he have to die? The unrecognized Christ who walked beside them said, "How foolish you are, and how slow to believe all that the prophets have spoken!" (Luke 24:25 NIV). Jesus then asked them, "Did not the Messiah have to suffer these things and then enter his glory?" (v. 26 NIV).

To consider his question in our own context, the cross was necessary from two points of view, God's and man's.

I. From God's point of view, the cross was necessary.

A. *The cross was necessary to reveal God's evaluation of human life.* In Jesus' day, human life was cheap. Unwanted children were disposed of. A slave might be killed by his master, and no questions were asked. Despots like Nero lighted their gardens with human torches. Human life is cheap in our day also. This attitude is what makes war possible. It makes poverty and slums, economic injustice, and abortion possible. Sin is rife and life is cheap. This is the attitude of a sinful world.

   But life is not cheap. In God's sight life is supremely valuable. The death of his Son on the cross demonstrates his point of view. Human life is not cheap when God was willing to give his only Son to die to save it.

B. *The cross was necessary to reveal the very essence of God's character.* "God is love" (1 John 4:8). Again John said, "Herein is love, not that we loved

God, but that he loved us, and sent his Son to be the propitiation for our sins" (4:10). We could never understand God's character without the cross. "But God commendeth his love toward us," Paul told the Romans, "in that, while we were yet sinners, Christ died for us" (5:8). The cross reveals God in his limitless love, his boundless mercy, and his pardoning grace.

The cross reveals God, not as a God of vengeance, nor as a despotic ruler, nor as a merciless judge, but as a loving Shepherd who followed the trail of suffering and death to find the sheep that was lost. God is a suffering Father who longs for his prodigal son to return from the far country and who receives and forgives him when he turns his steps toward home.

C. *The cross was necessary to reveal God's estimate of sin.* Only as we look at the cross can we realize how awful sin is in God's sight. To many sin is cute, chic, in good taste; but to God sin is a horrible thing.

We call our sins mistakes, weaknesses, slips, complexes. Even when we use the word, we use it lightly, emptied of its real meaning. What is sin? It is sin that takes the holy God, incarnate in the flesh, and treats him as no beast should ever be treated. It is sin that takes the sinless Jesus and strips him, lashes him, spits on him, pierces him with nails, and then laughs at him.

How bad is sin? Sin is so bad that only the shed blood of the Son of God could do anything about it. A pastor was waiting in a hospital with an anxious father whose little girl was in surgery. Presently, the surgeon came in and described how the surgery had gone. An incision ran more than halfway around the little girl's body. One of her ribs had been removed, and a nerve had been deliberately clipped. After the surgeon left, the father turned to his pastor and said, "If it took all that to make her well, my baby must have been terribly sick." If it took the death of God's Son to heal the world, this world must have been terribly sick. The world is still terribly sick. Only the blood of Christ can heal it.

II. From a human point of view, the cross was necessary.

Apart from Christ's death on the cross, we have no salvation; and apart from his sacrifice for our sakes, no hope. The cross is necessary for us. It is the power of God (1 Cor. 1:18).

A. *The cross is the power of God to challenge our sinful hearts.* Jesus said, "I, if I be lifted up from the earth, will draw all men unto me" (John 12:32). Nothing but the cross could have such arresting, lifting power. Paul spoke of Christ in the most personal terms when he referred to him as "the Son of God, who loved me, and gave himself for me" (Gal. 2:20).

To have someone willing to die for us is an arresting experience; and when someone does so, the experience can be traumatic. Several years ago a hunter and his dog became temporarily separated. As the hunter was trying to cross a swift river in a flimsy boat, the boat capsized. The dog reappeared at the river's edge just in time to see his master float to the water's surface. The dog immediately plunged into the swirling waters to help him. The hunter grasped hold of the limbs of a tree floating downstream and eventually reached the shore, but the dog was not so fortunate. His master stood helplessly on the riverbank and saw his faithful dog drown. Later he said, "It is a challenging thing to have someone die for you—even a dog." But consider this: it was the *Son of God* who loved us and gave himself up for us.

B. *The cross is the power of God to atone for our sins.* The New Testament has no fine-spun theories about the atonement. It presents it plainly, repeatedly, and emphatically. Paul said, "We are convinced that one died for all, and therefore all died" (2 Cor. 5:14 NIV). And Titus 2:14 refers to Jesus as the one "who gave himself for us to redeem us from all wickedness" (NIV). The writer of Hebrews tells us, "Without the shedding of blood there is no forgiveness" (9:22 NIV). John wrote, "He is the atoning sacrifice for our sins, and not only for ours but also for the sins of the whole world" (1 John 2:2 NIV). But no one stated this more clearly than Peter: "He himself bore our sins in his body on the cross" (1 Peter 2:24 NIV).

C. *The cross is the power of God to change us.* In 2 Corinthians 5 Paul came to this conclusion: "Therefore if anyone is in Christ, the new creation has come: The old has gone, the new is here!" (v. 17 NIV).

As an English Methodist minister came out of his church one day, he saw a young workman staring incredulously at a large crucifix. The young man saw the minister and remarked, "I don't see what good it did the Father that his Son should die like that." The minister replied, "It wasn't for the good of the Father; it was for the good of undone sinners our Lord went to the cross." Paul said it exactly: "For he hath made him to be sin for us, who knew no sin; that we might be made the righteousness of God in him" (2 Cor. 5:21).

Conclusion

May we never question God's ways or God's love. The cross was necessary for him, and it is necessary for us. Hallelujah for the cross!

WEDNESDAY EVENING, APRIL 5

Title: Selfishness Separates Families

Text: "Now therefore, my son, obey my voice; and arise, flee thou to Laban my brother to Haran" **(Gen. 27:43)**.

Scripture Reading: Genesis 27:30–45

Introduction

Jacob and Esau, twin sons of Isaac and Rebekah, differed from the start. Esau, the older, was a man of the field, while Jacob was a "home boy." Twice during their days at home, Jacob took advantage of Esau. First, he enticed his older brother to sell his birthright to him for a bowl of pottage. The second time, he and his mother, Rebekah, deceived Isaac and made him grant the major family blessing to Jacob rather than Esau.

Because of his deception, Jacob had to flee and spent twenty years in a distant land waiting for Esau's anger to cool. Even when Jacob returned, he was still not certain that he was safe from his older brother's wrath. We can learn several valuable lessons from this story.

I. Parents should never "play games" with their children.

One of the saddest scenes in contemporary family life is to see one parent take the side of one child and another take the side of the other. This can lead to domestic suicide. Of course, parents do not always "play the game" the same way Isaac and Rebekah played it. This quest for popularity with our children has variations. Sometimes one parent bestows secret and even lavish gifts on a child with the instructions, "Don't let your sibling(s) know about it." This game can be fatal. Usually when parents play games, they do so because something is lacking in their relationship with each other. The old cliché still shouts loudly, "The best thing a father can do for his children is to love their mother." This applies the other way also.

II. There are no shortcuts to realizing our life goals.

Jacob tried to con his way upward, but his plan backfired. We never gain for ourselves when we take advantage of another person's weakness or shortsightedness. When the morning of reality arrives, the consequences are terrible.

III. Gratifying our appetites immediately can be dangerous.

We do not always need what we think we do at a given moment. We can bring years of regret and grief on ourselves because we make a foolish bargain on impulse.

IV. A divided family is tragic.

Look at the terrible result of the competitive nature in Isaac and Rebekah. On the surface, Rebekah seems more at fault than Isaac because she was the aggressive one. Isaac, however, should have shown more awareness. He seems to have allowed his wife's dominating spirit to have full sway. Regardless of how we assess the blame, both parents suffered tremendously. Esau married several Hittite women. And although Jacob married Leah and Rachel, Semitic girls from Rebekah's family background, he didn't return with the grandchildren until twenty years later. We don't even know if Rebekah ever saw Jacob's children, because we have no record of when she died. What a terrible price to pay for sowing seeds of discord by showing favoritism.

Conclusion

Let's not end on a negative note. How can we have a united family? The best way is for a mother and father to keep their love for each other meaningful and vital. The greatest security children will ever have and the thing that will bind them closest together is to know that their mother and father genuinely love each other. With the divorce rate so high today and with many other couples staying married in name only, how necessary it is for us to take inventory of our home life and make the necessary adjustments. The greatest help to family solidarity and marital unity is to let Jesus Christ be the Lord of our home.

SUNDAY MORNING, APRIL 9

Title: The Sound of a Familiar Voice

Text: "[Jesus] asked her, 'Woman, why are you crying? Who is it you are looking for?'

"Thinking he was the gardener, she said, 'Sir, if you have carried him away, tell me where you have put him, and I will get him.'

"Jesus said to her, 'Mary.'

"She turned toward him and cried out in Aramaic, 'Rabboni!' (which means 'Teacher')." **(John 20:15–16 NIV)**.

Scripture Reading: Luke 8:1–3; John 20:1–18

Hymns: "This Is the Day the Lord Hath Made," Watts
"The Head That Once Was Crowned," Kelly
"Christ, the Lord, Is Risen Today," Wesley

Offertory Prayer: Lord God, author of life and conqueror of death, we rejoice in the privilege of worship. On this Resurrection Day, we thank you for the signs of new life that abound in your beautiful creation. We thank you even more for making us new, for saving us from sin and giving us abundant life. We pray for guidance and strength in bearing one another's burdens. Help us to minister to each other. May no breach of fellowship make our offerings unacceptable. Pierce our hearts with the probing light of the Spirit so that we can see ourselves as you see us. Convict us of the need to forgive as we have been forgiven, to love as we have been loved, and to give as we have received. We pray this in Jesus' name. Amen.

Introduction

Each of us can recall moments when the sound of a familiar voice was an especially meaningful experience. It might have been a long-distance call from someone special, the voice of an old friend in a crowd of strangers, a recording of a son or daughter away from home, or words of assurance following surgery. The sound of a familiar voice is powerful medicine. I doubt if any of us has experienced the feeling Mary Magdalene had when she heard the familiar voice of Jesus in the garden of his burial! This was not their first encounter. Jesus had spoken important words to her in the past. He still speaks and waits for us to hear and respond.

I. The word of conversion.

A. *Life in need of change.* Mary first heard the Lord speak the words of conversion. Luke records that seven demons had come out of Mary Magdalene (Luke 8:2). This woman, possessed by evil, had lived a life of torment and suffering. Tradition says she was a prostitute. That label may have fixed itself on her because of the extremely wicked town from which she came. The people knew Mary; they had seen how the devil had used her and captivated her body and made her a public shame.

I wonder what happened at the first meeting between Mary and Jesus—the divine Son of God face-to-face with a demon-possessed woman! Did she cry out in scorn at Jesus, as others had? Did she cower in fear in a dark corner, afraid of his power? The circumstances do not matter. What is significant is that this woman, so desperately in need of transformation, met the Master and heard the words of conversion: "Be whole!"

Is your life in need of change? Does some kind of evil spirit possess you? The spirit of selfishness? Fear? Hate? An anonymous poet expressed our longings:

> Oh, I wish there were some wonderful place
> Called the Land of Beginning Again
> Where all our sins and mistakes
> Could be laid aside like a shabby old coat
> And never be put on again!

There is such a place! The place where you meet Jesus. He can change your life just as he changed the life of Mary Magdalene.

B. *The power of resurrection.* It is significant that Mary was the first person to see the risen Lord. She had one of the more dramatic conversion experiences. God is telling us something here about resurrection and conversion. Without Christ's resurrection, there can be no conversion. Paul wrote to the Philippians of his desire "to know Christ—yes, to know the power of his resurrection" (3:10 NIV). The resurrection power is what changes people. A dead Christ can change no one. Paul told the Corinthians, "If Christ has not been raised, your faith is futile; you are still in your sins" (1 Cor. 15:17 NIV).

The power of sin nailed Jesus to the cross; the power of God raised him. That same power continues to work, and if you will repent of sin and trust Jesus, his power will change you today.

II. The word of appreciation.

A. *Involved in ministry.* After her conversion, Mary Magdalene assumed a place of service in the disciple band. She and several others traveled with Jesus and the disciples and "were helping to support them out of their own means" (Luke 8:3 NIV). We are not told the exact nature of Mary's ministry. She might have washed their clothes, helped prepare food, and provided funds for needs in the group. Her ministry was a result of the love she had received from Christ.

Conversion should result in committed service. "For we are God's handiwork, created in Christ Jesus to do good works, which God prepared in advance for us to do" (Eph. 2:10 NIV).

B. *Appreciation for service.* How often Jesus must have said to Mary, "Thank you, Mary!" She frequently heard the word of appreciation for her service; and if the Lord said it to Mary, he will say it to us. If the Lord noticed the widow's small copper coin and offered praise for her faithfulness, he notices what we do. He appreciates our ministry, whether great or small.

I sometimes hear the elderly and homebound express the sentiment of feeling forgotten and unappreciated. They have faithfully served in the past but now are no longer able. Some of them may be forgotten by the church, but the Lord remembers. He appreciates every labor, and in eternity they will hear his word of appreciation: "Well done, good and faithful servant! . . . Come and share your master's happiness!" (Matt. 25:21 NIV).

III. The word of commission.

A. *Go tell.* The third word Jesus spoke to Mary was the word of commission. When Jesus spoke her name, Mary realized who he was and embraced him in adoration. But Jesus said, "Do not hold on to me" (John 20:17 NIV). It was not a time of worship. The resurrection is not a doctrine to hold on to selfishly but an experience to share selflessly. We are not to hold on to it but give it away. Mary Magdalene obviously understood, because she "went to the disciples with the news: 'I have seen the Lord!' " (v. 18 NIV).

A newspaper had this interesting editorial about Easter: "Easter is usually a quiet occasion. . . . Millions of Americans make a special effort to go to church on Easter Sunday. Easter is a wholesome kind of holiday. It gives all of us an opportunity to recuperate in a small measure from the harassments of daily life." That is not what the Lord intended. The resurrection is the impetus to enter the harassments of life and change the world. It is ironic that for Christians, Easter events take place inside the church building. We dress up and go to church where we enjoy our programs and flowers and decorations. Jesus said the big event should be outside the church—go tell!

B. *Every disciple telling.* Mary's commission illustrates the Lord's desire to use every disciple to share the resurrection news. The Lord's appearance to Mary—a woman with a scandalous past—sent a shock wave throughout the disciple band. The eleven disciples probably thought that Jesus should have appeared to them first. Isn't that just like Jesus to use the person others consider unlikely? The ingredient that makes the difference is love. He will use any of us to tell the good news.

Conclusion

Jesus still speaks. His voice can be heard today. Are you listening? He says, "Here I am! I stand at the door and knock. If anyone hears my voice and opens the door, I will come in" (Rev. 3:20 NIV).

Sunday Evening, April 9

Title: The Theology of the Cross

Text: "For while we were yet weak, in due season Christ died for the ungodly. For scarcely for a righteous man will one die; for peradventure for the good man some one would even dare to die. But God commendeth his own love toward us, in that, while we were yet sinners, Christ died for us" **(Rom. 5:6–8)**.

Scripture Reading: Romans 5:1–11

Introduction

When we look at the cross, we can easily become preoccupied with the details of the agonizing death, the mocking crowd, and the darkened skies. While we should never forget what people did to Jesus that day, the significance of the cross lies in what Jesus did for people.

Paul turned again and again to the cross and made it central in his theology; the cross was the instrument of the amazing act of love and self-sacrifice that set people free. Paul preached Christ as crucified because on the cross he finished his work as mediator between God and people. Paul told the Galatians: "Far be it from me to glory, save in the cross of our Lord

Jesus Christ, through which the world hath been crucified unto me, and I unto the world" (6:14).

As we seek to understand the "theology of the cross," let's think in the broadest terms possible beginning at the outer rim of the circle and moving in toward the center.

I. The cross conceived.

Three questions cry out for an answer.

A. *When?* The cross was no afterthought with God. It was the plan of the ages. To the Ephesians Paul said, "[God] chose us in him before the creation of the world" (1:4 NIV). Exactly what that may or may not mean, it surely indicates that God's plan was not foiled when man fell into sin. God's plan of the ages was ready. It centered on a cross. Indeed, the Lamb of God was slain from the foundation of the world.

B. *Where?* Where was the cross conceived? The answer is in the mind and heart of the Father God, conceived in love. The cross does not make God love us; it is the outcome and measure of his love to us. In the Old Testament, we see types or foreshadowings of the cross. There was the sin offering, the scapegoat, and the Day of Atonement. But when the fullness of time came, these types were fulfilled.

C. *Why?* Jesus died on the cross for two reasons.

   1. He died because of our sins, "the just for the unjust, that he might bring us to God" (1 Peter 3:18). We were such sinners that God's Son had to die in our place.
   2. He died because of God's love for us. The heart of the gospel is this: "God so loved the world, that he gave his only begotten son" (John 3:16). Moved by love, God sent his Son to live as a man among other men. In earthly terms, the cross is not a sign of God's majesty and power but an unforgettable reminder of the lengths to which he will go to bring people to himself.

II. The cross achieved.

We will never understand the mystery of the cross nor agree on our ideas of the atonement. But we will not go far astray if we remember one thing: *God did it!* Paul told the Corinthians: "God was in Christ, reconciling the world unto himself" (2 Cor. 5:19).

But you might wonder, *I thought Jesus was crucified because of the betrayal of Judas, the envy of the high priests, and the weakness of Pilate.* There is some truth in this analysis, but it is not the whole truth. Emil Brunner said, "The cross was the consequence of Judas's treason, of the jealousy and blindness of the high priests, of the human fears of the Roman governor. Yet it was God's work (*I Believe in the Living God* [Philadelphia: Westminster, 1961], 33).

God is not defeated by the sins of men, as demonstrated by the cross at the heart of our faith. Though God did not condone the cross, he wrought it into his final design, which was and is the salvation of the world. George W. Cornell, a reporter and theologian, described what God did this way: "There on the cross, Christians believe, a loving God was a stand-in for all mankind, substituting himself for man, taking on himself in some mysterious way the result of man's pervasive sin, as demanded by his consistent moral order, so that sinners could be accepted without sin's consequences" (*The Way and Its Ways* [New York: Association Press, 1963], 141).

The Old Testament foretold Jesus' coming and the suffering he would endure. In the fullness of time, Jesus came. His birth is the centerpiece of history. His life was perfect. He could die for our sins because he had no sins of his own. His atonement was perfect and complete, superseding all that foreshadowed it (see Heb. 9:11–12).

III. The cross perceived.

The world agrees on the historical fact that two thousand years ago, in a tiny province of the Roman Empire, an itinerant Jewish prophet named Jesus was crucified on a Roman cross, but the world does not agree as to what that event means.

A. *Some, like the Greeks, seek after wisdom.* To them the preaching of the cross is foolishness. But as Paul reminded the Corinthians, "The world through its wisdom knew not God" (1 Cor. 1:21).

B. *Some, like the Jews, are offended by the cross.* It is to them a stumbling block (1 Cor. 1:23). In Galatia Paul felt the pressure to tone down or dilute the gospel. If only he would yield on one point and agree with the Judaizers that not only faith but also the old Jewish rites were necessary for salvation, his troubles and persecutions would be over. "In that case the offense of the cross has been abolished," Paul said (Gal. 5:11 NIV). The offense of the cross is its exclusiveness. There is no other way.

C. *Some, like the modern sophisticates, rebel at the idea of the cross.* Some people cannot believe that a loving God would allow his own Son to suffer such a violent death. They think, *Certainly God could have found a better way!* But this notion is quite in contrast to what is revealed to us on the cross. Through his death, Christ manifested absolute love. "Greater love has no one than this: to lay down one's life for one's friends" (John 15:13 NIV). And we were not even Christ's friends; we were his enemies.

D. *Genuine Christians understand and embrace the cross.* One of two things happens when a person really sees what the cross is and what it means.

1. One result is *unbelief.* When God meets us in the fullness of his love, we don't want him because his demands are too high; instead, we join those who shouted long ago, "Crucify him!"

2. The other result is *conviction for sin.* It is only as we see God in his mercy taking our place that we see ourselves as we are in all our poverty and nakedness, our sin and wickedness.

IV. The cross received.

When we do see, when we do understand, what will we do? Will we accept the love Jesus offers us? The cross stands with open arms to welcome every sinful soul. It is the door through which the Father welcomes the prodigal back to the family and home.

To receive the cross is to enter a new way of life. As Jesus himself said, "If any man would come after me, let him deny himself, and take up his cross daily, and follow me" (Luke 9:23). Taking up our cross does not mean devoting ourselves to some form of asceticism. Rather, it means constantly refusing to gratify our self-life, perpetually dying to pride and self-indulgence in order to follow Christ in his redemptive mission for the salvation of all humankind. "Let him take up his cross daily," Jesus said. The cross means sharing the good news of Christ to the last and to the fullest.

Conclusion

Let's take this time to gaze upon the cross, for that is the only place we discover absolute love—love that endures beyond all reason and convinces beyond all argument. "While we were yet sinners, Christ died for us" (Rom. 5:8). At the cross, love brings home the truth to us until, all doubts and questions silenced, we want only to worship and adore.

Let's thank God, as we say with poet Harry Webb Farrington:

> I know not how that Calvary's cross
>   A world from sin could free;
> I only know its matchless love
>   Has brought God's love to me.

Wednesday Evening, April 12

Title: Finding God for Yourself

Text: "Surely the Lord is in this place" **(Gen. 28:16)**.

Scripture Reading: Genesis 28:1–22

Introduction

Do you find God, or does God find you? In a sense it works both ways. When an outstanding evangelist asked a young boy, "Have you found Jesus?" the lad replied, "Mister, I didn't know Jesus was lost." Of course, that's true. On the other hand, God is lost to us if we don't know him.

Today's Scripture reading tells how a young man, away from home for perhaps the first time, discovered God for himself—an experience that surpassed any previous knowledge he may have had of the Lord. Jacob may have made it all the way to Bethel his first night away from home. Remember, he was fleeing from Esau and was a young man. He probably traveled light and fast.

The spot he chose to spend the night was the site of an old Canaanite worship place. God, however, used this location as a sanctuary for his glory. Our Lord can always give new meaning to old things, and he delights in transforming the ungodly into something or someone that will bring praise to his name.

Jacob had a marvelous dream that night and awoke to find that his life had new meaning. For perhaps the first time in his life, God was real to him. This firsthand experience transformed him and sent him on his way to Haran with a new attitude toward life and changed goals. Some great lessons come to us from this experience.

I. We often find God in unlikely places.

Moses found God in a burning bush, but Jacob found him in an old Canaanite sanctuary. We usually associate the occasion of being born again with a formal church meeting, a revival, or some other religious assembly. Indeed, these are all good places. On the other hand, people also have been convicted of their sins while they were at a place that was seemingly not conducive to spiritual encounters. Of course, a previous experience at worship or a previous testimony by a friend may have paved the way for this experience occurring in an unlikely place. The point is that God can speak to anyone anywhere he chooses. We cannot limit God nor rigidly circumscribe how he will do his work in the world.

II. Sometimes it helps to get away from home.

Jacob's family environment was not the best. His mother, as best as we can understand the biblical record, tried to do his thinking for him. When this happens, a young person often needs to get away for a while and become his or her own person. We should remember, of course, that leaving home is not necessary for all children because not all parents "operate" the same way. In Jacob's case, however, he needed to find out "who he was"; and what better way than a quiet place where God could speak to him!

III. A hasty commitment can be immature.

We generally don't like to find fault with the great biblical characters, but the Bible presents them as they were, "warts and all." We must be honest enough to admit that Jacob's vow was not a completely mature Christian commitment For instance, it was too "iffy" and was based on the fact that God would bless him. He said, "*If* God will be with me, and will keep me in this way that I go, and will give me bread to eat, and raiment to put on, so that I come again to my father's house in peace; *then* shall the LORD be my God" (vv. 20–21).

Mature Christians know that you don't bargain with God in promising to be dedicated. God does not always give us the things we want and think we need. Our promise to tithe should not be based on the fact that God gives us plenty. Some great Christians have been called to suffer tremendously but have still maintained their faith in God. If we take Jacob's vow literally, he would not have been obligated to serve God or bring the tenth to him until God brought him back safely to his father's home, which did not happen until twenty years later. We should carefully monitor our promises to God.

IV. God accepts us as we are.

The glorious thing about Jacob's experience and our own is that God is willing to receive us and bless us even when our understanding of him is inadequate or immature. Someone has said that becoming a Christian is surrendering as much of ourselves as we understand today to as much of Jesus as we understand today. How true! God blessed Jacob even though his understanding of divine things was far from perfect.

Conclusion

All of our motives are mingled. A lost person cannot expect to understand everything about the Christian faith at the beginning. Spiritual birth requires growth and development much the same as physical birth. Jacob learned much about God at Bethel, but he had more to learn as he faced the experiences before him. So do we!

SUNDAY MORNING, APRIL 16

Title: Life in the Son

Text: "This is the testimony: God has given us eternal life, and this life is in his Son. Whoever has the Son has life; whoever does not have the Son of God does not have life" **(1 John 5:11–12 NIV)**.

Scripture Reading: 2 Timothy 1:12; 1 John 5:9–12

Hymns: "I Know Whom I Have Believed," Whittle
"Blessed Assurance, Jesus Is Mine," Crosby
"Standing on the Promises," Carter

Offertory Prayer: Father, we thank you that because of Jesus we can be part of the family of God. Thank you for loving us and providing us with all we need. Lord, we believe; help our unbelief. Forgive us of the sin that darkens our lives. Cleanse us, and in the joy of our closer relationship may we be zealous to witness and willing to serve. May these gifts we now present come from cheerful givers who have the assurance that this offering will be used to bring others to you. May your name be glorified in this worship. In Christ's name. Amen.

Introduction

The words of this song by Bill Gaither confidently express the basis of our Christian hope:

> Because He lives, I can face tomorrow;
> Because He lives, all fear is gone;
> Because I know He holds the future,
> And life is worth the living just became He lives.

After the spiritual high of Resurrection Sunday, some might ask, "Where do we go from here?" Because Christ lives, we can be sure of several truths that change our lives into a daily experience worth living. The key word in John's first letter is *know*—the word is found thirty times in 105 verses. John was certain of the gifts that came with Christ. One of these gifts is life in the Son—"God has given us eternal life, and this life is in his Son" (1 John 5:11 NIV).

I. God gives life.

A. *Life in the Son.* It is not God's will for anyone to perish; he wants each person to live. But we can find fulfillment only in Jesus, who said, "I am the resurrection and the life. The one who believes in me will live, even though they die; and whoever lives by believing in me will never die" (John 11:25–26 NIV). Jesus' resurrection assures us of life. No "resurrection spirit" can give us victory over death. Paul asked, "'Where, O death, is your victory? Where, O death is your sting?' . . . But thanks be to God! He gives us the victory through our Lord Jesus Christ" (1 Cor. 15:55, 57 NIV).

   Lofton Hudson wrote that "death, for many, if not most modern Western men and women, is a four-letter word—obscene, vulgar, nasty, not to be used on stage or in polite society" (R. Lofton Hudson, *Persons in Crises* [Nashville: Broadman, 1969], 110). Jesus' death and resurrection have changed the face of death. Death need not be the grim reaper but the doorway to eternal life—life in the Son.

B. *New quality of life.* The life God gives in Jesus is more than living forever. He imparts a new quality of life. The words *eternal life* refer to the very life of God at work within us now. Jesus said, "I have come that they may have life, and have it to the full" (John 10:10 NIV). An extraordinary quality of life is available in Jesus Christ. But those without Jesus are "dead in trespasses and sins" (Eph. 2:1). Jesus promised, "Whoever hears my word and believes him who sent me has eternal life and will not be judged but has crossed over from death to life" (John 5:24 NIV). Life in the Son is more than just living—it is life with quality.

II. Do you have life?

A. *Received through faith.* The gift of life comes to those who have the Son, and the Son must be received through faith. "I write these things to you who believe in the name of the Son of God so that you may know that you have eternal life" (1 John 5:13 NIV). Faith was the essential element to which Jesus responded. Four men lowered a paralytic through the roof into the house where Jesus was teaching. "When Jesus saw their faith, he said to the paralyzed man, 'Son, your sins are forgiven'" (Mark 2:5 NIV).

   Faith is a common ingredient of daily existence, yet many claim they cannot have faith in Christ. Aldous Huxley once wrote, "Theology claims the just shall live by faith. Science says the just shall live by verification." Yet the scientist believes in a logical universe. He believes in principles used to verify presumptions. What is a theory? It is something *believed* to be true but unproven. We believe in education, democracy, ourselves. Belief is common; why not believe the best and have life in the Son?

B. *Lost because of unbelief.* If this uncommon life comes to those who believe in Jesus, those who refuse to believe are lost—"whoever does not have the Son of God does not have life" (1 John 5:12 NIV). Can a good person really be lost? Yes. Can a churchgoer be lost? Yes. Can the lovable, generous neighbor who has simply delayed her commitment to Christ be lost? Yes. Faith in Christ is the crucial test: "Whoever believes in him is not condemned, but whoever does not believe stands condemned already because they have not believed in the name of God's one and only Son" (John 3:18 NIV).

> Brethren, see poor sinners round you
> Slumbering on the brink of woe,
> Death is coming, hell is moving,
> Can you bear to let them go? . . .
> Tell them all about the Saviour,
> Tell them that He will be found.
>
> —*George Atkins*

Realizing that life is only in the Son should motivate us to "rescue the perishing, care for the dying, snatch them in pity from sin and the grave."

III. Life—for keeps!

A. *Trust God's testimony.* Maybe as a child you responded to a person's gift by saying, "Is this mine, for keeps?" Life in the Son is a permanent possession. God is the basis of this security. A personal testimony about new life is great, but "God's testimony is greater. . . . Whoever believes in the Son of God accepts this testimony" (1 John 5:9–10 NIV). To doubt the certainty of life on the basis of the requirements set forth by God is to make God a liar. If you have done what God said to do, then trust his word and rejoice!

B. *God keeps us.* Paul's confident word to Timothy included a testimony of God's keeping power. "I know whom I have believed, and am persuaded that he is able to keep that which I have committed unto him against that day" (2 Tim. 1:12). The word *keep* means "guard" and evokes the image of a garrison of heavenly troops protecting the individual. Christ is able to keep us and present us one day at the throne of glory. Because he was able to defeat death, he is adequate for everything in this life and the next.

Conclusion

I share the sense of mystery about which Daniel Whittle wrote:

> I know not why God's wondrous grace
> To me He hath made known,
> Nor why, unworthy, Christ in love
> Redeemed me for His own.

I do know I believe Christ. Life in the Son is real. Life is worth the living because he lives.

SUNDAY EVENING, APRIL 16

Title: The Message of the Cross

Text: "For the message of the cross is foolishness to those who are perishing, but to us who are being saved it is the power of God" **(1 Cor. 1:18 NIV)**.

Scripture Reading: 1 Corinthians 1:18–25

Introduction

On the horizons of history, many mountain peaks tower high. There is Mount Sinai, where God's people, Israel, received the law. There is Mount Tabor, where "the stars in their courses fought against Sisera" (Judg. 5:20). There is Mount Carmel, where Elijah defeated the prophets of Baal and God answered by fire. There is Mount Hermon, the probable mountain of the transfiguration. But above them all is Mount Calvary. No mountain towers so high in its influence on people's hearts and minds as that skull-shaped knoll outside the city wall of Jerusalem.

Paul told the Corinthians, "For the message of the cross is foolishness to those who are perishing, but to us who are being saved it is the power of God" (1 Cor. 1:18 NIV). The gospel is essentially the story of the cross, and that story is God's message to the world. The message of the cross has never lost its power. The cross was a divine event. How so?

I. The cross is God's supreme declaration to humankind.

God has many ways of speaking to people, but his supreme way is in the cross (Heb. 1:1–2).

A. *The cross is God's declaration of man's guilt.* Here the sin debt of the human race is fully computed, the bankruptcy of humankind is vividly portrayed. Christ's death, the most undeserved and crudest conceivable, epitomized the tragic condition of humanity. And remember, "Christ died for our sins according to the Scriptures" (1 Cor. 15:3 NIV). The great Catholic scholar John M. Oesterreicher said, "Anyone who denies his part in the crucifixion, also thereby excludes himself from any need of, or share in, the redemption" (quoted by George W. Cornell in *The Way and Its Ways* [NewYork: Association Press, 1963], 135).

   We might moralize and philosophize about sin, but the only way to grasp its enormity is to see what it does. A man was driving while drunk with his wife and two young children in the car. Though his wife pleaded with him to slow down, he would not heed. He wrecked the car and killed his wife and two children, yet he survived almost unscathed. Two days later as he stood by the three caskets side by side in the funeral home, he said, "Never did I realize how awful my sin is until I see now what it has done." Before the gaze of a sin-wrecked world, God raises the cross of his Son, and the first declaration of that cross is "Guilty!"

B. *The cross is God's declaration of man's helplessness.* If people could have atoned for their sin and guilt in any way, the cross would have been unnecessary; but they could not. Jesus died on the cross because people had been rendered helpless by their sin. Morality and good works are not enough to settle humankind's debt of sin.

   As the Israelites, bitten by the fiery serpents in the wilderness, had to confess their helplessness by looking to the uplifted brazen serpent, so must we confess our helplessness by looking to the uplifted Christ. Each one of us is not only guilty before God but helpless to do anything about it. The cross is the power of God offered to powerless sinners.

C. *The cross is God's declaration of his justice.* The nature of humankind's sin called for the most drastic action. That drastic action was God's taking the penalty of our sin on himself through Christ's death on the cross. If God were to blot out our sins and remember them no more, he was faced with a problem. How could the law be satisfied and his forgiving mercy be made possible at the same time? The law says, "The soul that sinneth, it shall die" (Ezek. 18:4) and "The wages of sin is death" (Rom. 6:23). There was only one way possible, and that was for someone who had no sin of his own to die in our place. Only the sinless Son of God met that requirement, and he died for us.

D. *The cross is God's declaration of his love.* Man's sin without God's love would not have sent Jesus to the cross. God could have dealt with our sin some other way. Had it not been for God's great love, he could have destroyed sin by destroying all sinners. But his love sought to save sinners from their sins. The cross was the only remedy. As the cross measures the enormity of our guilt, it also measures the depth of God's love.

Pilate chose the words for the sign that hung on the cross: "JESUS OF NAZARETH THE KING OF THE JEWS" (John 19:19). He should have written: "For God so loved the world" (John 3:16). The cross of Christ stands as a supreme declaration of God's love for a guilty world.

II. The cross is God's supreme offer to man.

A. *By the cross God in his love offers his hand to people in their sin.* The message of the cross is the word of life. It is the message of salvation to all who believe.

Botanists tell of a certain plant in the West Indies called the manchineel. It exudes a substance extremely poisonous to the human touch, producing a terrifying rash and skin eruptions. Fortunately, in this same locality, a plentiful and effective antidote is available. This remedy is the sap of a certain fig that is secured by bruising the body of the fig tree. All people have sinned. We have touched the poison plant of sin, but by faith we each can have access to the tree of healing. The cross is that tree of healing.

B. *In the Bible, God's offer of love and healing is made plain.* The captain of an old sailing vessel lay dying in his cabin. Knowing that his ship was too far from port to reach it before he died, he asked if any member of the crew had a Bible. The cabin boy, the only crew member so equipped, was brought to the captain. Looking at the boy with the Bible in his hand, the dying man asked, "Son, can you find something in that book that will help an old sinner who is soon to meet his Maker?" Turning quickly to Isaiah 53, the lad read it through slowly. The captain listened intently and finally said, "That's pretty, but I'm not sure I understand what it means."

Then this boy, with his mother's Bible in his hand, became the old man's teacher. "Sir," he said, "if you will repeat after me as I read again, I believe you will understand." He read the chapter again, changing only one word: "Surely he hath borne *my* griefs, and carried *my* sorrows. . . . But he was wounded for *my* transgressions, he was bruised for *my* iniquities; the chastisement of *my* peace was upon him; and with his stripes *I* am healed." Suddenly the old man, who had been following with a weakening voice, broke in to say, "Wait a minute, lad, I think I have it. He was wounded for *my* transgressions and with his stripes I am healed. That's it! I see it all now, lad!

Jesus took my place on the cross, and he offers me salvation." The captain had caught the message of the cross, and accepting its offer, he had experienced the saving power of the cross of Christ.

III. The cross is God's supreme power among men.

A. *The cross endures.* The cross of Christ knows no failures. For many centuries the forces of hell have loosed all their fury against it, but still it stands, the mightiest power among humankind.

B. *The cross attracts.* The message of the cross is still the most engaging message ever proclaimed. Rhetoric and philosophy and the wisdom of the world all grow stale, but the sincere proclamation of the simple story of the cross remains wondrously new and continues to attract our interest and attention (see John 12:32).

C. *The cross has power.* The cross has drawing power. It has lifting power. It is the spiritual magnet of the world. The cross draws us from empty creeds and lifts us up out of our sins.

D. *The cross is timeless.* It is timeless in its appeal. The message of the cross is old, yet it is new in its relevance, its urgency. It attracts people when all else fails.

E. *The cross changes people.* It transformed Simon the fisherman into Peter the rock. It changed Saul, the persecutor of the church, into Paul, the apostle to the Gentiles. In a garden in Milan, Aurelius Augustine of Thagasta was mightily converted and became the saintly scholar of the fourth century. The roguish and dissolute son of Pietro Bernardone became the beloved Francis of Assisi. After John Wesley's heart was "strangely warmed" in a meeting at Aldersgate Street, he was used of God to turn England upside down. In a country Baptist church in Clay County, North Carolina, George W. Truett was converted and became one of the most effective preachers of his time.

Conclusion

No other religion can have the power of Christianity because no other religion is built around a cross, with its message of humankind's guilt and helplessness and God's redeeming love. May we always preach Christ and him crucified (1 Cor. 2:2).

Wednesday Evening, April 19

Title: We Reap What We Sow

Text: "What is this thou hast done unto me? did not I serve with thee for Rachel? wherefore then hast thou beguiled me?" **(Gen. 29:25)**.

Scripture Reading: Genesis 29:16–28

Introduction

The eager lad went with exuberance on his journey. His steps must have been lighter as he anticipated the experiences of a new country. With the help of the Lord, Jacob immediately found the country where his mother's kinfolk lived. The adrenaline must have been flowing in his system, because when he saw Rachel, he was able, by himself, to roll the stone from the well's mouth, a task that usually required several men. When he identified himself to Rachel, she was delighted to know him and ran to tell her father.

Jacob the schemer met his match in Laban, his mother's brother. Jacob remained as a guest for a month, but after that Laban suggested that a contract be drawn up for work. Jacob proposed that he work seven years for Laban's daughter, and at that time she would become his wife. However, Jacob did not count on Laban's craftiness.

The wedding feast was a great one, with all the customs of that day. The morning after the wedding had been consummated in the darkness of the tent, Jacob discovered he had slept with Leah, Laban's elder daughter, rather than Rachel. Of course he raised great objections, but Laban showed him the "fine print" in the contract and explained that it was a custom of their country never to give the younger daughter in marriage until the firstborn was wedded. As a result, Jacob had to serve another seven-year term for Rachel. Naturally, Jacob loved Rachel more than Leah. However, God blessed Leah with many children. It was a long time before Rachel bore even one child, and then she died giving birth to the second one. Some great lessons stand out for us from this story.

I. God leads his children along.

Jacob had set out on a dangerous journey, and many things could have happened to him. However, God was with him, and the text indicates that he came quickly to the country where his mother's people lived. In fact, on first inquiry he found Rachel. This seems to have been more than coincidence. God was working in Jacob's life.

How refreshing for us to know that in spite of our shortcomings and sins, God can use us. The Lord had chosen Jacob as the channel through which the Messiah would come. If we had been choosing, no doubt we would have picked Esau, for in many ways he was a more likable character. Yet Jacob, with all of his undesirable traits, had a nature sensitive to God's will. He did not always act in accordance with his knowledge, but he genuinely loved God in spite of his personal ambition and inconsistent nature. Esau, on the other hand, was a worldly wise sophisticate who felt no need for religious affiliation or divine support.

God blesses us when we are earnestly trying to do his will. He will lead us if we will only keep ourselves in tune with him. He does not count our mistakes, but only our good intentions. His mercy is always ready to wipe the slate clean and give us a fresh start. The land of Laban was the place of "beginning again" for Jacob. We, too, can know the joy of starting afresh if we will honestly seek the Father's face and his will.

II. The web of deception is a tangled one.

Sir Walter Scott wrote, "Oh, what a tangled web we weave, when first we practice to deceive." Jacob learned this truth firsthand. He started out as a supplanter. Nothing mattered to him except getting what he wanted. He did not care if he hurt anyone in securing the things he felt he must have at a given moment. Then he met someone who operated from the same base. Experts do not agree as to whether or not we inherit emotional qualities, but we cannot help but wonder if Jacob's "craftiness" was from his mother's side of the family. After all, she aided him in deceiving Isaac, and now we discover that her brother has the same characteristics. Even Jacob the schemer was not going to gain the upper hand with Laban because Laban had more resources to work with and therefore had Jacob at a disadvantage.

What do you imagine Jacob thought the morning after his wedding when he found Leah in his tent? Do you suppose he saw any relationship between the darkness of the tent the night before and the darkness of his father's eyes when Jacob tricked him to receive his blessing? The similarities are too great to go unnoticed. Jacob must have felt great remorse. We do not, however, see any repentance at this moment. Sin had stalked its victim! Jacob was now getting a dose of his own medicine.

III. God always sends compensation.

The relationship between Jacob and his wives is an interesting one. God blessed Leah with children, which was the greatest honor that could come to a woman of that day. I remember talking to a Jewish guide in Israel several years ago. He no doubt reflected the feeling of his people even to this day as he suggested that Rachel was the "beauty queen" who did not want to work, while Leah was the better of the two. We do not have dogmatic evidence of this, but the text seems to imply it. Also, Rachel died earlier and was buried by the side of the road near Bethlehem. She never enjoyed the blessings and fruits of old age. Leah, however, lived a long time and was finally buried in the cave of Machpelah with Jacob, her husband, and the other two patriarchs and their wives. Nearly four millennia have passed, but the grave of Leah is still honored. Also, God sent the Savior through one of Leah's sons, Judah. Life indeed has a strange way of sending compensating blessings for our inadequacies and adversities.

Conclusion

Jacob's life is a strange mixture, a paradox, a dilemma. On one hand, he was a schemer and suffered for it. On the other hand, God stood within the shadows and kept watch over Jacob. He overruled Jacob's mistakes and sins and blessed him in spite of them. Aren't you happy that we serve a God who, because of his mercy, forgives our sins?

SUNDAY MORNING, APRIL 23

Title: Where the Spirit of the Lord Is

Text: "And when the day of Pentecost was fully come, they were all with one accord in one place. . . . And they were all filled with the Holy Ghost" **(Acts 2:1, 4)**.

Scripture Reading: Acts 2:1–21

Hymns: "All Hail the Power," Perronet
"Breathe on Me," Hatch
"Sweet, Sweet Spirit," Akers

Offertory Prayer: Father, as we give to your church this morning, we give in the spirit of your Word that says, "For ye know the grace of our Lord Jesus Christ, that, though he was rich, yet for your sakes he became poor, that ye through his poverty might be rich." May your work be enriched by the gifts you enable us to give. For your glory, we pray. Amen.

Introduction

Acts 2 records an awesome historic event that changed the church forever—the coming of the Holy Spirit into the life of the church on the day of Pentecost. It happened just as definitely as Jesus' birth and resurrection, and the believers were never the same. The church really became the church at Pentecost.

We don't need Pentecost again as such, just as we don't need Jesus' birth, death, or resurrection to occur again. But we constantly need the person of Pentecost, the Holy Spirit, in control of our lives and the church.

Acts 2 is a fascinating chapter of Scripture. It has much to teach us as a church if we are to know the Spirit of Pentecost. Where the Spirit of the Lord is, there is something spiritually special. This is the story of Acts. This is the story of the church through the centuries. This is its message to us today.

Where the Spirit of the Lord is, there are four results.

I. The presence of the Lord.

There was a sudden and strange awareness of supernatural happenings. A sound from heaven like a mighty, rushing wind filled the house where the Christ followers were waiting, and tongues of fire came to rest on each of them. They were filled with the Holy Spirit and began speaking in languages not previously learned. The crowd heard them speaking and banded together in amazement. A very special moment in God's eternal plan was taking place—the coming of the Holy Spirit. The Holy Spirit was entering a new temple—believers. The tabernacle was just an empty tent until Exodus 40:34: "Then a cloud covered the tent of the congregation, and the glory of the Lord filled the tabernacle." The temple of Solomon was an empty building until

1 Kings 8:10–11: "The cloud filled the house of the LORD." Now in the New Testament, the Lord has filled a new temple, not one of skins and tapestries nor of stones and ornaments, but his new temple, the church. Christ is the foundation, and born-again believers are the living stones.

On the day of Pentecost, the Holy Spirit began to indwell all believers just as the glory of God had filled the tabernacle and the temple with his awesome presence! He indwells the church because he dwells in each believer in a personal, intimate way (John 14:17; 1 Cor. 6:19; Eph. 2:21–22).

Where the Spirit of the Lord is, there is the manifestation of his power and the awareness of his holiness in relation to sin. This is what the mighty wind and tongues of fire represent. It is personal to those who sense that something wonderful is happening. It is perplexing to many who do not know the Lord.

II. Power for evangelism.

The day of Pentecost reveals that the Holy Spirit uses and blesses two primary methods of evangelism.

A. *The first method is personal witnessing.* Acts 1:8 says, "Ye shall receive power, after that the Holy Ghost is come upon you: and ye shall be witnesses unto me." Acts 2:4 says, "They were all filled with the Holy Ghost, and began to speak with other tongues." Then verse 11 says, "We do hear them speak in our tongues the wonderful works of God."

The early believers did not receive the fullness of the Spirit to give them a spiritual uplift, but rather to make them powerful witnesses and equip them for service. Not all of us have the gift of evangelism, but every Christian is a witness! Being filled with the Spirit precedes personal witnessing (Acts 4:31).

B. *The second method is powerful preaching.* Acts 2:14 refers to Peter's preaching when he stood up and raised his voice. He preached powerfully with the Spirit in control.

1. Such preaching leads people to repentance (2:37).
2. Such preaching is anointed (2:4).
3. Such preaching is bold (2:22–24, 36).
4. Such preaching is Christ honoring (2:22–24).

The Holy Spirit still honors these methods of evangelism.

III. Victory of the harvest.

Pentecost was called the Feast of Harvest and celebrated the summer harvest. It was on that day as recorded in the book of Acts that the Holy Spirit harvested three thousand souls. The number itself was significant because that was exactly how many were killed on the day that Moses brought the law down from Mount Sinai and found the people worshiping the golden calf. The letter kills; the Spirit gives life.

This is the age of the Spirit. He is still harvesting souls. We are still under the order of Pentecost. George Whitefield saw thirty thousand converted in his revivals in America. In the 1858 revival about fifty thousand people were saved each week. Through Billy Graham's ministry 3.2 million came to Christ. The harvest of the Holy Spirit is seen throughout the world.

IV. A pattern for doing God's work.

The marks of a church that does things God's way are found in Acts 2:41–47.

A. *Atmosphere.* The new believers had a fear, a reverence of the Lord, an awareness that God was at work.

B. *Activities.*
   1. Teaching (v. 42).
   2. Fellowship (vv. 42, 46).
   3. Breaking of bread (vv. 42, 46), including fellowship meals and the Lord's Supper.
   4. Prayer (v. 42).

C. *Attitudes.*
   1. Generosity (vv. 44–47).
   2. Oneness of spirit (v. 46).
   3. Gladness (v. 46).
   4. Praise (v. 47).
   5. Favor (v. 47).

D. *Additions (vv. 41, 47).* The Lord continually builds his church, and as the church grows, believers join together in a spirit of enthusiasm and excitement.

Conclusion

It is not the size of the church that counts, but the working of the Spirit. Lord, touch us with the freshness of your Holy Spirit. Work in us and through us for your glory!

SUNDAY EVENING, APRIL 23

Title: Glorying in the Cross

Text: "May I never boast except in the cross of our Lord Jesus Christ" **(Gal. 6:14 NIV).**

Scripture Reading: Galatians 6:11–18

Introduction

Paul's argument in Galatians is that if these gentile Christians submit to circumcision as a symbol of their commitment to the Jewish law, they have nullified the power of the cross of Christ. Their circumcision would be a sign of dependence on the law and not grace for salvation. The law is not the gospel of Christ; it is not a gospel at all (Gal. 1:6–7). This thought is at the heart of our Scripture reading today. It is summed up in our text: "May I never boast except in the cross of our Lord Jesus Christ" (Gal. 6:14 NIV). Paul gloried not in the law but in the cross.

I. Paul gloried in the cross as the test of motivation (Gal. 6:12–14).

What were the motives of these Judaizers? What was Paul's motive?

A. *Their first motive was human pride.* "Those who want to impress people by means of the flesh are trying to compel you to be circumcised" (Gal. 6:12 NIV). Paul was saying, "They would make capital out of your compliance; they would boast of having won you over to carnal rites." The teaching of the Judaizers was only a pious form of human pride.

B. *Their second motive was fear.* "[They] are trying to compel you to be circumcised. The only reason they do this is to avoid being persecuted for the cross of Christ" (Gal. 6:12 NIV). In effect, Paul was saying, "Those who would force circumcision on you have no sincere faith in its value. Their motive is quite different. They merely hope to save themselves from persecution for professing the cross of Christ." Both Judaism and the Roman authorities would tolerate a Christianity that was only a sect of the Jewish religion. But the cross set the Christians apart in such a way as to bring persecution from both Jews and Romans.

C. *Their third motive was selfishness or worldliness.* Paul said, "Not even those who are circumcised obey the law, yet they want you to be circumcised that they may boast about your circumcision in the flesh" (Gal. 6:13 NIV). In other words, "Look at their inconsistency. They advocate circumcision, and yet they themselves neglect the ordinances of the law. Their motives are those of worldly men. Their basic motivation is selfishness. They want to be able to boast of the number of Gentiles to be circumcised as a result of their efforts."

D. *Paul's motive was pure and true to the gospel.* He said, "May I never boast except in the cross of our Lord Jesus Christ" (Gal. 6:14 NIV). Paul placed no value here on his impeccable credentials as a Jew. He could describe himself as "a Pharisee, descended from Pharisees" (Acts 23:6). And in writing to the church at Philippi, he listed his entire pedigree (Phil. 3:4–6). From the Jewish standpoint, these were real credentials. But how did Paul regard them? As rubbish. He said, "Whatever were gains to me I now consider loss for the sake of Christ" (Phil. 3:7 NIV). Paul gloried only in the cross. If he could be in one of our church services today, no doubt he would gladly sing with us:

In the cross of Christ I glory,
Tow'ring O'er the wrecks of time,
All the light of sacred story
Gathers round that head sublime.
—*John Bowring, "In the Cross of Christ I Glory"*

II. Paul gloried in the cross as the means of separation.

The cross separates believers from unbelievers. The Jews deplored the offense, or scandal, of the cross. Some Jews might have accepted Jesus as the Messiah, but they could not accept a crucified Messiah, a Savior on a cross. They wondered, *How could God permit this wonderful being to experience the degrading, agonizing penalty of the cross?*

The apostles pointed to the Old Testament, explaining that the crucifixion was a part of the Messiah's experience described and predicted hundreds of years earlier. Preaching in the temple courts after the healing of the man who was crippled from birth, Peter said, "But this is how God fulfilled what he had foretold through all the prophets, saying that his Christ would suffer" (Acts 3:18 NIV). For the most part, the Jews would not accept this teaching, nor would many of the Gentiles. To the Jews, the cross was a stumbling block and to the Gentiles foolishness. To Paul the cross was God's means of salvation.

In personal terms, Paul said of the cross, "May I never boast except in the cross of our Lord Jesus Christ, through which the world has been crucified to me, and I to the world" (Gal. 6:14 NIV). Paul considered his acceptance of the crucified Christ as the end of his life in the world and the beginning of a new life in Christ. To him the world's appeal was dead. Earlier in Galatians, Paul declared, "I have been crucified with Christ and I no longer live, but Christ lives in me. The life I now live in the body, I live by faith in the Son of God, who loved me and gave himself for me" (2:20 NIV).

The cross is primary. All other things are secondary. Paul made his boast in Christ and him crucified. "The world has been crucified to me" (6:14 NIV). He was saying, "What is the world to me now? What are all the things of which I once boasted? They are crucified." Paul also said that he had been crucified to the world. He said farewell to the world, and the world said farewell to him. His life's work was a continuous protest against the spirit of worldliness. Paul, like his Master, was "despised and rejected of men" (Isa. 53:3). And all because of Christ crucified. The cross separates believers from the world. It separated Paul. It separates us.

III. Paul gloried in the cross as the way of salvation.

Paul continued, "Neither circumcision nor uncircumcision means anything; what counts is the new creation" (Gal. 6:15 NIV). A new creation! Externals do not count. What counts is being a new creature in Christ Jesus, being transformed by the power of God's Spirit. The acceptance of Christ crucified is the only way of salvation. Jesus said on his last journey to Jerusalem,

"Whoever does not carry their cross and follow me cannot be my disciple" (Luke 14:27 NIV).

Commentator Frank Stagg wrote, "The cross stands for death. In principle it is death to self in the act of surrender to Christ. It is the denial of the self that would have its own being apart from God and others. Although it is death, it is also life. The cross is life through death. It is finding a new way of life by rejecting the way of self-love, self-trust, and self-assertion" (*Studies in Luke's Gospel* [Nashville: Convention Press, 1967], 99). The cross is God's way of salvation. There is no other.

IV. Paul gloried in the cross as the touchstone of Christian unity.

A faithful pastor once said, "I have little time for ecumenism, the four-dollar word for church union, with the proposition, 'You surrender a little of what you believe and I will surrender a little of what I believe, and by and by we will get together.' Let me say frankly and bluntly, that until, by the Scriptures, it is shown me that I am in error, I will not give up one jot nor one tittle of what I believe, but I will meet any man at the foot of the cross. That is the touchstone. The man who trusts in the redeeming merits of Christ's death on the cross for his sins, and only in that, is a Christian; and the one who does not is not a Christian. The man who throws himself like an empty rind upon the grace of God, made possible by the cross, is my brother in Christ; and I care not what the other factors may be."

Listen to Paul again in Galatians 6:15: "Neither circumcision nor uncircumcision means anything; what counts is the new creation" (NIV). God is willing to accept Jews and Gentiles alike. It makes no difference. He blesses all who agree to live by his principles. But the key phrase here is in verse 16: "Peace and mercy to all who follow this rule—to the Israel of God" (NIV). The "Israel of God" is in implied contrast to the "Israel of the flesh." It stands here not for the faithful converts from the circumcision alone, but for spiritual Israel generally, the whole body of believers whether Jew or Gentile.

The entire argument of Galatians is against creating two groups of believers—Jewish and gentile. Paul's clear position is that Jews and Gentiles are one in Christ (3:28). Thus the true "Israel of God" is a bold way of stressing this truth. Paul pronounces a benediction of peace and mercy on a third race of people—neither Jews nor Gentiles, but Christians. The cross is the touchstone of Christian unity.

Conclusion

The cross is not simply a historical event that occurred two thousand years ago; it is a spiritual fact now. We are involved. Jesus' choice of the cross as God's way to redeem humankind has been vindicated by thousands who, like Paul, have gloried in the cross. What about you and me?

Wednesday Evening, April 26

Title: Struggling for Our Faith

Text: "I will not let thee go, except thou bless me" **(Gen. 32:26)**.

Scripture Reading: Genesis 32:22–32

Introduction

Jacob's life with Laban was a stormy one. Surely Laban did not completely despise his son-in-law; after all, Jacob presented him with a number of grandchildren. Yet the scheming between the two carried on constantly, and finally Jacob left the country. Even then, a stormy scene ensued. But ultimately they "mended their fences," and Jacob journeyed back to the land of his father and mother.

The scene at the Jabbok is a strange one. Jacob sent his company on before him and was left alone. He was greatly disturbed because he did not know how Esau would receive him. Jacob prayed earnestly that night, and his experience with the mysterious stranger was no doubt a great part of his encounter with God. We cannot dismiss this episode as a dream. Even though we cannot understand it completely, the account is historical. Who was the mysterious stranger? Jacob later said concerning the incident that he had "seen God face to face" (Gen. 32.30), and we must leave the account there. Some valuable lessons from this incident stand out for us.

I. Old sins still haunt us.

Twenty years had passed. Surely Esau had mellowed! This thought must have crossed Jacob's mind, but he was not sure. Jacob had treated his brother despicably, and crafty soul that he was, he was afraid that Esau possessed similar characteristics.

Sin often comes back on us. In God's moral world, the law of sin and retribution often dishes out its own punishment and reward.

II. God can enter directly into the affairs of humans.

None of us understands God's workings. Paul said, "Without controversy great is the mystery of godliness" (1 Tim. 3:16). God does not choose to intervene directly on all occasions, but when his redemptive program needs his personal attention, he gives it. Jacob needed to learn a great lesson. If we count his experience at Bethel as the beginning of his "saved life," we must look at this incident at the Jabbok as the time when he made a complete surrender of himself to the Lord with the full knowledge of what it cost.

Ideally, of course, when we accept Jesus as Savior, we also accept him as Lord. Unfortunately, we often don't understand enough about God to accept his full claim upon us until later in our Christian life. Jacob needed to be completely subdued by the Lord. Ambition, greed, pride, and all of the accompanying vices still held sway in his life. God refused to give up on Jacob. He had chosen him for himself and insisted on keeping him as a special person in his redemptive program.

III. Jacob met the test.

In the New Testament, we are taught that salvation comes by grace through faith and not by works. In some of these Old Testament stories, we must be careful not to push too far in order to find an analogy of "salvation by grace" in the experiences of the great people God chose and used. The simple point of this story is that Jacob hung on doggedly and literally fought for his faith. He felt unworthy, subdued, frustrated. The years at Haran had taken a toll on his life. If he once felt that God had a great purpose for him, he was not so sure now. Yet he was not willing to give up the experience at Bethel. He would not let God cast him off. He continued to grapple, although perhaps he did not understand the exact nature of the conflict.

How like our lives is this experience! Sometimes we fight the fight of faith when we do not understand the true nature of the battle. Sometimes God nudges us with adversity to humble us and make us usable in his service. Although we must accept this story as literal history, many spiritual lessons also emerge. As God touched Jacob, so he has touched us many times. When we come through the conflict, we understand God in a greater way. We need the storms of life as much as we need the blue sky.

Jacob was never the same after the Jabbok experience. He still had hang-ups from his old life, but something happened by the brook that refined and mellowed him, making him able to cope with the remaining years and the problems they would bring.

SUNDAY MORNING, APRIL 30

Title: The Spirit Within and the World Without

Text: "You, dear children, are from God and have overcome them, because the one who is in you is greater than the one who is in the world" **(1 John 4:4 NIV)**.

Scripture Reading: Acts 1:8; 1 John 3:23–4:4; 5:4–5

Hymns: "Come, Thou Almighty King," Anonymous
"Breathe on Me, Breath of God," Hatch
"Seal Us, O Holy Spirit," Meredith

Offertory Prayer: Our Father in heaven, we adore you and come to worship you this morning. We are not ashamed of the good news of Jesus, for through it we have come to possess abundant life. We thank you for the power of your daily presence. Help us to walk by faith and not by sight.

We pray that you would forgive us of giving in to Satan's deception and trying to cope with our world in our own strength. Thank you for keeping us to this day. We are glad we can offer these gifts to spread the news of life in Christ. Use our gifts for your glory. We pray this in the name of Jesus, who pleads our cause at the throne of grace. Amen.

Introduction

With what do you associate the word *power*? The power of a river—constructive when harnessed at a dam but destructive in a rampaging flood? The power of atomic energy, capable of leveling Hiroshima or fueling a mighty ship? The powerful influence of a government leader? The power of peer pressure? *Power* can be defined as "the means to achieve the assignment."

A car without a motor is only good for display. The car needs engine power to accomplish its purpose. Likewise, Christians are to be more than showpieces of morality. We need the power of the Holy Spirit to accomplish our mission in the world. We are called to be salt and light, a preserving and uplifting influence among people—God's change agents in the world.

Jesus assures us that the power we need to fulfill this mission is available: "You will receive power when the Holy Spirit comes on you" (Acts 1:8 NIV). The Spirit within is the power to face the world without. This gift of victorious power is affirmed in 1 John: "The one who is in you is greater than the one who is in the world" (4:4 NIV).

I. The Spirit within.

A. *The Spirit assumes residence (1 John 3:23–24).* Much controversy surrounds the person and power of the Holy Spirit. The debate causes many Christians to completely ignore this vital area of relationship to God. Paul warned that in the last days there would be many "having a form of godliness but denying its power" (2 Tim. 3:5 NIV).

The initial realization of God's power is the fact his Spirit assumes residence in a Christian at the moment of repentance and faith. Obedience to the commandment of faith opens the door for the Spirit's entry. It is impossible to be a Christian without the Holy Spirit. The Spirit convicts us of sin and turns us toward God. "Through Christ Jesus the law of the Spirit who gives life has set you free from the law of sin and death" (Rom. 8:2 NIV). Jesus promised to send the Comforter and to be with us always. The only way his promise can be fulfilled is through the Holy Spirit—"Christ in you, the hope of glory" (Col. 1:27).

B. *The sign of the Spirit (1 John 4:2).* Someone asks, "How can I be sure the Spirit is within me? Is there a certain sign?" The only sign is the confession of faith in and commitment of life to Jesus. "This is how you can recognize the Spirit of God: Every spirit that acknowledges that Jesus Christ has come in the flesh is from God" (NIV). Jesus also said the Spirit would testify about him (John 15:26) and bring glory to him (John 16:14).

II. The world without.

A. *Antichrist at work (1 John 4:3).* In opposition to the Spirit's work within us is the spirit of antichrist. The Antichrist is not just a powerful evil entity to be revealed in the end times; the spirit of antichrist is in the world already. "The god of this world" (2 Cor. 4:4) opposes Christ. Moreover, our "enemy the devil prowls around like a roaring lion looking for someone to devour" (1 Peter 5:8 NIV).

B. *Test the spirits (1 John 4:1).* The spirit of antichrist is a master at deception—"Satan himself masquerades as an angel of light. It is not surprising, then, if his servants also masquerade as servants of righteousness" (2 Cor. 11:14–15 NIV). The devil can and does perform supernatural phenomena. Just as important as faith in Christ is the commitment to test every spirit. If we are gullible, we will find ourselves "carried about with every wind of doctrine" (Eph. 4:14). Every teaching should be subjected to the standard of God's Word. The Spirit within leads in this search for truth.

III. The Spirit overcomes.

A. *His power is greater (1 John 4:4).* The Word assures us of victory in this conflict with the spirit of antichrist. The Holy Spirit within is greater than he who is in the world. Second Kings 6 records the dramatic account of Elisha before the troops of Syria. Elisha's servant exclaimed in fear, "What shall we do?" That same debilitating fear grips us when we face problems, sin, and an uncertain future. Elisha answered, "Don't be afraid. . . . Those who are with us are more than those who are with them" (2 Kings 6:15–16 NIV). The prophet prayed, "Open his eyes, Lord, so that he may see" (v. 17 NIV). The servant's fear was overcome when he saw the mountain full of the Lord's army. We need a fresh vision of the spiritual resources within us. Nothing, and no one, is greater than the Lord.

B. *Appropriate the power (1 John 5:4–5).* The unbeliever says, "Seeing is believing." But God says, "Believing is seeing!" The same Lord we trust to save us from hell is adequate to keep us in life, but his power is limited by our lack of faith. "This is the victory that has overcome the world, even our faith" (v. 4 NIV).

The Spirit is within us, but does the Spirit control us? We have faith in Jesus, but do we live by the faith of Jesus (Gal. 2:20)? Paul's injunction to "be filled with the Spirit" (Eph. 5:18) refers to the continual control of the Spirit in our lives. It means to avoid sin and submit to God's will. The extent of our victory in the world without depends on the Spirit's control within.

"Now the Lord is the Spirit, and where the Spirit of the Lord is, there is freedom" (2 Cor. 3:17 NIV). Freedom to be what God wants us to be. Freedom to love as Christ loves. Freedom to courageously resist temptation and sin. Freedom to witness without fear or intimidation. The Spirit within sets us free to win the world (Acts 1:8).

"[Christ] was crucified in weakness, yet he lives by God's power" (2 Cor. 13:4 NIV). Appropriate that power!

Conclusion

Because we know the living Christ, we can be sure of life in the Son, forgiveness and control of sin, the love of God, and the ability to love others. "The Spirit himself testifies with our spirit that we are God's children" (Rom. 8:16 NIV). Do you have that confidence? Have you received God's love in Christ?

> Come Holy Spirit,
> Dark is the hour—
> We need Your filling,
> Your love and your mighty power;
> Move now among us,
> Stir us, we pray.
> Come, Holy Spirit,
> Revive the church today!
>
> *—John W. Peterson, "Come, Holy Spirit"*

Respond now to the Spirit.

SUNDAY EVENING, APRIL 30

Title: The Triumph of the Cross

Text: "When you were dead in your sins and in the uncircumcision of your flesh, God made you alive with Christ. He forgave us all our sins, having canceled the charge of our legal indebtedness, which stood against us and condemned us; he has taken it away, nailing it to the cross. And having disarmed the powers and authorities, he made a public spectacle of them, triumphing over them by the cross" **(Col. 2:13–15 NIV)**.

Scripture Reading: Colossians 2:8–15

Introduction

Colossians includes three great teachings.

A. *The incarnation of Jesus Christ.* He was a real human being of flesh and blood and bones and not an apparition as some of the false teachers said. Jesus was (and is) God in all that God is and not just an intermediary being as others had taught the Colossians. The high-water mark of the New Testament is this: "For in Christ all the fullness of the Deity lives in bodily form" (2:9 NIV).

B. *The supremacy of Jesus Christ.* He is supreme in creation and over all created beings (1:15–16); he is supreme in the church (1:18); and he is supreme over all principalities and powers (2:10, 15).

C. *The crucifixion of Jesus Christ and its meaning.* These heretical teachers had attacked the Christian teaching of redemption through Christ's death in two ways.

1. "Christ did not have an actual physical body," some of them said; "he only appeared to have one." Therefore, they maintained that the crucifixion was not an actual event but only a nonhistorical apparition.
2. Others among these heretics said, "Christ had a real physical body, but he was not God's Son. Hence," they contended, "the crucifixion, though a historical event, had no saving power."

Paul wrote his letter to the Colossians largely to refute these views. Thus the teaching about the crucifixion is the main thrust of his letter. The heart of the Christian religion is this: We are redeemed "through his blood, shed on the cross" (1:20 NIV). Through the death of his Son, God has triumphed over sin and death and the devil.

Tonight's Scripture reading presents a fact and the implications of that fact.

I. The fact is this: the triumph of the cross.

Notice the phrases Paul stacks one after another to emphasize the triumph of the cross: "God made you alive with Christ. He forgave us all our sins, having canceled the charge of our legal indebtedness . . . he has taken it away, nailing it to the cross. And having disarmed the powers and authorities, he made a public spectacle of them, triumphing over them by the cross" (Col. 2:13–15 NIV).

A. *The triumph of the cross is a historical fact.* That Christ died an actual death on the cross cannot be disputed. "His blood, shed on the cross" (1:20 NIV) was an actual, witnessed, historical event (John 19:34). "Christ died for our sins according to the Scriptures" (1 Cor. 15:3 NIV).

B. *The triumph of the cross is a theological fact.* In his first letter, John tells us, "The blood of Jesus . . . purifies us from all sin" (1:7 NIV). Consider Jesus in the garden of Gethsemane, with the shadow of the cross looming in front of him. What did he do with it? He laid hold of it. He made it an instrument of redemption, offering himself as a full, perfect, and sufficient sacrifice for the sins of the whole world.

C. *The triumph of the cross is a spiritual and personal fact.* "When you were dead in your sins . . . God made you alive with Christ" (Col. 2:13 NIV).

The triumph of the cross becomes a personal victory in our lives when by faith in Christ we accept what he has done for us on that cross.

II. The scope: the vast reaches of the triumph of the cross.

The triumph of the cross has both a legal and spiritual aspect.

A. *The legal aspect of the triumph of the cross.* Colossians 2:14 tells us that the penalty for our sin was the death sentence. That sentence has been taken from us, satisfied by another, canceled forever. Through the cross, Jesus has done three things about this sentence of death.
   1. He "canceled the written code, with its regulations, that was against us and that stood opposed to us." Our debt is canceled, marked "Paid" like a canceled check; and we have peace with God.
   2. "He took it away." It's gone, thank God! That sentence is no longer over our heads. How could it be removed from us? The perfect law of God must be satisfied. Nothing can thwart it, escape it, or rewrite it.
   3. "Nailing it to the cross." What does that mean? It was customary for the Romans to nail a sign with the condemned man's crime on the cross just above his head. On the sign over Jesus' head, Pilate had written: "JESUS OF NAZARETH, THE KING OF THE JEWS" (John 19:19 NIV). But that was not the real indictment. Had Pilate known, he could have written: "Crucified for the sins of humankind."

B. *The spiritual aspect of the triumph of the cross.* Listen to Paul: "And having disarmed the powers and authorities, he made a public spectacle of them, triumphing over them by the cross" (Col. 2:15 NIV). What appeared to be God's defeat and the triumph of the powers of darkness proved instead to be God's triumph and the doom of Satan and sin. The cross was God's field of victory, the implement of his triumph.

Conclusion

In closing, let's ask ourselves this question: "What is or what should be the significance of the triumph of the cross in our own personal lives?"

A. *Death to sin.* "We are those who have died to sin; how can we live in it any longer?" (Rom. 6:2 NIV).

B. *Life in Christ.* We ought to say and think and do those things worthy of a life redeemed by Christ's blood.

> At the sign of triumph
> Satan's host doth flee,
> On, then, Christian soldiers,
> On to victory.
> —*Sabine Baring-Gould, "Onward, Christian Soldiers"*

SUGGESTED PREACHING PROGRAM FOR THE MONTH OF MAY

■ Sunday Mornings

This month begin a series called "The Christian Family: Living for Christ in the Present." Marriage and the family are under great stress today. The church has a vital stake in the husband-wife relationships and in the parent-child relationships of those who constitute its membership.

■ Sunday Evenings

"Beneath the Cross of Jesus" is the theme for a series of eight biographical sermons about the people who were present when Jesus was dying on the cross. "Were You There When They Crucified My Lord?" is also a good theme for these sermons.

■ Wednesday Evenings

On the first Wednesday evening of the month, complete the series on Jacob, "Lessons from a Changed Man." Follow up with a four-part series on Jacob's son Joseph titled "Lessons from Joseph."

WEDNESDAY EVENING, MAY 3

Title: Start Over Where You Began

Text: "God said unto Jacob, Arise, go up to Bethel . . . make there an altar unto God, that appeared unto thee when thou fleddest from the face of Esau thy brother" **(Gen. 35:1)**.

Scripture Reading: Genesis 35:1–10

Introduction

To Jacob, Bethel was more than a geographic location. It was the place where he had first come to know the Lord in a personal way. All of us have our Bethels. For some of us, it is where we accepted Jesus Christ as personal Savior. We also may have smaller Bethels in our lives—those times when we awakened to a more meaningful relationship with God. Whatever Jacob may have known about God before his Bethel experience, we do not know. We can be certain, however, that this was the dearest place on earth to Jacob, because there he entered into a relationship with the Lord that, though clouded over at times by sin, remained his moment of inspiration that sent him forth with a song in his heart.

Now God wanted Jacob to follow up the Jabbok experience with a time of fresh dedication. He called on him to go back to the place of spiritual origin.

The text does not tell us that God commanded him to do it, but Jacob took his household with him and told them to put away the strange gods they had become attached to during the days in Haran, to purify themselves, and to put on fresh clothes as a symbol of a new spiritual beginning.

How Jacob's heart must have beat faster when they handed him the various pieces of jewelry that represented dedication to foreign gods and practices. He hid them and most likely never went back to recover them. We can find some great teachings in this account.

I. We all need periods of fresh beginning.

We are too intermeshed with the world. We cling, too often and too long, to the superficial things that the secular way of life offers. Even though we have surrendered to Jesus, our dedication is far from complete. We do not bow down to gods as the pagans did, but we often imitate their value system in our lifestyles. Although technically we cannot "rededicate" something that has once been dedicated, we can reaffirm our dedication and loyalty. We can ask God to help us make a fresh start. We can tell him once more that we love him and seek to lead our families into closer fellowship with him.

II. A truly saved person never forgets.

If we have once experienced deliverance from sin, that experience will always remain special in our lives. The doctrine of "once saved always saved" is reflected, in some senses, in this story. Jacob had been delivered by God at Bethel, and he never forgot it. Years of sinning and selfishness had driven a wedge between him and proper fellowship with God, but the relationship was still there.

We cannot always find perfect analogies between the Old Testament and New Testament in spiritual experiences, but here we can see enough to make a comparison. At Bethel God delivered Jacob from fear and distress. At Calvary he paid the price to deliver us from the fear of sin and the distress of guilt. We need to come back to our initial experience often to secure renewed grace for living and strength for service.

III. For maximum happiness, sin must be put away.

Even though we are saved from the guilt of our iniquities by Christ's atoning sacrifice at Calvary, the influence of worldliness is an ever-present threat. How much Jacob was personally influenced by the gods of Laban's family we cannot be sure, but his family seemed to have picked up the habit of idol worship. Perhaps Jacob did not personally participate, but his influence was not strong enough to keep his family from this sin.

How often the same is true of us! Our lives are not so much terrible as they are empty. There is not enough spirituality in our homes to lead our children to faith in Christ. We need to go back to the Bethel experience and secure fresh motivation. We need to clean out the cobwebs and take out the trash. God had given Jacob a new name at the Jabbok. He renewed this truth at Bethel, expecting Jacob's life to take a new direction.

Conclusion

Do you need the Bethel experience? What direction would your life take if you genuinely returned to the eager desire to serve Christ that you had on the day you were saved? Why not spend some time by yourself to review the time you were saved and to reaffirm your life in the Savior?

SUNDAY MORNING, MAY 7

Title: Healthy Families Are No Accident

Text: "'Do not judge, or you too will be judged. . . . So in everything, do to others what you would have them do to you'" **(Matt. 7:1, 12 NIV)**.

Scripture Reading: Matthew 7:1–14

Hymns: "Oh, for a Faith That Will Not Shrink," Bathurst
"Onward, Christian Soldiers" Baring-Gould
"Come, Come, Ye Saints," Clayton

Offertory Prayer: Father, in your Word you have taught us that if we are to know your presence, we must be still. So in this quiet moment, we are still before you. Sometimes we are so broken by our doubts that we live with an empty spirit and don't know quite how to find you. You promised that if we will quit talking for a while and allow our ears to listen and our hearts to respond, that you will speak to us again and our doubts can be erased with a hope and confidence that come from you.

We bring our offerings this morning, not so that we can buy assurance from you, nor in a vain attempt to pay you for those times you were clearly present with us. Our gifts are signs of our love even when we, for a while, may have lost sight of the way. We wait upon you and worship today, through Jesus our Lord. Amen.

Introduction

Healthy families are no accident, and they are usually happy families. But happiness is not what I'm talking about this morning. Happiness should not be our goal. It is not something we find at the end of the rainbow. It is what happens to us along the way to building a meaningful, purposeful life.

Families, like people, get sick sometimes. We are not always healthy. But when we get sick, we want to get well. Sometimes it is harder for sick families to get well than it is for sick bodies to heal, because we have trouble admitting that our families are sick. Sick families can get well, but healing doesn't happen automatically. It happens only when people are determined to change their lifestyle. In our text from the Sermon on the Mount, we learn some exciting truths that can be applied to family life.

I. Healthy families are the result of deliberate choices (Matt. 7:13–14).

God's way is not easy to find, nor is it easy to walk in once we find it. There are easier ways to live than to live God's way. The traffic that moves in the direction of the world follows a crowded thoroughfare. People who justify their choices by saying, "Everybody's doing it," are walking on that well-traveled path.

But God's Word is clear. If we want to find life, we will often be on a lonely road. That's one reason churches are so important to Christian families. If we had to live our lives isolated from one another, we really would feel isolated in this world. We gather together in the church, not because we're perfect and not because we're always what we ought to be, but because we understand the ground rules and we know when we're in foul territory. The world doesn't even know there is an out-of-bounds. They live bouncing off one wall to the other, never quite understanding why their lives keep getting shaken out of joint.

We know that our church has many healthy families, but we also know that many of us are really hurting. As a church, we are here to help one another, not only when we're well but also when we're sick. Nevertheless, the church must be more than a hospital, more than a place that treats pain with quick fixes. To be well, we must make deliberate choices to that end. It isn't easy. It's costly. Sometimes we have to go against the current to escape the easy flow the world offers us. We need to step out and feel the breeze that comes when we're all alone, striving to be a family used of God to be different and healthy.

II. Healthy families are built on thoughtful behavior toward one another (Matt. 7:12).

Matthew 7:12 is the Golden Rule for families: "So in everything, do to others what you would have them do to you" (NIV). A free translation might be, "So whatever you wish your husband would do for you, do that for him. Whatever you wish your wife would do for you, do that for her. Whatever you wish your children would do for you, do that for them. And whatever you wish your parents would do for you, do that for them."

A healthy family is not a fifty-fifty proposition. Every member has to give 100 percent. If you want more attention from your husband, give him more attention. If you want more love and affection from your wife, then ask yourself, *How can I be easier to love and to be affectionate with?* And then give affection as you would like to receive it. If you're a child in your family, ask yourself, *How would I like for my children to treat me when I'm a parent? What kind of children do I want to have?* That will help you every time to know how to relate to your parents.

The saddest thing about child-parent relationships is that the things we miss most in our parents are often the very things that are the hardest for us to give to our children. Parents, touch your children, hold them, be proud of them, believe in them, even if your parents weren't able to do that for you. It's not how others have treated you, but how you *wish* they had treated you. We all have scars. Some are more visible than others, but we don't have to inflict the same ones that were inflicted on us if we only stop and cry out to God, "Oh, God, forgive whoever hurt me and let me down, but don't let me do the same. Remind me that I am loved, that you love me. Remind me that I am important. I belong to you. And now, out of who I am before you, let me give myself to the man or woman or children who are special to me. You have given them to me. I will treasure them as you have treasured me."

III. Healthy families are honest with one another (Matt. 7:1–5).

When a husband and wife refuse to judge one another, they are on their way to being a healthy family. Parents are to respect one another and their children. Criticism and judgmentalism are not to be known in a Christian family. Parents who put their children into competitive modes, judging one child over the other, create heartache that can never be fully measured. Long after the parents are gone, that kind of mishandling will continue to exact a price. These verses in Matthew 7 mean that we are not to set ourselves up as though we're perfect and the others in the family are somehow unworthy. We can't hide a plank in our eye. We will never be healthy until we admit, "Yes, that's a plank in my eye; let's get it out so we can work on the speck in yours." Parents who understand this concept do better with their children. And children who understand this concept don't have to judge their parents as harshly as they might otherwise.

IV. Healthy families are more interested in giving than getting (Matt. 7:2).

We usually interpret this verse in terms of money, but it also has to do with loving and caring and being a family. We can't outgive God. Nor can we outgive a spouse or children or parents who give with no strings attached. When we give our hearts and start to love others unconditionally, our gifts of love come back to us. To receive love, we have to give it. It's a reciprocal process.

V. Healthy families are protected by faithfulness (Matt. 7:6).

Matthew 7:6 has generally been used to describe how Christian witnessing ought to be done, but perhaps it has even more to do with marriage. A husband and wife are not to take the precious gift of their sexuality and cast it out before "dogs" or "hogs." Beware, because if you do, they will turn and trample you underfoot as they attack you. Healthy families are protected by fidelity and trustworthiness. You cannot get so modern or so sophisticated that you are permitted to ignore that admonition. Treasure your sexuality. Used within marriage, it is indeed holy and as precious as pearls. But nothing can tear a family apart as much as giving that which belongs only to each other to someone on the outside.

IV. Healthy families are enriched by prayer (Matt. 7:7–11).

A. *If our family isn't healthy, we shouldn't abandon it any more than we would abandon a child who has gone to the hospital sick.* Just because we're sick doesn't mean we're dead. Just because we're ill doesn't mean we can't get well. Prayer changes us and makes us ready for what God is ready to do in our lives.

B. *If we're healthy, we shouldn't be proud, but grateful.* We should make our prayer one of thanksgiving and sensitivity to improve our decision making, our thoughtfulness, our honesty with one another, our willingness to give, and our fidelity. We should be thankful for what God is doing in our family to help us remain strong against the evil all around us that threatens our most precious possessions.

C. *We shouldn't insist that everyone around us pray just as we pray.* Some Christian homes would be healthier if there were no contest to see who is the most "spiritual." It is important to share our prayers together, and every child ought to hear his or her father and mother pray. But we must not try to make everyone fit one particular spiritual mold, or we will miss what God can do in each individual life.

Conclusion

Healthy families are no accident. It takes everybody giving his or her best. Each member of the family has a part in determining how healthy our families will be.

Sunday Evening, May 7

Title: The Face of Fortune: Barabbas

Text: "Now at that feast the governor was wont to release unto the people a prisoner. . . . Then released he Barabbas unto them: and when he had scourged Jesus, he delivered him to be crucified" **(Matt. 27:15, 26)**.

Scripture Reading: Matthew 27:15–26

Introduction

Pilate presented Barabbas to the crowd as an alternative, seeking to escape his responsibility in the ordeal. His training in Roman justice made it difficult for him to condemn an innocent man.

Pilate's offer takes on special significance if both of these men had the same name. Many scholars believe that the full name of Barabbas was Jesus Barabbas. Some manuscript evidence supports this theory. And if this was the case, the crowd had to choose between Jesus of Nazareth and Jesus Barabbas.

The face of Barabbas is truly the face of good fortune. Never has a better thing happened to a man on the day of his expected crucifixion. Jesus of Nazareth probably died on the cross that had been prepared for Jesus

Barabbas. When the Sabbath came, Jesus was lying in a tomb and Barabbas was sleeping in his own bed. This graphically sets forth the central truth of the gospel, "Christ died for us."

I. An undeserved fortune.

Barabbas deserved to die. Justice had finally caught up with him. But are we not all worthy of death when we are measured by God's perfect standard of righteousness?

A. *Because of wasted opportunities.* "Barabbas" means "son of a father." This probably indicates that he was the son of a rabbi. His full name, then, would have been Jesus, the Son of the Rabbi. Growing up in the home of a rabbi would have given him the opportunity to know the things of God. It would have brought many special opportunities for spiritual development. But apparently Barabbas had failed to take advantage of those opportunities.

   Does that sound like your story? You may not have been raised in a minister's home, but God has graced you with special opportunities.

B. *Because of the broken law.* Barabbas had broken the law of man and the law of God. He had been a terrorist against the Roman government. He was a devoted member of the Zealots, who were committed to the overthrow of Roman rule. In the process of pursuing this goal, he had broken many of God's laws. He had been guilty of violating almost all of the second table of the Ten Commandments. Disobedience to parents, murder, stealing, lying, and covetousness were characteristics of his life.

   If Jesus was going to die in place of someone else, certainly he wouldn't die in place of someone like Barabbas! But in the providence of God, Jesus did take the place of Barabbas so the great truth of the gospel might be revealed. "But God commendeth his love toward us, in that, while we were yet sinners, Christ died for us" (Rom. 5:8). He died for sinners!

II. An unsought fortune.

A. *For Barabbas.* As Barabbas stayed in his cell awaiting his crucifixion, he never thought to ask someone else to take his place. He simply assumed that his crimes had caught up with him. No one was more surprised than Barabbas with the outcome. He must have received the news of his release with some skepticism. He may even have thought the soldiers were playing a twisted prank on him. But the news was true. Jesus of Nazareth was going to die in his place.

B. *For the sinner.* Jesus Christ did not die for us in response to any appeal on our part. Indeed, instead of sinners pleading with him to bear their sins on the cross, they were busy rejecting him. "He came unto his own, and his own received him not" (John 1:11). The only explanation for Jesus' action is love. He died for us because he wanted to save us from hell.

III. The unrestricted fortune.

A. *The freedom of Barabbas.* All Barabbas had to do was walk out of the jail and he was a free man. Since Jesus was going to die in his place by Pilate's decree, the Roman law had no claim on him. His debt to society was paid.

It must have taken Barabbas a long time to realize what had really happened. He may have continued to hide every time he saw a Roman soldier coming. He may have expected some word that it was not really true. But it was! Barabbas had the good fortune to receive unrestricted freedom at the expense of another man.

B. *Freedom through the gospel.* Forgiveness must be God's greatest gift to humanity. It means that God has canceled the entire debt of our sin. But we must never forget that God is free to cancel the debt only because Christ paid it. "He himself bore our sins in his body on the cross, so that we might die to sins and live for righteousness; 'by his wounds you have been healed'" (1 Peter 2:24 NIV). And Ephesians 1:7 says, "In [Christ] we have redemption through his blood, the forgiveness of sins" (NIV).

This means that we can know freedom from condemnation, freedom from guilt, freedom from the stains of sin—all through the death of Jesus Christ. No wonder Paul exclaimed, "God forbid that I should glory, save in the cross of our Lord Jesus Christ" (Gal. 6:14).

Conclusion

Barabbas accepted Jesus' death in his place. He gladly walked out of the jail and allowed Jesus to die in his place. I don't know if Barabbas ever realized the meaning of the substitution, but we have no excuse to neglect its significance today.

Dr. Charles Allen shares a story from William L. Stidger about a young man named Bill who joined the navy when World War II began. One night his ship came into Boston, and he decided to visit Dr. Stidger, his former pastor and friend. During their visit together, Dr. Stidger said, "Bill, tell me the most exciting experience you have had so far."

Bill hesitated. It wasn't that he had trouble selecting the most exciting experience. Rather, the experience he had in mind was so wonderful and sacred that he had trouble putting it into words. Bill was the captain of a large transport that, along with a convoy, was making its way across the Atlantic. One day an enemy submarine rose in the sea a short distance away. Bill saw a torpedo coming directly toward his transport loaded with hundreds of young men. He had no time to change course. Through the loudspeaker, he shouted, "Boys, this is it!"

Nearby was a small escorting destroyer. The captain of the destroyer also saw the submarine and torpedo. Without a moment's hesitation, he gave the order, "Full speed ahead!" The tiny destroyer eased into the path of the torpedo, taking the full impact of the deadly missile midship. The destroyer blew apart and sank quickly; every man of the crew was lost.

For a long time, Bill remained silent. Then he glanced up at his beloved pastor and said, "Dr. Stidger, the skipper of that destroyer was my best friend." Again Bill was quiet awhile, then he said slowly, "You know there is a verse in the Bible that has special meaning for me now. It is, 'Greater love hath no man than this, that a man lay down his life for his friends.'"

But we were not Jesus' friends when he laid down his life for us. We were his enemies. Nevertheless, he took our place on the cross. Will you receive him as your Savior and Lord tonight?

Wednesday Evening, May 10

Title: Dream, but Don't Make Dreams Your Master

Text: "'Here comes that dreamer!' they said to each other" **(Gen. 37:19 NIV)**.

Scripture Reading: Genesis 37:1–28

Introduction

Joseph, like Jacob, stands out as one of the most delightful and exciting characters of the Old Testament. All but one of Joseph's brothers were born of different mothers, making for a diversity of interest and intensely competitive spirit among the brothers and ultimately leading to hostility. The tension between Joseph and his brothers is reminiscent of the conflict between Jacob and Esau.

Even though Jacob and Esau had their differences, in the end they seemed to have become reconciled to the point that they did not seek harm for one another. Joseph, on the other hand, remained a possible threat to his brothers, at least in their own minds, until the very end. Although he had forgiven them and given them positions of privilege in Egypt, they feared that after their father died Joseph would retaliate for the evil they had done to him.

Today's Scripture reading concerns Joseph's early years. God had given him several meaningful dreams, and he rather brashly reported them to his family. Even though we recognize that Joseph was chosen of God for a great mission, he was still a human being, and we are not irreverent to point out certain signs of his immaturity.

I. Dreams are important.

The prophet Joel said that young men would "see visions" (2:28). Youth is the time when we perceive with piercing distinctness because our faculty of vision is fresh. The true test of our ability to cope with life is our vision. People live by visions. Foolish people laugh at ideas they cannot understand, but dreams are not, as they have been called, "the vaguest things we know." They represent ideals, and we cannot dismiss a matter by saying, "That's a nice idea, but it's only an ideal." The world owes much to good people who have dreamed and then worked hard to make their dreams come true.

II. Dreams can be dangerous.

If it is wrong never to dream, it can also be wrong to dream and then act on that dream rashly or indiscreetly. We should be careful about disclosing our secrets. When Joseph recounted his dreams for his brothers, they were highly irritated. He let his family know that he considered himself a man with a great future; likely the implication of his words was that God had spoken to him in the dreams.

When we feel that God has revealed something to us privately, we should deliberate thoughtfully before we tell others. After all, what we feel God has revealed to us may be only our subjective egotism, a projection of our own desires. Even when we are correct in discerning God's will, others may not be ready to learn all that we know. God has revealed the truth to us because it is something he wants to entrust to us, so we need to prudently consider when others are ready and able to hear our word from the Lord.

III. Making dreams come true requires hard work.

Many years ago, I heard a message titled "Dreams Plus." I don't remember the entire outline or the illustrations the speaker used, but I do remember his suggestions for what we need to add to our dreams to turn them into a reality. The one I remember most is "hard work," which he emphasized more than any other point. God helps us when we are in his will, but God does not do for us the things we can do for ourselves.

Let it be said to Joseph's credit that he added hard work to his dreams. As we will see in other studies of his life story, he stayed morally pure, waited patiently, and took advantage of every opportunity. We must do these same things if we are to see our dreams become realities.

Conclusion

An old popular song contains two lines that forever ring true: "If your heart is in your dream, no request is too extreme." God will give us the strength, if we are faithful to him, to realize our ambitions—provided, of course, they are worthy of his help. We all need to be dreamers, for without vision an individual or even an entire nation perishes. But we must not let our dreams master us. We need to "stay on top of them" and not give up until the dream of yesterday becomes the fact of tomorrow. That's what faith is all about. One writer said that faith is "an affirmation and an act that bids eternal truth be present fact."

Sunday Morning, May 14

Title: The Gospel for Women

Text: "'Jerusalem, Jerusalem, you who kill the prophets and stone those sent to you, how often I have longed to gather your children together, as a hen gathers her chicks under her wings, and you were not willing'" **(Luke 13:34 NIV)**.

Scripture Reading: Luke 13:34–35; 15:8–10

Hymns: "God, Give Us Christian Homes," McKinney
"Oh, Master, Let Me Walk with Thee," Gladden
"Oh, God in Heaven," Martin

Offertory Prayer: Heavenly Father, we thank you for our mothers' love and patience and confidence in us. We have been graced by our mothers' watch care over us and by their prayers for us. We also have been graced by your salvation, which we have not earned but, like our mothers' care, is given freely and abundantly. As we bring our offerings to you today, we acknowledge that we have been given more than we can ever repay. Amen.

Introduction

Our message today comes from Luke 13:34–35 and Luke 15:8–10. What do these two texts have in common? They both describe the compassion of God in feminine terms. Has it ever occurred to you that Jesus understood God in a feminine as well as a masculine dimension? Most often Jesus taught us that God is Father—a loving, caring, patient Father who desires good things for his children and longs for them to put the kingdom of God first in their lives. But Jesus also used, at least twice, feminine analogies to illustrate God's nature toward his people.

Perhaps Jesus took his cue from Genesis 1:27. Or perhaps he simply believed that the marvelous fullness of God's nature required a variety of human analogies to help us understand God's greatness, his compassion, his will for the people of the earth. It is well known that Mary, as the virgin mother, provides the image of mothering warmth for those in the Catholic tradition, almost to the point of deification. But we need not go to extrabiblical sources to find the feminine, mothering aspects of God's nature. Jesus himself provides them for us in our Scripture readings today.

I. God as a mothering hen (Luke 13:34).

Jesus knew that his destiny could not be worked out unless he went to Jerusalem. But he knew that the record for God's people in Jerusalem was not good. With just a hint of satire in his voice, he insisted to his disciples that he must go on to Jerusalem, because, "Surely no prophet can die outside Jerusalem!" (Luke 13:33 NIV). (See also Jesus' story in Luke 20:1–20.) But in spite of Jerusalem's record with the prophets, Jesus loved that wayward city. In a voice clouded with deep sorrow and pathos, he cried, "How often I have longed to gather your children together, as a hen gathers her chicks under her wings, but you were not willing" (v. 34 NIV).

The Jews were a displaced people in Jesus' time. They belonged with one another, but conquest and God's judgment on their sin had left them scattered across the Roman Empire. Jesus yearned to bring them together in his messiahship. Jesus knew also that the storm was gathering. It would not be long until another judgment would fall upon Jerusalem, and in that storm Jerusalem would be lost to the Jews for all the centuries until now. So Jesus used the feminine image of a mothering hen who protects her scattered chickens.

II. God as a seeking woman (Luke 15:8–10).

In the famous trilogy of parables concerning God's nature, Jesus speaks of a woman seeking her lost coin, of a shepherd seeking a lost sheep, and of a father seeking his lost son. The woman had lost one of her ten coins. It was a serious loss. Perhaps it was a treasured coin that had been given to her in her dowry. Its value was more than what it could be used to buy. It stood for all the good memories of her life and her hopes for her own children. Or perhaps it was a coin that represented savings for a treasured purchase for her family. In any case, the coin was lost, and the woman would not give up until she had found it.

Perhaps the coin represents the children of God, meaning that God does not want to lose even one of his children to the evil one; each child is important. The woman did not say, "Well, I only lost one; I have nine left." She was not satisfied until the treasure was complete. So it is with God. We may appear to be one of many and not worth very much to some who would set a value on our lives, but to God we are extremely valuable. We are worthy of the search. Not one of us can slip through the cracks of life without God's knowledge. We can be sure that anytime we become lost in sin, God will search for us to bring us back to himself.

III. Jesus' regard for women.

Jesus' respect for women does not seem so radical today, but in his day Jewish men prayed, "Praise be to God that he has not created me a Gentile. Praise be to God that he has not created me a woman. Praise be to God that he has not created me a slave or an ignorant man." The Manichaeans, one of the most popular religious groups of Rome, prohibited women from membership. The place of women most often in pagan religions was as temple prostitutes. But Jesus changed women's standing.

A. *A woman's place (Luke 10:38–42).* The Jews believed that a woman was not worthy to handle the Law. Her place was as a house servant. But in this remarkable incident, Jesus clearly indicated that a woman's place is not only in serving, but in learning. One of the highest signs of respect that someone can give another is to take his or her mind seriously and attempt to teach truth. Jesus taught many women, including Mary. Notice also that Mary was not a mother, so he was not teaching her for her children, but for herself. He taught her for her mind's sake.

B. *A woman's sin (Luke 7:36–50).* There is no double standard with Jesus. He accepted the woman who poured perfume on his feet. Her repentance and sorrow were great; she wept and poured out an expensive gift. She was greatly forgiven (v. 47). Those who have hit bottom know how to glorify God most fully.

C. *A woman's gift (Luke 21:1–4).* A poor widow gave two copper coins that far surpassed the rich offerings of those who had more left than they gave. Jesus praised the woman for her willingness to be generous with what she had.

D. *A woman's distress (Luke 21:20–24).* In times of warfare, women have suffered particularly brutal treatment. Our Lord's compassion for women in the days of the destruction of Jerusalem serves as a model for all people.

E. *A woman's witness (Luke 23:55–24:11).* Who had the love required to go visit the tomb and bathe the dead body of the Savior with spices and ointment? Who had the courage to go and see if anything could be done for Jesus with Roman soldiers everywhere around? Who was the first to say, "Jesus is risen from the dead"? The disciples thought they were hearing an "idle tale" (v. 11). But that only reveals their reluctance to hear what God had ordained to tell them through women.

Conclusion

It is no wonder Paul could say, "There is neither Jew nor Gentile, neither slave nor free, nor is there male or female, for you are all one in Christ Jesus" (Gal. 3:28 NIV). The gospel for women is that God cannot be fully understood without the feminine dimension. He came to seek and to save that which was lost, both men and women. God's respect for persons applies equally to male and female. Because of his great love for us, God, like a mother hen, seeks to draw us near to himself. He will seek until we are safely under his wing.

Sunday Evening, May 14

Title: The Face of Favor: Simon of Cyrene

Text: "A certain man from Cyrene, Simon, the father of Alexander and Rufus, was passing by on his way in from the country, and they forced him to carry the cross" (**Mark 15:21 NIV**).

Scripture Reading: Mark 15:15–25

Introduction

"Were you there when they crucified my Lord?" Simon of Cyrene was. As we study the faces beneath the cross, we find the face of this favored man. He carried the cross to Golgotha, where Jesus was crucified. We will use our imaginations this evening to fill in some of the implied details and see his story as it may have been.

Simon was born into a dedicated Jewish home in the North African city of Cyrene. His parents expressed their faith at his birth by naming him Simon, the name of one of the famous sons of Jacob the patriarch.

As Simon grew into manhood, he probably dreamed of going to Jerusalem to observe a Passover. Such a pilgrimage was the aspiration of all the faithful Hebrew people scattered across the world. Finally, Simon of Cyrene was about to realize his dream. We can imagine his heart beating with excitement as he entered the Holy City for the first time. When he arrived in Jerusalem, he found the city in an uproar. Everyone was talking about the teacher from Galilee. They were sharply divided over Jesus' identity. Some felt certain that he was the long-awaited Messiah, but others considered him a false prophet. There were reports that the leaders of the people were plotting his death.

On the day of the great Passover, Simon stumbled upon a strange spectacle as he entered the city. He saw a noisy crowd clustered around a band of soldiers. In the midst of the soldiers was an obviously weary man bearing a Roman cross. Most of the crowd was heckling the condemned man. The soldiers were prodding him to hasten his steps. Any observer could see that the man was about to fall beneath the weight of the cross. When Simon saw what was happening, he decided to stay in the shadows.

Just then the soldiers decided they had had enough of the slow pace of the tired criminal. They wanted to finish their assignment. They glanced around for someone to carry the cross, and their eyes fell on Simon. One of them grabbed Simon. "You!" he growled. "You take this cross out to the hill." Because he was a Jewish man, Simon was powerless to refuse. Roman soldiers had the power to conscript any non-Roman anytime they pleased. Reluctant and embarrassed, Simon shouldered the cross and followed the soldiers to Golgotha. Maybe it was the outcry of the women that caused Simon to take a second look at the condemned man. Somewhere along the way, he became aware that he was bearing the cross of Jesus of Nazareth.

It is easy for us to see that the soldiers unknowingly granted Simon a tremendous favor. Any of us who know Jesus would have been glad to carry the cross. Yet in a real sense the opportunity to bear his cross is always with us. The cross symbolized all of the shame and reproach that accompanied the life and death of Christ. The cross was what it cost our Lord to do the will of his Father. If we choose to walk in his ways, we, too, will bear his cross. This event changed Simon's life forever. What a favored man!

I. The favor of cross bearing may be hidden.

No doubt Simon saw nothing good in the ordeal at first. At best he viewed it as an inconvenience. Bearing the cross took time away from other activities he had planned for this special day. He had not planned on such an interruption.

Simon's resentment probably went even deeper. Being treated like a common slave on what was to be the greatest day of his life was just too much. Would the people think he was a disciple of Jesus, or would someone think it was his cross? What if he met one of his friends on the way? Cross bearing never seems to be a favor at first.

What was your first reaction to cross bearing? Were you surprised by how others treated you simply because you were a Christian? How could anyone question your motives and accuse you so wrongly? Jesus knew this would be a problem for his disciples, so he gave frequent and thorough instructions on the matter, exhorting his disciples to rejoice whenever they bore the shame of the cross.

The favor of cross bearing may be hidden to the natural eye, but it is seen by those who walk in the Spirit. The apostle Paul described such suffering as a "gift." We are favored by the Lord when we suffer shame with him.

II. The favor of cross bearing should be acknowledged.

A. *In public commitment.* We are not told when Simon actually became a disciple of Jesus. The fact that his name is given here can be taken as proof that the story of his conversion must have circulated widely among the early Christians.

Likely Simon was born again on the day of Pentecost. Luke reports that men from Cyrene were among the three thousand converts that day. The manner in which Jesus died must have impressed Simon. Jesus showed no fear throughout the ordeal but showed a remarkable peace instead. The only times he said anything were to pray to God or to help someone. He never appealed to the soldiers for mercy nor accused them of injustice.

Also, the report of Jesus' resurrection had been circulating throughout the city. Simon had been thinking about the Man and his death for fifty days. Then he heard Simon Peter, a disciple who had faltered during the ordeal because of fear, declaring boldly that this same Jesus is both Lord and Christ. Simon of Cyrene was compelled to believe. He stepped out from the crowd and willingly accepted baptism in water by one of the apostles, a public acknowledgment that bearing the cross was a favor. He was ready and willing to bear shame for this Jesus.

B. *In active service.* Simon of Cyrene translated this public commitment into active service. It is probable that he is the Simon who became a leader in the great missionary movement in Antioch. He continued to be identified with Jesus by aggressively seeking to make disciples for him.

Are we holding back from this public identification with Jesus Christ? Have we been afraid of the consequences? Do we consider the potential cost too high? Simon had no choice the first time he was identified with him, but what he learned about Jesus made him a willing cross bearer. He learned that bearing the cross of Jesus was actually a privilege. We also should make a public acknowledgment.

III. The favor of cross bearing can be shared.

Simon of Cyrene led his two sons to be cross-bearing Christians. He shared the privilege with them. We are not given the details, but we are given the names of Alexander and Rufus. The inclusion of their names indicates that they had become well known among the early Christians.

The Gospel of Mark was written to be used as a gospel tract in the city of Rome. When Paul wrote a letter to the Roman church, he sent greetings to Rufus and his beloved mother (Rom. 16:13). Could his relationship to Rufus and his mother date back to Paul's ministry with the church in Antioch? There is a tradition that Rufus became an effective church leader and that his brother Alexander became a martyr for the cause of Christ. And it all began with Simon bearing the cross.

At first Simon felt as though it was the worst thing that could happen to him, but it soon became his greatest blessing. It changed his life and the life of his family. If we bear the cross of Christ, we will influence others. Wouldn't it be wonderful to influence our own sons and daughters to bear the cross of Christ as well?

Conclusion

We sing, "Must Jesus bear the cross alone and all the world go free? No, there is a cross for everyone, and there is a cross for me." Dr. John Broadus noted that the original version of the hymn was, "Must Simon bear the cross alone, and the saints go free? Each saint of thine shall find his own, and there is one for me." Each one of us is called to bear the cross of Jesus.

You find this place of favor willingly. The cross will not be forced on you. You must make a public commitment of your life to Jesus Christ. You must be willing to bear any shame or suffer any loss in his service. Will you join Simon of Cyrene beneath the cross?

Wednesday Evening, May 17

Title: Without Purity We Cannot Please God

Text: "'How then could I do such a wicked thing and sin against God?'" **(Gen. 39:9 NIV)**.

Scripture Reading: Genesis 39:1–20

Introduction

Whatever immaturities Joseph may have had as a young lad, his dedication and genuineness of character more than made up for them. When Joseph arrived in Egypt as a slave, Potiphar, one of the pharaoh's chief officials, bought him. Joseph immediately advanced in position and was soon trusted with great responsibilities. His trouble, however, began when his master's wife sought to entice him. Joseph refused, but she would not give up. Later the wicked woman accused Joseph of doing the very thing he had consistently refused to do.

This incident, Joseph's refusal to compromise his moral integrity, is perhaps the most remembered fact about his life in Egypt. If Joseph had yielded to the woman's advances, the history of his life probably would have been far different. He stood firm on his convictions and was forced to go to jail, but he emerged victorious a few years later. One interesting sidelight to the story is that Potiphar probably didn't really believe his wife's story. If he had, Joseph would have been executed immediately. When Potiphar placed him in jail, he was actually showing mercy. Several interesting lessons speak to us from this story.

I. You can't keep a good man down.

Joseph performed his tasks well in Potiphar's household. We don't know exactly how long Joseph worked for Potiphar before he was recognized as a man of responsibility, but the text indicates that he was soon promoted. We read, "From the time he put him in charge of his household and of all that he owned, the LORD blessed the household of the Egyptian because of Joseph. . . . So Potiphar left everything he had in Joseph's care; with Joseph in charge, he did not concern himself with anything except the food he ate" (Gen. 39:5–6 NIV). Joseph was not boasting but simply stating a fact when he told Potiphar's wife, "No one is greater in this house than I am. My master has withheld nothing from me except you" (v. 9 NIV). God's blessing was on Potiphar's household, but we can infer that part of the reason Potiphar prospered was that Joseph was a good administrator.

II. Sin of any kind is against God.

When Potiphar's wife insisted that Joseph yield to her advances, he said to her, "How then could I do such a wicked thing and sin against God?" (v. 9 NIV). Joseph's response indicates that he thought first in terms of his relationship to God. He knew that taking another man's wife would have dire consequences, but his foremost concern was obedience to God's moral law. All sin is against God. When we mistreat another person, we mistreat one of God's creatures. When we abuse our body, we abuse the temple in which the Lord dwells. So-called sins against society are, first of all, sins against God.

III. Personal purity is essential for successful living.

No other sin will mar the lives of young people and stifle their chances for happiness in the future as much as sexual immorality. When young people cross the line of physical indulgence and allow themselves to become impure in this realm, something happens to their lives. Things are never the same. Even if they are saved and forgiven, they carry with them the crippling consequences of their actions.

More than a century ago, a young man led a young woman into a passionate affair. As a result, she became weaker and proceeded from one promiscuous experience to another, ultimately destroying her happiness and self-worth. Later the young man had a genuine salvation experience, and the Lord called him to preach. He carried with him the memory of what he had done to this young woman. He could not rest until he searched and found her. He pled with a broken heart for her to forgive him and sought to help her find forgiveness in Christ and the beginning of a new life. Unfortunately, she was weak and unable to repent as he had done. This man carried a broken heart to the grave.

Conclusion

Guard your personal purity! Like the little white ermine that protects its white fur even at the cost of its life, remember that purity is the dearest thing you possess. When you compromise the sanctity of your body, you usually, if not always, will compromise in other areas too. Paul said it simply but succinctly to Timothy: "Keep thyself pure" (1 Tim. 5:22).

SUNDAY MORNING, MAY 21

Title: Friends of the Family

Text: "'Everyone who hears these words of mine and puts them into practice is like a wise man who built his house on the rock'" **(Matt. 7:24 NIV).**

Scripture Reading: Matthew 7:24–29

Hymns: "Word of God across the Ages," Blanchard
"Built on the Rock the Church Doth Stand," Grundtrig
"At the Name of Jesus," Noel

Offertory Prayer: Father, you have taught us to love one another as you have loved us. Help us today to see that many of your best gifts to us are the people you put in our lives. We are your people, and you have made us to be friends. May our friendships always strengthen one another and bring glory to you.

Great God of gifts, we bring our gifts to you this morning. Much of what we have and now give is made possible through the help and encouragement of the friends you have given to us. Help us to be worthy friends to others. In Christ's name. Amen.

Introduction

It was front-page news. Two houses in Arlington, Texas, that had been built overlooking the Trinity River lost their backyards when after days of heavy rain they began to slide down into the river. Flooding had occurred in the low areas. The people who lived on the cliff probably felt secure from the flood, but they had not counted on the silent erosion of their entire backyards. We can imagine what they must have felt as all the work they had invested in those houses started to slide down into the river. They were forced to leave their homes in fear that next their back porches and then their entire houses would disappear into the river bottom.

Many kinds of enemies, often unseen ones, eat away at the foundations not only of our houses but of our homes. The financial investment we have in our houses is not all that is threatened; the very survival of our families is vulnerable. To paraphrase a common Scripture verse, "What good is it for someone to gain the whole world, yet forfeit their [family]?" (Mark 8:36 NIV). But just as surely as there are enemies of the family (see the June 4, Sunday mornining sermon), there are also certain friends of the family. Jesus not only taught us what to guard against but what to embrace. He not only taught us what to do, but he helps us see how to do it. In today's Scripture reading, Jesus gave us the clues we need for building healthy families.

I. God's Word is a friend of the family.

Jesus said that if we hear his words and do them, we will be like the wise man who built his house on the rock (Matt. 7:24). We almost always interpret this verse as an admonition for personal ethics, but it also applies to building healthy families. The words of Scripture give us a strong authority base for making decisions in our families. Some families make decisions about what they will allow their children to do by calling the neighbors to find out what they are going to let their children do. Many families decide their spending priorities by watching what their neighbors buy.

People who decide what is appropriate and inappropriate simply by taking the popular temperature get into trouble quickly. They are like the man who built his house on the sand. Every wind and storm that comes shakes them to their foundation; but those who build their families on the written Word of God have a strong foundation for the building of their lives together. We have to be cautious, though. If we build our homes on the Word of God, we must be careful to interpret the Word correctly.

Scripture can be taken out of context and have devastating consequences; for example, it could empower a husband to be a tyrant without reminding him of his responsibility to love his wife as Christ loved the church. God's Word is not to be used as a hammer to beat other people down but to foster thoughtful concern for one another and sacrificial compassion for each member of the family. God's Word provides the family with the standard against which to examine issues and to make thoughtful, moral, and equitable decisions.

Here are four of Jesus' precepts that apply especially to the family.

A. *Forgiveness (Matt. 6:12).* Jesus said that when we pray we should pray to be forgiven in the same way that we have forgiven those who have sinned against us. In Matthew 18:22 Jesus said that we are to forgive not seven times but "seventy times seven." Nothing is more devastating to a home than old hurts and offenses that have not been forgiven. If we make forgiveness a priority in our family and forgive even when it isn't easy to forgive, we will be able to withstand the storms. It is especially important that we forgive our parents for the times they were not able or willing to be the parents we needed them to be. Many families are still torn apart because of misunderstandings related to wills and inheritances. The ironic truth is that those who are hurt most by an unforgiving spirit are not those who are unforgiven, but those who will not forgive (cf. Matt. 5:21–24).

B. *Love (Matt. 5:43–46).* Jesus made it clear that his followers are to love their enemies as well as their friends. Sadly, we often find it difficult to love even within the family. Jesus provided us with the direction we need. The apostle Paul picked up on Christ's strong example of love in Ephesians 5:25. A husband is to love his wife as Christ loved the church and gave himself up for her. When Christ lives in us, we begin to discover resources for a love that can give itself away. As we prayerfully remember how our Lord has loved us, he will create in us the energy to love those around us. The best definition of this kind of love is found in 1 Corinthians 13. Here we discover excellent guidelines for showing love within the family.

C. *Faithfulness (Matt. 5:27–30).* The fabric of the family is a tightly woven material. Extramarital affairs introduced into the marriage relationship tear it apart. Jesus called the Christian family to fidelity and to a love that keeps the eyes focused on each other. The physical love relationship between the mother and the father is absolutely essential for a healthy family. Indeed, the best gift a father can give his children is to love their mother.

D. *Supremacy of God (Matt. 22:37).* Because the family is so significant and can bring us so much happiness, we may be inclined to worship our family and elevate it to a place only God ought to have. Matthew 10:37–39 reminds us of the absolute primacy of our allegiance to God. He must come before all other allegiances in life, even before our loyalty to family. As important as the family is to Christian life, it is not the ultimate for us.

II. The church is a friend of the family.

When Jesus described the founding of his church, he spoke of building it on a rock (Matt. 16:18). As we consider Jesus' parable about the wise builder who built on the rock, we remember that he took his own teaching to heart.

The house he built—the church—is the second great friend to your family. It is the place where God's Word is taken seriously and authoritatively. A man who had not been as active as he ought to have been in his church said to his pastor, "This church has been a great gift to my family. Even in those times when I wasn't doing what I should have been doing, the church ministered to my children. The reason my children are what they are today is because of the adult friends and the peers of my children who knew them and cared for them within the life of this congregation. The church has been the most important institution for my family."

A. *The church provides needed support through the many relationships it makes possible for its families.*
   1. Older families become a model for the younger families. This witness helps the younger families make decisions and plan how they want to raise their children and build their families.
   2. Older families are strengthened as they provide guidance for younger families. When a family knows there are younger families who believe in them and admire them, they are encouraged to be faithful to the Lord and to the task of building the finest families they can.
   3. All families are helped by their peer families. Knowing that we are part of a whole body of people who are sharing the same joys and struggling with the same concerns gives us courage to press forward and not give up.
   4. All kinds of families find a place of belonging in the church. The church is a place of refuge for those who are mentally or physically impaired. It provides a family for those who have no family of their own. It also offers a network of support to families broken by death or divorce. The church stands beside them as the hurts are healed and as God helps them begin again.
   5. Families need friends who have the same goals. We tend to adopt the standards, goals, attitudes, and ambitions of our friends. Friends shape our futures. One of the best gifts a church can give to a young couple is a place where they can meet couples their age and make lasting friendships that will be a bulwark of encouragement and support through the years.

B. *The church helps families learn how to worship together.* As families worship in church Sunday after Sunday, they learn how to praise God and rejoice in his creation outside the church. Worship becomes a natural part of daily living. Children who learn how to worship in church and outside in the beauty of God's world are prepared for a lifelong appreciation of God's power and majesty. They become more sensitive to the transcendent dimension that overarches all of life.

III. The community can be a friend of the family.

Christians should want to support good schools and teachers who care. A stable community and honest government are the products of people who are willing to get involved. The libraries, medical resources, marriage enrichment opportunities, and cultural activities in a community are all important to the health of family life in the city. Christian people are doing God's work for families when they reinforce positive and healthy attitudes in their local communities.

Conclusion

Healthy families are no accident. They are built under the authority of God's Word, in the fellowship of his church, and in a community where people encourage one another in healthy living. Let's build our families on the sure foundation—our Lord Jesus Christ.

SUNDAY EVENING, MAY 21

Title: The Face of Failure: Simon Peter

Text: "While Peter was below in the courtyard, one of the servant girls of the high priest came by. When she saw Peter warming himself, she looked closely at him.

"'You also were with that Nazarene, Jesus,' she said.

"But he denied it. 'I don't know or understand what you're talking about,' he said, and went out into the entryway.

"When the servant girl saw him there, she said again to those standing around, 'This fellow is one of them.' Again he denied it.

"After a little while, those standing near said to Peter, 'Surely you are one of them, for you are a Galilean.'

"He began to call down curses, and he swore to them, 'I don't know this man you're talking about.'

"Immediately the rooster crowed the second time. Then Peter remembered the word Jesus had spoken to him: 'Before the rooster crows twice you will disown me three times.' And he broke down and wept" **(Mark 14:66–72 NIV)**.

Scripture Reading: Mark 14:53–72

Introduction

Any of us could have done what Peter did. Failure as a disciple does not require exceptional weakness or extreme character flaws. This careful record of Peter's failure is a good reminder of this fact. Peter, a chief apostle, was present at the cross as a failure.

Let's review the facts we know about Peter so that we can put his failure in proper perspective. He joined the followers of Jesus very early after his brother, Andrew, brought him to Jesus. He gave up a fishing business to become a "fisher of men." Jesus chose him to be one of the twelve apostles and later included him in the "inner circle." He was present at the transfiguration of our Lord and was an "eyewitness" of most of his miracles. He had received personal instruction from the Lord on a daily basis for over three years before his failure.

Peter had not always been a failure. He was the one who gave the bold confession that so delighted Jesus' heart. Peter had never been without words before. But now under the pressure of the circumstance, facing the scrutiny of the group in the courtyard of the high priest, he vehemently denied three times that he knew the Lord. Though he had loved the Lord, he denied him.

Most of us who have been disciples a while can identify with Peter. We know the pain of failure. We can learn from Peter's experience.

I. The shame of our failure.

Failure is always shameful but is especially so when detected in the life of someone so privileged.

A. *The failure represents a misjudged evil.* Peter had no intention of failing. His intentions were to be faithful to the Lord regardless of what might happen. He sincerely expressed these intentions in the Upper Room as the disciples observed the Passover. But in making his spiritual calculations, Peter misjudged the power of the evil one. Jesus tried to sober his calculations by reminding Peter that Satan had made a request to sift Peter "as wheat in a sieve," but Peter ignored the warning. He felt sufficient in his own strength for any power that might rise against him.

   Wise men and women are careful to measure the strength of their enemy. Those who succeed in discipleship are always mindful that the enemy is like a "roaring lion seeking whom he may devour." Peter learned this truth the hard way.

B. *The failure represents a mistaken concept of self.* Peter did not know himself as well as he thought. Peter could not do all that he thought he could do. More of the "old Simon" was still present in him than he wanted to admit.

   Peter's words of dedication spoken in the upper room did not come from his faith in God, but rather from his faith in himself. They were the bold claims of a self-sufficient man. On the contrary, the person best prepared for the way of discipleship is the one who confesses, "In my flesh there dwelleth no good thing" (Rom. 7:18). Our only hope of avoiding failure is by wholly depending on the Lord and his strength.

C. *The failure involves a denial of Christ.* As Peter tried to be inconspicuous in the courtyard, he was discovered. Three times he was asked if he was a follower of Jesus, who was then on trial. Each time Peter's response was the same. He denied that he had ever known the Lord. Because he suspected that his denial was not convincing the crowd, the third time even included a religious oath and curses.

Many of us have done the same shameful thing. It may have been by our words or by our deeds, but we denied Christ. Likely the circumstance under which we did it was not nearly so threatening, but failing our Lord is a shameful deed under any circumstance.

II. The sorrow over our failure.

A. *A sign of repentance.* True disciples weep over their failures. They are never proud or boastful about such shameful matters. Peter's sorrow began the moment he heard the rooster crow, reminding him of the warning the Lord had spoken to him. Then there was the look that he received from Jesus as he remembered. The look must have emanated sorrow and hurt. It sent Peter out into the night to express his sorrow with tears.

Peter was not merely sorry that he had been caught in his denial, but was sorry for his failure and for how it had hurt Jesus. There is no real repentance without this type of sorrow. Such sorrow is a proper response when we know we have failed.

B. *A step toward recovery.* The Scriptures assure us that God is near to those with a "broken and contrite heart." If Peter had approached the whole ordeal with the same broken spirit that he had when he came out of it, he never would have failed. But he was soon to discover that his tears were not in vain. Our forgiving and compassionate God takes note of such sorrow. It is a true step toward recovery.

III. The solace after our failure.

Peter's experience is good news for every failing disciple. Our failures do not have to be final.

A. *The solace of forgiveness.* Tears of repentance will bring us to the solace of forgiveness. A poem by Dylan Thomas describes God's commission of a man to find the world's greatest treasure. The man finally locates a tear of repentance that proves to be the most precious thing earth can produce.

Martin Luther wrote, "No article of the creed is so hard to believe as this: I believe in the forgiveness of sins. But look at Peter. If I could paint a portrait of Peter, I would write on every hair of his head forgiveness of sins."

How do we know that Peter was forgiven? After Jesus rose from the dead, he sent a special message to his disciples, and he instructed the women who carried the message to deliver it to Peter personally. Our Lord forgave Peter fully, and he will forgive us when we fail.

B. *The solace of fellowship.* Much of the sorrow related to failure comes from our broken fellowship with Jesus. Knowing that we have disappointed him makes us uncomfortable in his presence. But after we receive his forgiveness, we can begin to enjoy his company again. This was true for Peter in the time he spent with Jesus after the resurrection. The fellowship was restored. He was not banished forever as he thought he might be.

Conclusion

How we deal with our failures is important. For Peter a shameful failure became a positive experience as he allowed his heart to be broken and struggled to gain another opportunity to show his loyalty. The record of Peter's ministry in the book of Acts after he was filled with the Holy Spirit is evidence enough of what a failure can become. How are you handling your failures?

Wednesday Evening, May 24

Title: Ingratitude Is a Marble-Hearted Fiend

Text: "The chief cupbearer, however, did not remember Joseph; he forgot him" **(Gen. 40:23 NIV)**.

Scripture Reading: Genesis 40:1–23

Introduction

Even while he was in prison, Joseph's sterling character shone forth. The prison warden recognized Joseph's integrity and put him in charge of all the prisoners. Like Potiphar, the warden gave Joseph free rein, and God blessed him even in prison. Some time later, the chief cupbearer and the chief baker were thrown in prison, and once again dreams entered Joseph's life. One night the cupbearer and baker both had strange dreams, and the next morning Joseph interpreted their dreams correctly. The cupbearer was restored to his position, but the baker was killed. Joseph refused to take credit for his wisdom but gave it to God. Also, he asked the cupbearer to remember him kindly and mention him to Pharaoh. The cupbearer agreed, but after he was restored to favor, he failed to keep his promise. Let's look at this story more closely and glean some truths.

I. God keeps his eye on his chosen ones.

We must never forget that the most important message of the Old Testament is that God was working redemptively through the nation he had chosen. Although our Savior did not come through the line of Joseph, God used Joseph to preserve the Israelites, and at this time he was the key person in the messianic story.

Of course, not all of us are chosen for such a strategic mission, but all of us are important to God. He has a place for each of us in his service; when we show him we intend to do his will and accomplish what he wants us to do, he will take care of us. An old truism says that Christians are divinely protected as long as they are in God's will and doing what God has mapped out for them. In spite of the opposition of the wicked people he encountered, Joseph continued to prosper because he was faithful in his living and loyal to the mission God had planned for him.

II. Evil people respect good people.

If people today live right and stay humble, even wicked people are impressed and show favor to them. Of course, both righteous living and a proper attitude are important. If we are overbearing in our righteous deeds, we can easily hurt our cause and even bring others' wrath on us. Joseph stayed humble even when he received great responsibility. When he was called on to interpret the dreams, he gave credit to God. Wisdom is a great virtue, but directing credit to God for our wisdom is greater.

Some have criticized Joseph for seeking to extract a promise from the cupbearer, claiming that he was not trusting God sufficiently. This is not a fair accusation, however, because God expects us to use every legitimate means to advance our cause as long as we do not violate Christian conscience or employ unchristian methods. Joseph did what any of us would have done under the same circumstances. He was patient, but he also saw a chance to better himself and took advantage of it. He provides us with an example of constructively using every opportunity that comes to us.

III. Selfishness and ingratitude are conjoined twins.

"The chief cupbearer, however, did not remember Joseph; he forgot him" (Gen. 40:23 NIV). Imagine Joseph's devastation when he realized the cupbearer must have forgotten his promise. Of course, the cupbearer did remember Joseph later, but only when he saw a chance to impress Pharaoh. How often our good deeds are mingled with selfish motives! If Satan cannot get us to do a bad thing, he will lead us to do a good thing with the wrong spirit and the wrong motive. We cannot condemn the cupbearer without considering our own lives and asking whether we have been fair with the people who have done favors for us. The greatest kindness ever shown is Christ's death on the cross for us. Have we been faithful to him? Have we returned the love he has shown to us?

Conclusion

We need to take a good look at ourselves! Do we remember friends who have helped us along the way? Maybe we remember the person who introduced us to Christ as Savior, or the person who helped us get a new job, or the teacher who opened up new areas of truth to us. What about our parents who made sacrifices for years in order to give us a good education? We have much to be grateful for. May we never forget it!

Sunday Morning, May 28

Title: The Family Deals with Death

Text: "'Lord, if you had been here, my brother would not have died.' When Jesus saw her weeping, and the Jews who had come along with her also weeping, he was deeply moved in spirit and troubled. 'Where have you laid him?' he asked. 'Come and see, Lord,' they replied" **(John 11:32–35 NIV)**.

Scripture Reading: John 11:1–4, 17–37

Hymns: "A Mighty Fortress Is Our God," Luther
"What Wondrous Love Is This?" American Folk Hymn
"Because He Lives," Gaither

Offertory Prayer: Heavenly Father, we thank you for our families, as they help us grow to be the people we have the potential to be. Especially in times of grief and heartache we turn to our families for comfort and strength. May we always remember that your love is what guides us through rocky times. We bring our gifts to you this morning in recognition that you first loved us and gave us your Son so that we might have abundant life. We pray in Christ's name. Amen.

Introduction

On this memorial Sunday, we have a good opportunity to talk about how families can deal with death. Everyone who has experienced the death of a loved one is grateful for the support a family can bring. In today's Scripture reading, we find two sisters suffering the tremendous loss of their brother, Lazarus. In response to Martha's straightforward statement in John 11:21, Jesus did not apologize for being late but rather answered in faith, "Your brother will rise again" (v. 23 NIV). Martha was the practical, no-nonsense housekeeper (cf. Luke 10:40), while Mary was the contemplative, sensitive sister whose heart worshiped her Lord (cf. Luke 10:39; John 11:2). What is interesting is that when Mary came to meet Jesus, she said the exact same thing to him that Martha had said earlier: "Lord, if you had been here, my brother would not have died" (John 11:32 NIV). But this time Jesus did not give a theological response; instead, he entered into her suffering. He asked, "Where have you laid him?" (v. 34 NIV) and then began to weep. Jesus shared in their grief, and he still shares in our grief today.

When a family is faced with death, they can find comfort by remembering several truths.

I. God can use death for good.

Death is a horrible, unnatural experience. It brings sorrow and pain, emptiness and loneliness, frustration and helplessness. Patiently a family needs to work with each other to admit the depth of the sorrow, the extent of the pain, the aching emptiness, and the fear of loneliness. A sense of guilt may linger with those who wish they could have been more helpful or had been more attentive.

But people of faith can see that death is more than the obvious; it is something God can use. In John 11:4 Jesus made the remarkable statement that God could be glorified even in Lazarus's sickness and death. We can easily see that God was glorified in Lazarus's case, because Jesus raised him from the dead a few days later. But we have a harder time accepting this truth today because we place our loved ones in the grave and by faith must await the resurrection in God's own time.

Still, the quiet testimony of many Christians has been that in the midst of their deepest loss, God has been able to bless and comfort them and ultimately bring glory to his great name. This kind of testimony must be what Paul had in mind in Romans 8:28–29: "And we know that in all things God works for the good of those who love him, who have been called according to his purpose. For those God foreknew he also predestined to be conformed to the image of his Son, that he might be the firstborn among many brothers" (NIV).

Paul did not mean that everything that happens to us is good. But God will bless those who love him so that everything that comes to us, whether good or bad or indifferent, can be worked out for good. The picture here is of God salvaging us from life's wreckage. In the junkyards of life God is fastidiously salvaging what he can so that out of our darkness and sorrow he can create a very good thing—more and more brothers and sisters who are "conformed to the image of his Son."

II. Christians don't need to fear death.

Jesus confronted the doubt of death with confidence. He challenged the despair of death with hope (John 11:25–26). Jesus said there is life on the other side of death. He said that death will never have the final victory: "The one who believes in me will live, even though they die" (John 11:25 NIV). Note, however, the necessity of faith in verse 25. To believe in Jesus means that he becomes the Lord of your life. When you surrender your life to him in faith, trusting that he is indeed God's power to deliver us and God's grace to save us, you are delivered from the worst death can do.

III. Friends can help.

In John 11:31 we see a picture of the common experience of all people through the ages. We see Mary surrounded by friends from the village who are seeking to comfort her. Friends know that even though they can't heal the pain, they can at least share in the grief. But the friend the sisters really wanted to see was Jesus because they knew he could have averted their brother's death, and they still had hope in Jesus' power.

Jesus often brings comfort to a family through the love of those who come in his name and offer their hands and hearts on his behalf. When a family has suffered the loss of a loved one, friends can help in many ways. The things that help most are practical activities, such as cleaning the house, taking care of the children, standing by to answer the phone or welcome visitors and accept food that is brought to the house.

The acts of service that mean most to the bereaved are those that don't require expertise on the part of the volunteer, but simply a desire and willingness to help. In a caring church family, the pastor is never the only one who is able to help the family. Indeed, the whole church body can, and should, offer help and communicate Christ's love.

IV. God's presence is never far away.

God knows about death. He warned Adam and Eve from the very beginning that disobedience would bring death. Even after they sinned, God did not abandon them, nor has he abandoned us. He shoulders our grief on his own back and bears the burden with us. The cross on which our Savior died became God's bridge to draw us back to himself. When a mother lost her only son to a car accident, she cried out, "Oh, where is God when I need him most?" A friend close by replied, "I suppose he's in the same place he was when he lost his Son."

The reality of God's grief is nowhere clearer than in the text before us (John 11:33–36). At this point, Jesus gave no words of explanation, no call to courage and great faith. He simply shared in their grief as they walked to the place where they had laid Lazarus. The Greeks would read John's gospel in disbelief. To them God is the Unmoved Mover. He is above our petty emotions. He cannot be touched by our sorrow and pain. But John's gospel is clear: God is not apathetic; he is empathetic with his people.

We should never be ashamed or feel guilty when we mourn the loss of a loved one. As Christians, however, we know that death is not the end. Paul wrote, "Brothers and sisters, we do not want you to be uninformed about those who sleep in death, so that you do not grieve like the rest of mankind, who have no hope. For we believe that Jesus died and rose again, and so we believe that God will bring with Jesus those who have fallen asleep in him" (1 Thess. 4:13–14 NIV). Because of our Lord's power over death, we don't have to grieve as those who have no hope.

V. Christians should bear witness to both the grief and victory in death.

Dwight L. Moody once said that when he was called to preach his first funeral sermon, he searched the Scriptures to find what Jesus said at funerals—only to discover that Jesus had no funeral sermons! Jesus turned around every funeral he ever attended. And Jesus still turns our grief into victory today. Jesus' resurrection of others was a sign of the great resurrection that would soon come in his own life. His own resurrection was the undeniable sign of God's victory over death, which he freely gives to those who trust him.

Conclusion

The greatest help a family could have when dealing with the death of a loved one is a vibrant faith in God and a close relationship with Jesus Christ. When the waves of grief threaten to engulf you, remember the words of Fanny Crosby:

> Down in the human heart, crushed by the tempter,
> Feelings lie buried that grace can restore;
> Touched by a loving heart, wakened by kindness,
> Cords that are broken will vibrate once more.

SUNDAY EVENING, MAY 28

Title: The Face of Faithfulness: John

Text: "Now there stood by the cross of Jesus his mother, and his mother's sister, Mary the wife of Cleophas, and Mary Magdalene. When Jesus therefore saw his mother, and the disciple standing by, whom he loved, he saith unto his mother, Woman, behold thy son! Then saith he to the disciple, Behold thy mother! And from that hour that disciple took her unto his own home" **(John 19:25–27)**.

Scripture Reading: John 19:17–27

Introduction

Christianity began with a group of men gathered by Jesus, but at the cross Christianity resembled a women's movement. Of the twelve men Jesus made apostles, only one was faithful to the end. Four faithful women stood with this one man until the end. One of them was Mary, Jesus' mother. Her sister was also there. Mary Magdalene was another of the four, and with her was the wife of Clopas. But today we want to focus our attention on John. His face beneath the cross is the face of faithfulness. A study of John's presence at the cross will help us in the pursuit of faithfulness.

I. The extent of faithfulness.

Years after Jesus' crucifixion and resurrection, John wrote a letter inspired by the risen Lord to the church in Smyrna. In the letter, the Lord admonished that suffering church, "Be thou faithful unto death" (Rev. 21:10). John would know about this kind of faithfulness. This is the kind of faithfulness each of us needs.

A. *Faithfulness until death.* The words could be understood to mean, "Be faithful for all of your life." It was a call for faithfulness regardless of what life might bring. John had this kind of faithfulness. It is the kind that a couple promises to each other in their wedding ceremony: "until death do us part." It is interesting to ask a couple as they approach marriage, "Under what circumstances will you seek a divorce?" Their answers are always revealing. Somc confidently reply, "Under no circumstances." As a pastor, I like that response, but I also know they will be surprised by the difficulties that will test this commitment to faithfulness.

The cross did not force John away from his commitment to Jesus. He intended to be faithful until the end of his life.

B. *Faithfulness unto death.* When the Lord admonished Smyrna, this is probably what he meant. "Faithfulness unto death" meant faithfulness even at the expense of life.

Scholars debate the extent of the danger facing John, but we can plainly see that the other apostles perceived danger at the cross. Anyone who has seen an angry mob knows that with a mob on the loose no one is safe. Jesus was on the cross because of such a mob movement. The danger to John must have been real. Yet he was ready to face even the possibility of death because of his desire to be faithful to the Lord. Even if it cost him his life, he would not run away. This is the quality of faithfulness that the Lord wants in each of us. If our faithfulness has limitations, it is flawed.

II. The inspiration for faithfulness.

Why did John stand beneath the cross while the others hid in fear? If we know this, we will know the secret of faithfulness.

A. *Not a sense of duty.* Was it a sense of duty that compelled John to stand beneath the cross? We must admit that such a sense of duty helps us to be faithful in hard times. A sense of duty keeps a soldier in his place of danger when others might flee. It keeps a son or daughter faithfully attending to the needs of aging parents. But the real secret of faithfulness goes much deeper than a sense of duty.

B. *The love of Jesus.* John gave a clue as to why he was there by the way he identified himself. He is the disciple "whom Jesus loved." His presence at the cross was a response to that love. Jesus loved all of the apostles just as much as he loved John, but this man seemed to have a special capacity to receive that love. He had a special awareness of that love. He seemed to know better than the others that Jesus was bound to the cross by his love for them. If Jesus could die on a cross out of love, could not John stand by the cross through the ordeal? Gratitude and love compelled him to do it.

This is the secret of Christian faithfulness. It will keep us faithful in our service. It will keep us faithful through all kinds of persecution. It will make survivors out of us. If we waver in our commitment, we need to be renewed by a fresh awareness of how much we are loved by Jesus.

III. The reward for faithfulness.

John's faithfulness beautifully illustrates the rewards that faithfulness to Christ will bring.

A. *The approval of Christ.* Jesus showed approval to John for his faithfulness. It must have been conveyed to him by a look from the cross. Can you imagine the difference in the look John must have received from that which Peter received in the moment of his denial? The look Peter received sent him into the night weeping in shame, but the look John received sent him home to take care of Jesus' mother. While John does not describe that look, I can imagine the look of gratitude Jesus must have conveyed to him. John, along with the women, was the one bright spot in a sea of darkness.

   Jesus promised that faithfulness to him will result in a final and blessed, "Well done, thou good and faithful servant."

B. *The trust of Christ.* His trust is the greatest reward for faithfulness. John received this trust in Jesus' special request from the cross. As Jesus neared death, he thought of his mother, Mary. While she stood by the cross brokenhearted, her firstborn Son made provisions for her needs. He said to her, "Woman, behold thy son!" Then he said to John, "Behold thy mother!" John reported, "From that hour that disciple took her unto his own home" (John 19:27). Although Mary had other children, John was the one who cared for her until her death years later in the city of Ephesus. Jesus trusted John with a very special responsibility.

   Responsibility is the primary reward for faithfulness. In his parable of the talents, Jesus said, "Thou hast been faithful over a few things, I will make thee ruler over many things" (Matt. 25:23). Could anything be greater than the Lord of glory trusting us with a special assignment? This kind of assignment is reserved for those who have proven themselves to be trustworthy through their faithfulness.

Conclusion

John's example of faithfulness is especially encouraging for those who are facing trials. Maybe you feel like you are in an extremely difficult place. What should you do? "Be thou faithful unto death." Do it because of Jesus' love for you! You will find the rewards for such faithfulness to be more than enough. As you meditate on Jesus' love, take a place of faithfulness with John beneath the cross.

Wednesday Evening, May 31

Title: To Err Is Human, to Forgive Divine

Text: "'Do not be distressed and do not be angry with yourselves for selling me here, because it was to save lives that God sent me ahead of you'" **(Gen. 45:5 NIV)**.

Scripture Reading: Genesis 45:1–13

Introduction

One more story remains in this series from the life of Joseph. Events moved rapidly after the cupbearer finally told Pharaoh about the prisoner who had such wonderful ability because of his God. Pharaoh called on Joseph to interpret his dream. Soon the Hebrew boy was made "prime minister" of the land, second only to the king himself. Later his brothers came to Egypt to buy grain during the famine. For a short time, Joseph played cat and mouse with them, but at last he revealed himself to them.

One of the noblest statements in God's Word is Joseph's address to his brothers. Not only did he forgive them for what they had done, but he went so far as to say that God was actually using them in his plan when they sold him as a slave. Of course, Joseph's forgiveness did not lessen their guilt, but it may have diminished their fears of his possible revenge. Let's consider several truths from this story.

I. God has his own way of doing things.

God knew exactly when to bring Joseph out of the dungeon. Often we do not have nearly as much of a problem with God's will as we do with his timetable. We want him to act on our schedule, not his! God sent the dream to Pharaoh at exactly the right time for Joseph to step in and interpret it.

How much better off we all would be if we simply trusted God to open doors for us. Our scheming often gets us into trouble because it can land us in places where God does not intend for us to be. That doesn't mean we should never put forth any human effort, but it does mean we should be cautious, accepting God's leadership and realizing that he will cause things to happen to us and for us at the time he knows is best.

II. Sin haunts us constantly.

Notice how the brothers said to each other while they were in Egypt buying grain, "Surely we are being punished because of our brother. We saw how distressed he was when he pleaded with us for his life, but we would not listen; that's why this distress has come on us" (Gen. 42:21 NIV). Many years had passed since the brothers had sold Joseph into slavery, but their consciences were awakened when Joseph acted harshly with their youngest brother, Benjamin. Likely this was not the only time over the years that they had recalled their terrible treatment of Joseph.

III. Forgiveness is Christlike.

The heart of the gospel is the merciful love of our heavenly Father. In Jesus Christ he sets us free from both the guilt and power of sin. Paul said, "Very rarely will anyone die for a righteous person, though for a good person someone might possibly dare to die. But God demonstrates his own love for us in this: While we were still sinners, Christ died for us" (Rom. 5:7–8 NIV). This is the ultimate in forgiveness!

Joseph did not retaliate against his brothers merely because he did not want to hurt his father. Yet years later, when Jacob died, the brothers became frightened. They came to Joseph, afraid that he would seek revenge; once more they begged for forgiveness. Joseph wept as he said to them, "Don't be afraid. Am I in the place of God?" (Gen. 50:19 NIV). He repeated many of the same things he had told them when he first revealed himself to them: They had meant to harm him, but God meant it for good. He assured them that he would continue to provide for them and their children.

Conclusion

How do you handle your desire for revenge? Even though all of us have sinned against other people, perhaps all of us have also had times when someone has sinned against us. Jesus said, "Blessed are the merciful: for they shall obtain mercy" (Matt. 5:7). Someone described revenge as the "costliest morsel that has ever been cooked up in hell," while someone else called forgiveness "the odor which a flower yields when trampled upon." Charles Spurgeon once said, "Cultivate forbearance until your heart yields a fine crop of it. Pray for a short memory as to all unkindness."

SUGGESTED PREACHING PROGRAM FOR THE MONTH OF JUNE

■ Sunday Mornings

Complete the series "The Christian Family: Living for Christ in the Present."

■ Sunday Evenings

Complete the series "Beneath the Cross of Jesus."

■ Wednesday Evenings

For the month of June, engage in a devotional study of Paul's letter to the Colossians, using the theme "Concerning Colossians."

SUNDAY MORNING, JUNE 4

Title: Enemies of the Family

Text: "Be very careful, then, how you live—not as unwise but as wise, making the most of every opportunity, because the days are evil" **(Eph. 5:15–16 NIV)**.

Scripture Reading: Ephesians 5:1–6:4

Hymns: "Jesus Calls Us o'er the Tumult," Alexander
"When We Walk with the Lord," Sammis
"God Will Take Care of You," Martin

Offertory Prayer: Dear Lord, thank you for our families. We want them to be healthy. We want them to bring joy to our lives, strength to our church, and glory to you. We know that sometimes we fail to obey you and thereby open our families to evil influences and dangerous temptations. We know there are enemies of the family that can destroy the vitality of our homes. We ask you to protect our families from evil and to place a wall of protection around us. May we be willing to live within your will and purpose for our homes. The offerings we give now are the shared expression of our love and obedience to you. Amen.

Introduction

How do Christians walk? We walk in love, as Christ taught us to walk (Eph. 5:1–2). This is a high calling, but it is nevertheless exactly what the Lord expects of his people. When we fail, he is willing to work with us; he knows how to forgive. But make no mistake about it—God wants us to grow continually in the fullness of life in Jesus Christ.

This may sound like an admonition for personal Christian living alone, but it also precedes a lengthy passage on family relationships (Eph. 5:21–6:4). Therefore we should apply these truths to the family as well as to our personal lives. Two weeks ago, we identified the friends of the family, but we should be aware of enemies of the family as well. While it is true that certain television shows and movies and the influence of non-Christian minds can be detrimental to the health of the family, these are not our primary enemies. We cannot isolate ourselves from the world if we are to have any impact on it. The real enemies of the family are those that arise out of our own disobedience to the Word of God. We can name these enemies by looking carefully at our Scripture passage.

I. Enemy #1 is permissiveness (Eph. 5:3–12).

The first enemy that will destroy a family is the permissive attitude that is popularly expressed as "anything goes." Sexual immorality, perversity, and coarse talk ought to be foreign to the people of God. When respect for the sexuality of the family is lost and no one sets standards for family attitudes toward sex, the bond of trust that must hold families together becomes frayed and soon breaks.

Children need to be taught the discipline that comes from obedience to God. We don't have to do all the things we want to do. We can say no so that at the right time and in the right way we can say yes. Young people, remember that the decisions you make now in your dating relationships will determine to a great degree the authority you will have as a parent to counsel your own children as to how they ought to treat their sexuality.

Parental immorality always undermines parental authority!

II. Enemy #2 is drunkenness (Eph. 5:18).

This warning includes not only wine, but all alcohol and drugs that alter the mental and emotional state and make us vulnerable to temptation and evil. A family is severely frustrated when one of its members becomes a different person in the aftermath of drug abuse. Alcohol is the worst drug problem in our world. Adults prefer to talk about the drug problems of the young because they don't want to deal with the drug problem they have installed in their own home bars. Pastors tend to be more vocal in their opposition to alcohol than most professionals because they so often counsel families that have been destroyed by the effects of alcohol. As strong as peer pressure may be in the lives of young people, parents can demonstrate a consistent Christian lifestyle along with fair and loving discipline to help protect their families from this enemy.

III. Enemy #3 is selfishness (Eph. 5:21–22, 25, 28–29).

Sermons on this text meet with one great difficulty. The men hear the part about how the wife should respect them and follow their leadership. The women hear the part about how their husbands should love them as Christ loved the church. The reason we hear the message in this way is selfishness. We first think of ourselves and later think of the other.

We must hear both of Paul's admonitions at the same time. In verse 21 we have the idea: "Submit to one another out of reverence for Christ" (NIV). Submission in a marriage should be mutual. First Corinthians 7:4 is a commentary on this very point. "The wife does not have authority over her own body but yields it to her husband. In the same way, the husband does not have authority over his own body but yields it to his wife" (NIV).

In a Christian home, the wife and children should be willing to allow the husband and father to provide leadership. He needs the respect of his family, not ridicule, if he is to be a successful leader of the family. Good leaders are good listeners. They are not tyrannical. They delegate authority and respect the decisions that others make. They are willing to provide leadership and accept the responsibility of articulating the vision for the family. Christian husbands are willing to let God make them into good leaders. Christian wives rejoice in helping God develop leadership in their husbands.

In a Christian home, the husband should love his wife with thoughtful attention. He should love his wife with the kind of devotion and courage that marked Jesus' love for the church. Jesus loved the church and gave himself up for her on the cross. No husband has begun to love his wife as God calls him to if he is more concerned about his own welfare, self-esteem, and future than he is about his wife's welfare, self-esteem, and future. Jesus died to save his church. A husband must be willing to die for his wife—to give himself away for her well-being and growth. A wife has a right to be loved by her husband nobly, faithfully, and always. A daily prayer of gratitude to God for the wife he has given you will strengthen your love for your wife.

Paul's admonition does not reserve respect for the husband nor love for the wife. Marriage is a blending of lives, and both husbands and wives are to be respected and loved. Selfishness is the enemy. Thinking of one another and doing loving things for one another are ways to overcome this enemy.

IV. Enemy #4 is carelessness (Eph. 6:4).

Fathers are advised not to provoke their children to anger. This means, obviously, that discipline must be fair and just. But it also means that fathers must not be careless of their children. No father is so poor that he cannot pay attention to his child! Children experience deep anger when they realize that one or both of their parents are not really interested in them. A man once said to his pastor, "My father was an excellent carpenter, but he never showed me how to do one thing. He could have helped me so much, but he never noticed me." Behind that complaint, the pastor was able to discern a latent anger that had blocked the son's emotional and spiritual growth for years.

Children know they have a right to be considered. They feel deep anger, which is usually repressed, when parents don't listen or don't set boundaries, show interest, or expect excellence. We must not be careless with our children, not only for their sakes, but also for our own. One way or another, fathers have to pay attention to their children. Ideally, fathers will be there to offer support to their children at the time in their lives when it can bring joy and growth. If support comes too late to help, all that is left to do is hurt.

V. Enemy #5 is ignorance of the Lord (Eph. 6:4).

The greatest strength in any home is the knowledge of the Lord. The Jewish fathers were given the high task of instructing their children about the Lord and his deliverance of their people from bondage (Deut. 6:1–9). Paul exhorted parents that children must be brought up "in the training and instruction" of the Lord (Eph. 6:4 NIV). If they are not taught, they are ignorant. It is not because children are dumb or stubborn that they don't know God's way; it is because their parents have not taught them. It is not the school's fault nor the church's fault if children are spiritually illiterate; spiritual knowledge is the responsibility of the parents. We cannot train our children in godly matters if we are not experienced. If we are not on speaking terms with God, we will not be able to teach our children what they need to know.

Conclusion

Beware of the enemies that seek to destroy your family. Ask God to help you defend against permissiveness, drunkenness, selfishness, carelessness, and ignorance. If you must confess that you do not know the Lord well enough to teach your children, then he invites you to start to walk with him in faith that you may indeed be wise and successful in making the most of the time you have with your family (Eph. 5:16).

SUNDAY EVENING, JUNE 4

Title: The Face of Folly: Judas

Text: "'The Son of Man will go just as it is written about him. But woe to that man who betrays the Son of Man! It would be better for him if he had not been born'" **(Matt. 26:24 NIV).**

Scripture Reading: Matthew 26:14–16, 47–50; 27:3–10

Introduction

Judas played the part of the fool. When he placed the kiss of betrayal on the face of the Lord Jesus, he acted as a fool. This is the consensus of history. Dante pictured Judas in the very bottom of hell. He pictured him as isolated from all other sinners and gripped by the most horrible torment.

Jesus said, "The Son of Man will go just as it is written about him. But woe to that man who betrays the Son of Man! It would be better for him if he had not been born" (Matt. 26:24 NIV). Only after his betrayal did Judas feel that he had played the fool. And then he considered that the only appropriate response was to end his life in suicide.

What was so terrible about Judas's crime? Actually, his crime is different only in degree from the crimes that many people commit. It is a matter of rejecting the claims of Christ and handing him over to his enemies. Let's consider this face of folly beneath the cross.

I. The decision of the fool.

A. *The basis of the decision.* We must go back to the beginning to understand Judas's decision. Judas was the only one of the Twelve from Judea. He was the only southerner in the group. Apparently he joined the company of Jesus with burning hopes for a glorious and powerful earthly kingdom. While some of the others were able to move from this kind of hope to an acceptance of Jesus as a different kind of Messiah, Judas could never make the change.

Judas made the final decision at the dinner meeting at which Mary broke the alabaster box and anointed Jesus' body. It was just too much for Judas. He spoke up to rebuke her gesture as being a waste. But Jesus hastened to Mary's defense. Up to this time, Judas had been the keeper of the funds for the Twelve, and John tells us that he had been stealing from them. Out of this experience Judas went to the enemies of Jesus and offered to deliver him to them for a reward. He agreed with the priests to do it for thirty pieces of silver. His decision seems to have been based on the profit principle. He was ready to salvage anything he could out of the situation.

B. *The nature of the decision.* Luke reports that Satan entered Judas (Luke 22:3). This indicates that Satan was responsible for the temptation to betray Jesus; and when Judas yielded to the temptation, Satan took possession of his life. Anyone who makes this kind of choice has responded to a satanic temptation and has become a tool of Satan. This insight gives spiritual and eternal significance to the decision.

II. The deed of the fool.

A. *He spurned genuine love.* Jesus loved Judas and expressed that love. Jesus' love for Judas is what prompted him to choose him as one of the Twelve. Jesus' love reached out to Judas at that last Passover. At that dinner, Jesus dipped a piece of unleavened bread into the bowl of herbs and handed it to Judas. This was a gesture of special friendship and love. Judas knew what it meant. At that same moment, out of love, Jesus warned him of the consequences of his present course of action. Even in the garden as Judas betrayed him, Jesus expressed warmth toward him by calling him "Friend." But Judas chose to commit his deed anyway. He shunned this great love with the kiss of betrayal.

B. *He acted with knowledge.* Judas had both eyes open to the truth. He knew what he was doing. He understood who Jesus was but wanted no part of that type of Messiah. He had enjoyed three years of helpful instruction from the Master. He had been confronted with the best evidence about Jesus' mission in the world. He acted not out of ignorance but out of foolishness.

How much do we know about Jesus? We may actually know more than Judas. We have the advantage of two thousand years of Christian history. We know the outcome of his death on the cross. If we refuse him a place in our lives, we, too, are sinning against knowledge.

C. *He aligned himself with the enemies of Jesus.* Some scholars believe that Judas was manifesting his inner resentment through the betrayal. They see Judas's frustrated ambition behind his deed. He would get even turning Jesus over to his enemies. Whatever the motivation, it made Judas one with the enemies of Jesus. What attitudes and actions have we taken toward the Lord Jesus?

III. The destiny of the fool.

A. *Temporarily, despair.* Judas's folly is best seen when we consider the end. When Judas realized that Jesus was going to be crucified, he went back to the priests with deep regret. He wanted to return the money they had given him, but they mocked him. In despair he cast the silver coins on the floor and rushed out to end it all. Suicide was the ultimate gesture of despair. It was his way of saying, "Nothing can ever bring meaning to my life. My life is no longer worth living."

Allowing Jesus Christ to be Lord of our lives is the only thing that puts us in touch with God's ultimate purpose for our lives. Any other center for your life will fail. Judas had refused the only one who could give meaning and purpose to his life.

B. *Eternally, hell.* According to Acts 1:25, Judas went to "where he belongs" (NIV). In other words, Judas went to hell, a place of eternal separation from Jesus Christ. Although his end was tragic, hell is the logical end of a life without Christ.

The destiny is directly related to the decision and the deed. If the decision is different, the destiny will be different. When we consider the end of Judas's life, we have to agree with Jesus that it would be better if he had never been born. He acted like a fool. Let's consider where our decisions and deeds are leading.

Conclusion

Judas kissed Jesus to signal the soldiers to arrest him. But there is another way Judas could have kissed him. It was customary in that day for a man to bow before a king and kiss his ring. The ring symbolized the king's authority, and the kiss symbolized submission to him. This is why the psalmist wrote, "Kiss his son, or he will be angry and your way will lead to your destruction, for his wrath can flare up in a moment. Blessed are all who take refuge in him" (Ps. 2:12 NIV).

Those who kiss the Son in submission to his authority are no fools. Their lives take on an excitement that will last for eternity. How will you kiss the Son? Will it be the kiss of a fool or the kiss of a wise person?

Wednesday Evening, June 7

Title: The Purpose of Prayer

Text: "Devote yourselves to prayer, being watchful and thankful. And pray for us, too, that God may open a door for our message, so that we may proclaim the mystery of Christ, for which I am in chains. Pray that I may proclaim it clearly, as I should" **(Col. 4:2–4 NIV)**.

Scripture Reading: Colossians 4:1–4

Introduction

A pastor is invited to a family's home for Sunday supper. Before anyone says grace, the children start to eat. The embarrassed mother gives them a quick reprimand, while the children stare in confusion. The pastor then offers grace in the strained silence.

The mother explains, "We don't always say grace before meals at our house."

Of course, this is fairly obvious, but the pastor butters his roll and waits, because he knows there is another line to this script.

"We just take it for granted that God knows how grateful we are!"

Why should we pray? God knows how grateful we are. That figures, according to the logic of the dinner table. The trouble with this kind of attitude is that it doesn't stay at the dinner table. It leaves the table and roams all over the house. And soon we find ourselves saying, "Why pray at all? God knows all that we need." Did not Jesus himself say that God knows all that we need before we even ask him? But Jesus' conclusion was, "Therefore, do pray." This same line of reasoning led Frederick B. Speakman, in his book *Love Is Something You Do,* to ask the provocative question, "What if God refuses to read his children's mail unless it is addressed to him?"

We are to pray in order that we might commune with God and share with him the most deeply felt needs of our lives. We are to express to God the gratitude and praise and joy we feel in him and in salvation. Paul elaborated on the purpose of prayer in Colossians 4:2–4.

I. The purpose of prayer is seen in the manner of prayer (v. 2).

A. *We are to pray with perseverance.* Prayer is not to be a spasmodic outburst in a moment of emergency, but persistent calling on God for his guidance and blessing.

B. *We are to pray with watchfulness.* This word literally means to be wakeful, to be alert when we pray. Prayer should not be reserved solely for times of crisis. We should pray before the crisis comes so that we have the spiritual resources to meet the testing time. Napoleon said that battles are not won on the battlefield; rather, they are won at the conference table in the planning meetings before the battle is ever begun.

C. *We are to pray with gratitude.*

II. The purpose of prayer is seen in the object of prayer (vv. 3–4).

A. *We are to pray that God will give us an open door of service.* Remember that Paul was in prison when he wrote his letter to the Colossians. He could have prayed for many things while he was in prison—release, the favorable outcome of the trial, comfort, rest—but Paul prayed that God would give him an opportunity to minister.

B. *We are to pray that God will help us take advantage of our opportunity for service.* To pray for the open door, an opportunity for service, is just half the prayer. We are to pray also for the courage and ability to take advantage of the opportunity that is there.

Paul wanted the Colossians to pray that he might be able to "proclaim the mystery of Christ." This should be our prayer too.

Conclusion

This is the purpose of prayer: We pray that we might commune with God with persistence, watchfulness, and thankfulness in order to have opportunities to witness for Christ and the strength to take those opportunities.

SUNDAY MORNING, JUNE 11

Title: You Can Have a Happy Family

Text: "'But seek first his kingdom and his righteousness, and all these things will be given to you as well'" **(Matt. 6:33 NIV).**

Scripture Reading: Matthew 6:25–34

Hymns: "Praise the Lord! Ye Heavens Adore Him," Anonymous
"God of Grace, and God of Glory," Fosdick
"Brethren, We Have Met to Worship," Atkins

Offertory Prayer: Eternal and everlasting God, who was and is and ever shall be, Creator of the earth and all therein, Savior and Redeemer of our lives, and ever-present Spirit, we can scarcely take it in when we recognize that you are our Father, loving us even more than any parent could love us, desiring good things for us even more than they can. You know us completely—where we go, what we do, when we cry, and when we laugh.

You hear us when we pray, and you guide us in your way. It is our joy to live before you and to offer our gifts of praise for your work in this world. Please accept the tithes and offerings we bring to you today, and use them for your glory. In Christ's name we pray. Amen.

Introduction

You might wonder about the worthiness of setting a goal for your family's happiness. Happiness is certainly not the goal of the gospel for our lives. Obedience to God must always take precedence over "the fleeting pleasures of sin" (Heb. 11:25). But if we define happiness as a sense of well-being, of contentment, of joyful purpose in living, then happiness is, at least, what most people are looking for in life.

In today's Scripture reading, Jesus had not dismissed happiness as a superficial desire but rather focused on how an individual and a family can find true happiness. We don't have to be anxious about life, although we often are (Matt. 6:25, 27–28, 31, 34). There is a way to find happiness in the midst of our living. And Jesus wants us to find it. But first we need to recognize that we can miss happiness in a frantic effort to gain it for our family.

I. Ways we miss having a happy family.

A. *We miss having a happy family when we are never satisfied with what we have.* It is fine to be people of vision and anticipation for the future, but we shouldn't miss the taste of now and the colors of the present moment. Happiness is not some magical state of existence that we finally discover over the next mountain of life. Happiness happens to you along the way, in the midst of life. People who seek happiness on the other side of the mountain are those who try to find the pot of gold at the end of the rainbow. They will never find it.

The tragic truth is that many families run right past happiness in the search for it somewhere else. Don't miss the gift of joy a child's smile can bring today. Don't miss the explosion of wonder a child's question can set off in your heart. Don't miss the gift of love your spouse can bring to you today. You will miss the moment if you are not paying attention!

B. *We miss having a happy family when we value happiness too much.* If you would rather be happy than committed to one another, if you would rather be happy than courageous, if you would rather be happy than responsible, if you would rather be happy than right, then you will never really be happy at all. Husbands and wives who value happiness more than sincere effort together in fidelity and love will not be happy for long. People who seek happiness in one marriage or affair after another are deceived into believing that happiness is a gift someone else can give when, in truth, happiness must come from within.

C. *We miss having a happy family when we are not willing to do God's will.* If we will not seek first the kingdom of God and his righteousness, he cannot add to us the needs and desires of our hearts (Matt. 6:33). God's will does not always lead us to easy tasks or give us smiles and laughter. Sometimes we walk with him through the darkness of suffering or in the outer reaches of rejection as we seek to follow him. But the testimony of Christians is that deep joy can be known in obedience and faithfulness to his will. Paul said, "I consider that our present sufferings are not worth comparing with the glory that will be revealed in us" (Rom. 8:18 NIV).

II. Ways we can have a happy family.

A. *We can have a happy family when we value each other (Matt. 6:26).* Our heavenly Father feeds the birds of the air. But what about us? He values us more than the birds, so we can be sure he will care for us. We are given value by our Creator, and no one can take that value from us. People are happy when each member of the family recognizes the value of every other member. People are unhappy in their homes when they don't treasure one another. We are each God's gift to the other members of our family. God stands behind the value of every person and guarantees it. The next time we are tempted to ignore our children or shout at our spouse or ridicule someone's efforts, we should remember that we are dealing with someone God loves and has created and shared with us for our joy and fulfillment.

B. *We can have a happy family when we understand that life is more than externals (Matt. 6:25).* Life is more than food and drink, clothes and shelter. As important as they are, they are not the goal of life. It is ironic that in most Christian congregations, talk about food, clothing, and houses is a discussion of status symbols, while in much of the world that same discussion is a debate about survival. It isn't just food, but dining at the "right" restaurants! It isn't just a pair of jeans, but designer jeans! It isn't just a house, but the address that we're interested in! God, save us from explaining our poor giving habits by pleading that our bills are so high, when much of our world does not have the luxury of even having bills!

A happy family puts sufficient emphasis on the necessities and desires of life to provide motivation for work and thrift, but it is not consumed by a passion for gadgets and expensive toys—nor by anxiety about life's essentials. Jesus doesn't tell us not to worry about food and clothing because they are unimportant. Just the opposite. In Matthew 6:32–33 Jesus asserts that the Father knows we need these things and will provide them. They are so important that God will not leave their provision entirely up to us. He intends to provide for his own.

C. *We can have a happy family when we find the purpose in life God has for our family (Matt. 6:33).* When a family sees itself as a unit of love and service that can be offered to God for his use in blessing and redeeming the world, that family is on its way to happiness. Happiness is what happens to us when we are doing God's will! A family is happy when its members are fully committed to seeking the kingdom of God *first.* This verse reminds us of the necessity of setting priorities for life. If God and his will are first, nothing can be above or before him. When God is at the center of life, everything else fits into place. Parents can help their children if, by example and precept, they teach them how to live by loving God as they love nothing else and loving their neighbor as they love themselves.

Conclusion

You can have a happy family. It won't be easy, but it is possible. You won't be happy every day—there will be times when you go through painful and difficult trials—but by the grace of God even those moments can contribute to the growing joy and happiness you will find as you live and grow together within his will and loving care.

SUNDAY EVENING, JUNE 11

Title: The Face of Forgiveness: The Thief

Text: "One of the criminals who hung there hurled insults at him: 'Aren't you the Messiah? Save yourself and us!'

"But the other criminal rebuked him. 'Don't you fear God,' he said, 'since you are under the same sentence? We are punished justly, for we are getting what our deeds deserve. But this man has done nothing wrong.'

"Then he said, 'Jesus, remember me when you come into your kingdom.'

"Jesus answered him, 'Truly I tell you, today you will be with me in paradise'" **(Luke 23:39–43 NIV).**

Scripture Reading: Luke 23:26–43

Introduction

Everything about Jesus' death was designed to bring him suffering and shame. His enemies crucified him between two thieves for the purpose of humiliating him. They wanted to present him as a common criminal dying with his kind. As usual, Jesus turned the evil plans of his enemies into something good. The presence of these condemned men provided him with an opportunity to demonstrate his grace and forgiveness.

Though the two thieves came to the cross from a common background and had perhaps been companions in sin, they responded to their situation differently. While at first both of them joined the crowd in ridiculing Jesus, one of them soon made a dramatic change in his attitude toward Jesus. The way that Jesus responded to the abuse being heaped upon him convicted the thief. It convicted him of his own guilt and of Jesus' innocence. The thief knew that he and his companion deserved death because of their guilt. He also knew that Jesus was innocent of the charges brought against him. He could see that Jesus was different. He was out of place hanging on that cross.

The way that Jesus was praying probably made an impression too. He said, "Father, forgive them; for they know not what they do." How could a man have such confidence in God in these circumstances? There was just something about the way he said the word *Father*. And surely he must be different to have such an attitude of forgiveness toward those who were crucifying him. All of these impressions led to the thief's appeal.

"Jesus, remember me when you come into your kingdom" (Luke 23:42 NIV). It was not a very strong appeal, but it was directed to the right person. Beneath this simple request was an unspoken plea for forgiveness. In mercy and love, Jesus answered, "Today you will be with me in paradise" (v. 43 NIV). *Today* stood in contrast to a distant time in a future kingdom. And the thief would be more than "remembered." He would *be with* Jesus in the dwelling place of God. Jesus assumed responsibility for all of the thief's sins and granted him full, free forgiveness.

This incident is a beautiful example of divine forgiveness. Forgiveness is the removal of our sins so they are no longer a factor in God's dealings with us. We have no greater need than the assurance of God's forgiveness.

I. The fullness of the divine forgiveness.

A. *God's forgiveness is full in that he forgives all kinds of sins.* Because of this man's reputation as a thief, he was sentenced to death on a cross. He was probably guilty of many other kinds of sins as well. He may have broken all of the Ten Commandments along the way!

When I find people burdened with guilt, I often ask them, "Have you ever done anything you feel God cannot forgive?" I am constantly surprised by the things that people feel God cannot forgive: for one person adultery seems unforgivable, for another homosexuality, for another divorce, for another murder, and I could go on. The account of Jesus' forgiveness of the thief shows us that God forgives all kinds of sins.

B. *God's forgiveness is full in that he forgives all sins, regardless of their number.* Can we accumulate so many sins that God cannot forgive them all? Is there a certain number of sins that mark the limit of divine forgiveness? The story of the thief is a witness to the fullness of God's forgiveness. God can forgive a multitude of sins just as easily as he can forgive one sin. Before we could have this forgiveness, however,

God had to send his Son as a sacrificial lamb. When Jesus died on the cross, he died for all. His death covered all our transgressions.

Isaiah realized this truth when he prophesied, "Come now, and let us reason together, saith the LORD: though your sins be as scarlet, they shall be as white as snow; though they be red like crimson, they shall be as wool" (Isa. 1:18). And John offered this assurance: "If we confess our sins, he is faithful and just to forgive us our sins, and to cleanse us from all unrighteousness" (1 John 1:9). The phrase "all unrighteousness" reminds us of the fullness of divine forgiveness.

II. The freeness of God's forgiveness.

Jesus' forgiveness of the thief exposes more erroneous thinking about how we receive forgiveness than any other incident in the Bible. Surely the Holy Spirit caused Luke to include this account for this very reason. God forgives people freely. There was no other way this condemned man could have known forgiveness.

A. *Divine forgiveness is extended apart from good works.* This man had no opportunity to do any good works. Again and again I encounter people who feel that if they just do enough good works, God will forgive their transgressions. When they feel pangs of guilt because of past sins, they redouble their efforts to cover their sins with a multitude of good works. But good works alone are worthless without sincere repentance. The thief received the forgiveness of his sins from Jesus as a free gift.

B. *Divine forgiveness is extended apart from religious affiliation or ordinances.* This man had no opportunity to be baptized, so baptism is not necessary to wash away our sins. He had no opportunity to receive Communion, so such an ordinance is not necessary to receive God's forgiveness. This man had no opportunity to join a religious group or institution, so such affiliation is not necessary to enter heaven. Forgiveness is a free gift apart from religious trappings.

C. *Divine forgiveness comes through repentance.* Repentance means to acknowledge our sins. This man openly confessed his guilt and his worthiness of the death sentence. Repentance is extremely difficult for many people. It means to reach the point where we can sincerely admit, "I have sinned. I am a sinner." Repentance is essential, because God cannot forgive a sin that we will not acknowledge.

D. *Divine forgiveness comes by faith.* After we acknowledge our sin, we must turn to Jesus for forgiveness. We must do what the thief did. We must ask Jesus for forgiveness. Though he did not say it in exact words, Jesus knew what the man meant and wanted. This was faith!

Freeness of forgiveness makes it possible for all people to be forgiven at any place and any time in life. Though the story of the thief does not encourage us to wait for deathbed repentance, it does encourage us to believe that it is never too late to turn to Christ. God forgives freely and fully.

Conclusion

God is a God of forgiveness. In the death of his Son on the cross, God made full provision for the forgiveness of your sins. Now he awaits your response. Will you, like the thief, ask him to forgive your sins and become the Lord of your life?

WEDNESDAY EVENING, JUNE 14

Title: A Witness to the World

Text: "Be wise in the way you act toward outsiders; make the most of every opportunity. Let your conversation be always full of grace, seasoned with salt, so that you may know how to answer everyone" **(Col. 4:5–6 NIV)**.

Scripture Reading: Colossians 4:5–6

Introduction

Professing Christians live a life of faith in God and obedient response to the Holy Spirit; they also live in a world that is often hostile to Christ, or worse still, indifferent to Christ. Their response to the world around them is crucial to their Christian walk and their witness for Christ. Too often Christians make the response of identification with the world. They so closely identify themselves with the world that their lives can hardly be distinguished from that of non-Christians. Another response that Christians sometimes make is withdrawal from the world. They try to shut out entirely the world around them and live in their own little, private, well-protected world.

Neither of these is the proper response. The proper response is for Christians to be responsible witnesses to the world. We live in the world. We make our living in the world. We associate with people of the world. Therefore, we should give a responsible witness of our faith to the world. Our faith should be the guiding principle for our lives. Our encounter with God in worship gives us strength and power for daily living. Our character, growing out of our relationship of faith in God, gives silent but eloquent witness of the meaning of faith and salvation. Through our very lives we are "salespeople" for salvation.

Elton Trueblood once said that faith lives or dies not by what goes on in churches, but by what, as a result of the churches, goes on outside of them. That is what the apostle Paul meant by these two verses in the last chapter of his letter to the Colossians. He urged them, "Be wise in the way you act toward outsiders" (v. 5 NIV), meaning those who are outside the Christian fellowship. He had both an offensive and defensive purpose in mind. The defensive purpose was to protect the good name of the Christian community.

The offensive purpose was to go after outsiders and bring them into the Christian fellowship and to faith in Christ. This is still our witness to the world.

I. Our witness to the world involves our time in the world.

A. *We should use our time well.* We are told to redeem the time, which means literally "to buy up the time."

B. *We should use our time to witness.* We must take every opportunity to witness. John A. Broadus said that opportunity is like a fleet horse that pauses for one moment by our side. If we fail to mount the horse in that moment, we can hear the clatter of its hooves down the corridors of time.

II. Our witness to the world involves our walk in the world.

A. *We should walk with wisdom in our witness.* Paul's instructions in Colossians 4:5–6 may be a gentle warning about the methods of witness. We must use wisdom and discretion in presenting the claims of Christ to those who do not know him.

B. *We should walk with wisdom in our practices.* The kind of life we live before the world is encompassed in the word *walk.* As we walk in the world, we must ensure that our walk is consistent with our talk.

III. Our witness to the world involves our talk to the world.

A. *Our talk should be full of grace.* As our conduct is marked by grace, so should our speech be marked by grace. Grace implies kindness, good will, and tact. This is the kind of talk that witnesses for Christ—kind, courteous, tactful, not loud, coarse, or rude.

B. *Our talk should be well seasoned.* This kind of talk has the ring of reality about it. Many years ago a Hindu woman was converted and subsequently suffered much persecution from her husband. When the missionary asked her what she did when her husband became angry with her, she replied that she cooked his food better. When he complained, she swept the floor cleaner. When he spoke unkindly, she answered him mildly. She tried to show him that when she became a Christian she became a better wife and mother.

C. *Our talk should be directed to individuals.* As we "answer everyone," we can be sure that we will talk to individuals. Stock answers and memorized replies won't suffice. We should meet each occasion with answers tailored to the person with whom we are talking.

Conclusion

Paul's instructions to the Colossians are important for us today. We have in this letter a challenge to take the initiative in witnessing for Christ. Will we accept the challenge?

SUNDAY MORNING, JUNE 18

Title: Fathers and the Father

Text: "'But the father said to his servants, "Quick! Bring the best robe and put it on him. Put a ring on his finger and sandals on his feet. Bring the fattened calf and kill it. Let's have a feast and celebrate. For this son of mine was dead and is alive again; he was lost and is found." So they began to celebrate'" **(Luke 15:22–24 NIV).**

Scripture Reading: Luke 15:11–32

Hymns: "Great Is Thy Faithfulness," Chisholm
"Faith of Our Fathers," Faber
"Lord, I'm Coming Home," Kirkpatrick

Offertory Prayer: Father, in your hands are all the fathers and mothers and children here today. We want to offer you our families for your blessing. Purify all our dreams and plans and make us holy by your presence in us. All our fears and failures we ask you to redeem so that we can be the families and people you want us to be. Through Jesus our Lord, we pray as he taught us to pray . . . (*lead into the Lord's Prayer*).

Introduction

Jesus called God "Father." In this intimate and intensely personal name, Jesus swept away all speculative attempts to name the Mystery. The "Unmoved Mover," "First Cause," and "Ground of Being" all suffer by comparison to Jesus' simple appeal to "our Father which art in heaven" (Matt. 6:9). In the story of the prodigal son, Jesus gave us a parable that can be mined again and again for its wealth of insight into God's way with his children. The story is the father's story. He is the central character when the story is heard as a whole (Luke 15:11–32). Jesus' point is clear: Our heavenly Father is like this earthly father who loves both of his sons and waits eagerly for each son's return and reconciliation.

Fathers who want to be like the Father can glean two great truths from today's Scripture reading: (1) fathers learn how to treat their children by considering God's way with them, and (2) fathers can enrich their understanding of God the Father from experiences they have as human fathers. The first truth helps fathers in a practical way to excel in the most important job a man can do—to be an effective father. The second truth helps fathers use the insights they have gained from being fathers to fulfill the most important privilege a man is ever given—to worship and rejoice in God the Father.

I. Men learn how to be fathers by watching God's way of fathering them.

A. *God the Father never stops loving, and neither should human fathers.* The father in the parable waited and watched for his son to return.

Jesus does not say how long, but we can infer that he would have waited and watched for as long as the son was gone. Fathers and mothers sometimes go through recurring anguish over the negligence and recklessness of their children. How long should we care? How long should we keep on watching? As long as it takes! God loves his people with an everlasting love, and fathers are called to love their children in that same manner (Jer. 31:3).

B. *God the Father balances freedom with responsibility, and so should human fathers.* The younger son was free to leave. The father does not forsake his own character and goals to chase after his son. The father painfully allows the son to find his own way back. When the boy returns, broken and repentant, the father rejoices; but he will not let his boy back home on the son's terms: "Make me like one of your hired servants" (Luke 15:19 NIV). The boy was born to be a son, and the father will not let him retreat from that responsibility. It is easier to be a servant than an heir. When we have been wounded and our self-confidence shaken, we are often willing to settle for security alone, but God's tough love places the responsibility of sonship squarely on our shoulders. God's confidence that we can be sons and daughters gives us courage to be just that.

C. *God loves all his children, and so should human fathers.* The elder brother was jealous because of all the attention being lavished on "this son of yours" (Luke 15:30 NIV). He would not call him his brother. "You never gave me so much as a kid goat, but for him you killed the fattened calf! How is that fair?" The elder son's feelings are mirrored in millions of elder brothers who feel they have been treated unjustly. But the father's attitude is, "Son, you have been with me. We have shared together, planned together, worked together, laughed together. Meanwhile your brother has been absent from our joy. Look what he has missed. He's been hurt, rejected, shamed. . . . We must try to make it up to him. He's home now, and we need to celebrate."

Many Christians betray a deeply pagan view of the world when they secretly think that the people in the world are the ones who are really enjoying life and having all the fun. Living with the Father is what heaven is all about. Those who live in his presence now are tasting in advance what heaven will be like. We are immature if we think we need more reward than his presence, and we are blind to think the sin of the world does not exact its own punishment from which a loving Father wants to redeem us. The father loved both his sons equally. Their different needs, however, required of him different expressions of that love. Wise earthly fathers also seek to be sensitive to the different needs of their children.

II. The experiences of human fathers can help them enrich their understanding of the heavenly Father.

A. *God cannot allow us to do everything we want to do.* When a young father first has to deny his child a request and is unable to fully explain to the child the reason for his decision, he knows something of the dilemma God faces with his children. In moments like these, a father learns to be thankful that neither does the heavenly Father give us everything we ask for in prayer. Indeed, we might pray more often, "Thank you, Lord, for not answering the prayer I prayed last year."

B. *God is quiet sometimes because his children aren't ready to listen.* A father held his four-year-old child in his arms. She was angry and hurt. She could not understand why he would not let her do what she wanted to do. He knew he couldn't explain his reasoning in a way she could understand. So for a while he just held her as she beat her little hands on his chest. After a while, she fell asleep, her fury exhausted. He held her while she slept. When his little daughter awoke, she looked up and smiled, hugged his neck, said, "I love you," and ran off to play.

   In that moment, the father understood a little better why the heavenly Father sometimes stays silent in the face of our bitter questions and angry accusations. We are not ready, maybe not yet able, to understand what God would like to say to us. So he holds on to us and waits. In his "not letting go," he speaks the most eloquent language of all.

C. *God wants his children to love one another.* God gains great joy and pleasure from the love and attention his children share with one another. On the other hand, he feels the sharp pain a father feels when his children turn on one another with divisive and bitter emotions. No wonder we are admonished in the Scriptures to love one another.

Conclusion

When Jesus called God "Father," he helped us to worship God with more understanding. He also helped us to be better fathers and mothers when he showed how the heavenly Father cares for his children.

All of us have been born into a natural family. Most of us have had a human father. But God also wants us to have a heavenly Father. He wants to be our Father now and forever. He wants to help make up for what a human father did not or could not give us. He wants to build on all the good experiences we have had with fathers to help us know fully how much we are loved. No matter where you have been or how discouraged you may feel, he is ready to help you become a son or daughter in his glorious, eternal family. Come home to the Father!

Sunday Evening, June 18

Title: The Face of Faith: The Centurion

Text: "Now when the centurion, and they that were with him, watching Jesus, saw the earthquake, and those things that were done, they feared greatly, saying, Truly this was the Son of God" **(Matt. 27:54)**.

Scripture Reading: Matthew 27:45–56

Introduction

Centurions represented the best of Roman men. They rose through the ranks to become commanders over one hundred men. Those who appear in the New Testament are presented as strong and good men. This unnamed centurion witnessed the climactic events connected with Jesus' death. He was probably at the arrest and the trial; we know he was at the cross. What he saw and heard had a profound effect on him.

Just after the earthquake at Jesus' death, the centurion confessed, "Truly this was the Son of God." He had become a man of faith in Jesus Christ. This is the confession that God wants to hear from each of us. If we look closely at this "face of faith" beneath the cross, perhaps we, too, can join him in his confession.

I. The evidence for faith.

This noble man changed his mind about Jesus in a relatively short time. He set out to help the Jews rid themselves of a nuisance but soon confessed the nuisance to be none less than the Son of God. What is the evidence that changed his mind?

A. *The manner of Christ's suffering.* Never had the centurion seen one human being undergo so much abuse. He had been harassed, beaten, mocked, whipped, spat on, and now crucified. But not once did the victim ever lose his poise or react in anger.

   Even as the soldiers nailed him to the cross, he was meek and submissive. The only words he spoke were a prayer: "Father, forgive them; for they know not what they do." Observing Jesus' behavior gave the centurion a strange feeling. What kind of man was this? Surely he must be more than human!

B. *Christ's love for his enemies.* The crowd's hatred for Jesus was obvious. The people relentlessly hurled insults and accusations at Jesus even as he died. But he responded to their ridicule with love, gasping, "Father, forgive them." He was concerned about the welfare of the crowd who was crucifying him. What love! Jesus' attitude impressed the centurion and made him wonder about the judgment of the crowd and Pilate. How could someone with such love deserve to die?

C. *The natural phenomena.* It was a strange day. After Jesus had hung on the cross about three hours, darkness came over the land. Even though it was high noon, there was no sun to be seen. As the centurion stood near the cross during the darkness, he heard Jesus exclaim, "My God, my God, why hast thou forsaken me?"

About three o'clock Jesus died. At that time the whole countryside began to shake with an earthquake. The centurion sensed that there was a connection between Jesus' death and the earthquake. Surely he was not a criminal!

D. *The manner of Christ's death.* The centurion had seen many deaths in the course of his duty. He knew that death by crucifixion followed a certain pattern. But Jesus' death was different. In his last moments, Jesus cried out, "It is finished." It was like a shout of triumph. Then quietly he prayed again, "Father, into thy hands I commit my spirit." He died as though he were the one in charge. He died with a quiet trust in God.

The evidence was just too much for the Roman. He knew in his heart that this man was more than a man. So he exclaimed, "Truly this was the Son of God." We have more evidence than the centurion, because we know of the glorious resurrection and continued work of Jesus. Look at the evidence carefully, and it will lead to faith.

II. The evidence of faith.

We have two separate accounts of the centurion's confession. According to Luke, the centurion declared, "Certainly this was a righteous man." And Matthew reported that he confessed Jesus to be the Son of God. No doubt both accounts are accurate.

A. *The act of confession.* The centurion's confession itself reveals faith. His voice is the only voice we hear at the cross commending Jesus. It is one thing to have some impressions in your heart but another thing to verbalize those impressions. True faith leads to confession. If you have never confessed, your faith is in question.

B. *The substance of the confession.* What the centurion confessed is the real evidence. He confessed the righteous character of Jesus, contradicting the judgment of the world. What a strong confession!

The centurion also confessed the uniqueness of Christ: "Truly this was the Son of God." Scholars still debate how much the centurion actually understood, and whether or not he meant to acknowledge the deity of Christ. Surely Matthew included this account because he saw it as being the logical end of Jesus' life and death. Both Matthew and Luke put it at the climax of the gospel story. Without trying to make a theologian out of the centurion, let's accept his confession for what it says. He had come to believe in the uniqueness of Christ. He had come to believe that Christ was the Son of God.

Conclusion

Dr. Russell Bradley Jones tells about an old English farmer who went to London and visited one of the great art galleries in the city. There he was attracted by a painting of the crucifixion. He sat before it, studying each detail with intense interest. At last, forgetful of his surroundings, he cried out, "Bless him! I love him!" Others nearby, startled by his words, came to see what was wrong with the old man. From different parts of the gallery they gathered around him. They saw the tears flowing down his bronzed cheeks. They, too, looked at the painting of the crucifixion. After a while, one man in the group, with tearful eyes, reached for the farmer's hand and said, "And I love him too!" Then another and another and still another took the old man's hand until there was a sizable group of sobbing believers rejoicing in front of the painting of Christ's crucifixion and declaring, "We love him too!"

Will you join the centurion in his confession, "Truly this man is the Son of God"?

WEDNESDAY EVENING, JUNE 21

Title: Transforming Friendships

Text: "Tychicus will tell you all the news about me. He is a dear brother, a faithful minister and fellow servant in the Lord. I am sending him to you for the express purpose that you may know about our circumstances and that he may encourage your hearts" **(Col. 4:7–8 NIV)**.

Scripture Reading: Colossians 4:7–18

Introduction

Some of our most meaningful relationships are those we have with friends. We can recall with warm feelings the hours we have spent together and the joys, sorrows, and experiences we have shared. The Bible speaks highly of friendships: "A man that hath friends must shew himself friendly: and there is a friend that sticketh closer than a brother" (Prov. 18:24).

Friendships help to make life beautiful and enjoyable. Elizabeth Barrett Browning once asked novelist Charles Kingsley the secret of his life. He thought a moment, then replied, "I had a friend." One of the most important things we can do in life is to make friends and cultivate lasting friendships.

When we come to the last section of the letter to the Colossians, we meet a whole host of Paul's friends who were with him in Rome. Remember that he was a prisoner, and it was probably highly dangerous to be his friend. But these men chose to demonstrate their friendship and loyalty to Paul by staying with him. Some of these names we identify immediately—Mark and Luke, for instance—but others are not so familiar.

In these names and references, we find a great message: the message of transforming friendships. We can see a lot of gospel in the names mentioned here.

I. A transforming friendship can change a life.

A. *A life can be changed.* Paul refused to write about his personal problems in this public letter. The bearer of the letter, Tychicus, would fill them in on those details. With him would be Onesimus, who was described as a "faithful and dear brother" (Col. 4:9 NIV) and who was evidently a native of Colossae.

Onesimus was the slave of Philemon, also of Colossae. He had stolen something from Philemon and fled to Rome to lose himself among the many people in the crowded streets. But while there he met someone—Paul—who introduced him to someone else—Jesus Christ. Now this man who once had been a fugitive slave was going back to Colossae with a letter to the Colossian church, but also with a letter to Philemon from Paul. In this letter, Paul appealed to Philemon to take him in and receive him as a Christian brother.

B. *The friendship that changes a life makes it profitable.* "Profitable" is the meaning of Onesimus's name. Before he was introduced to Christ, Onesimus had been anything but profitable. But his friendship with Paul and his new relationship with Jesus had transformed his life, making him profitable indeed.

II. A transforming friendship can develop steadfastness.

A. *A steadfast friend shares experiences with you.* Aristarchus was a native of Thessalonica who was a Jew by birth. Called a "fellow prisoner," he willingly shared the bondage of all believers in Christ.

B. *A steadfast friend stays with you.* Aristarchus is seen three times in the New Testament: during the riot in Ephesus at the temple of Artemis when he was captured by the mob (Acts 19:29), when Paul sailed as a prisoner for Rome (Acts 27:2), and here with Paul in Rome. He was a man who stood by Paul in a crisis, always at hand in times of need.

Someone has described a friend as one who steps in when the whole world steps out.

III. A transforming friendship can build a life.

A. *Hasty decisions can hurt friendships.* Mark is the next name mentioned. Mark had set out with Paul and Barnabas (he was a relative of Barnabas) on the first missionary journey but soon left them and went home to Jerusalem. Paul refused to take him with them on the second missionary journey. Their mission team broke up because of Mark.

B. *Friendship can rebuild and reclaim lives.* Mark's life was mended because of friendship. Now Paul had Mark with him in a place of difficult service.

IV. A transforming friendship can weld a heart of loving service.

A. *Loving service can renew a church.* Paul mentioned Epaphras, who was likely the founder and pastor of the church at Colossae as well as those at Hierapolis and Laodicea. The concern that he had for the people there was manifested as he prayed daily for them that they might stand within the will of God.

B. *Loving service can show a contrast infidelity.* Luke, the beloved physician, and Demas are mentioned. Demas is mentioned only here, in Philemon 24, and in 2 Timothy 4:10, where these sad and haunting words appear: "Demas hath forsaken me, having loved this present world." The following verse reads, "Only Luke is with me now." Demas and Luke show a contrast in fidelity.

C. *Loving service is willing to share one's home for Christ.* The last name listed is Nympha, who offered her home as the meeting place for the church. She shared what she had with Christ.

Conclusion

We show friendship to God and others when we serve them faithfully. We are friends of Christ when we obey what he commands and witness to others of what he has done for us. And we do all this because Christ showed his love for us by laying down his life for us.

SUNDAY MORNING, JUNE 25

Title: Guidelines for Strengthening Family Relationships

Text: "Whatsoever ye do in word or deed, do all in the name of the Lord Jesus, giving thanks to God and the Father by him" **(Col. 3:17)**.

Scripture Reading: Colossians 3:17–21

Hymns: "The Solid Rock," Mote
"A Child of the King," Buell
"Love Divine," Wesley

Offertory Prayer: Holy Father, we acknowledge that every good and perfect gift comes from your merciful and bountiful hand. We thank you for all spiritual blessings. We thank you for social and family blessings. We thank you for material and economic blessings. We thank you for your blessings on the work of our hands. We come now bringing tithes and offerings as an expression of love and as an indication of our desire to give ourselves afresh to you. Bless these gifts to the glory of your name and to the good of a needy world. We pray in Jesus' name. Amen.

Introduction

Four basic institutions contribute to a stable society: the church, the school, the state, and the home. Each of these four institutions plays a vital role and has a tremendous contribution to make to individuals, to communities, and to the nation.

There are many things that vitally affect our lives over which we have very little or no control at all. This is true concerning each of the four basic institutions that make up our society. However, we do have some contribution to make and some control over the most basic of these four institutions—the home.

In considering some guidelines for strengthening family relationships, let us recognize some presuppositions that should be made as we face the question "What can I do to strengthen my family relationships?" The first assumption we should make is that marriage and the family are of divine origin (Gen. 1:27–28, 31). God instructed his creation to be fruitful and multiply, and he proclaimed that his creation was very good. We can conclude that God intended for man and woman to live together in a relationship of love and trust and mutual helpfulness.

A second assumption we can make is that God has provided divine laws to safeguard marriage and the home. One of the Ten Commandments emphasizes the responsibility of the children toward their parents (Ex. 20:12). The seventh commandment emphasizes the sacredness of sex and the preservation of purity in the marriage relationship (v. 14). The final commandment forbids the lust that would destroy family stability (v. 17). A third assumption that we can make concerning marriage and the family is that God has placed responsibility on the parents to teach divine truth to the children (Deut. 6:4–9).

Before the church, the school, or the state, God established the home. It is the most important of the basic institutions of our society.

I. Consider some reasons for failure in family relationships.

A. *Some marriages fail because they are based on nothing more than romanticism.* The marriage that has no greater foundation than "chemistry" is built on an unstable foundation to begin with.

B. *Many marriages fail because the partners refuse to recognize that each must work diligently to achieve success.* Success is not automatic or accidental; it must be achieved.

C. *Some marriages fail because of a collapse of character on the part of one or both parties in the relationship.*

D. *Some marriages fail because as parents the couple fails to be unified in child rearing.* Parents must present a united front, particularly in the matter of disciplining and training children.

II. Some guidelines for those facing marriage.

A. Recognize that many people are involved in your marriage—your parents, the community, the church, the school, the state, unborn children, you personally, and God.

B. Recognize and respond to the truth that marriage is a divine institution. It should not be entered into lightly or without genuine commitment.
C. Evaluate the importance of a Christian marriage—the union of two people who recognize and respond to the lordship of Jesus Christ in every area of life.
D. Remember that marriage is for adults and that it is for keeps. It should be considered as a bond of honor in which the couple makes an unconditional lifetime commitment to so live as to bring happiness to each other and to their children.

III. Some guidelines for wholesome family relationships.

A. *Counsel to both husbands and wives (Eph. 5:21).* The husband and the wife are responsible to God for the manner in which they relate to each other in marriage. God holds each responsible for achieving success.
B. *Counsel to wives (Col. 3:18).* It is interesting to note that the apostle Paul addresses the wives first. By this is he implying that the wife makes the greater contribution toward the happiness and the well-being of the home? The wife is instructed to adapt to her husband being the head of the household (Eph. 5:22–24, 33).
C. *Counsel to husbands (Col. 3:19).* It is interesting to note in Paul's epistle to the Ephesians that the husband is instructed to love his wife as Christ loved the church (Eph. 5:26). Christ revealed the measure of this love by dying for the church. He also suggests that the husband is to love his wife even as he loves his own body (Eph. 5:28–32). The apostle Peter urged husbands to be kind and considerate to their wives. Failing to do so will hinder the effectiveness of their own prayer life (1 Peter 3:7).
D. *Counsel to children (Col. 3:20).* Children are to recognize that God has appointed their parents as teachers and guides. The authority of parents is to be recognized and responded to in a positive manner. The only time children are free to be disobedient is in a situation in which the parents are commanding them to do something contrary to God's will (Eph. 6:1–3).
E. *Counsel to fathers (Col. 3:21).* Parents are instructed to guard against having a harsh, unkind, unchristian, and unwise attitude toward their children. While the parents are to discipline, they must be on guard lest they harass and irritate their children in such a manner as to provoke a destructive and hurtful spirit within them. Wisdom from the Lord is required at this point.

Conclusion

If young singles want to achieve success in marriage, it is of vital importance that they follow a program of making themselves worthy of the very best. They should keep themselves in such condition that they will be worthy of the best when the time of choosing a companion arrives.

Husbands and wives must recognize that there are many ways to spell the experience we call love. One of the best ways is w-o-r-k. We must work for success as husbands and wives and as parents. Parents need to recognize that they are responsible to God for the manner in which they work in family relationships. Children also need to recognize that they are responsible to God for the contribution they make to the family.

Christ was interested in marriage. We know this because on at least one occasion, he helped at a wedding (John 2). Invite Christ to come into your heart and make his home there. Invite Christ to come into your wedding if it is still in the future. Let him help you select your future companion. Invite Christ to come into your home relationships now. He can help you with whatever the problems may be.

SUNDAY EVENING, JUNE 25

Title: The Face of Fear: Joseph

Text: "Joseph of Arimathea asked Pilate for the body of Jesus. Now Joseph was a disciple of Jesus, but secretly because he feared the Jewish leaders. With Pilate's permission, he came and took the body away. He was accompanied by Nicodemus, the man who earlier had visited Jesus at night. Nicodemus brought a mixture of myrrh and aloes, about seventy-five pounds" **(John 19:38–39 NIV).**

Scripture Reading: John 19:38–42

Introduction

The cross of Christ changed two cowards. They came to the cross bound by fear but left with a life filled with courage. Many of us find it easier to identify with Joseph and Nicodemus than with anyone else at the cross. We have known what it is to be silent when we should have spoken, to keep our relationship with Christ a secret when it should have been shared.

In many ways Joseph of Arimathea is a man of commendable character. He is so presented on the pages of the New Testament. Each of the gospel writers tells of Joseph's part in Christ's burial. They tell us that he was a successful businessman and a community leader. Luke tells us that he was a good and righteous man. He was also a part of that remnant that looked for the kingdom of God. In spirit he was akin to Simeon and Anna who appeared early in the life of Jesus.

Joseph was probably a member of the Sanhedrin along with Nicodemus. This placed him in a unique position to act on behalf of Jesus. Since the Sanhedrin's decision was unanimous, Joseph and Nicodemus evidently stayed away from the important meeting. Being absent would be easier than speaking up for Jesus. They would not have to make known that they were his "disciples."

After Christ's death, however, Joseph and Nicodemus could keep their secret no longer. The cross overcame their fear and allowed them to act in a responsible way. Joseph displayed courage by asking for Jesus' body to bury in his own tomb. This was surely a public sign of friendship and support for the dead Christ.

I. The cause of fear.

John analyzed Joseph like this: "Now Joseph was a disciple of Jesus, but secretly because he feared the Jewish leaders" (John 19:38 NIV). Yet the Jews did not cause the fear; their presence simply caused it to be revealed. What really caused Joseph's fear?

A. *Valuing position before men more than position before God.* The riches and the position on the Sanhedrin had come to mean too much to Joseph. They were the products of a lifetime of effort. He could not just cast them away without thought. What would it mean to lose them? Surely a bold confession of Christ Jesus would cause him to lose his position on the Sanhedrin, and it would probably hurt his business. These misguided values were at the root of the fear that silenced him. Indeed, such a value system has bound countless people with fear throughout the ages.

What impact does your value system have on your relationship to Jesus Christ? Those who are prepared to give a bold witness to Jesus must be ready to set their minds on things above (Col. 3:2).

B. *Valuing the praise of men more than the praise of God.* Gaining the approval of others can become very important; losing the approval of others can become a major crisis. This was the reality that faced Joseph. If he made an open stand for Christ, the price would be high. Losing the approval of others would have immediate consequences. What others think can cause us to do many hurtful things.

You probably don't need to fear a physical attack if you become a Christian, although you may have to face ridicule from your peers or from some member of your family. But which is more important: having their approval or the approval of God?

II. The cost of fear.

Here we must read between the lines and attempt to put ourselves in the situation of this Jewish businessman.

A. *The opportunity for fellowship with Jesus.* This opportunity was lost forever. Joseph missed seeing many miracles, hearing many lessons, and sharing many conversations with Jesus. He, too, could have walked with Peter and the others in his company. Is fear keeping you from a close walk with God?

B. *The assurance of eternal life.* There may be room for debate about whether a person can have eternal life and be a "secret disciple." Regardless of what position you take in the debate, surely you will agree that there can be no real assurance of salvation. Fear brings only torment, guilt, and self-accusation. Joseph must have been ashamed to face himself in the mirror when he considered his cowardly actions toward Christ. Assurance comes with a bold confession of Jesus as Lord (Rom. 10:9–10).

III. The cure for fear.

A. *The cross cures our fears by revealing the end of fear.* As Joseph and Nicodemus saw Jesus hanging on the cross, they could see the end of cowardly actions. Deep within they knew their silence had played a part in this terrible tragedy. Realizing what their silence had done prompted them to take action. Do you realize that Jesus' body might have been thrown in the trash heap or buried in a common grave with the thieves if these two had not acted? Have you ever considered the end of your fearful way of life?

B. *The cross cures our fears by revealing God's love for us.* Nicodemus probably remembered his first meeting with Jesus. In the protective shadows of the night, Jesus had said to him, "As Moses lifted up the serpent in the wilderness, even so must the Son of man be lifted up: that whosoever believeth in him should not perish, but have eternal life" (John 3:14–15). As Nicodemus and Joseph saw Jesus hanging there, Nicodemus may have told Joseph about his earlier conversation with Jesus. They could see just how far he was willing to go for them.

How could they be silent before such love? How can you? This kind of love casts out fear.

Conclusion

In the light of the love of the Lord Jesus Christ, I call you to action. I call on you to cast aside your secrecy and your fears and to boldly declare him as your Lord. Let all the world know that you rest your hopes of eternal life on Christ alone. He promises, "Whosoever . . . shall confess me before men, him will I confess also before my Father which is in heaven. But whosoever shall deny me before men, him will I also deny before my Father which is in heaven" (Matt. 10:32–33).

WEDNESDAY EVENING, JUNE 28

Title: A Reminder for Ministry

Text: "Tell Archippus: 'See to it that you complete the ministry you have received in the Lord'" **(Col. 4:17 NIV)**.

Scripture Reading: Colossians 4:17

Introduction

Included in Paul's list of personal greetings and miscellaneous matters with which he characteristically closed his letters was a special reminder to Archippus. Although we know almost nothing about Archippus, some think he may have been Philemon's son or the pastor of the church that met in Philemon's house. It is not really known what church he served or whether he served in a pastoral ministry at all. Tonight we are going to make a general application from this verse to the ministry that we all have as Christians.

I. The reminder for ministry is personal.

A. *Our ministry is personal.* Paul addressed his reminder to one person—Archippus. All Christians have a ministry to which we have been called. God calls some of us to special ministries, but all of us have been called to ministry.

B. *Our ministry has precedent.* Jesus assured us that he had come into the world to minister rather than to be ministered to. God called Moses, Samuel, and Paul, for instance, into special kinds of ministry for his sake. We have good biblical precedent for the ministry that we will perform in Christ's name.

C. *Our ministry is permanent.* In *The Christian Persuader* Leighton Ford told of the Billy Graham team stopping at Dakar, West Africa, while en route to the African Crusades in 1960. A French missionary met them for coffee. They found out that he had labored in that Muslim center for ten years. One of the group asked him how many converts he had. He thought a moment and replied that there had been one or two, perhaps three converts. The group was stunned. If there were only three converts in ten years, why did he stay? He answered that he stayed because Jesus put him there.

II. The reminder for ministry is practical.

A. *Watch what is done.* "See to it" is Paul's advice. In ministry we watch what is done. Christian ministry encompasses many different jobs, but some of them have priority. Jobs such as pastoral care, the ministry of encouragement, and personal preparation through prayer and study are always priority items in ministry.

B. *Watch how it is done.* We must perform our various ministries in a way that honors God and leads people to faith in God, not in a way that brings glory to ourselves.

III. The reminder for ministry is purposeful.

A. *The source of ministry.* Paul's reminder was for Archippus to finish the ministry he had "received in the Lord." The source of all ministry is in the Lord, meaning that God gives us the place to serve and the call to service.

B. *The strength for ministry.* It is by God's strength that we serve. A spider once spun a large and intricate web. He became proud of his web and snapped the filament that hung down from the top because it did not fit into the design he had spun. But in snapping the filament, he snapped the anchor of the web and it fell to the ground.

IV. The reminder for ministry is pointed.

A. *Ministry must be fulfilled.* If we are called by God, we must fulfill the ministry he has given us. Otherwise we will lose our right standing with him.

B. *Ministry cannot be transferred.* We each have a personal responsibility for our own ministry that we cannot transfer to someone else.

C. *Ministry cannot be measured by inaccurate models.* Our models for ministry have too often come from the commercial world or from the athletic arena. We do not consider ourselves to have fulfilled our ministry unless we have "won," whatever form winning may take. But Jesus gave us a different model by which to evaluate ministry. It is the model of his own life. Even our apparent failures may become successes in God's hands. On the surface, the cross seemed like a dismal failure, but the resurrection showed it to be the fulfillment of God's purpose in the redemption of humankind.

Conclusion

This is our reminder for ministry. Take it. Heed it. Make your ministry as a Christian all that God wants it to be.

SUGGESTED PREACHING PROGRAM FOR THE MONTH OF

JULY

■ Sunday Mornings

On the first Sunday of the month, you may wish to do a sermon appropriate for the celebration of Independence Day. The theme for the next eight weeks is "The Seven Deadly Sins." These seven sins are inward attitudes that affect character as well as conduct. Through Jesus Christ and the power of the Holy Spirit, we can be delivered from the seven deadly sins.

■ Sunday Evenings

"The Inward Attitudes of a True Disciple" is the theme for a nine-part series of sermons based on the Beatitudes, found in the beginning of the Sermon on the Mount.

■ Wednesday Evenings

"Amen and Amen" is the theme for a series of studies from the Psalms, in which the psalmist gives voice to prayers that resound in our hearts today.

SUNDAY MORNING, JULY 2

Title: Christian Citizenship: The Salt That Saves

Text: "'You are the salt of the earth. But if the salt loses its saltiness, how can it be made salty again? It is no longer good for anything, except to be thrown out and trampled underfoot'" **(Matt. 5:13 NIV)**.

Scripture Reading: Matthew 5:13–16

Hymns: "God of Our Fathers, Whose Almighty Hand," Roberts
"He Leadeth Me! O Blessed Tho't!" Gilmore
"I Would Be True," Walter

Offertory Prayer: Heavenly Father, we thank you today for your blessings on our nation. We thank you for our form of government. We thank you for the freedoms and liberties we enjoy as citizens of this fine country. We pray, Father, that you will help us to be a godly people. Help us to serve you in such a way that we might become better citizens of this country in which we live. Help us to give ourselves supremely to you as we seek to be good citizens in our community. In Christ's name we pray. Amen.

Introduction

As we come to the anniversary of the signing of the Declaration of Independence, we should take time to ask ourselves, "Are we being responsible citizens of our country?" I saw a bumper sticker that read, "America: Love It or Leave It." Christians would be wise to change that bumper sticker to read, "America: Love It and Lead It." We need to lead our nation to worship God and to be a responsible nation among the nations of the world.

Our text and Scripture reading emphasize the influence of the ideal followers of Jesus Christ. The text declares that we must function as salt, and the Scripture reading indicates that we are to serve as the light of the world.

A. *Dr. Foy Valentine had some excellent observations on a Christian's responsibility to be a good citizen within the community and country.* He noted, "Christian citizenship is applying the principles and values of the Christian faith in our world through appropriate involvement in the political process." As followers of Christ, we should be more than eager to apply spiritual and moral principles based on our faith in and obedience to God to all of life.

   We can take one of four different stances toward our country, our church, or our denomination.

   1. We can be critical but not loyal. We could specialize in identifying problem areas but fail to generate constructive ideas for solutions.
   2. We can be loyal but not critical. We could give a blind but superficial loyalty to the group of which we are a part.
   3. We can be neither critical nor loyal. Consequently, we would have no real dedication in our hearts.
   4. We can be both critical and loyal. In this case, our commitment is genuine. Love and respect often demand discipline and rebuke.

   We need a renewed faith in and obedience to God and service to our country and to its people.

B. *Dr. Valentine has also said that "the first demand of Christian citizenship is involvement."* In his book *Citizenship for Christians,* he lists some guidelines for responsible Christian citizenship.

   1. Christians need to mix religion and politics. We must not eliminate religion from politics.
   2. Christians need to understand the real issues that confront them as citizens.
   3. Christians need to be politically active.
   4. Christians need to work with special-interest groups who are promoting worthy causes or interests.
   5. Some Christians need to run for office.
   6. All Christians need to vote intelligently.

7. Christians must have a higher loyalty. Loyalty to God takes precedence over all other loyalties.

I. Salt is a valuable item.

In the days in which Christ lived, salt was extremely valuable, so this sentence from the Sermon on the Mount could mean "You are extremely valuable." When foods, especially vegetables, taste flat and need seasoning, more salt is the remedy. The tiny white crystalline cubes are necessary for the health of the human body. Throughout history salt has played an important part in people's lives. People living close to the sea could obtain a plentiful supply. Inland dwellers had to barter for it. Part of a Roman soldier's pay was given to him in salt and was called *salarium.* From this Latin word comes our English word *salary.*

II. Salt is an essential part of the human diet.

Salt is necessary for the digestion of food. We cannot live without salt. In fact, some people who sweat excessively in the heat of summer need to take salt pills to maintain their strength. Jesus was saying to his disciples that they were an essential part of a good society. Without Christians who live out their faith, no society can be what God wants it to be.

III. Salt is a substance used to prevent decay.

In the days before modern refrigeration, salt was used almost exclusively to preserve meat from decay. Most likely Christ was thinking of this use for salt when he called his followers the salt of the earth.

A. *Followers of Jesus Christ prevent personal decay.*
B. *Followers of Jesus Christ serve as salt in the home and prevent moral and spiritual decay.*
C. *Followers of Jesus Christ act as a purifying agent in their community.*
D. *Christian citizens preserve their nation from deterioration.*

IV. Salt is used universally to bring out the flavor of foods.

A. *Followers of Jesus Christ should bring out the best in their family members.*
B. *Those who love God and purpose to do right in all circumstances can bring a refreshing zest to the business world.*
C. *Christian teachers and students can have a wholesome effect in the classroom, on the playground, and at extracurricular activities.*
D. *From the courthouse to the statehouse and to the White House, Christians should prevent decay and bring good taste to all government activities.*

Conclusion

In Matthew 5:13 Jesus pointed out the possibility of disaster: The salt can lose its saltiness and become worthless. The basic chemical nature of salt can be destroyed through erosion or contamination. What is true in the physical world can also happen in the spiritual realm.

What can we do to prevent this calamity from befalling us as followers of Christ?

1. We need to recognize and respond to who we are and what we are. We are followers of Jesus Christ, and we are to function as the salt of the earth.
2. We should read the Scriptures not just as lessons to learn, but as God's instructions to us that we should carry out in our daily lives.
3. We should listen to the voice of the Holy Spirit as he leads us forward in commitment to God and in service to others.
4. We need to beware of the peril of drifting through life and accomplishing nothing.
5. We need to respond to correction and rebuke so that we might be blameless in God's sight.

SUNDAY EVENING, JULY 2

Title: Questions about the Beatitudes

Text: "And he opened his mouth and taught them, saying . . ." **(Matt. 5:2)**.

Scripture Reading: Matthew 5:1–12

Introduction

Perhaps no sayings of Jesus are more familiar but less understood by the average Christian than the Beatitudes. Most congregations could be classified as belonging to one of three groups on the basis of their attitudes toward the Beatitudes.

A. *In one group there are those whose attitude is: Come to think of it, I don't know what they mean. I've never tried to learn, and I don't care.* Not many of this group come to church.

B. *In a second group there are those whose attitude is: I have thought about the Beatitudes. I have wished I could have these qualities in my life, but this quest is not for me. These ideals are too high. I cannot attain to them.* A large percentage of the average congregation would fall into this group.

C. *In a third group are those whose attitude is: The Beatitudes are idealistic. Only Jesus ever exhibited them perfectly. Being meek and merciful and pure in heart are qualities we'll have in heaven, but they aren't for now.* Not so! The Beatitudes are for the here and now. If Jesus had not wanted these qualities to be exhibited in our lives until we get to heaven, he would have waited until then to tell us.

What about the Beatitudes? What is the correct attitude toward these sayings of Jesus? Consider three questions about them taken as a unity.

I. What are the Beatitudes?

A. *The Beatitudes are plain, simple statements of fact or truth, not promises of reward.* Jesus did not say that if a person is "poor in Spirit," he will give him the kingdom in order to make him happy. The poor in spirit are happy "for theirs is the kingdom of heaven" (v. 3). Jesus did not give gifts to make us happy. He creates conditions within us that enable us to find happiness everywhere. Jesus gives people a character that radiates happiness regardless of outward circumstances.

B. *The Beatitudes describe not seven different classes of people, but seven different character traits, or elements of Christian excellence, in one individual.* Who is a Christian? A subject of the kingdom. Jesus is here describing what he came to create in the subjects of his kingdom. The whole Sermon on the Mount treats the character and conduct of members of the kingdom, those who become Christians. Here at the very outset we have the character Christ desires and requires of his followers sketched in these seven characteristics. These traits do not exclude one another but are mutually dependent. Those who are meek also need to be merciful; those who are merciful also need to be pure in heart.

II. What do the Beatitudes teach?

A. *The Beatitudes teach Christ's doctrine of the kingdom.* The multitudes in Jesus' day, for lack of knowledge, degraded and materialized the teachings of the coming kingdom. They believed the kingdom of God to be a perpetual banquet where they would eat rich food and make merry. The more privileged classes were not more spiritual than the masses. They thought of the coming kingdom as a political revolution when the hated Romans would be overthrown. The Beatitudes and the Sermon on the Mount as a whole were a flat contradiction of both of these misconceptions. They taught, rather, that the kingdom is a spiritual realm that is not of this world, though in it. The kingdom of heaven is wherever the laws of heaven rule in the hearts of people. When Jesus spoke of his kingdom, he was speaking from a level of spiritual elevation into the blessedness of which he would lead humankind.

B. *The Beatitudes teach Christ's doctrine of happiness.* In this the Beatitudes cut straight across the ideas of the world. Who are the happy people? If carnal man were to draw up a list of Beatitudes, they would go something like this: "Blessed are the rich, the famous, the well-born, the cultured, those who live in ease and luxury." But not so Christ! People look to outward circumstances for happiness; Christ looks to character. Happiness is decided not by what we have but by what we are. Happiness is never dependent on outward conditions but always on an inward spirit. Therefore, Jesus said, "Blessed are the poor in spirit . . . they that mourn . . . the meek . . . the merciful . . . the pure in heart." All of these are inward qualities of heart and not outward circumstances.

III. How may we profit from a series of studies on the Beatitudes?

A. *Studying this perfect picture of Christian character, we will be able to see ourselves as we are.* By this standard, we will be able to take stock, to see how far short we fall. Are we poor in spirit, meek, merciful, pure in heart, peacemakers? We are not, but why not?

B. *Studying this perfect picture of Christian character, we may see ourselves as we could be, as Christ intended us to be.* Seeing this, let us "press on toward the goal" (Phil. 3:14).

C. *Studying this perfect picture of Christian character, we may be challenged to make some progress toward bridging the gap between what we are and what we ought to become.*

Conclusion

For the next eight Sunday evenings, we will consider the Beatitudes. Seven of these are found in Matthew 5:3–9. The eighth, an often forgotten but authentic beatitude of Jesus is found in Acts 20:35.

WEDNESDAY EVENING, JULY 5

Title: Prayers We Need to Pray

Text: "With my whole heart I seek thee; let me not wander from thy commandments!" **(Ps. 119:10 RSV)**.

Scripture Reading: Psalm 119:9–16

Introduction

It is altogether appropriate for us to say "Amen" either audibly or inaudibly when we listen to the prayers of others and those prayers express the deep desires of our hearts. The Hebrew word *amen* means "let it be so." It is an affirmation of concurrence and agreement. Each of us can participate more meaningfully and more profitably in the public prayers uttered by others if we listen intently and appropriately say "Amen."

With great benefits coming to us, we can study the written prayers of others. Often they verbalize the prayers that we would like to utter, and we can then say "Amen" as we read written prayers.

Psalm 119 is an artistic record of the psalmist's devotions and dialogues with God. The psalm contains many prayers that we could profitably pray as our very own prayers.

Tonight we look at the second of twenty-two stanzas of this acrostic poem. It contains some prayers that each of us needs to pray.

I. "Let me not wander from thy commandments" (Ps. 119:10).

The psalmist recognized the human tendency to wander away from the proper path and offered a prayer that he might be saved from a life of aimless wandering. Why do people wander away from God's truths?

A. *Perhaps it is because we have a fallen nature.*
B. *Perhaps it is because we are forgetful.*
C. *Many of us are preoccupied with other things, and we find it easy to drift.*
D. *We can be tempted by the promises and the possibilities of what the world has to offer.*
E. *Some of us wander because of weariness. The psalmist prays that God will so work in his life that he will be saved from straying from God's precious commandments.*

II. "Teach me thy statutes" (Ps. 119:12).

Throughout this longest psalm in the Bible, we hear the psalmist repeating the petition, "Teach me thy statutes." Each of us should repeat this prayer and mean it with all of our heart.

In this petition, the psalmist was saying, "I want what God wants." God's grace had worked within the innermost being of this man to cause him to want to follow God's statutes.

We need to remember that our Savior was thought of as the great Teacher (Matt 5:1–2; 7:28–29). Only as we understand the teachings of God through Jesus Christ can we truly walk in his ways and do the things he wants us to do.

III. Putting feet on our prayers.

For prayer to be meaningful and productive, we must do more than just talk to Father God. We must cooperate with him as he works to bring about the fulfillment of the desires we have expressed in the petition we have offered.

A. *We can keep our lives pure by bringing our thoughts and actions under the searchlight of God's Holy Word (Ps. 119:9).*
B. *We can avoid a life of sin by storing up God's Word in our hearts that it might serve as both a restraint and as a challenge (v. 11).*
C. *We can verbalize the great truths and the great insights that come to us from God's Word in our conversations with others (v. 13).*

Conclusion

To pray effectively, we need to delight ourselves in God's precepts, his ways, his statutes (vv. 14–16).

Devotional Bible study can be the listening side of prayer. God will speak to our needs through his Word if we study it with trust and with a willingness to be obedient.

Let us consider the prayers that the psalmist has given voice to in this stanza, and let us say "Amen" from the heart to the prayers that we need to pray for our own spiritual good.

SUNDAY MORNING, JULY 9

Title: The First Deadly Sin: Pride

Text: "Pride goes before destruction, a haughty spirit before a fall" **(Prov. 16:18 NIV).**

Scripture Reading: Proverbs 16:5, 18; 29:23

Hymns: "Come, Thou Almighty King," Anonymous
"The Rock That Is Higher Than I," Johnson
"Just When I Need Him Most," Poole

Offertory Prayer: Loving Father, we approach your throne assured of your love and conscious of the rich gifts that you have bestowed on us through faith in Jesus Christ, your Son and our Savior. We thank you for your generosity and thoughtfulness on our behalf. We come now to express our gratitude and our worship in the form of tithes and offerings. Accept these gifts as tokens of our love and as indications of our partnership with you in ministering to the world. Help us, Father, to give ourselves totally to you and in service to others. We pray in Christ's name. Amen.

Introduction

Pope Gregory the Great (AD 590–604) divided all sins under seven headings. He believed that every sin a person commits can be classified under these seven categories. These seven words have come to be called "the seven deadly sins." Sometimes they are referred to as "the seven cardinal sins." They are *pride, anger, envy, impurity, gluttony, slothfulness,* and *avarice.* Although these sins are never found listed together in any single passage, they are continually condemned in Scripture.

Today and for the next six Sundays, we will look at each sin separately. We begin with the sin of pride. Pope Gregory put this sin at the head of the list because he believed that all other sins grow out of this one.

Our Scripture readings for today each make a point about pride. I have chosen three verses from the book of Proverbs, and each verse will make a point for the sermon.

I. Pride is often the source of our troubles.

Proverbs 16:18 says, "Pride goes before destruction, a haughty spirit before a fall" (NIV).

A. *Synonyms for* pride *are arrogance, haughtiness, insolence, contempt, snobbery, presumptuousness, rudeness, sassiness, audacity, disdain, and impudence.* Actually, the list could be longer, but such an endless listing would serve no purpose beyond that which has already been made—that is, pride soon leads one to a multitude of sinful attitudes and actions.

B. *Pride that is unchecked alienates us from our fellow humans.* It may be a feeling of superiority based on racism, nationalism, intellectualism, social station, spirituality, or materialism. Regardless of its basis, smugness that causes one to swagger before humankind and strut in the presence of the Almighty is a harmful detriment to anyone's future.

C. *No one lives out his life without making mistakes.* Most of us make some serious error that requires our families' or our friends' support. When that happens, the boastful braggart is often left "to stew in his own brew."

II. Pride is hated by God.

"The Lord detests all the proud of heart. Be sure of this: They will not go unpunished" (Prov. 16:5 NIV).

A. *The pride that God hates is not a healthy self-respect.* Some Christians have the impression that it is a sin to believe in yourself, your talents, or your capabilities. These people try to develop an attitude of false humility that denigrates or belittles their musical talent, wealth, intellect, or spiritual maturity.

Such efforts are many times a kind of "reverse" pride. The more they play down their God-given abilities, the more others will heap praises on them. These people are playing at humility in order to get others to build them up.

B. *The pride that God hates is an arrogant haughtiness.* This is one who thinks more highly of himself than he ought. Believing that God has given one the wisdom to always be right in judgments or leadership is arrogance. Other members of the church are also guided by God's Holy Spirit, and their collective wisdom might be truer to God's will than one self-appointed leader.

C. *The punishment of God is promised to the conceited, self-inflated soul.* The latter part of Proverbs 16:5 says, "Be sure of this: They will not go unpunished."

The country expression I often heard as a boy was "The chickens come home to roost!" Whatever seeds one sows in life, he or she reaps (Gal. 6:7). Sooner or later there is a day of accounting.

III. Pride leads to humiliation.

"Pride brings a person low, but the lowly in spirit gain honor" (Prov. 29:23 NIV).

A. *Unhealthy pride is a form of self-deification.* Bertrand Russell wrote, "Every man would like to be God, if it were possible; some few find it difficult to admit the impossibility" (*Power: A New Social Analysis* [New York: Norton, 1969], 11). Adam and Eve's sin was one of a desire to be like God—knowing the difference between good and evil (Gen. 3:5).

Humans' desire to control their own destiny leads them to believe—falsely—that they actually can control their emotions, attitudes, abilities, and intellect without God's help. Such faulty reasoning has led to secular humanism.

B. *Adam and Eve were brought low for their sin of pride.* God promises to do the same to all who do not accept their dependence on God.

Sadly, some churches have such a well-oiled, institutional machine that they can keep the organization moving temporarily even without God's leadership.

C. *But the reverse is also true—that is, a truly humble person is elevated to leadership.* If you are talented, you seldom—if ever—have to tell people. Admirable qualities usually find their way to surface.

This last verse tells us that the humble man gains honor. Jesus put it another way. He said, "Blessed are the meek, for they will inherit the earth" (Matt. 5:5 NIV).

Conclusion

We have seen that God abhors the common sin of pride and brings judgment on the one who lets pride become a lifestyle. But God has many rewards for the one who is genuinely humble. True humility is found in Jesus Christ. He is a perfect example of intelligence, power, fame, ability, and leadership. Yet he never used these qualities selfishly or in conceit. Consequently, we are encouraged to become "like Christ," and this is done by believing that he is God and that he alone can guide our lives.

Will you accept Jesus as your Savior now?

SUNDAY EVENING, JULY 9

Title: The Poverty That Possesses

Text: "'Blessed are the poor in spirit: for theirs is the kingdom of heaven'" **(Matt. 5:3).**

Scripture Reading: 2 Corinthians 8:1–9

Introduction

The person who is truly poor in spirit is blessed because such poverty enables that person to possess the supreme possession of all, "the kingdom of heaven." For our sakes, Jesus set the example: "For ye know the grace of our Lord Jesus Christ, that, though he was rich, yet for your sakes he became poor, that ye through his poverty might become rich" (2 Cor. 8:9).

Poverty of spirit is the first character trait Jesus wants in his followers, the subjects of his kingdom. It is a trait that carries its own reward: "theirs *is* the kingdom of heaven." Note the tenses carefully here: "Blessed *are* the poor in spirit," not "have been," not "shall be," but "*are*."

Two questions about this beatitude call for an answer.

I. What is poverty of spirit?

Jesus said that the ones who are poor in spirit are blessed. How so? What does he mean? Consider the answer from two points of view.

A. *Negatively.*

1. Poverty of spirit does not mean *poverty of material possessions.* It is true that earthly poverty does sometimes produce conditions in which Christian virtues may thrive. It is also true that the Bible warns us against "the cares of this world and the deceitfulness of riches" (Matt. 13:22) because of their power to distract us from the desire for heaven's treasure. But happiness is a matter of character, not conditions. It issues from the rightness of our hearts, the relationships of our lives, and not from external conditions. A person may be a millionaire and yet be poor in spirit. One may be penniless but also proud and arrogant.
2. Poverty of spirit does not mean *poverty of native endowment.* No life was ever richer in natural endowment than Jesus' life, yet he was poor in spirit.
3. Poverty of spirit does not mean *poverty of spiritual life* in the sense of being feeble and neutral in one's life. Jesus came to bring the abundant life (John 10:10). He had patience with those of little faith, those weak in spirit, and those impetuous in actions. But he wanted to help them grow, to be of great faith, to be strong in convictions.
4. Poverty of spirit does not mean *pretension of humility.* Some are profuse in self-deprecation. Jesus had no patience with the sort of "worm in the dust" mock piety that is always saying, "I am nothing and nobody and not worth your notice." Often, deep down in their hearts, these are as desirous of "salutations in the marketplace" as the proudest of the proud. The pride that apes humility is more detestable than the pride that casts off all disguise.

B. *Positively.* What then is this poverty of spirit that Jesus calls blessed?

1. Poverty of spirit is *that quality of spirit that accurately perceives that man, as he is, has no virtue inherent in himself, that each gift and each grace of the spirit comes from God.* The great expositor Alexander

Maclaren said, "To me it means a just and lowly estimate of myself, my character, my achievements, based upon a clear recognition of my own necessities, weaknesses and sins."

When we see how completely dispossessed of virtue and grace and righteousness we are in ourselves, pride, self-esteem, and self-righteousness must fall away. When we see how rebellious against God and his righteousness our wills have been, we want to cry out with Paul, "Wretched man that I am!" (Rom. 7:24). Poverty of spirit is the realization that spiritually we are dispossessed, bankrupt, and without merit of our own.

2. Poverty of spirit is *that quality of spirit that recognizes that, apart from God, man is forever incomplete, that the true center of life is God.* The world has little time and no admiration at all for such a person. Rather, it admires the self-sufficient man, the self-confident man, the self- made man (so called), the man who feels he is complete within himself. The Greek philosopher Plato, discussing the good man, the happy man, places one condition upon him: he must be "self-sufficient." Such was the spirit of Jean Jacques Rousseau in his impious boast that he would stand before the judgment bar of God with his "book of confessions" in his hand and challenge anyone living to say, "I am a better man than that man." How much better to cry out with Augustus M. Toplady:

   Nothing in my hand I bring,
      Simply to Thy cross I cling;
   Naked, come to Thee for dress,
      Helpless, look to Thee for grace;
   Foul, I to the fountain fly,
      Wash me, Saviour, or I die!

3. Poverty of spirit is *that quality of spirit that intensely desires that God will supply the true needs of the soul.* Jesus told a story of "two men" who "went up into the temple to pray." One, a Pharisee, did not actually pray. Instead, he gave God a recital of his qualities and virtues. He was self-righteous, self-satisfied. This is exactly what poverty of spirit is not. The other, a publican, was so conscious of his need, so full of the sense of his own shortcomings, he would not even lift his head. Yet, so desirous was he of God's blessing that he cried out, "God, be thou merciful to me a sinner" (Luke 18:13). This is poverty of spirit.

II. How does this poverty of spirit bless us?

In what sense is it true that the poor in spirit are happy in the blessings of possessing the kingdom? Here are five links in a chain that must not be broken.

A. *Poverty of spirit causes us to seek in Christ the grace we need.* We need not mere conviction of sin, for conviction does not always lead to repentance and conversion. Poverty of spirit is that appraisal of our lack on the one hand and of our sins on the other that cause a person to seek salvation.

B. *Poverty of spirit conditions us for receiving the gift of God.* All of the prophets have realized this. Isaiah said, "Thus saith the high and lofty One that inhabiteth eternity, whose name is Holy; I dwell in the high and holy place, with him also that is of a contrite and humble spirit, to revive the spirit of the humble, and to revive the heart of the contrite ones" (57:15). David said in Psalm 51, "The sacrifices of God are a broken spirit: a broken and a contrite heart, O God, thou wilt not despise" (v. 17).

C. *Poverty of spirit releases the saving grace of God upon us.* That is our only hope. This is effective only when we empty our hearts of self and throw ourselves like broken vessels on his mercy.

D. *Poverty of spirit fits us for service in the kingdom.* God loves to use the life that keeps self out of sight and honors only him.

E. *Poverty of spirit opens the eyes of the heart (Eph. 1:18) on the broad horizons of heaven's possessions.* This vision says, "You are a child of the King. These things are yours."

Conclusion

Let's test ourselves. Let each one ask, "Am I poor in spirit, or am I self-satisfied, self-righteous, and arrogant?" An unknown poet has said:

He that is down, needs fear no fall,
    He that is low, no pride:
He that is humble, ever shall
    Have God to be his guide.

Wednesday Evening, July 12

Title: A Prayer for Eyes That See

Text: "Open my eyes that I may see wonderful things in your law" **(Ps. 119:18 NIV).**

Scripture Reading: Psalm 119:17–24

Introduction

In this third stanza of the longest chapter in the Bible, we find more prayers that we can profitably pray along with the psalmist.

I. The motive behind our praying is important (Ps. 119:17).

Jesus had much to say about praying with the proper motive (Matt. 6:5–8).

James declared that an unworthy motive can deprive us of an affirmative answer from God when we pray (4:3).

The psalmist prayed for the abundance God is able to provide. The Revised Standard Version translates his petition, "Deal bountifully with thy servant, that I may live and observe thy word" (Ps. 119:17). The New International Version translates it, "Be good to your servant while I live, that I may obey your word." This saint of long ago was requesting that God deal generously with him so that he might be able to live a life of obedience and helpfulness to others.

A. *He could have prayed for riches.*
B. *He could have prayed for acceptance and popularity.*
C. *He could have prayed for that which would be pleasurable to his appetites.*
D. *He could have prayed for that which would have contributed to his comfort.*

The psalmist prayed with a proper motive. We should examine our motives and try to bring them into conformity with the character and will of our Father God.

II. A prayer for spiritual sight.

"Open my eyes that I may see wonderful things in your law," prayed the psalmist (v. 18 NIV).

It seems as if sin and selfishness create a film over our eyes that makes it difficult for us to see anything except that which is tangible. Paul taught that Satan's strategy was to put a blindfold on the minds of unbelievers so that they could not see the truth of God as it was revealed in Jesus Christ (2 Cor. 4:3–4). Throughout Jesus' ministry he was seeking not only to cure those who were physically blind, but to open the spiritual eyes of his disciples that they might see God's truth. It is significant that, following his resurrection, "he opened their minds to understand the scriptures" (Luke 24:45 RSV).

Every time we open up God's Word, we need to pray for eyes that truly see the marvelous things that spring up out of God's truth.

A. *We need eyes to see God as we study his Word (cf. Isa. 6:1).*
B. *We need eyes that will enable us to see ourselves as we read God's Word (cf. Isa. 6:5).*
C. *We need eyes that see the needs of others as we study God's Word (Matt. 9:36–38; John 4:35).* In our praying, we should ask the Lord, "Take the veil from over my eyes and help me to see what you want me to see."

III. A prayer of gratitude (Ps. 119:24).

In verses 21–24 the psalmist speaks of troubles and of enemies who were plotting to bring about his downfall. During this time of great travail of soul, he found strength, comfort, and help by listening to the great truths of God's Word. He had discovered that studying God's Word could be a listening experience. It is more important that we hear what God has to say than to give voice to our petitions.

Conclusion

Do you want God to deal bountifully with you? Then examine your motives as you pray.

Do you understand all of the mysteries and problems that perplex you? If not, then pray that God will open your eyes as you study his Word.

As you read God's Word, listen to the voice of his Spirit.

SUNDAY MORNING, JULY 16

Title: The Second Deadly Sin: Anger

Text: "He that is slow to anger is better than the mighty; and he that ruleth his spirit than he that taketh a city" **(Prov. 16:32)**.

Scripture Reading: Psalm 37:8; Proverbs 16:32; Matthew 5:21–22

Hymns: "O Worship the King," Grant
"Guide Me, O Thou Great Jehovah," Williams
"Jesus, Lover of My Soul," Wesley

Offertory Prayer: Thank you, Father, for the sunlight of this day. Thank you for the air that we breathe. Thank you for the food that nourishes our bodies. Thank you, Father, for the gift of eternal life through faith in Jesus. Thank you for the joy of fellowship in your family. Thank you, Father, for the privilege you grant to us of being earners and givers. Help us now, Father, as we come bringing tithes and offerings to indicate our love for you and our desire to see others come to know Jesus Christ as Savior. Help us to give ourselves totally to you. In his name we pray. Amen.

Introduction

The second deadly sin is a highly destructive sin: anger. Pride is at the head of this infamous list of sins, but following close on the heels of pride comes anger. Like pride, anger is a sin that infects us all. No one is immune. From the smallest child to the oldest adult, this sin stalks humankind like a predatory animal looking for an unsuspecting sheep.

Parents are aware of the fierce temper of infants. Babies cry out until they are red with anger. Childhood is no better. Fits of anger lead to bickering and self-centered fighting among siblings. Outward displays in childhood degenerate to sulking and pouting in teenagers. Anger causes a wife to develop a headache and a husband to slam doors. Older adults may suffer from ulcers, hypertension, and stress, which may be aggravated by violent outbursts of temper.

I. Uncontrollable anger is a sign of weakness.

"He that is slow to anger is better than the mighty; and he that ruleth his spirit than he that taketh a city" (Prov. 16:32).

A. *The majority of people are able to subdue their anger into a controlled reaction on most occasions.* However, all of us have had circumstances that have sorely tried our patience. During those stressful periods, we become different persons.

   Excuses to downplay our temper tantrums are offered. We say that we were "just letting off steam" or that we were "temporarily insane." The truth is that we lost control. We let our passion go unchecked. When this occurs, our personalities become repulsive, irrational, and border on being animalistic rather than human.

B. *Our Scripture passage tells us that such conduct is the opposite of strength; it is a weakness of character.* It shows a lack of discipline. Anger that is uncontrolled motivates us to action. It leads us to say and do things we later regret. It is so highly destructive that a longtime friendship can be destroyed in a few minutes of unchecked fury.

C. *Our Scripture also implies that not "all" anger is evil.* It says, "He that is slow to anger"; it does not say, "He that *never* gets angry."

   The Bible indicates on more than one occasion that God became angry with both people and circumstances. But God's anger is slow in coming and is usually tempered by a chance for one to be forgiven.

II. Uncontrollable anger leads to personal harm.

"Cease from anger, and forsake wrath: fret not thyself in any wise to do evil" (Ps. 37:8).

A. *Anger is such a strong emotion that when it subsides, it generally leaves a person emotionally drained.* Some people are better than others at getting over a fit of rage. Anger can be so upsetting that any of a number of physical maladies may occur—loss of appetite, inability to sleep, headaches, indigestion, and high blood pressure, among others. At times physical symptoms may disappear, only to reappear later when one sees the person who caused the anger. Anger in such cases soon becomes hatred, which leads to even more serious disturbances.

B. *Rage can rob one of self-esteem.* People get angry with themselves because they allowed themselves to lose control. They chastise themselves, which causes guilt, confusion, and frustration.

C. *Such uncontrolled anger leads one's thinking and attitudes to be marred.* One Scripture passage says, "Fret not thyself in any wise to do evil." Fretting causes us to think in evil ways of how to get even. Plotting evil makes us more like Satan than like God.

III. Uncontrolled anger leads to evil activity.

"But I tell you that anyone who is angry with a brother or sister will be subject to judgment. Again, anyone who says to a brother or sister, 'Raca,' is answerable to the court. And anyone who says, 'You fool!' will be in danger of the fire of hell" (Matt. 5:22 NIV).

A. *Jesus explained in this passage that the sin of murder begins in anger.* For those who take temper tantrums lightly or excuse their emotional displays of fury as being "just my fiery nature" need to realize that they have broken one of the Ten Commandments. Jesus does not take it so lightly. He counts it as disobedience.

B. *One who goes a step further by calling someone "a stupid fool" or "Raca!" (which means "You good-for-nothing") has progressed further in his degeneration.* Jesus said that he is dangerously close to hell fire.

Conclusion

Pride and anger are the first and second deadly sins. Anger that is out of control is as dangerous as murder. Anger causes physical harm to oneself and can lead to physical harm to others.

People can seldom change their nature by personal resolve. They need outside help. Jesus Christ was able to change the Gadarene demoniac from a wild, rampaging beast into a calm, quiet, effective witness (Mark 5:1–20), and he can do the same for your temper. If you would like to change, I invite you to come to Christ.

Sunday Evening, July 16

Title: Joy Comes in the Morning

Text: "'Blessed are they that mourn: for they shall be comforted'" **(Matt. 5:4)**.

Scripture Reading: Psalm 30:1–12

Introduction

Having never fully understood all that it means to be a Christian, we have never fully appropriated the full blessedness of the Christian life. "Blessed are they that mourn: for they shall be comforted" (Matt. 5:4). This is a plain statement of simple truth. Blessed is the man in whose heart the "consolation in Christ" (Phil. 2:1) has been, is, and ever shall be effective. Blessed is the Christian, even in sorrow, grief, and pain, because for the Christian, God's comfort is sure.

As a child of God, the psalmist of our Scripture reading—having passed through the fires of grief, pain, and trial—had found the balm of Gilead sufficient for his soul. His experience was this: "Thou hast turned for me my mourning into dancing: thou hast put off my sackcloth, and girded me with gladness" (v. 11). He believed by faith that "weeping may endure for a night, but joy cometh in the morning" (v. 5). Any English translation must miss the picture of the word here rendered "endure." The figure is "to come in to lodge as a guest." The psalmist was saying, "Weeping may come in to lodge with us at eventide, but joy comes in as a guest in the morning." This is not a mere promise to a Christian; it is the unfailing result of being a Christian, the natural consequence of the Christian life.

Other than Christianity and its forebear, Judaism, every religion says that weeping, trials, and pain are things to be escaped; and those who do not escape them are unfortunate. Only Christianity knows any way of dealing with these unwelcome guests that does not involve arresting, perverting, or even abandoning life itself. In substance, Buddhism says, "Sorrow and pain are universal. Therefore endure, for all must suffer." Not much comfort here! The Stoic seeks to become calloused in soul and therefore indifferent to suffering, a remedy worse than the disease. A dead heart is worse than a broken heart. Christian Science offers escape from the ills of life by denying and ignoring their reality, thus supposedly destroying their hold on human consciousness.

Opposed to all of these is Jesus' solution, which lies in the opposite direction in the abundant life, the happy Christian life, the eternal life that he came to give. Christianity would swallow up grief and pain in victory, mortality in life, and transmute the sorrows and trials of life into the joys and fellowship and love of heaven's own citizens. Only Christ can give "beauty for ashes, the oil of joy for mourning, the garment of praise for the spirit of heaviness" (Isa. 61:5).

"Blessed are they that mourn: for they shall be comforted." These words are true to the facts, especially in three relationships.

I. These words are true to the facts of the conversion experience.

A. *The mourning of conviction for sin is comforted by the joy of forgiveness.* Every Christian remembers the long "night" of weeping under sin's conviction before conversion came in the "morning." We were miserable and wretched; and then after weeping had endured for the night, the joy, the comfort, and the peace of God came in the morning. Then we understood David's exulting words: "Blessed is he whose transgression is forgiven, whose sin is covered" (Ps. 32:1). We may paraphrase our text: "Blessed is the sinner who mourns because of his sin, for he shall be comforted as he finds the peace of God unto salvation."

B. *Not all mourning is blessed.* "Godly sorrow brings repentance that leads to salvation and leaves no regret, but worldly sorrow brings death" (2 Cor. 7:10 NIV).

1. The mourning that issues from our own folly is not blessed but has a curse on it.
2. The mourning over the failure of treacherous schemes, or of the hurt of passion untamed, or of the loss of hoarded treasure is not blessed.

C. *All mourning over sin is blessed.* "Blessed are they that mourn" refers to those who show repentant sorrow for sin that results in God's pardon and peace. The New Testament abounds with illustrations. If the prodigal son was a sorrow-stricken sinner, his reception by his father represents the comfort God has ready for the sinner who mourns over his sin. The woman who wept scalding tears of repentance and gratitude on Jesus' feet was comforted when he said to her, "Thy sins are forgiven" (Luke 7:48). The thief on the cross turned in his agony to cry, "Jesus . . . remember me" (23:42); and he was comforted, even in death. But the most telling illustration is not in the long ago, nor even in the Scriptures, but in the here and now, in your heart and mine where God's salvation has spoken comfort to our souls.

II. These words are true to the facts of a developing, enlarging, deepening Christian life.

In pressing on toward the goal of the Christian life, weeping often comes in to lodge as a guest for the night, but always, again and again, and in a more and more wonderful way, "joy cometh in the morning." As we grow toward "the measure of the stature of the fulness of Christ" (Eph. 4:13), our capacity for life enlarges, our sensibilities to its wrongs and ills quicken, and our struggle with sin deepens into a deadlier and more and more desperate conflict. It is also true that our capacity for the true joy of heaven's realm in like measure increases.

As the prophet had said, Jesus was preeminently "a man of sorrows, and acquainted with grief" (Isa. 53:3). He was so because, as Adam Smith said, "He felt all the sin of man with all the conscience of God."

A. *Growth in Christ enlarges our capacity to live and therefore increases our capacity for pain and joy.* The biologist ranks living creatures according to their capacity for pain on the one hand or joy on the other. Near the bottom of the scale lies the earthworm, with few capacities for life. Then comes the turtle, whose hard shell guards it from suffering and whose cold blood makes it sluggish. Near the top of the animal kingdom is the horse, a finely coordinated, sensitive, spirited, intelligent animal. It lives much and suffers much. At the top of the scale stands man, the apex of creation. Man rejoices in the richness of a mental and spiritual nature yet is the supreme mourner.

Man does not reach the summit, however, until in Christ he becomes a new creature. Then his capacity for life is brought to its fullest. No one can suffer like the full-grown, mature man in Christ; but, on the other hand, no man can rejoice as he can. "Blessed are they that mourn," as only the true Christian can, "for they shall be comforted" with all the comfort of God that the world knows not.

B. *Growth in Christ quickens our sensibilities to the wrongs and woes and ills of the world.* We cannot grow in the knowledge and likeness of Christ without taking to ourselves some of his love for the world and therefore some of his sorrow for its sins. Christ is a man of sorrows because he loves the world and knows its sins. He feels all the sin of the world with all the heart of God. "Blessed are they that mourn" because of the sorrows and sins of the world, "for they shall be comforted" by being made ministering saints (see 2 Cor. 1:3–5).

C. *Growth in Christ deepens the conflict with sin in our lives.* If we develop the power to resist sin, we sorrow all the more for our failures when we do stumble and fall. Here is the obvious fallacy of the doctrine of sinless perfection. Our sensitivity to sin, our hatred of sin, deepens as, through Christ, our power over it increases; and no mature Christian ever thought of himself as sinless and perfect. "Blessed are they that mourn" the deepest over their shortcomings and sins, "for they shall be comforted" to the full.

III. These words are, and ever shall be, true to the facts of eternity.

While I was a guest in the home of a man who was an excellent amateur photographer, I came in from visiting one afternoon to find him missing. When I asked his wife, "Where is Harley?" she replied, "He is in his darkroom. He will be out soon." In a few minutes, he did come out, his prints developed, their images clear. The photographer always takes his negatives into a darkroom to develop them; and in the darkroom the image gradually appears clearer and clearer.

Isn't that, in part at least, what suffering and sorrow mean in our lives? Compared with the unfading light of heaven's realm, this world is God's darkroom; but the Artist of our souls is patient, and little by little the image appears. One day he will take us out, the image clear, into the light of heaven's perfect day; and then shall come to pass the saying "Just as we have borne the image of the earthly man, so shall we bear the image of the heavenly man" (1 Cor. 15:49 NIV). After earth's night of weeping is past, heaven's joy comes in the morning.

> Heaven's morning breaks, and earth's vain shadows flee—
> In life, in death, O Lord, abide with me.
>
> —*Henry Lyte, "Abide with Me"*

Conclusion

Whence comes this comfort with which we are comforted? Not from ourselves, for we are like landlocked pools with limited reserves, but from the "God of all comfort" (2 Cor. 1:3), as his power like a river flows through our lives.

The last scene of all is this: "He shall wipe away every tear from their eyes; and death shall be no more; neither shall there be mourning, nor crying, nor pain, any more: the first things are passed away" (Rev. 21:4). There will be no weeping in heaven. We will enter heaven with the stain of tears on our faces. God himself will wipe our tears away, and it will be for the last time.

Wednesday Evening, July 19

Title: Prayer and the Word of God

Text: "Make me understand the way of thy precepts, and I will meditate on thy wondrous works" **(Ps. 119:27 RSV)**.

Scripture Reading: Psalm 119:25–32

Introduction

Psalm 119 is an acrostic poem composed of twenty-two stanzas, each of which uses and emphasizes one of the letters of the Hebrew alphabet. It is a poem that exalts the law, the testimonies, the ways, the precepts, the statutes, the commandments, the words, and the promises of God.

One of the finest ways to pray effectively is to pray the prayers of biblical characters. We can pray the same prayers the psalmist prayed with great profit. Let us look at some of the prayers in this stanza of Psalm 119 that we might have some assistance in our prayer life.

I. "Revive me according to thy word!" (Ps. 119:25 RSV).

We hear the psalmist praying for a revival or for a renewal in his innermost being. He is discouraged and depressed. He feels as if he is down in the very dust of life. He cries out to God for a revival and a restoration of the vital energies of life. At times each of us needs to pray this prayer.

II. "Make me understand the way of thy precepts" (Ps. 119:27 RSV).

The psalmist is here praying for insight into the inner meaning of the teachings of God's Holy Word.

We can discover truth by research and by reason and logic. But the greatest discovery of truth comes through divine revelation. The psalmist is crying out to God for inward spiritual understanding so that he will then be able to speak of all of God's wondrous works.

III. "Strengthen me according to thy word!" (Ps. 119:28 RSV).

The psalmist was aware of his weakness and his inability to do what he needed to do. He felt overwhelmed with heaviness and grief and sorrow. He stood in need of divine spiritual resources. He cried out to God for strength to face life.

A. *In the New Testament, we are encouraged to be strong in the Lord and the power of his might (Eph. 6:10).* The implication is that we have no hope of overcoming evil and achieving what we need to achieve apart from the strength that comes from God.

B. *Paul found strength through Jesus Christ and was confident that he could make all adjustments in all of the things that he needed to do through faith in Jesus Christ (Phil. 4:13).* Not a day goes by when we, as the children of God, do not need to say "Amen" to this petition offered by the psalmist.

IV. "Put false ways far from me" (Ps. 119:29 RSV).

The psalmist was eager to have removed from him the ways of falsehood, the ways of untruth that would lead to the wrong kind of destination in this life and to failure as far as the next life was concerned. He felt a need to be delivered from deception, falsehood, and untruths. We, too, need to pray this prayer so that we might be able to see through the sham of much that is presented in our world today. The psalmist was eager to enjoy the grace of living according to God's truth rather than being destroyed by falsehood.

V. "Let me not be put to shame!" (Ps. 119:31 RSV).

The psalmist had a healthy fear of failure. He did not want to experience humiliation and embarrassment. Nor did he want to cast a poor reflection upon his God. Thus he prayed that he might be saved from failure.

A. *Paul warned the followers of Christ at Corinth against the danger of failure and expressed his determination that through discipline and dedication he would avoid personal disappointment and failure (1 Cor. 9:24–27).*

B. *When Paul wrote to the Roman Christians, he expressed great confidence in the power of the gospel to save.* He declared that the gospel had never disappointed him up to this point.

Conclusion

In the words of this stanza in Psalm 119 we find many petitions from the heart of the psalmist with which we can and should concur. As we read this prayerfully, we should be able to say a sincere amen to each of these petitions. The psalmist has prayed our prayer for us.

SUNDAY MORNING, JULY 23

Title: The Third Deadly Sin: Envy

Text: "A heart at peace gives life to the body, but envy rots the bones" **(Prov. 14:30 NIV)**.

Scripture Reading: 1 Peter 2:1–3

Hymns: "Holy Ghost, with Light Divine," Reed
"God Will Take Care of You," Martin
"Does Jesus Care?" Graeff

Offertory Prayer: Blessed Father, for all of the influences that have combined under your guiding hand to bring us to this place of prayer and worship, we thank you. Here with your people we are reminded of the many blessings that you have bestowed on us both in the past and in the present. Today we respond to your grace with joy and gratitude and praise. We come bringing the fruit of our labor in the form of tithes and offerings as expressions of our love and as indications of our partnership with you in ministering to a needy world. Through these offerings, bless the preaching of the gospel to the ends of the earth that others might come to know Jesus Christ and worship you as Father. Minister to the needy, and help us always, Father, to give and serve and be a blessing to others. In Jesus' name. Amen.

Introduction

Envy and jealousy are identical twins. They walk hand in hand through our lives. Like the sins of pride and anger, envy is an all-too-common sin. Few of us escape its clutches. It creeps into our relationships and destroys our confidence in ourselves and in others.

Some claim to be exempt from this third deadly sin. "I don't have a jealous bone in my body" is more often talk than reality.

There are many examples of envy and jealousy in the Bible. King Saul was jealous of David's growing popularity. First Samuel 18:28–29 says, "When Saul saw and knew that the Lord was with David, and that all Israel loved him, Saul was still more afraid of David" (RSV).

Joseph felt the jealousy of his brothers. Genesis 37:11 records, "And his brothers were jealous of him" (RSV).

Jesus also was a victim of jealousy. "'Do you want me to release to you the king of the Jews?' asked Pilate, knowing it was out of envy that the chief priests had handed Jesus over to him" (Mark 15:9–10 NIV).

I. Envy is the least understandable of the seven deadly sins.

A. *Envy has no rewards!* It does not make one's position or status more secure. Jealousy destroys relationships without ensuring that one's status can be enhanced. It is never gratified and does not gain a profit.

B. *Envy grows out of fear.* Jealousy fears that someone else's success will be the beginning of one's own demise. Mistrust and suspicion are the beginning of an evil attitude. Such fear invades marriage, family, the marketplace, school, professions, and the church. Christianity's history is littered with the ugliness of coveting. Church history reveals persecution and death by those who felt their status was threatened.

C. *Envy creates a grudging spirit.* Doubt gives way to bitterness. A person who has a happy marriage, successful employment, and intelligent children may be the target of jealousy. A sister may hate a brother because he does well in school. An employee may dislike another employee who gets a promotion. A church member may resent another Christian's being selected for the office of deacon. And in all these cases, not one person profits by letting such a bitter spirit enter his or her life.

II. Envy needs no justification.

A. *This point is seen continually in the Scripture.* David did not pursue the throne of King Saul, yet Saul let envy grow to the point where it blinded his judgment and his relationship to God. David was willing to be a loyal and faithful servant. Even when David had the chance to kill Saul, he didn't. If David had killed Saul, most would have called it self-defense. There was no justification for Saul's jealous rage.

B. *Jesus would have willingly spread the Christian message through the Pharisees.* Their religious knowledge could have been as useful as the apostle Paul's was to him. Yet their jealousy kept them from becoming the tools of God. Eventually the ugly envy in the hearts of the religious leaders led them to contrive false charges against Jesus and deliver him to Pilate. Yet Jesus loved the Jewish leaders and would have rejoiced in their salvation. He meant them no harm. Their jealousy was unjustified.

C. *Therefore, let us remember that jealousy is seldom a proper response.* Coveting destroys spiritual health. It attacks its opponent with vengeance.

III. Envy takes away the joy of living.

A. *King Saul became a madman.* Finally, with his son dead and his enemies surrounding him, Saul fell on his own sword. The joy of life had long since departed.

B. *Envy isolates one from other people.* It sows the disposition that causes people to see life in a begrudging manner.

The book of Esther tells the story of jealousy. It is the history of a man named Haman whose jealousy of the Jews centered on the Jewish leader Mordecai. Haman became obsessed with hatred, and his hatred led to deceit and a desire to enhance his own status with the king. By the strange twist of God's hand on history, Haman was hanged on the very gallows he built for Mordecai. Haman was trapped by his own envy.

C. *Happiness and contentment are two qualities all of us seek in life.* Yet our Scripture text, Proverbs 14:30, tells us that the opposite of such peace is envy.

Conclusion

Since envy and jealousy constantly stalk humanity, we must constantly guard our souls against their destructive power. They do not enhance our status and often cause us to lose more than we gain.

Jesus Christ, the Prince of Peace, is the way to peace, and he alone is capable of putting the mind at peace. If jealousy is one of your major sins, I bid you to turn to Jesus for help. As the proverb says, "A heart at peace gives life to the body" (Prov. 14:30). So give your heart to Jesus and live!

Sunday Evening, July 23

Title: Rest unto Your Souls

Text: "'Blessed are the meek: for they shall inherit the earth'" **(Matt. 5:5)**.

Scripture Reading: Matthew 11:25–30

Introduction

As Americans, our heritage has hardly prepared us for this beatitude. Our heritage is one that encourages contempt for what we understand to be "the meek" and admiration of the self-assertive. On the one hand, we have inherited, through the classics, the Roman ideal of greatness in which meekness has no place. On the other hand, we are the heirs of Anglo-Saxon self-assertiveness and insistence on personal rights and privileges. Under these influences, we have come to admire power, domination, and personal success.

"Blessed are the meek: for they shall inherit the earth" (Matt. 5:5). On hearing this, the average American will say, "To tell you the truth, I just don't admire that. Doesn't that mean a weak and spineless creature, a namby-pamby, milquetoast type of individual, flabby in character and lacking in self-respect?" Laboring under this false impression of what meekness is, they ask, "Who wants to be meek? More than that, the statement, 'They shall inherit the earth,' is ridiculous. Maybe some of them will go to heaven someday, but 'inherit the earth'? Forget it! I don't believe it!"

This beatitude meets with a poor reception by most people. Perhaps none in the list is as unpopular as this. To the popular mind this beatitude is undesirable and unbelievable. But popularity is no reliable test of anything and certainly not of things that pertain to Christ and his kingdom. The popular conception of Christian meekness is both erroneous and inadequate, and these ideas are therefore false. This is not a popular beatitude, because in the world's failure to understand what true meekness is, it neither admires nor desires it.

But there are some other more reliable tests to apply to this saying of Jesus. "Blessed are the meek: for they shall inherit the earth." Jesus was stating a simple fact, and that fact is demonstrated to be true by three important tests.

I. The test of God's Word.

The word *meek* and injunctions to be meek are sprinkled throughout the Bible. Our attention is called to the profitableness of meekness. Moreover, meekness is enjoined as one of the most commendable traits of a saint. The psalmist said it will meet the test of survival: "The meek shall inherit the earth; and shall delight themselves in the abundance of peace" (Ps. 37:11). Jesus took these words and expanded them into our beatitude.

A. *Paul urged the virtue of meekness on those to whom he wrote.* In a great passage in Galatians (5:22–23), Paul described this fruit, which the Spirit will plant in our hearts: "the fruit of the Spirit is . . . meekness." To the Colossians, Paul exhorted how, as "God's elect," they were to clothe themselves: "Put on therefore, as God's elect, holy and beloved, a heart of . . . meekness" (3:12 ASV). To Timothy, Paul's own son in the faith, he wrote, "But thou, O man of God . . . follow after . . . meekness" (1 Tim. 6:11).

B. *The apostle Peter also urged the virtue of meekness on those to whom he wrote.* In his first epistle, he said to his female readers, "Your beauty should not come from outward adornment. . . . Rather, it should be that of your inner self, the unfading beauty of a gentle and quiet spirit." Peter knew the mind of the world in these things, so he added, "which is of great worth in God's sight" (1 Peter 3:3–4 NIV).

C. *The Bible, in general, demonstrates that the people most conspicuous for meekness are God's greatest people.*

   1. In the Old Testament. The outstanding example of meekness is not some person of colorless character without spirit, passion, or vitality, but Moses, one of the greatest men of all time. "Now the man Moses was very meek, above all the men which were upon the face of the earth" (Num. 12:3). And what a man he was: courageous, resourceful, able, high-spirited, and strong. He was "broken to God's bridle" (for that is what meekness is), amenable to correction, teachable in God's hands, and submissive to God's yoke. He was enduring, forbearing, suffering, not because of cowardice or fear, but for God's sake, his work's sake, and his people's sake.

   2. In the New Testament. In his list of the Twelve, Mark said of two of them: "James son of Zebedee and his brother John (to them he [Jesus] gave the name Boanerges, which means 'sons of thunder')" (3:17 NIV). Think of it! John, the beloved apostle, who had once been described by Jesus as a "Son of Thunder," became meek and lowly in heart, bowing to Christ's yoke, learning of him.

      Above all, Jesus himself is the world's supreme example of meekness. He demonstrated his own beatitude to be true.

II. The test of Jesus Christ's character and person.

What is meekness? In a word, meekness is Christlikeness. To become meek is to become like Christ. How do we attain it? In our Scripture reading, Jesus said, "Take my yoke upon you, and learn of me" (Matt. 11:29).

A. *We become meek by submission to Christ.* "Take my yoke upon you" was a figure the rabbis used for going to school, but it carried with it the idea of submission to the teacher. The actual word used to express the idea of meekness is the word used by the Greek writer Xenophon to speak of a horse "broken to the bridle." He was not speaking of some old "plug" without spirit, strength, or sensitivity, but a horse strong, sensitive, and high-spirited yet submissive to its master's bridle. One has translated this beatitude "Blessed are the God-tamed." That is meekness. We may paraphrase our text "Blessed are those whose strength is great, whose sensibilities are well developed, whose spirit is hot and quick, but who yet have taken Christ's yoke upon themselves, who have submitted to his bridle, who have become God-tamed."

The great Russian pianist and composer Sergei Rachmaninoff had large and powerful hands. After one of his concerts, a critic wrote that he played as if "his hands were steel gloved in velvet." That is meekness—strength under control. Meekness is the courage to fear God rather than men.

B. *We become meek by learning of Christ.* "Take my yoke upon you and learn of me." The basis of Christ's appeal is not his power and wisdom, but the fact that he is "meek and lowly in heart." He wants us to imitate that, to cultivate it.

1. We are to learn the unselfishness of Christ—the unselfishness of the one who "came not to be ministered unto, but to minister, and to give his life a ransom for many" (Matt. 20:28).
2. We are to learn the gentleness of Christ. Peter said of him, "Who, when he was reviled, reviled not again; when he suffered, he threatened not" (1 Peter 2:23). The greatest heroism is the strength of gentleness, to bear, to endure for Christ's sake.
3. We are to learn the humility of Christ. "Lowly in heart" means teachable, thoughtless of self, thoughtful of others, depending not on self but on God for strength. Humility is an inseparable corollary of meekness.
4. We are to learn the courageousness of Christ. At the bottom of the world's bravery lurks a miserable cowardice, the terrible fear that people will think we are afraid. Jesus had the courage to follow the will of the Father all the way to the cross, regardless of people or malice, of custom or convention.
5. We are to learn the strength of Christ. Paul caught the meaning of this when he said, "When I am weak, then am I strong" (2 Cor. 12:10). Dependence on God releases his power in us.

III. The test of results.

Jesus assured us that the power of meekness is vindicated by the results. "Blessed are the meek; for they shall inherit the earth." Who owns the earth?

Those who, like Jesus, are meek and lowly in heart and have found "rest unto their souls." We may understand the word *rest* in three ways.

A. *Cessation from strife.* The quiet and tranquility of inner peace. The world belongs to those who have peace in their hearts.
B. *To rest on something as on a foundation.* The meek person rests on Christ. As Paul said, "For other foundation can no man lay than that which is laid, which is Christ Jesus" (1 Cor. 3:11).
C. *To rest in the sense of a legal term.* The lawyer, having finished his plea for his client, turns to the court and says, "We rest our case." The meek man rests his case in the hands of Jesus; for if indeed he is meek, he has faith in the final vindication of the right, the triumph of love.

Conclusion

God help us to follow and to imitate him who is "meek and lowly in heart," for to him heaven and earth belong. "Blessed are the meek: for they shall inherit the earth."

WEDNESDAY EVENING, JULY 26

Title: Amen and Amen

Text: "Teach me, O LORD, the way of thy statutes; and I will keep it to the end" **(Ps. 119:33 RSV)**.

Scripture Reading: Psalm 119:33–40

Introduction

Amen is a transliteration of the Hebrew word into both Greek and English. Amen means "faithful" in reference to God, his testimonies, and his promises.

At times the people of God used *amen* to express their assent to a law and to their willingness to submit to the penalty attached to the breach of that law (cf. Deut. 27:15; Neh. 5:13). *Amen* is also used to express acquiescence to another's prayers (1 Kings 1:36). It is also used by some to show agreement when another is offering thanks to God (1 Chron. 16:36). These verses would suggest that we need to let others help us with our prayers. That is, when someone else prays a prayer that expresses the deep desires of our heart, it is permissible and proper that we say "Amen" either audibly or inaudibly.

The psalmist offered up many petitions to which we can say "Amen."

I. A prayer of agreement and affirmation (Ps. 119:33).

The psalmist was praying to God, saying, "Teach me, O LORD, the way of thy statutes, and I will keep it to the end." This is a prayer in which all of us should participate.

A. *To pray this prayer is to make the law of God personal.*

B. *To pray this prayer internalizes the law of God and writes it on the walls of our hearts.*

II. "Lead me in the path of thy commandments" (Ps. 119:35 RSV).

A. *David, in the great Shepherd Psalm, wrote, "He leadeth me in the paths of righteousness for his name's sake" (23:3).* This means that God leads us in the paths that are right because God's character is at stake. The only way God can lead us is in paths that are right. In this petition the psalmist is praying for divine leadership that he might walk in the right paths throughout life.

B. *Through Jeremiah, God said, "Stand ye in the ways, and see, and ask for the old paths, where is the good way, and walk therein, and ye shall find rest for your souls" (Jer. 6:16).*

III. "Incline my heart to thine testimonies, and not to gain!" (Ps. 119:36 RSV).

A. *Feelings of insecurity pull us toward the desire for profits in the economic world.*

B. *Greed can capture our minds and hearts, and we can become the servants of mammon.*

C. *The psalmist was praying that God would deliver him from the lure of the material and lead him to that which was eternal and permanent.* He was eager that God would help him guard his heart, because out of the heart come the issues of life. This verse has been translated, "Bend my heart to your will and not to the love of gain."

This is a prayer to which all of us should say, "Amen and amen."

IV. "Turn my eyes from looking at vanities" (Ps. 119:37 RSV).

The writer of the book of Ecclesiastes came to recognize that many of the things we look upon with desire produce emptiness and despair once they are obtained. The psalmist was here praying that he might be delivered from all the pursuits and ambitions that lead to emptiness and disappointment. All of us need to join with the psalmist in praying this prayer.

V. A prayer for deliverance from failure (Ps. 119:39).

The New International Version translates verse 39, "Take away the disgrace I dread." A healthy fear of failure can be positive and helpful. Here the psalmist is earnestly praying that God will so work in his life that he will be saved from making decisions and choosing ways that will lead to disappointment and shame.

Conclusion

These petitions are very personal. The psalmist was giving voice to a strong cry for deliverance from subtle dangers. To his petitions we can say, "Amen and amen."

Sunday Morning, July 30

Title: The Fourth Deadly Sin: Impurity

Text: "A man who commits adultery lacks has no sense; whoever does so destroys himself" **(Prov. 6:32 NIV).**

Scripture Reading: Proverbs 6:32–33

Hymns: "Love Divine, All Loves Excelling," Wesley
"Let Others See Jesus in You," McKinney
"I Would Be True," Walter

Offertory Prayer: Our heavenly Father, we are aware of our debts to you and to others. We come asking your forgiveness and, at the same time, thanking you for the gift of forgiveness. Today we come bringing tithes and offerings as expressions of our love and gratitude. Accept them and bless them in ministries that will honor your holy name. In Jesus' name. Amen.

Introduction

The fourth deadly sin was labeled "impurity" by the ancient fathers. We know it better by the word *lust.* It is the category of sin that deals with the immorality of sexual sins. Lust, premarital and extramarital sex, prostitution, pornography, homosexuality, pedophilia, incest, and rape are all sins that may be classified as "impurity."

I. Lust demonstrates a lack of maturity.

A. *Our Scripture text for today makes this point.* "A man who commits adultery has no sense" (Prov. 6:32 NIV). A lack of judgment indicates a lack of maturity.

The world declares otherwise, and unfortunately even some Christians have been fooled. The world calls some movies "adult movies" or rates some "For mature audiences only." The Christian should rightly ask, "If this is maturity, then what would be immaturity?"

B. *Lust is built on the world of fantasy, not reality.* Lust dreams of activities that either are impossible or require the misuse and disregard of another's personal rights. It is selfishness in its lowest form.

C. *Lust is not the admiration of physical beauty.* It is perfectly natural to appreciate an attractive person. But real maturity does not let such "appreciation" become an obsession. That is the essential difference.

Lust is coveting, uncontrolled craving, unleashed passion. Man should not behave like an animal, for he is more than an animal; he is a creature made in the image of God and should act as such.

II. Lust demonstrates a lack of good judgment.

A. *Our Scripture text makes a second point about sexual depravity.* It states clearly that adulterers lack judgment. Adultery, fornication, incest, rape, homosexuality, masochism, and all other sexual sins demonstrate a lack of wisdom.

It is readily apparent that such actions do not take into consideration the consequences. On the other hand, if one does know the consequences of such activity and still proceeds, then he or she is indeed lacking in good judgment.

B. *Sincerity and responsibility are two qualities of good judgment.* People who practice free love hide under the guise of enlightened intellectualism; they actually demonstrate a childish emotional level.

Babies demonstrate almost total selfishness and self-centeredness. This is necessary for their development, and hardly anyone expects them to act otherwise. They cry to gain our attention and have temper tantrums to express their feelings of frustration. The only way to end such behavior is to mold our world around their needs and desires.

Lustful people behave like babies. They resent any restrictions on their behavior and lack the judgment to be able to understand that they cannot always have what they want when they want it.

III. Lust produces self-destruction.

A. *Our Scripture text says that anyone "who commits adultery has no sense; whoever does so destroys himself" (Prov. 6:32 NIV).* There are so many ways this verse proves true. Ministers, doctors, lawyers, psychologists, and social service personnel regularly see evidence of this. Sexual sins cause grief, destruction of trust, guilt, divorce, anger, frustration, jealousy, deceit, murder, physical injury, wrecked futures, loss of friendships and jobs—the list seems endless!

B. *Many believe they should be allowed to live their sexual lives as they choose.* Perhaps if one lived in a vacuum, such logic would make more sense. But because "no man is an island," such logic is absurd. Nearly every one of the professionals listed above can tell you how adultery, incest, homosexuality, and the whole list of sexual sins has destroyed the lives of others.

C. *If you think you can violate the laws of God to your own selfish desires with impunity, you are wrong.* "Do not be deceived: God cannot be mocked. A man reaps what he sows. Whoever sows to please their flesh, from the flesh will reap destruction, whoever sows to please the Spirit, from the Spirit will reap eternal life" (Gal. 6:7–8 NIV).

Conclusion

Let us see our sexual appetite as a good gift from God to be used wisely and for enhancing marriage. By viewing our sexuality in a Christian manner, we will honor God, demonstrate maturity, and contribute to a dependable and responsible society. Failing to harness our sexuality will cause our culture to disintegrate.

If you are already a Christian and are having difficulty with lust, then turn back to Christ. Return to the basics of following Christ and his teachings for a rich and satisfying view of your sexual needs.

Sunday Evening, July 30

Title: Delighting the Soul in Fatness

Text: "'Blessed are they which do hunger and thirst after righteousness: for they shall be filled'" **(Matt. 5:6)**.

Scripture Reading: Isaiah 55:1–13

Introduction

It is a great blessing to desire earnestly and to receive the things of the Spirit that God will give to those who ask. Three things stand out about this beatitude.

A. *The universality of the figure in which the beatitude is conveyed.* Hunger and thirst are elemental instincts known to all people, so Jesus' words strike a responsive chord in every heart. Taken together, hunger and thirst form a universal figure for an intense desire that is perpetual. The word translated "filled" is from a word that means "to fatten," as to fatten cattle on fodder, grain, or grass. Hence, Jesus' meaning is "Blessed are those who desire, intensely and perpetually, what God has to give, for their souls shall be made fat on God's fodder." Long ago the prophet Isaiah quoted God as saying, "Hearken diligently unto me, and eat ye that which is good, and let your soul delight itself in fatness" (55:2).

B. *The definiteness of the terms to which the beatitude is confined.* Jesus speaks about those who are hungering and thirsting after righteousness. Upon no other desire does the blessing fall. Again the prophet said, "Wherefore do ye spend money for that which is not bread? and your labour for that which satisfieth not?" (Isa. 55:2). There is a bread that is not the Bread of Life and drink that does not satisfy.

   Like a coin too long in circulation, the word *righteousness* has so lost weight and value through years of misuse that it is almost too light and thin to convey Jesus' meaning. As Jesus used it, righteousness means a right standing before God, a right relationship with God through Christ. Blessed are those who long to be right with God, for upon the atoning merits of Christ they shall be. But to a Christian, righteousness should also mean what it meant to Christ—to do the will of the Father (see John 4:34). We are filled when the righteousness of Christ is imputed to us (2 Cor. 5:21) and when his Holy Spirit works the works of God through our lives.

C. *The quality of the condition that is called blessed.* This beatitude describes a blessed process by which the soul grows to be like God. We hunger and thirst. We eat and drink and are satisfied; but in a matter of hours hunger and thirst return, and we repeat the process. Blessed is the process of hungering and thirsting after righteousness and of being filled, for by this process we grow and develop as Christians. Blessed is the one whose appetite for spiritual food and drink is growing, for he or she will be filled again and again.

Consider three questions about this beatitude.

I. Wherein are these blessed?

How are those hungering and thirsting after righteousness blessed?

A. *By the freeness of God's invitation to be filled.* This is a steady refrain in the Bible. "Ho, every one that thirsteth," cried the prophet after the manner of the water peddler in the arid upland villages, "come ye to the waters, and he that hath no money; come ye, buy, and eat; yea, come, buy wine and milk without money and without price" (Isa. 55:1). Jesus said, "If any man thirst, let him come unto me, and drink" (John 7:37). And the examples may be multiplied (see also John 4:14; Rev. 22:17).

The intensity of our desire to be filled can never exceed the freeness of Jesus' invitation to feed our souls on his righteousness, which is manna to the hungry heart—life and health and peace.

B. *In the bounty of God's supply.* "They shall be filled." As we grow in God's grace, capacity enlarges, and hunger and thirst for righteousness intensify; but our desire can never exceed God's resources. Still he says, "My grace is sufficient for thee" (2 Cor. 12:9).

C. *In the certainty of the result.* "They shall be filled." Oh, the blessed certainty of the gospel. This note runs throughout the Bible and sings its way through the Gospels' pages. "Him that cometh to me I will in no wise cast out" (John 6:37). Paul gave this assurance: "Whosoever shall call upon the name of the Lord shall be saved" (Rom. 10:13). John's gospel preserves Christ's picture not only of the initial experience of salvation, but also of the provision for the Christian that follows (John 10:9). "And [shall] find pasture." No hunger is too great, no thirst too deep. "They shall be filled."

II. Why are these blessed?

In our thinking, the pain of unsatisfied desire is not a happy condition. But Jesus said it is—if that hunger and thirst are for righteousness.

A. *Hunger and thirst are proof of spiritual life and health and vitality.* This is true in every realm.
   1. In the realm of the mind. A child asks questions because her mind is hungry, healthy, and growing.
   2. In the realm of the physical. An ordinary beech tree will draw up sixty-five gallons of water in a single spring day.
   3. In the realm of the spiritual. Above all, this is true of the hunger and thirst for righteousness. To desire intensely the things of the Spirit is a sign of spiritual life and vitality and health. The person who wants to be vitally in touch with God wants spiritual food. When no hunger and thirst for the things of God are apparent, there is cause for alarm.

B. *Hunger and thirst are a means of spiritual growth.* When your child refuses to eat, you become alarmed, fearing the child is sick and not growing. Likewise, in the spiritual realm, we become alarmed when we see that people are not partaking in the reading of the Word and other spiritual growth activities and therefore not growing spiritually. On the other hand, how wonderful it is to watch a growing Christian hungering and thirsting after righteousness.

C. *Hunger and thirst carry the promise of maturity.* Have you ever been a guest in a home and noticed marks on a doorframe with names and dates by those marks where someone was charting the growth of a child? As Christians we should be able to chart our spiritual growth. In Philippians Paul called attention to his own growth chart: "Brothers and sisters, I do not consider myself yet to have taken hold of it [that for which Christ Jesus took hold of me]" (3:13 NIV). He was not satisfied, for he went on to say, "I press on toward the goal to win the prize for which God has called me heavenward in Christ Jesus" (3:14 NIV). The end and promise of the Christian life is maturity. We reach maturity in Christ as we press on, as we hunger and thirst after righteousness and are filled.

III. When are these blessed?

Wonderful is the word of our beatitude, matchless is the blessing, but when does it apply? When shall those who hunger and thirst after righteousness be filled?

A. *The answer is now; the blessing is for this life.*
   1. This blessing is subjective, within the heart and life now. This is the blessedness of advancing toward maturity, the blessedness of having joy and peace in the mind and heart.
   2. This blessing is also objective. It is apparent to the world surrounding the Christian. Those people of science and education and letters whose work has blessed the world are those whose

hungry minds did not stop short of fulfillment. They hungered and continued onward. This is true also of Christians. Those who have been the saving salt of the earth and lights on a hill have been those whose hearts hungered and thirsted after God.

B. *The answer is also hereafter.* Our idea of heaven as a place where all limitations will be removed is true. The Bible teaches that. But it also teaches that there will be growth in heaven and that our capacity to enjoy it will grow forever and forever.

Conclusion

One description of heaven is as a banquet where "many shall come from the east and west, and shall sit down with Abraham, and Isaac, and Jacob, in the kingdom" (Matt. 8:11). Whatever else it means, here is certainly the suggestion that even then the divinely blessed alternation of hungering and thirsting and being filled shall go on and on and on.

Suggested Preaching Program for the Month of August

■ Sunday Mornings

Complete the series "The Seven Deadly Sins."

■ Sunday Evenings

The Beatitudes vividly set forth the inward spiritual characteristics of those who are ideal citizens of the kingdom of God. Continue with the theme "The Inward Attitudes of a True Disciple." Only when we are right in our inward attitudes can we be right in our outward conduct.

■ Wednesday Evenings

Complete the devotional study of the Psalms using "Amen and Amen" as the theme.

Wednesday Evening, August 2

Title: Prayer and the Promises of God

Text: "Let thy steadfast love come to me, O Lord, thy salvation according to thy promise" **(Ps. 119:41 RSV)**.

Scripture Reading: Psalm 119:41–48

Introduction

Again we look at some of the prayers prayed by the psalmist and let his prayers become our prayers. As we read these prayers from Holy Scripture, it is entirely appropriate that we say "Amen" to his prayers and thus make them personal.

I. A prayer for the pouring out of God's love (Ps. 119:41).

The New International Version translates this verse, "May your unfailing love come to me, O Lord, your salvation according to your promise." Here the psalmist was asking God to demonstrate his love for him. Perhaps we ought to pray that the Lord will open our eyes and help us to see his continuous efforts to show us his love.

II. A prayer for adequate speech at all times (Ps. 119:43).

Often we find ourselves speechless when we have opportunity to witness or to help someone. Later we say to ourselves, *Well, why didn't I think of it at the time?* The psalmist had similar experiences.

A. *He speaks of those who taunt him because of his faith in the Word of God (v. 42).* The people of God have enemies who taunt them and criticize them.
B. *Some try to intimidate us, and we are afraid to speak to them as we ought (v. 46).* The psalmist prays that God will give him adequate speech.

The New International Version translates verse 43, "Do not snatch the word of truth from my mouth, for I have put my hope in your laws." Let us pray that God will help us always to speak for him as he would have us do.

III. Prayers of affirmation.

A. *"I will always obey your law" (v. 44 NIV).*
B. *"I will walk about in freedom, for I have sought out your precepts" (v. 45 NIV).*
C. *"I will also speak of thy testimonies before kings" (v. 46 RSV).*
D. *Expressions of love and praise:* "I delight in your commands because I love them" (v. 47 NIV); and "I reach out for your commands, which I love, that I may meditate on your decrees" (v. 48 NIV).

Conclusion

In each of these great affirmations, we should be able to unite with the psalmist in petition to God. Let us join him in prayer and say from our hearts, "Amen and Amen."

SUNDAY MORNING, AUGUST 6

Title: The Fifth Deadly Sin: Gluttony

Text: "If anyone has material possessions and sees a brother or sister in need but has no pity on them, how can the love of God be in that person?" **(1 John 3:17 NIV)**.

Scripture Reading: 1 John 3:17–18

Hymns: "O Worship the King," Grant
"Grace Greater Than Our Sin," Johnston
"Blessed Assurance, Jesus Is Mine," Crosby

Offertory Prayer: Our heavenly Father, we offer thanks for your blessings upon us. We come bringing gifts that are but indications of the generosity of your provisions for us. We remind ourselves that every beast of the forest is yours and the cattle on a thousand hills are yours as well. Help us to use our gifts to proclaim the gospel to the ends of the earth and to minister to the needs of the unfortunate about us. Bless these gifts and multiply them to your honor and glory. In Jesus' name. Amen.

Introduction

Gluttony is not a sin we hear much about today, and when we do, it is usually in reference to overeating. However, the sin of gluttony is more than overindulgence in food or drink. It is the sin of excess and intemperance. It is unrestraint, self-indulgence, and inordinate extravagance. Gluttony seeks to satisfy our senses and our greed while disregarding the needs of others. Thus gluttony covers a large number of sins. Certainly in our affluent society, we can readily see the extent of this sin and the many heartaches it causes.

I. Gluttony is the sin of the affluent.

A. *The possession of wealth is not a sin.* Occasionally ministers and churches may have given people the impression that affluence in and of itself is a sin. This is certainly untrue.

Although the Bible tells of many wealthy people who used their material blessings to serve God, there are many more illustrations in Scripture about how prosperity became a stumbling block. As a matter of fact, the Bible generally tends to be skeptical of the use of great wealth by those who have it.

B. *In 1 John 3:17 John was pointedly condemning those who have much but are stingy about sharing with the needy.* If you have no pity, how can you say that you are a reflection of God? How can you say God's love is in you? John implied that this is impossible.

C. *Holding on too tightly may ensure that you will always have possessions, but it will not ensure friendship or God's approval.*

Most churches have benevolence programs—either through their local congregations or through their denomination (or sometimes both). These are usually exhausted early or are funded by token amounts in comparison to needs.

Churches must be judicious in the distribution of benevolence money, clothing, and food, because unfortunately there are those who prey on a church's generosity or gullibility. But we must not let this keep us from doing as much as possible. Jesus did not promise us that people will not take advantage of us; frankly, he said they will try. Nevertheless, we are given this instruction: "Let us not love with words or speech but with actions and in truth" (1 John 3:18 NIV).

II. Gluttony is a sin of sensual gratification.

A. *Gluttony is a gratification of our fleshly appetites.* It is often based on pleasure, amusement, excitement, or comfort. Drugs, alcohol, food, and tobacco are representative of this point. But this point of selfishness to the exclusion of others' needs can also be seen in our use of the world's natural resources. It appears that many Americans believe somehow that it is our divine right to use water for irrigation and industry, oil for heating and fuel, and coal for electricity without regard to future generations or to pollution or to the extinction of parts of God's creation.

B. *I do not doubt that God abhors a godless communism, but I strongly suspect he also hates a greedy capitalism.* In Philippians 3:18–19 Paul wrote, "Many live as enemies of the cross of Christ. Their destiny is destruction, their god is their stomach, and their glory is in their shame" (NIV). Caring for the poor and poverty-stricken should not be entirely the government's responsibility. We are called to share our wealth.

C. *Many new automobiles cost more than some have paid for their houses.* A man told me the other day that he had bought a new car, and it was the first time in his life he had ever paid that much for anything that did not have a lawn or shrubs.

III. Gluttony is the sin of too much without sharing.

A. *Too much, too often, too expensively, too soon is another way to define gluttony.*

Most people in Jesus' day were relatively poor. The average daily wage was one denarii—about sixteen to eighteen cents. A yearly income was equal to about fifty to sixty dollars. In one's adult lifetime, he had only two coats (or outer garments worn for warmth and protection from the elements).

Thus what John the Baptist said in Luke 3:11 has more meaning if you understand how rampant poverty was among his hearers. He admonished, "Anyone who has two shirts should share with the one who has none, and anyone who has food should do the same" (NIV). Please notice that John did not admonish us to give away all that we have. He simply commanded us to share part of our prosperity.

B. *James, the half brother of Jesus, wrote in his epistle a similar thought:* "Suppose a brother or a sister is without clothes and daily food. If one of you says to them, 'Go in peace; keep warm and well fed,' but does nothing about their physical needs, what good is it?" (2:15–16 NIV).

The implied answer to James' question is, "Nothing! It is no good! It is useless!" Having a lot or too much is not a sin. But having a lot or too much and not sharing is a sin.

Conclusion

Gluttony is not a sin we hear much about these days. Some would categorize preaching and Bible teaching about gluttony as meddling rather than gospel preaching. But most of the prophets and the followers of Jesus had a lot to say about gluttony. The Lord himself warned his followers not to be anxious about food and clothing but to seek first God's kingdom (Matt. 6:25–34).

SUNDAY EVENING, AUGUST 6

Title: As I Had Mercy on Thee

Text: "'Blessed are the merciful: for they shall obtain mercy'" **(Matt. 5:7)**.

Scripture Reading: Matthew 18:21–35

Introduction

The parable of the unmerciful servant illustrates in reverse the truth of the beatitude "Blessed are the merciful: for they shall obtain mercy." To the debtor to whom the king would have forgiven all of his enormous debt, had he in turn been willing to forgive his fellow servant a paltry sum, the king said, "I forgave thee all that debt, because thou besoughtest me; shouldest not thou also have had mercy on thy fellow-servant, even as I had mercy on thee?" (Matt. 18:32–33 ASV).

"Even as I had mercy on thee"—that is the moral of this parable; and in substance it may be phrased like this: "Woe unto the unmerciful: for they shall not receive the mercy of God"—exactly the reverse of tonight's beatitude. This is a law of the moral realm that never fails and for which there is no appeal. It is an absolute in the kingdom of God. If God's mercy has not awakened in our hearts some sense of mercy toward our fellow humans, we should not deceive ourselves by thinking that we have received God's mercy, for we haven't.

"Blessed are the merciful: for they shall obtain mercy." Three things about this beatitude demand our attention. Each can be stated in one word.

I. Mercy's explanation.

Remember that in these beatitudes Jesus is not speaking of seven different individuals; rather, he is describing seven qualities of excellence he desires in one person. But before Jesus commended these qualities to others, he exhibited them himself. His own life is the best commentary on them. In him all of the strength and tenderness, all of the patience, longsuffering, and compassion, all of the love of a God of love was illustrated before human eyes in his gracious life for our example and in his atoning death for our redemption.

A. *Christ was longsuffering with error, patient with failure, and kind with stupidity.* How thankful we ought to be for that. He was gracious and generous in his appraisal of people who were sincere. Andrew brought his brother Simon to Jesus. Looking past the rough qualities, the impetuousness of the man as he was, Jesus spoke of him as he would become: "Thou art Simon the son of John: thou shalt be called Cephas (which is by interpretation, Peter)" (John 1:42 ASV). To be kind, generous, and gracious in our appraisal of our fellow humans, to look for the best rather than the worst—this is merciful.

B. *Christ was forgiving in spirit toward those who wronged him and sinned against him.* His great love for sinners overflowed in free pardon and forgiveness. On the cross, he prayed for forgiveness for those who crucified him, pleading, "They know not what they do" (Luke 23:34). The only hindrance to Christ's forgiving love was in the refusal on the part of sinners to receive it. This is mercy—the forgiving spirit that longs to restore the fallen to their place.

C. *Christ was compassionate in heart and deed toward all those who needed the care of "the great shepherd of the sheep" (Heb. 13:20).* Jesus' heart went out in deeds of love toward the suffering, the sorrowing, the needy, the distressed, the bereaved. He was moved with compassion for the unloved, leaderless multitudes, "distressed and scattered, as sheep not having a shepherd" (Matt. 9:36 ASV). He helped them because he loved them. Peter's benediction on his life was that he "went about doing good" (Acts 10:38). He had mercy on the sick, the lame, the blind. His word to his followers was, "Heal the sick, raise the dead, cleanse the lepers, cast out demons: freely ye received, freely give" (Matt. 10:8 ASV). Mercy is Christlikeness.

II. Mercy's demonstration.

Who are the merciful? Not those who can shed oceans of tears about the sins and woes of the world without ever harnessing their emotions to concrete action. Some who think they exhibit the quality of mercy are like Lincoln's steamboat, which had a four-foot boiler and a six-foot whistle; every time it blew the whistle, it had to pull over to the riverbank and get up steam again. They talk a lot, but by the time they get through blowing their whistle, they have no steam left to make progress against the world's woes. Being sentimental is not being merciful.

To be merciful is to exhibit, to some degree at least, the mind and spirit of Christ in this hard and loveless world that knows so little of him and has so little of his spirit. We are to do this not for our own glory or reward but for his sake and for his glory, that the world may come to know him.

A. *If we are merciful, as Christ was merciful, we will exhibit the generosity of his judgments of others.* Like Christ, we will search for the best, not the worst, in our fellow humans. Like our Master, we will be slow to condemn and quick to commend our brother, and this not out of a sense of duty but as the natural expression of a loving heart.

B. *If we are merciful, as Christ was merciful, we will exhibit his spirit of forgiveness.* We will be forgiving in spirit, refusing to hold a grudge, casting hate—by the Spirit's power—out of our hearts, blessing those who curse us and praying for those who persecute us. How we need the compassion of Christ to flood our unfeeling hearts and to send us out to give and forgive and serve for his sake.

C. *If we are merciful, as Christ was merciful, we will give ourselves for a world's need as he did.* Is there any spark of his love for a lost and dying world in our hearts? Are any of the tender mercies and compassion of Christ in us at all? Mercy is to have its demonstration in the minds and hearts and deeds of those who have received God's mercy and grace freely shed abroad in their hearts.

III. Mercy's benediction.

"Blessed are the merciful." What is the benediction pronounced on the merciful? "They shall obtain mercy." The blessing on the merciful is that they shall receive in the same manner in which they give. This is a self-acting law of the moral realm. It never fails. The certainty of that blessing is based on the reciprocal law of life that Jesus stated so often, a law more dependable than the law of gravity.

It is true of general experience that persecution never produces tolerance, nor hate love, nor cruelty kindness. Life will pay off in like coin. As we give, we get. As we sow, we reap. This holds true in an infinitely higher sense. As between God and man, the merciful obtain mercy.

A. *To be like Christ in his judgments is to claim this blessing.* To be gracious, generous, seeking and thinking the best—what if we are like that in our judgments? Jesus said, "For with what judgment ye judge, ye shall be judged: and with what measure ye mete, it shall be measured unto you" (Matt. 7:2 ASV). James told us, "For judgment is without mercy to him that showeth no mercy: mercy glorieth against judgment" (2:13 ASV).

B. *To be like Christ in his forgiving spirit is to claim this blessing.* To have an unforgiving spirit is to forfeit the same. Jesus said, "For if ye forgive men their trespasses, your heavenly Father will also forgive you. But if ye forgive not men their trespasses, neither will your Father forgive your trespasses" (Matt. 6:14–15). One of the petitions of the Lord's Prayer is: "And forgive us our debts, as we also have forgiven our debtors" (6:12 ASV). The unforgiving heart cannot receive forgiveness, nor the unmerciful, mercy.

C. *To be like Christ in deeds of compassion is to claim the blessing.* In the story of the good Samaritan, Jesus answered the question, "Who is my neighbor?" When he had completed the story and asked, "Which of these three, thinkest thou, proved neighbor unto him that fell among the robbers?" his questioner was compelled to reply, "He that showed mercy on him" (Luke 10:36–37 ASV).

Conclusion

In that picture of judgment in Matthew 25, to whom did Jesus say, "Come, ye blessed of my Father, inherit the kingdom prepared for you from the foundation of the world" (v. 34)? He said this to those who had exhibited mercy in their lives. To whom did he say, "Depart from me, ye cursed, into the eternal fire" (v. 41)? He said this to those who showed no mercy.

Wednesday Evening, August 9

Title: The Prayers of the Psalmist

Text: "Thou art my portion, O Lord: I have said that I would keep thy words" (Ps. 119:57).

Scripture Reading: Psalm 119:57–64

Introduction

We continue our study of Psalm 119, the longest of the Psalms and one arranged in an acrostic comprised of twenty-two stanzas, each of which uses and emphasizes one of the letters of the Hebrew alphabet. It is a poem that exalts the law, the testimonies, the ways, the precepts, the statutes, the commandments, the words, and the promises of God. As we read the psalmist's words, we'll find ourselves saying, "Amen and amen."

I. Prayer and positive self-esteem (Ps. 119:57).

The psalmist rejoiced as he took a spiritual inventory and recognized that God was his greatest and dearest possession. The Revised Standard Version of the Bible says, "The Lord is my portion," while the King James Version is more personal and says, "Thou art my portion." The New International Version also personalizes it: "You are my portion, Lord." As the psalmist talked to God, recognizing that he belonged to God and that God was committed to him, he was spiritually enriched and felt better about himself.

II. Prayer and sincerity (Ps. 119:58).

"I entreated thy favour with my whole heart" (v. 58). The New International Version translates it, "I have sought your face with all my heart; be gracious to me according to your promise." Faith and sincerity are essential if we would pray effectively.

III. Prayer and God's promises (Ps. 119:58).

"Be merciful unto me according to thy word" was the petition offered by the heart of the psalmist (v. 58). The Revised Standard Version translates it, "Be gracious to me according to thy promise." The psalmist was in the habit of clinging to and claiming the promises of God when he prayed. This is a habit we, too, should form.

IV. Prayer and repentance (119:59).

Repentance is not just the beginning point of the life of faith and discipleship. The life of faith is to be characterized by continuous repentance. The psalmist said it in beautiful words: "I thought on my ways, and turned my feet unto thy testimonies" (KJV). The New International Version translates this, "I have considered my ways and have turned my steps to your statutes." Each time we pray, we are to search our hearts and let God help us so that we might turn from evil.

V. Prayer and praise to God (Ps. 119:62).

Most of us think of thanking God and praising him when prosperity comes. Some of us think of praising and thanking him when we go to church. In this verse the psalmist tells us that midnight is a good time to arise and give thanks to the Lord for all of his righteous judgments.

The psalmist suggests that when we have difficulty getting to sleep, we can thank God for the many blessings he has bestowed upon us and praise him for his goodness to us. This might help us to relax and get a better night's sleep.

VI. Prayer and the recognition of God's love (Ps. 119:64).

The psalmist was rejoicing that the earth was full of God's mercy and steadfast, never-failing, never-ending love. This is a truth that all of us need to recognize and respond to positively.

The closing line in this stanza of this great acrostic poem closes with words of petition: "Teach me thy statutes." To these prayers of the psalmist, let each of us say, "Amen and Amen."

SUNDAY MORNING, AUGUST 13

Title: The Sixth Deadly Sin: Slothfulness

Text: "'The one who is unwilling to work shall not eat'" **(2 Thess. 3:10 NIV).**

Scripture Reading: 2 Thessalonians 3:6–10

Hymns: "Love Divine, All Loves Excelling," Wesley
"At Calvary," Newell
"Love Lifted Me," Rowe

Offertory Prayer: Our loving heavenly Father, we thank you for the warmth of the sunlight, for the refreshing breezes that blow, and for the beauty of the world in which we live. We thank you for life, for health, and for friends. We thank you for your grace and mercy toward us, which you have revealed in Jesus Christ. Today we bring tithes and offerings to you because we want others to experience your love. Bless these gifts to the proclaiming of the good news around the world. Bless these offerings toward the relief of suffering. Bless these offerings for the coming of your kingdom in the hearts of people. In the name of our Lord we pray. Amen.

Introduction

Slothfulness is not a common word today. We use other words to describe the attitude of slothfulness, such as *idleness*, *listlessness*, *apathy*, *indifference*, *goofing off, wasting time, sluggishness, procrastination,* and *laziness.* Actually, there are even more synonyms and adjectives that describe this human condition, but the listener should understand the breadth of the problem by this meager listing.

The sloth is a lethargic animal with coarse hair. It builds no nest or home, sleeps eighteen hours a day, and wakes very slowly. The sloth is so inactive that a green algae grows in its hair. Some humans imitate the sloth. Slothfulness permeates schoolwork, the marketplace, the home, friendships, and Christianity. Almost no area—except leisure—seems to be immune. Laziness is soundly condemned in the Bible. Proverbs 21:25 says, "The craving of a sluggard will be the death of him because his hands refuse to work" (NIV).

Our text is very explicit: "If a man will not work, he shall not eat."

I. Laziness is the neglect of duty.

A. *Slothfulness is really a sin against ourselves as much as it is a sin against society.* It shows the difference between the person you are and the person you could be.

Paul's letter to the people at Thessalonica indicates that while he was with them, he and his companions did work. They accepted no gifts of food or other things without paying for them. Indeed, they worked "night and day" to keep from being a financial drain on anyone and to be a model for them (2 Thess. 3:8–9).

B. *God expects us to work.* It is our duty. When God put Adam in the garden of Eden, he charged him to work and care for the garden (Gen. 2:15). Work is not punishment for Adam's sin; work is the privilege of man to serve God.

Laziness is the opposite of God's plan for humankind. Children should learn minor chores that prepare them for major responsibilities later. Husbands and wives are to work at their marriage, at being parents, and at their jobs. A wife's job may be to serve as a homemaker. If both spouses work outside the home, household chores should be shared.

C. *To do less is to neglect your duties.* Some are too lazy to care. Some children are allowed to practice sloppiness at home because it is easier for parents to leave them alone than to correct and teach them. As they grow into adulthood, they carry their laziness with them.

II. Laziness is a violation of Christian living.

A. *Some might ask, "How can doing nothing be a sin?"* In theology there are basically two kinds of sins: sins of commission and sins of omission. Sins of commission are the sins we commit; sins of omission are the things we know to do yet do not do.

In the parable of the talents, the servant who hid his talent in the ground was chastised because he did nothing with his talent. In fact, the master said, "Throw that worthless servant outside, into the darkness, where there will be weeping and gnashing of teeth" (Matt. 25:30 NIV). Likewise, those who do absolutely nothing about their salvation will be lost.

B. *Some Christians are slothful in their prayer life, Bible study, church attendance, witnessing, financial support, and Christian service.* The reason our world does not have an effective Christian witness can be directly traced to laziness and inactivity by Christians throughout Christian history. We do not work as hard as we should to live as Christian examples.

C. *Christians should be preparing for Jesus' return.* Five of the ten virgins failed to prepare for the return of the bridegroom because of laziness (Matt. 25:1–13). Whatever else this parable may mean, it demonstrates that the Lord is going to come again, and we as Christians must prepare for his return.

III. Laziness is a threat to God's plan.

A. *God does not intend for a person to be idle.* The author of Proverbs draws on nature to illustrate God's plan for man. In Proverbs 6:6–11 he graphically draws the analogy of the ant as a picture of how diligent one should be about living. The ant has no commander, overseer, or ruler per se, but still he knows to work. He works because unless he works he will perish. He works hard in summer in order to enjoy the fruit of his labor in winter.

B. *Humankind must do the same.* God never intended for other humans to support the lazy. Welfare programs are wonderful for the disabled, infirm, and unfortunate in society. Many souls are severely limited by physical, emotional, and mental handicaps that prevent them from working side by side with the healthy and able-bodied. But social programs that encourage one who is not disabled or mentally incompetent to remain unemployed should be eliminated. Such programs build resentment among people that spills over against the deserving. To reward laziness is a sin.

Conclusion

Slothfulness is found in the workplace, schools, churches, and government offices. Every Christian should do his or her best at all times. We should labor as though God were our employer (Eph. 6:5–8).

Jesus Christ has commanded us to be an active and effective witness for him. To do less is wrong. If you want to have the joy of solid biblical living, you must obey the commands of Christ.

If you are not a Christian, I challenge you to serve and accept the only one who can bring joy to your work.

Sunday Evening, August 13

Title: The Hill of the Lord

Text: "'Blessed are the pure in heart: for they shall see God'" **(Matt. 5:8)**.

Scripture Reading: Psalm 24:1–10

Introduction

Psalm 24 is often given the title "The Hill of the Lord," because the verses containing this expression form its very heart (vv. 3–5). The question "Who shall ascend into the hill of the Lord?" (v. 3) is equivalent to asking, "What is true religion?" The psalmist answers, "He that hath clean hands, and a pure heart" (v. 4).

True religion is more than a matter of having clean hands; it is first of all a matter of a pure heart. True religion is not a matter of deeds or observances or worship at all, except as these outward appearances, which are seen, are a sincere expression of a pure heart within. If the heart is pure in the sense Jesus wants it to be pure, the rest will take care of itself. Mixing our two Scripture passages, we might paraphrase our beatitude thus: "Blessed are the pure in heart: for they shall ascend into the hill of the Lord, and stand in his holy place; they shall receive the blessing fresh from the Lord himself."

A. *How complimentary this beatitude is to humankind: "for they shall see God."* Created as humans are, in the image of God, they have the faculty of spiritual sight (Eph. 1:18). They can see God.
B. *How beautifully this beatitude expresses the deepest longing of the human heart: "for they shall see God."* The desire to see God, to look upon his face, is a longing as old as man yet as contemporary as physical hunger. Throughout the ages, humans have cried out with Job, "Oh, that I knew where I might find him! that I might come even to his seat!" (Job 23:3). And the better a person comes to know God, the deeper this yearning becomes.
C. *How truly this beatitude tells us our deepest need: "for they shall see God."* Spiritual blindness is a great tragedy in our world. Sin and self-seeking, lust and pride, have put cataracts over "the eyes of the heart"; and our world cannot see God. But the blessing is available to all who will look. "Blessed are the pure in heart: for they shall see God."

The sixth beatitude brings us face-to-face with the nature and the demands of true religion, which is first of all a matter of the heart. Four questions demand an answer if Jesus' words are to mean anything to us.

I. What is the purity of heart of which Jesus speaks?

It is important to heed exactly what Jesus said.

A. *Jesus did not say, "Blessed are the pure."* That would have gone straight into our minds with an exact meaning, and many have so understood this beatitude. But Jesus did not say, "Blessed are the pure." Neither did he simply make a parallel statement of the seventh commandment: "Thou shalt not commit adultery" (Ex. 20:14). Purity in our relationships with others is only one of the fruits of a pure heart.

B. *Jesus did not say, "Blessed are the perfect."* That would have ruled out all of us, and this beatitude would not touch our lives at all. It is true that perfection is the only standard worthy of Jesus, and that he did say, "Ye therefore shall be perfect, as your heavenly Father is perfect" (Matt. 5:48 ASV). But he did not say that we shall never be happy this side of perfection.

C. *Jesus did say, "Blessed are the pure in heart: for they shall see God."* Pure here means unmixed, without alloy, unadulterated. To speak of your watch as a "gold watch" is not technically correct. The case is probably ten-karat gold, which means that it is alloyed with another harder metal to give it better wearing qualities. The pure heart, however, is a single heart, a heart devoted to the purposes of God. According to Jesus' meaning, a pure heart is an unmixed heart, unadulterated, with no cross-purposes, no crosscurrents in loyalty, no reservations in devotion. There is no true happiness for the one who says, "I will follow you, Lord; but first . . ." (Luke 9:61 NIV).

II. How may we attain to the purity of heart of which Jesus speaks?

Purity of heart, in the sense Jesus had in mind, is attainable for all Christians who desire it with all their hearts. This beatitude is not only for some aged saint in the late winter of life, nor simply for some exalted servant or prophet of God, some choice soul here and there. Purity of heart is a prize of supreme worth within the reach of every heart willing to receive it. But how do we attain it?

A. *By surrender.* A surrender to Christ, full and entire, brings the cleansing power of God's forgiveness flooding the heart to cleanse and purify. An Old Testament beatitude throws light on this beatitude of Jesus. Out of his experience, the psalmist cries, "Blessed is he whose transgression is forgiven, whose sin is covered" (Ps. 32:1). This beatitude is not for the sinless but for forgiven sinners, not for the perfect but for the purified in heart. No sinner is excluded in the sweep of its possibilities. "Wash and make yourselves clean," God said through the Old Testament prophet (Isa. 1:16 NIV), and he continued, "Come now, let us settle the matter. Though your sins are like scarlet, they shall be as white as snow; though they are red as crimson, they shall be like wool" (1:18 NIV).

How do we become pure in heart? By a full surrender to Christ to be cleansed by his power. But that isn't all of the answer.

B. *By a complete consecration of the life to God.* Not all Christians are pure in heart. Too many are borderline Christians; and like the Israelites settling in the promised land, many of us stop before we drive out all our enemies. The pure in heart must drive out every alien thought and purpose to give Christ full possession. Too many of us have mixed motives and desires. Our hearts need to be single, set on him and on him alone. To such is the vision promised.

III. What blessing does Jesus pronounce upon the pure in heart?

"Blessed are the pure in heart: for they shall see God." In this, the highest faculties of human nature are exercised; the deepest yearnings of the soul are gratified; the most compelling needs of the human heart are met.

What is the blessing for a heart pure before God, a heart unmixed, without alloy, unadulterated by love for the world, and single to his service? "They shall see God," Jesus said. They shall see him now; they shall see him in hours of worship in God's house; they shall see him in the circle of family worship; they shall see him in holy hours of private prayer and meditation on his Word. Behind the dark background of the world's confusion and misery, they shall see God as the one, single, sovereign, unifying purpose in the world and in history.

The promise is that one day the pure in heart shall look upon Jesus, not by implication, not indirectly, not "through a glass, darkly" (1 Cor. 13:12), but face-to-face.

IV. What are the abiding results in human personality of this vision of God?

A. *This vision of God causes us to see the unseen resources of God.* Paul saw Jesus on the Damascus road and found the strength to carry him through every trial. In his death agony, Stephen saw "the Son of Man standing at the right hand of God" (Acts 7:56 NIV). This gave him the martyr's courage to die for Christ. Of Moses, the writer of Hebrews said, "For he endured, as seeing him who is invisible" (11:27). Think of all Moses endured. How steadfast he was! How courageous! How dauntless! What was his secret? "He endured, as seeing him who is invisible."

B. *This vision of God causes us to see the infinite needs of humankind and gives us a sense of personal obligation.* Having seen the infinite resources of God and the infinite needs of the world, this vision causes us to see that we are to be used to bring the two together. Moses, Isaiah, and

Paul each saw the resources and the need, and each volunteered. The vision of God that does not send us out to serve is a spurious vision.

C. *This vision of God causes us to see what will one day be the consummation of the Christian life and undergirds our lives with hope.* Paul told the Corinthians, "For now we see through a glass, darkly; but then face to face" (1 Cor. 13:12). John promised those to whom he wrote, "We shall be like him; for we shall see him as he is" (1 John 3:2).

Conclusion

What a blessed hope we have! In the day when Christ returns, our hope will be fulfilled.

WEDNESDAY EVENING, AUGUST 16

Title: The Prayer of a Depressed Saint

Text: "How long, O Lord? Wilt thou forget me for ever? How long wilt thou hide thy face from me?" **(Ps. 13:1 RSV)**.

Scripture Reading: Psalm 13:1–6

Introduction

The Psalms present a record of the life of God's people in all of its dimensions. In the Psalms, we find high worship experiences in which praise is being offered to God, but we also find sorrow and grief. We find perplexing questions and expressions of faith. But we also find expressions of despair. Psalm 13, for instance, presents the prayer of a man in deep depression.

Today we know that depression may be the result of many different factors. Some people have a tendency toward depression because of heredity factors. Others experience deep depression because of a chemical imbalance. One may go into depression because of mistreatment by someone near and dear. One may also experience depression because of a negative way of thinking. Depression is often the result of weariness and physical collapse. Some experience deep depression because of their utter helplessness. Depression often accompanies illness. Others experience depression as death approaches. All of us experience some depression because of impatience. Divine chastisement is also a cause for depression. Maybe this was the reason David was depressed and gave voice to this psalm.

I. A prayer during a time of depression (Ps. 13:1–2).

A. *Have you ever prayed to God when it seemed as if he had forgotten you (v. 1)?* Does God really forget his children?

B. *Have you ever prayed when it seemed as if God had turned his face away from you (v. 1)?*

C. *The psalmist was depressed by the length of the suffering he was experiencing in his soul (v. 2).*
D. *The psalmist was so depressed that he experienced sorrow in his heart throughout the day (v. 2).*
E. *The psalmist was depressed because of the victory of his enemy over him (v. 2).* Many have experienced depression because of the victory of Satan over them.

II. A cry for help while in a state of depression (Ps. 13:3–4).

It is exceedingly difficult to pray effectively when one is in the depths of despair, suffering the pains of depression. Nevertheless, one may need to pray a prayer of confession and ask for cleansing. The psalmist continued to pray even in his despair. In times like these, we need to study God's Word and recognize our relationship to him and continue to come before him as needy children (Heb. 4:16).

III. The faith of the psalmist in depression (Ps. 13:5–6).

A. *The psalmist was able to continue to trust in the steadfast love of God (v. 5).* Many times a person suffering depression finds it impossible to believe that God continues to love him or her.
B. *The psalmist had faith to believe that he would yet rejoice in the great salvation of God (v. 5).* Perhaps the psalmist had this assurance because he believed that God would forgive him and cleanse him.
C. *The psalmist decided to sing unto the Lord because he was confident that God would deal bountifully and graciously with him (v. 6).*

Conclusion

Depression in one form or another will be the experience of all of us somewhere along the road of life. Depression must be dealt with or one will live a life of misery.

God is good. He loves us. He works for good in everything that life brings to us (Rom. 8:28). If our depression is due to the discipline of our heavenly Father, let us rejoice rather than give way to discouragement. Let us look up because something good is going to happen (Heb. 12:5–13).

SUNDAY MORNING, AUGUST 20

Title: The Seventh Deadly Sin: Avarice

Text: "Then he said to them, 'Watch out! Be on your guard against all kinds of greed; life does not consist in an abundance of possessions'" **(Luke 12:15 NIV).**

Scripture Reading: Luke 12:15–21

Hymns: "Come, Thou Almighty King," Anonymous
"He Leadeth Me! O Blessed Tho't!" Gilmore
"Have Thine Own Way, Lord," Pollard

Offertory Prayer: Holy Father, it is impossible for us to express our thanks adequately for the abundance of your blessings upon us. You are so gracious to grant us the privilege of being your children. We thank you for the gift of eternal life. We also thank you for all the material gifts you provide in the world about us. We make our gratitude tangible by bringing tithes and offerings to your altar. Bless the use of these gifts in communicating the wonders of your love and the measure of your mercy. Bless them to the relief of human suffering and to the enrichment of the human spirit, and may your name be honored and glorified in it all. Amen.

Introduction

Avarice is much like the word *slothfulness* we had last week. It is not a word we use very often today. Instead, we use the word *greed.*

Avarice is the last of the seven deadly sins, and it is also related to the last sin listed among the Ten Commandments: "You shall not covet" (Ex. 20:17 NIV). Coveting is the beginning of greed, the inordinate desire to grasp and possess material goods. It can lead to deceit, theft, envy, jealousy, murder, war, and selfishness.

"The Midas touch" has become a desirable virtue rather than a detestable and seriously sad sin. Many wish they had the "Midas touch." Forgetting the fable that was composed to teach the folly of greed, some Christians are hooked on materialism. It has become an obsession to gain more expensive possessions to add to or replace other possessions.

Jacob wanted Esau's birthright; Ahab wanted Naboth's vineyard; Judas sold Jesus for thirty pieces of silver; and Ananias and Sapphira held back land because of greed.

In our text for today, we read Jesus' words from the introduction to the familiar parable of the rich fool who tore down his barns to build bigger ones—all because of greed.

I. Greed usually means someone else must suffer.

A. *Whatever it takes to make a dollar becomes all right.* Greed is based on expediency. A criminal who traffics in illegal drugs believes only in caring for himself and his own comfort. He does not care about the lives that are destroyed or the thievery it takes for a junkie to maintain his habit.

People who sell alcohol seldom show concern for traffic victims, broken homes, battered wives and children, or alcohol-related crimes.

B. *Car thefts, burglaries, embezzlement, assaults, shoplifting, robbery, and most murders have their origin in greed.* All of these crimes cause someone else to suffer.

Gambling is also based on greed. To their shame, some professing Christians flock to gambling centers—casinos, race tracks, tourist areas, county or state fairs—or gamble online, hoping to gain more with little effort.

C. *Suffering is caused by cheating, lying, and the deceit involved in practicing greed.* Confidence games are played on the elderly every year. Police departments report a growing number of older or more trusting Americans being taken in by con men.

II. Greed is a quest for more than just necessities.

A. *There are at least five items we need in order to live a reasonably happy life.* They are food, clothing, shelter, medical care, and a means to get enough money to purchase the first four. Having the best-tasting food, the finest clothes, the nicest home, and the most expensive medical specialist is not necessary for living a full and happy life.

B. *Advertising creates desires for things we don't need.* The sleekest sports car is hardly a necessity. Jewelry, electronic equipment, sporting equipment, recreational vehicles, and brand-name clothes can all become traps of greediness.

Jesus said in our text that "a man's life does not consist in the abundance of his possessions" (Luke 12:15). Most of us—preachers included—believe he was speaking to others and not to us.

III. Greed is a sophisticated form of idolatry.

A. *Most Christians would destroy a man-made figure of some god that was worshiped by a member of their family.* We do not believe in idolatry. Yet greed is a man-made god that commands our money, time, and even that we sacrifice our families to it.

Some people will eventually give up friends, parents, spouses, church, and Jesus Christ in the pursuit of possessions. Parents allow youth to take jobs that require them to work on Sunday and thus miss church. A father will work on Saturday, Sunday, and late nights to have extra money for Christmas—the birth celebration of Jesus—and will thus neglect his children and spouse. Some wives will push their husbands to earn money in order for them to keep up with friends or their own selfish goals. Amos the prophet condemned wives who pushed their husbands toward greed (Amos 4:1).

B. *Credit debt is out of hand.* Many Christians are deeply in debt. Credit card debt has put these people of God on an endless treadmill. Likewise, some churches are so deeply in debt that they cannot provide enough money for necessary programs, missionary giving, or evangelistic thrusts.

Conclusion

The seven deadly sins rob us of the "good life." At first they each seem to offer us a good and abundant life, but they are subtle satanic lies that will destroy us. The good life is found only in Christ. God does not condemn these seven attitudes because he wants to spoil our fun. He forbids pride, anger, envy, impurity, gluttony, slothfulness, and avarice because these pursuits destroy life.

Let us return to God. Let us lay aside these sins that so easily beset us, and let us return to the teachings of Jesus Christ. Will you turn to Jesus and receive the rich, full life he intended for you?

SUNDAY EVENING, AUGUST 20

Title: The Children of God

Text: "'Blessed are the peacemakers: for they shall be called the children of God'" **(Matt. 5:9)**.

Scripture Reading: 1 John 3:1–10

Introduction

No work is more in imitation of God's work than that of making peace, for God is a "God of peace." No one is more clearly demonstrated to be a child of God than the peacemaker, the person who by his or her own character, example, and testimony is a reconciling influence in the world.

"Blessed are the peacemakers." How strange these words sound in our world today. For two thousand years people have been honoring these words of Jesus with their lips while their hearts have been far from him. By our lives, our actions, and our words, we have said, "Blessed are the sowers of discord, the fomenters of strife." But, to paraphrase, Jesus said, "Blessed are the peacemakers: for they are, they shall be called, they are acting like the children of God." All of those described in Jesus' beatitudes are the children of God, for Jesus is describing seven facets of one character. Yet nothing demonstrates more clearly the character of Christ and the nature of God than the effort to make peace.

Three observations will set forth the truth of this seventh beatitude.

I. The need for peacemakers.

Why are peacemakers needed so desperately in our time?

A. *Because of the enmity and strife on every hand.*

1. Enmity exists between man and God. This strife is as old as the human race and dates back to the garden of Eden. Because of sin, man became separated from God and became God's enemy. Our enemies fall into three classifications: enemies according to

the natural order, enemies by virtue of certain relationships that exist, and enemies because of the acts and words of our lives. Until we are reconciled to God through Christ, his Son, we are enemies of God on all three scores.

2. Enmity exists between man and his higher nature. When a man is reconciled to God, civil war exists within his own soul, and his heart is a house divided against itself. In *The History of Mr. Polly*, H. G. Wells said of one of his characters, "He was not so much a human being as a civil war." This is true of every person before he or she is reconciled to God.
3. Enmity exists between humans. People glare at and fight one another as individuals. Group rises up against group, race hates race, and nations make war against one another. Oh, the need for peacemakers!

B. *Because enmity and strife are so costly.*

1. Think of the cost of a person's being unreconciled to God. Jesus tells us plainly, "Except ye repent, ye shall all likewise perish" (Luke 13:3). Enmity against God is the source of all wretchedness. A personality divided against itself is unhappy and ineffective, and it means eternal death in the end.
2. Think of the cost of hatred and strife between people. Hatred works havoc to the hated and more seriously damages the one who hates. Many a church has had its work all but nullified by the petty but bitter hatred of a few. How infinite is the cost of hatred between nations. No good can come out of war, and its cost is beyond calculation. Peacemakers are needed in all these areas.

C. *Because someone must take the initiative.* This is true if enmity and strife are ever to cease, if enemies are ever to be reconciled. The heart of the gospel is that "all things are of God who reconciled us to himself through Christ" and that "God was in Christ, reconciling the world unto himself" (2 Cor. 5:18–19 ASV). God took the initiative that we might be at peace with him.

Christ is the great peacemaker in our hearts, because, as Paul said, "He is our peace" (Eph. 2:14). He keeps in perfect peace those whose hearts steadfastly trust God (Isa. 26:3).

II. The identity of the peacemakers.

A. *Negatively.*

1. Peacemakers are not passive bystanders who in a cowardly fashion leave things alone or give in to wrong and injustice. Peacemaking does not necessarily mean one will live a quiet life. On the contrary, peacemakers are often activists. One may let the other guy have his way because he is bigger or shouts louder. This may seem prudent, but it is hardly peacemaking. The peace-at-any-price

people who cry, "Peace! Peace!" when there is no peace may be the real foes of peacemaking.

2. Peacemakers are not meddlers. Many times people think they are making peace when they are just sticking a finger into somebody else's pie, meddling in some quarrel that is really none of their affair. Peacemaking is often thought of as intervening in a quarrel; it ought to mean preventing a quarrel from arising in the first place.
3. Peacemakers are not indifferent. The peace of indifference is counterfeit. Some couldn't care less that there are millions of homeless refugees and displaced persons in the world. Some take for granted the need of the sick and lonely around them just as the rich man in Jesus' story accepted the beggar Lazarus as a part of the street scenery. From his self-contained vantage point of plenty, he simply ignored him. His was a peace of soul that was dead like the peace of a stagnant pool with green scum on top.
4. Peacemakers are not compromisers. A formula of compromise may end a controversy, but compromise is not peace. Jesus never accepted any terms of compromise or agreed to any truce in the warfare for truth and righteousness.

B. *Positively.*

1. Peacemakers are those whose work is grounded in the reconciling work of Christ. Isaiah prophesied that he would be the "Prince of Peace" (9:6). At his birth, angels sang, "Glory to God in the highest, and on earth peace" (Luke 2:14). He lived as a man of peace. He spoke of his own peace, which he would bestow upon humans (John 14:27). He went to the cross to pay the price of peace. Well did the prophet say centuries before, "The chastisement of our peace was upon him" (Isa. 53:5). And in retrospect Paul said that Christ "made peace through the blood of his cross" (Col. 1:20).
2. Peacemakers are those whose work stems out of an experience whereby the peace of God, in Christ, has become effective in their own lives. Listen to Paul: "Therefore being justified by faith, we have peace with God through our Lord Jesus Christ" (Rom. 5:1). No man can be a peacemaker, either between God and man or between man and man unless he is first at peace with God himself.
3. Peacemakers are those whose work finds its imperative and authority in a divine commission. In 2 Corinthians 5 Paul speaks of God, "who reconciled us to himself through Christ and gave us the ministry of reconciliation" (v. 18 NIV). He goes on to say, "He has committed to us the message of reconciliation" (v. 19 NIV). In the next verse, he states the business of a Christian: "We are therefore Christ's ambassadors, as though God were

making his appeal through us" (v. 20 NIV). After the close of World War II, one of America's top executives said, "We have been making the implements of war in great abundance and in great perfection; but the tools of war are not my company's real business. Peace is our business." Let every Christian say, "Peace is our business."

4. Peacemakers are those whose lives exhibit, in some measure at least, the character and likeness of God whose children they are.

III. The blessing pronounced on the peacemakers.

At first glance, this seems the strongest blessing in the list: "For they shall be called the children of God." And when the meaning of those words sinks in, we see that it is also the most wonderful blessing of them all. Two results follow.

A. *The first result is recognition.* Not only are the peacemakers the children of God, but they are recognized as being so. This is not a self-recognition, nor necessarily a recognition by the world—which is more apt to persecute them and call them traitors (Matt. 5:10–11)—but by God himself. In his first epistle, John said, "Behold, what manner of love the Father hath bestowed upon us, that we should be called the children of God" (3:1 ASV). Who calls the peacemakers "children of God"? God does.

B. *The second result is realization.* Peacemakers realize in their own hearts that they are children of God when, by the Spirit's leadership, they are used by him to lead another into peace with God.

Conclusion

A pastor was seeking to win a thirteen-year-old girl to Christ in her home when her mother interfered. The pastor asked that mother, "Are you a Christian?" "Well," she said, "I have a hope." She had five children. Not one of them was a Christian. All were in danger of hell, while she mouthed pious phrases. How could she have known? Had she tried to be a peacemaker between any one of her children and God, and had she succeeded, she could have said, "Now are we children of God, and it is not yet made manifest what we shall be" (1 John 3:2 ASV).

Wednesday Evening, August 23

Title: A Prayer for Divine Correction

Text: "Search me, O God, and know my heart! Try me and know my thoughts! And see if there be any wicked way in me, and lead me in the way everlasting!" **(Ps. 139:23–24 RSV).**

Scripture Reading: Psalm 139:1–12, 23–24

Introduction

A devotional study of the Psalms can be particularly helpful in nourishing our faith and assisting us in our prayer life.

Psalm 139 emphasizes that God has unlimited knowledge (vv. 1-6) and also that God is always and everywhere present (vv. 7–12). This great psalm celebrates the truth that God is our Creator (vv. 13–18). It closes with a prayer against the wicked and a prayer for divine correction as the psalmist faced the present and the future.

I. A prayer for divine probing (Ps. 139:23).

The psalmist was positioning himself on the Physician's examining table and asking him to examine the motives of his heart and the thoughts of his mind. He recognized that the source of actions and conduct is found in the thoughts and emotions of the inward man.

Perhaps David was motivated to pray this prayer for divine probing because he was being severely tested by his enemies. He considered himself to be the enemy of those who were the enemies of God (vv. 19–22). Perhaps he was disturbed by some of his hostile thoughts toward these ungodly enemies of God who were also his enemies.

II. A prayer for divine directions (Ps. 139:24).

The psalmist brought his mind and heart under the searchlight of God's watchful eye, not merely so that he might be informed about himself, but that he might correct his way.

We read in the book of Proverbs, "Every way of man is right in his own eyes" (21:2). We also read, "There is a way which seemeth right unto a man, but the end thereof are the ways of death" (14:12).

God spoke through Isaiah and urged the wicked to forsake his way and the unrighteous man his thoughts (55:7). God spoke further and said, "For my thoughts are not your thoughts, neither are your ways my ways. . . . As the heavens are higher than the earth, so are my ways higher than your ways and my thoughts than your thoughts" (vv. 8–9 NIV).

A person may be quite sincere and yet be thinking the wrong kind of thoughts and walking in the wrong way. The psalmist recognized this truth and urged God to reveal to him whether there was some wicked way within his heart.

The psalmist prayed, "Lead me in the way everlasting." He wanted to forsake any false paths that would lead to the wrong destination. He wanted to be delivered from self-deception. He wanted to be saved from inaccurate thought processes and decision making. He prayed that God would guide him into paths that would be pleasing to God and that would bring peace to his own heart and mind.

Conclusion

How long has it been since you have had a thorough physical examination? How long has it been since you have taken your temperature to see if you had an undetected infection in your body? How long has it been since you looked into your mouth to see if you had a red spot in your throat? These are some of the techniques that are used to detect the presence of infection or illness.

How long has it been since you brought yourself into God's presence for a spiritual examination? It might be a painful experience, but it could be highly profitable.

We would be exceedingly wise if day by day we would pray, "Search me, O God, and know my heart! Try me and know my thoughts! And see if there be any wicked way in me, and lead me in the way everlasting!" (Ps. 139:23–24 RSV).

SUNDAY MORNING, AUGUST 27

Title: The Deliverer from Sin

Text: "Wretched man that I am! Who will deliver me from this body of death? Thanks be to God through Jesus Christ our Lord!" **(Rom. 7:24–25 RSV)**.

Scripture Reading: Romans 8:31–39

Hymns: "O Worship the King," Grant
"Christ Receiveth Sinful Men," Neumeister
"Thou, My Everlasting Portion," Crosby

Offertory Prayer: Loving Father, thank you for the gifts of light and love and life. Thank you for hope and health and all of the help that you have given to us. Thank you for the privilege of being in your house with your people today. As we bring our tithes and offerings, we pray that you will accept them and bless them to the end that your name will be honored and glorified. In Jesus Christ our Lord. Amen.

Introduction

Romans 7 pictures the tragic failure and disappointment of a believer who tries to find peace of heart through human effort to keep the holy law of God. Paul would declare that he who seeks to overcome the seven deadly sins in willpower and human effort alone will experience the despair of one who finds a fatal flaw within that produces repeated failure.

There are two powers that would claim the right to rule in the heart of man. Paul described these as "flesh" and "Spirit." By the term *flesh* he was referring to our human nature, which is defiled by sin. It is that portion of ourselves that remains unregenerate and does not experience the new birth. It is that part of our human nature that provides a bridgehead for sin. It is the inward tendency that we all have to drift downward rather than to move upward.

When Paul spoke of "the Spirit," he was speaking of the indwelling Holy Spirit, who comes to live within the believer at the moment of conversion and makes it possible for the child of God to grow in Christlikeness.

Romans 7 describes the pain and disappointment, the failure and despair of one who tries to live a Christian life without a conscious dependence on Christ and the filling of the Holy Spirit. Yielding to the unregenerate nature described as "flesh" is the road to ruin. Recognizing and responding to "the Spirit" is the road to life and peace.

Romans 8 begins with "no condemnation" and closes with "no separation." The contents of Romans 8 declare that there need be no defeat in the Christian life. However, it should be recognized that Christian victory over the seven deadly sins is not automatic and inevitable. We must accept responsibility for our spiritual response to the indwelling Spirit. Romans 8 contains twenty references to the person and work of the Holy Spirit in the life of the believer. It is through this living, present power of the Holy Spirit that we are to be delivered from the tyranny of sin.

From Romans 7 into Romans 8 we move from the prostration of defeat to the promise of victory. We move from spiritual depression to spiritual delight. We move from a sigh to a song. The indwelling Holy Spirit makes possible spiritual victory and high ethical conduct that reflects the grace and the glory of God.

I. The indwelling Spirit sets us free from the law of sin and death (Rom. 8:1–4).

The Holy Spirit of God liberates us from the law of sin and death and makes it possible for believers to five righteously. When sin would serve as an oppressing tyrant, the Holy Spirit comes in to deliver us with a strength greater than the law as a governing principle had for Old Testament believers.

II. The indwelling Spirit delivers us from the weakness of the flesh (Rom. 8:5–13).

Even after we have come to know Jesus Christ as Savior, we are still plagued by the power of an inward tendency to sin. This is where the devil seeks to do his work in the hearts and lives of believers. Paul was affirming that through the power of the Holy Spirit we can have victory. In his epistle to the Galatians, he affirmed that instead of serving the flesh, we can reap the harvest of the Spirit if we will trust in him and walk in him and obey him (5:16–25).

III. The indwelling Spirit provides leadership for God's children (Rom. 8:14).

The Holy Spirit wants to lead us in thought and word and deed. By faith we are to recognize and obey these divine impulses that could have no source except the heart of a loving God. The Holy Spirit is the creator of a quality of life in which the will of God is loved, accepted, and obeyed.

IV. The indwelling Spirit gives testimony to our divine sonship (Rom. 8:15–17).

The Holy Spirit communicates with the believer that he is now a child of God and a member of the family of God.

As Satan tries to defeat us by tempting us to fall into any of the seven deadly sins, we need to firmly grasp our new relationship with God in order that we might overcome evil and achieve victory.

V. The indwelling Spirit is God's pledge of our final and complete redemption (Rom. 8:18–25).

In Romans 7 Paul described the despair of one who finds it impossible to overcome the seven deadly sins by human strength alone. Here in these verses he told of the glorious expectation and the assurance of the final victory God has provided for those who trust Jesus Christ as Savior. God not only promises us victory over our evil nature in the present, but he promises us final and ultimate and complete redemption beyond history.

VI. The indwelling Spirit aids us in our efforts to pray according to the will of God (Rom. 8:26).

All of us have difficulty praying properly. Paul said that it is the ministry of the Holy Spirit, who wants to deliver us from the seven deadly sins, to aid us in our prayer life.

VII. The indwelling Spirit makes intercession for us according to God's will (Rom. 8:27–28).

No one can overcome the flesh in human strength alone. No one can overcome an evil nature by trying to obey the law. Our help comes from God. The Holy Spirit not only seeks to aid us in our prayer efforts, but Jesus intercedes in heaven for us according to God's will.

Conclusion

Who is to deliver us from the power and presence of sin? Let us thank God that through Jesus Christ and the precious gift of the Holy Spirit we can have deliverance now from the power of sin, and ultimately we will have complete redemption and salvation from the very presence of sin.

SUNDAY EVENING, AUGUST 27

Title: The Forgotten Beatitude

Text: "Remember the words of the Lord Jesus, that he himself said, It is more blessed to give than to receive" **(Acts 20:35 ASV)**.

Scripture Reading: Acts 20:17–35

Introduction

An experienced pastor tells of hearing both the pastor of his college church and the pastor of his seminary church preach a series of sermons on the Beatitudes of Jesus. Neither included this beatitude that Paul preserved for us. Later, in a pastorate of his own, this pastor also preached a series on the Beatitudes, and he did not include this beatitude either. Why not? His testimony was, "I forgot it." Then he added, "I suppose the two pastors I heard and the authors of the six books I read in preparation for my series forgot it also." Ask almost any Christian, even the most careful Bible student, to name the beatitudes of Jesus, and he or she will name those listed in Matthew 5. Not one out of a hundred would name the one given in Acts 20.

Thus it is fair to call Acts 20:35 "the forgotten beatitude."

A. *There is no question as to the authenticity of this beatitude.* That this is a genuine saying of Jesus there can be no doubt. Beyond doubt, this was a current saying of Jesus with which the Ephesian elders were familiar. Moreover, the writer, Luke, who heard Paul's address to these pastors and preserved it, also wrote the gospel that bears his name; and his gospel preserves, in slightly varied form, Jesus' beatitudes (Luke 6:20–23).

B. *There can be no doubt that Jesus demonstrated this beatitude in his life and ministry and death.* Just as surely as he demonstrated meekness, mercy, and purity of heart, so did Jesus demonstrate that "it is more blessed to give than to receive."

C. *There can be no fault found with the form in which this beatitude is given.* Paul prefaces his statement of the beatitude with a twofold caution: "Laboring," he said, "ye ought to help the weak, and to remember the words of the Lord Jesus, that he himself said, It is more blessed to give than to receive." His caution "to remember" is certainly in place for us, for this is the forgotten beatitude.

Let's look at three questions concerning this beatitude.

I. Why is this beatitude the forgotten beatitude?

A. *We have never understood it.* Taken together, the full impact of these words has never hit us as Jesus intended they should. We tread lightly on the first half of this saying and let our minds dwell on the latter half. But Jesus' emphasis is the other way around: "It is more blessed to give than to receive." This turns the normal attitude of the carnal mind upside down. There is a blessedness in receiving, and our Lord does not discount the fact. None of us could live for ten minutes apart from what we receive. It is blessed to receive, but it is more blessed to give.

B. *We have never believed it.* If we doubt that this is the most disbelieved truth in the Word of God, we need but to look first at the average church treasury and after that into the faces of the average congregation when the offering is being received or when the pastor mentions money. Many look upon giving to the church as a necessary nuisance, a bother, a thing to be dreaded. It isn't so at all if our hearts are right. The sense of our text then is this: "It is a far happier experience to give than to receive." And it surely is if our hearts are right with God.

C. *We have never actually tested it.* Oh, a few have! And their testimony tells us that it is the very Word of God. They say, "It is more blessed to give than to receive." Those who love the most give the most. But the majority of Christians cannot testify one way or another. They haven't tried it out!

II. What results from this beatitude's being the forgotten beatitude?

A. *We have missed the main emphasis of Jesus' teachings.* This beatitude stands supreme among all the beatitudes of the Bible. It is the center of the Bible's teaching, the supreme emphasis of Jesus. To give was the purpose of his coming: "The Son of man came not to be ministered unto, but to minister, and to give his life a ransom for many" (Matt. 20:28). Selfishness is self-destructive; giving is redemptive, creative, permanent. We lose what we keep and keep forever what we give to God.

B. *We have missed the greatest joy, the supreme blessing of Christian living.* What is Christian living? It is doing our best to give more than we receive for Christ's sake because we love him and because we love a lost world. What is the Christian philosophy of life? It is believing in and trying to live by this Word of the one who redeemed us: "It is more blessed to give than to receive."

No amount of earthly things can ever satisfy the spiritual part of us that God made to be blessed by giving. The writer of Ecclesiastes said, "He that loveth silver shall not be satisfied with silver; nor he that loveth abundance with increase: this is also vanity" (5:10).

C. *We have failed to take the gospel to the whole world.* Why has the gospel made such slow conquest of the world? Why have missions and evangelism lagged and dragged? It is because preachers have been so timid about preaching the joyous truths of the Bible about giving and because people have been so rebellious and unbelieving when they have presented it.

There is no danger of exaggerating the measure in which this beatitude has been discredited in the world and even by Christ's own people. Selfishness is the dominant note of humanity, the cancer of society, the mud on the chariot wheels of God's army; and selfishness finds its supreme expression in man's attitude toward money. The world believes it is more blessed to get than to give, and therefore for two millennia we have not carried the gospel to all the world.

III. What blessings would follow a wholesale recovery of this beatitude?

A. *Blessings on us as individuals.* "It is more blessed to give than to receive." That is true for each one of us as individuals. We love our Lord because there was no trace of selfishness in him. He gave and gave and gave, and it was his joy to give. The writer of Hebrews said of him, "For the joy set before him he endured the cross, scorning its shame" (12:2 NIV). Jesus demonstrated the truth of this beatitude as he did all the others. We are to be like him.

   When pastors persuade their congregations to give "not grudgingly, or of necessity" (2 Cor. 9:7), but joyfully and liberally, they are doing a real service to their souls.

B. *Blessings on our churches.* Recovering this beatitude would mean that our churches would have the means, the resources, but above all, the spiritual power to attempt to carry out the Great Commission.

   A young seminary graduate was in his first pastorate in a rural setting. Both the church and his salary were small. With three young children, he was having a hard time making ends meet. One kind farmer in his church brought him a fine milk cow and the feed to feed her. "Pastor, milk this cow. She'll give all the milk your children need." Some weeks later, when the farmer asked about the cow, the young pastor replied, "She went dry. I don't know why. We were very careful. We milked only the milk we had to have." That is bad for a cow. It is bad for a church. Because of their failure to give liberally, most of our churches have gone dry spiritually.

C. *Blessings on an unsaved soul.* "It is more blessed to give than to receive." If they would only heed these words, churches would challenge an unsaved world by an exalted testimony and witness. The churches would begin to do the thing they were brought into existence to do. They would start knocking on the doors of the world with the gospel, the world would heed, and some would be saved.

Conclusion

The Beatitudes describe the character traits of a happy Christian, and this one, so often forgotten, is the most joyous of them all.

Wednesday Evening, August 30

Title: A Prayer of Praise and Thanksgiving

Text: "Enter into his gates with thanksgiving, and into his courts with praise: be thankful unto him, and bless his name" **(Ps. 100:4)**.

Scripture Reading: Psalm 100

Introduction

Prayer is first of all an approach to God and not the presentation of a celestial shopping list. We come first to give rather than to take, offer rather than request. The psalmist described the priority of prayer: "Enter into his gates with *thanksgiving*, and into his courts with praise." In prayer we should approach the loving Father with our praise and thanksgiving. This is the picture of true worship found in Revelation. The four living creatures praise the Lord and give "glory and honor and thanks to him." The twenty-four elders "fall down before him . . . and worship him . . . singing, 'Worthy art thou, our Lord and God, to receive glory and honor and power'" (4:9–11).

I. Praise and thanksgiving acknowledge the nature of God.

A. *To pray with praise and thanksgiving is to acknowledge God's holiness and majesty.* Remember he is the Lord. "It is he that hath made us, and not we ourselves; we are his people, and the sheep of his pasture" (v. 3). In prayer we affirm our dependence on the Lord. We adore him and express our reverent praise for his steadfast love and faithfulness.

B. *Jesus taught us to approach the Father with praise and adoration.* "Our Father which art in heaven, hallowed be thy name" (Matt. 6:9). To hallow the Lord's name means to regard him as holy and separate and to respond with awe and reverence. Thus we are to enter in with praise and thanksgiving.

II. Praise is an action of the will.

A. *A problem in our prayer life is the vacillation of our emotions.* Sometimes we do not *feel* like praying. If we let our emotions determine our prayer life, we will certainly fail. With the will, we must decide to pray. Emotion frequently limits the meaning of prayer, but we can still will to praise and thank God. Paul instructed, "Rejoice always, pray constantly, give thanks in all circumstances; for this is the will of God in Christ Jesus for you. Do not quench the Spirit" (1 Thess. 5:16–18 RSV).

B. *God does not tell us to always feel grateful.* He does, however, command us to give thanks always. Even when we do not feel emotionally grateful, we can still choose to give thanks and praise to God: "I will bless the LORD *at all times*: his praise shall continually be in my mouth" (Ps. 34:1 RSV, italics added). Psalm 43 reflects the depressed emotions of one caught in difficult circumstances. Yet, with a decision of the will, he determines to praise God. Our feelings do not alter the Lord's loving presence and powerful nature.

III. Some encouragements for praise and thanksgiving.

A. *The will is prompted to praise by various encouragements.* Recollection of God's nature—his creative power, his personal presence, his steadfast love, and his abundant mercy—will bring much praise to our lips.

B. *The memory of blessings encourages praise.* "Count your many blessings, name them one by one" is good advice for praise. Ten lepers met Jesus and sought healing of their dreaded disease. They were all cleansed, but only one came back to offer thanks (Luke 17:11–19). This one leper then received full communion with the Lord through faith. Failure to offer thanks can clog the channel of blessings. Count your blessings and praise the Lord.

C. *Praise is encouraged through the use of God's Word.* Meditate on Scripture. The words will become your own expression of praise and thanks. Put yourself in the place of the author; feel his experiences of deliverance, joy, and spiritual blessings. Praise and thanksgiving will erupt.

D. *The psalmist utilized "joyful songs" (v. 2) to praise and thank the Lord.* Christ placed a new song in the heart of the redeemed. With music we, too, can "praise God from whom all blessings flow."

Conclusion

Entering into prayer with praise and thanksgiving brings the results John Greenleaf Whittier had in mind when he prayed:

> Drop thy still dews of quietness,
> Till all our strivings cease;
> Take from our souls the strain and stress
> And let our ordered lives confess
> The beauty of Thy peace.

SUGGESTED PREACHING PROGRAM FOR THE MONTH OF SEPTEMBER

■ Sunday Mornings

The focus for Sunday mornings in September is on evangelism—sharing the gospel with a sense of urgency, seeking to persuade the noncommitted and nonbelievers to put their faith in Jesus Christ. The theme is "Today Is the Day of Salvation.

■ Sunday Evenings

"The Master's Recipe for Effective Praying" is the theme for an eight-part study of the petitions found in the Lord's Prayer.

■ Wednesday Evenings

"The Christ of John's Gospel" is the theme for a series of expository studies that focus on John's unique portrayal of the Christ. This series will run through the end of the year.

SUNDAY MORNING, SEPTEMBER 3

Title: The Lostness of the Lost Man

Text: "'For the Son of man came to seek and to save the lost'" **(Luke 19:10 RSV).**

Scripture Reading: Luke 15:1–7

Hymns: "Amazing Grace," Newton
"He Included Me," Oatman
"The Way of the Cross Leads Home," Pounds

Offertory Prayer: Holy Father, we pray today that you will open our eyes and help us to see more completely the evidences of your grace to us. Help us to recognize that every day is a gift from you. Help us to accept this hour of worship as a divine appointment. Give us the faith we need to experience the living presence of the Christ in this service. As we come now to bring tithes and offerings, help us to place them in the hands of him who gave himself for us on a cross. In his precious name we pray. Amen.

Introduction

The New Testament clearly teaches that God so loved a lost and needy world that he gave his Son to die on a cross that the world might be saved (John 3:16). On every page of the Gospels, we see that Jesus Christ was concerned about the lostness of people; he wanted to rescue and restore them to the

Father. And the lostness of people was such a pressing burden on the apostle Paul's heart that it caused him to become a spiritual "workaholic" for God as he sought to evangelize the world (Rom. 10:1).

Why is it that modern-day Christians have no sense of urgency to help save lost people from the fate that follows a life of no faith in Jesus Christ? Is it possible that we have let the devil blind our minds as he has blinded the minds of unbelievers so that they cannot see the way to become children of God (2 Cor. 4:4)? Surely if Satan can blind our minds to the lostness of people, we will not urgently press on them the claims of Christ or point out to them their need to trust him as Savior.

Let's consider some of the losses lost persons experience because they are apart from God and living in unbelief.

I. Lost persons lose the very life of God.

When we become believers, we receive in the miracle of the new birth the very life of God. We receive eternal life, which is more qualitative than quantitative. Jesus said, "I give them eternal life, and they shall never perish, and no one shall snatch them out of my hand" (John 10:28 RSV).

II. Lost persons lose the nature of God.

The miracle of the new birth brings with it the very nature and character of God in embryonic form. Through faith we become partakers of the divine nature (2 Peter 1:4). In the new birth we become the children of God (1 John 3:1–2). Those who reject Jesus Christ as Savior and Lord lose the privilege of receiving God's nature.

III. Lost persons lose the presence of God.

The disciples were greatly strengthened and blessed by the presence of Jesus Christ during his earthly ministry. He encouraged them with the promise of his abiding presence as they carried out the Great Commission (Matt. 28:20). He accomplished this by sending his Holy Spirit to live within believers (John 14:16–18).

IV. Lost persons lose the guidance of God.

Isaiah described unbelievers as sheep who have gone astray, having turned to their own way (Isa. 53:6). He urged them to seek God while he may be found and to return to him so that they might obtain pardon and mercy (55:6–7).

The psalmist, speaking from experience and out of a heart of great faith, said of God's guidance, "He leadeth me in the paths of righteousness for his name's sake." God is pictured as a Shepherd who leads his sheep along the paths of life that lead to abundant living in the here and now.

Through the Holy Spirit, God wants to guide us and give us directions throughout life.

V. Lost persons lose the comfort of God.

Sooner or later we all experience the pain of separation from those near and dear to us through death. Only those who have accepted Jesus Christ as Lord and Savior can claim and be comforted by the precious promises of God found throughout the Bible. Paul said that Christians don't grieve as those who have no hope, those who have either rejected Christ or neglected to trust him (1 Thess. 4:13).

VI. Lost persons lose the privilege of going to the Father's home at the end of life.

Heaven is being prepared for those who receive and believe in Jesus Christ as Lord and Savior (John 14:1–6). It is not the will of the Father God that any should perish but that all should repent and receive the gift of forgiveness and eternal life (2 Peter 3:8–9).

The losses unbelievers experience in this life are too numerous to list. And those who shut out Jesus Christ from their lives rob themselves of eternal life.

Jesus Christ loved you so much that he went to a cross and died there for you. He was so powerful that he conquered death and the grave. He is so gracious that he offers you forgiveness that is full and free forever.

Conclusion

Today is the day you should turn from a life without faith and ask Jesus Christ to forgive your sins and receive you into God's family. You have already lost much. Don't take a chance on losing eternal life. Jesus is waiting for you today. Come to him now.

SUNDAY EVENING, SEPTEMBER 3

Title: Our Father

Text: "After this manner therefore pray ye: Our Father which art in heaven, Hallowed be thy name" **(Matt. 6:9)**.

Scripture Reading: Matthew 6:1–15

Introduction

If we are to come boldly to the throne of grace to receive help in our time of need, we must know who sits on the throne. We must know who God is, and we must know what kind of person he is.

We can learn much by considering our Lord's most basic instruction on prayer. What we have commonly called the Lord's Prayer contains some of the most profound thoughts on prayer found in all of the Bible. Every word in that model prayer is important. The prayer was given again in Luke's gospel in response to a specific request from the disciples concerning prayer. They felt their inadequacy in prayer and wanted Jesus' aid. He responded by giving this beautiful pattern to follow.

How are we to understand the prayer? It was not given just to quote as a prayer to God, even though it is useful for this. All of us have experienced some beautiful moments with God as we uttered these words to him. Dr. Martyn Lloyd-Jones contends that the prayer is actually meant to be an outline for prayer. It is to guide us in our prayers as an outline guides a speaker in his sermon. The prayer presents two major concerns that we may present to the Father. The first three petitions are concerned with the glory of God: his name, his kingdom, and his will. The last four are concerned with our needs. This should always be the order of our concern when we come to present ourselves to the Father in prayer.

First, we will gather from it the light it gives about the God to whom we pray. He is to be addressed, according to our Lord Jesus, as "Our Father which art in heaven."

I. We must know that God is our Father.

There were a few scattered references to God as Father in the Old Testament; but it was Jesus, our Lord, who really gave meaning to this address. Jesus came from the bosom of the Father, speaking of God as Father in very personal terms. What are we admitting or affirming when we address God in prayer as "our heavenly Father"?

A. *The resourcefulness of God.* This address is an acknowledgment of the resourcefulness of God. The root of this word translated "Father" includes the idea of originator. It points to a source, a cause, a point of origin. God is the Source.

   The God who is the source of our physical life is also the God of all mercy and grace. As such, he is the source of our eternal life. The relationship we have with him is at his initiative. He is the originator of the relationship. Every address of God as Father by a person in worship should be acknowledgment of this. It is an affirmation that the relationship that each has with him is his work, his creation.

B. *The responsibility of God.* This address also indicates that since God is our heavenly Father, he is the one who is responsible for us. None of us would have dared to push off on God this responsibility, but fortunately he himself made it so. Since God has revealed himself as the one who accepts responsibility for us, it is not presumptuous for us to bring our joys and our needs to him. This is exactly what he expects and even encourages.

C. *The responsiveness of God.* A third thing suggested by this title of God is responsiveness. To address God as Father is to affirm that he is the responsive God of love whom we know him to be. Do you remember that helpful word about the Father that Jesus gave? He assured Thomas that "he that hath seen me hath seen the Father" (John 14:9). It is safe to assume that God is just as responsive to our needs as Jesus was to need wherever he met it. If you will read the Gospels with discernment, you will be reassured that Jesus was always accessible and responsive.

II. We must know that God is our Father in heaven.

The phrase that our Lord added to "Our Father" is significant. It reveals some things about the God to whom we pray, things that we need to know if we are going to pray confidently.

A. *His position.* First, Jesus' saying that our Father is in heaven is surely an affirmation that God is separate from all earthly fathers and personalities. Some people mistakenly approach deceased human beings in prayer. They select great saints of the past and address prayers to them. This is surely a mistake. There is no need to come to some mere mortal—a deceased one at that—when you can come before the living God himself. Furthermore, it separates him from all living fathers. He is the one in heaven in contrast to all of those on earth. Prayer is not to be addressed to our physical or spiritual fathers.

Second, related to this is the affirmation that God is sovereign. The heavens were understood to be the very seat of God. God is seen as the Ruler over all things. All things are under his control. So, to approach God as the heavenly Father is to approach the one who has the right to do whatever pleases him. There is no other one in all the universe who has this kind of authority.

B. *His power.* "Our Father which art in heaven" addresses God as the one who has the power to do whatever needs to be done. "Father" would indicate that he would want to do it, but his position indicates that he has the power to do it. Some of the titles with which people approach God today fail to acknowledge this. Some refer to him as the "man upstairs." This is not the same thing as saying, "Our Father which art in heaven."

The apostle Paul surely caught hold of this truth. He affirmed in a prayer, "Now unto him that is able to do exceedingly abundantly above all that we ask or think, according to the power that worketh in us, to him be glory . . . for ever and ever!" (Eph. 3:20–21). When you address God as "Our Father which art in heaven," this is what you are acknowledging.

Conclusion

Your prayer life will grow as your knowledge of God grows. Prayer has no meaning apart from this personal knowledge of him. The great essential in a growing knowledge of God is fellowship with him. One of the greatest means of fellowship with God is prayer. Do you see where this leads? If you want to become more effective, bolder, and more confident in your prayer life, then pray more. The more you pray, the better you will know the God who answers prayer and the more your position in his family will mean to you. The more he means to you, the more you will enjoy the experience of prayer. This will be true for eternity. So let's go pray!

Wednesday Evening, September 6

Title: The Greatness of Christ

Text: "And the Word was made flesh, and dwelt among us, (and we beheld his glory, the glory as of the only begotten of the Father,) full of grace and truth" **(John 1:14)**.

Scripture Reading: John 1:1–18

Introduction

The prologue to the Gospel of John is like the overture to a great symphonic composition, in which the themes are stated with stunning force. The dominant note in 1:1–18, a poetic portrait of Christ, is his greatness.

This hymn was composed by John under the divine inspiration of the Holy Spirit. The poem is a marvel in word choices—beginning, word, life, light, witness, glory, grace, and truth. It is also a marvel in arrangement—the Word and God (vv. 1-5), the Word and the world (vv. 9–13), the Word and the flesh (vv. 14, 16–18). John commences his story of Jesus not with a narrative about birth, wise men, or John the Baptist. He begins it with a song of praise. It is a hymn worthy of our study, so let's examine its teachings.

I. Jesus is the eternal Christ.

A. *Jesus has coexistence with the Father.* "In the beginning was the Word, and the Word was with God" (John 1:1). "All things were made by him; and without him was not any thing made that was made" (v. 3). There has never been a time when Jesus was not. Finite human beings have difficulty understanding this profound truth, for in our world there is a beginning and an end. But Christ is eternal.

B. *Jesus has equality with the Father.* "And the Word was God" (John 1:1). Though there is a distinction between the Father and the Son, there is not independent existence as if there were two wholly separate divine beings. Whenever you look at Jesus, you observe the essence and being of God.

II. Jesus is the incarnate Christ.

A. *The incarnation is a reality.* "The Word was made flesh, and dwelt among us, (and we beheld his glory, the glory as of the only begotten of the Father,) full of grace and truth" (John 1:14). The term "flesh" suggests human nature. Jesus did not cease to be God when he became a man, and he did become fully human. He became the God-man.

The reality of the incarnation may be seen in the expression "dwelt among us." Literally, it could be translated "tabernacled among us." In the Old Testament, God dwelt in a tabernacle in the midst of Israel. In the New Testament, God came to live among human beings in the human form of the Son of God.

B. *The incarnation has a significant meaning.* To acknowledge that Jesus became a man is to recognize that he can understand us. "For we have not an high priest which cannot be touched with the feeling of our infirmities; but was in all points tempted like as we are, yet without sin" (Heb. 4:15).

III. Jesus is the enabling Christ.

A. *Jesus makes himself available.* "The true light that gives light to everyone was coming into the world. He was in the world, and though the world was made through him, the world did not recognize him. He came to that which was his own, but his own did not receive him" (John 1:9–11 NIV). Jesus made himself available to many people. Oddly enough, many chose not to receive the Lord. One of the hardest truths to understand is that people reject the eternal Christ.

B. *Jesus gave the power to become God's children.* "But as many as received him, to them gave he power to become the sons of God, even to them that believe on his name" (John 1:12). If one makes himself or herself available to the Lord, the Lord will give the status of a child of God. The entrance into God's family does not depend on heredity or inheritance, personal resolution, or environment. Life in God's family is imparted by the power of God.

Conclusion

Don't miss the theme of this hymn. It focuses on the greatness of Christ. This Christ is speaking to you today. Listen, God is speaking!

SUNDAY MORNING, SEPTEMBER 10

Title: Harvesttime

Text: "Do not be deceived; God is not mocked, for whatever a man sows, that he will also reap" **(Gal. 6:7 RSV)**.

Scripture Reading: Galatians 6:7–10

Hymns: "The Kingdom Is Coming," Slade
"Must I Go, and Empty-Handed," Luther
"To the Work," Crosby

Offertory Prayer: Precious Father, you have invited us to come to your house so that we might worship you in Spirit and in truth. We bow before you in gratitude and praise. We rejoice in your kindness and thank you for your blessings to us. We thank you for the privilege of letting us share in your kingdom's work through tithes and offerings. Bless these gifts as they are used to spread the gospel in this community and around the world. We pray in Jesus' name. Amen.

Introduction

Even though we may not all be farmers, we will all reap a harvest in the future. The apostle Paul painted a picture of life as an opportunity to plant in one of two fields:

1. We all have the opportunity to do our planting in the realm of our fleshly nature (Gal. 6:8; cf. 1 John 2:15–16).
2. We all have the opportunity to plant in the realm of our spiritual nature (Gal. 6:8; cf. 1 John 2:17).

Paul pictured life as an opportunity to reap a harvest. We will reap a harvest in the area of our fleshly nature if that has been the area in which we have done our planting (Gal. 5:16–17).

We will reap a harvest in the realm of the Spirit if we have been sowing to the Spirit (Gal. 5:22–23). It is highly possible that many of us have not interpreted the words of our text as fully as we should have. The apostle Paul was not speaking primarily to nonbelievers in this text. He is warning believers against the peril of living only in the dimension of their fleshly nature. Many of us may be sowing only in the realm of the flesh and may be totally neglecting the Spirit.

The words of our text should speak loudly both to the unsaved person who sows only in the realm of the flesh and to the saved person who faces the peril of neglecting the Spirit while sowing to the fleshly nature.

I. We harvest exactly what we plant.

This is both a law of nature and a law of God. When you sow wheat, you do not reap oats. When you plant cotton, you do not reap turnips. When you plant beans, you do not reap popcorn. When you plant potatoes, you do not reap pumpkins.

If you have neglected or rejected Jesus Christ as Lord and Savior, you are sowing in the realm of your flesh. If you have received Jesus Christ as Savior, it is still possible that you are neglecting to sow in the Spirit as you could and should.

II. We reap the harvest where we plant.

A. *If your life is spent sowing to your fleshly nature, you will reap a harvest only in the realm of the flesh.*

B. *If you recognize and respond to the spiritual, you can reap a harvest in the realm of the Spirit.* We are made in the image and likeness of God and have the potential for fellowship with him. We can be in partnership with God. To the degree that you cultivate this part of your life, you will reap a harvest in the realm of the Spirit.

III. We harvest more than we plant.

It is interesting to see how many tomatoes grow on a single tomato vine that was produced by a single tomato seed. It is interesting to see how many grains of wheat are produced by a single grain of wheat. It is interesting to see how many kernels of corn are on an ear of corn produced by a single kernel of corn.

In the realm of the flesh, you reap more than you sow. And in the realm of the Spirit, you reap more than you sow. If you want to reap an abundant harvest, then plant many seeds in the realm of the Spirit.

IV. We harvest later than when we plant.

No farmer expects to reap a harvest the same day he plants his seed. Some seeds produce a crop in a matter of a few weeks. Other seeds produce a crop that takes months to mature. We will reap the harvest of the flesh as well as the Spirit during our lifetime. Many of the fruits come to us here and now.

We can also reap the harvest of the Spirit in the life beyond. What we are and do lives on and bears fruit after our lips have become silent and our hands have been stilled by death. God rewards his children for the total impact of their lives; and consequently, it is possible to sow seeds that will produce fruits after our earthly life is over.

Conclusion

Harvesttime is coming. What will the harvest be? Are you sowing only to your flesh? If so, you need to turn from the life of no faith and the life of selfishness that leads to destruction. You need to come to God through faith in Jesus Christ and begin to live as God meant for you to live.

If you have already received Jesus Christ as Savior, you would be wise to cooperate fully with God's Holy Spirit as he seeks to work within you.

A harvest day is coming, and the harvest will be determined by the sowing that is being done in the present.

Sunday Evening, September 10

Title: Hallowed Be Thy Name

Text: "After this manner therefore pray ye: Our Father which art in heaven, hallowed be thy name" **(Matt. 6:9)**.

Scripture Reading: Luke 11:1–13

Introduction

The Lord's Prayer is a useful guide for disciples to follow in their prayer life. It gives us some priorities by which to establish our prayer life. Most of us have quoted this prayer since childhood, but we may not have looked carefully at what it really says.

What should be the primary burden of your prayer when you approach the heavenly Father? In this prayer, Jesus set forth seven petitions. The first three are concerned with the things of God. The last four are concerned with the things of man. This reflects God's priorities that should be observed in prayer.

The first petition is "Hallowed be thy name." The biblical use of "name" is a little strange to modern minds. In understanding the Bible, you cannot separate the name from the person. Alexander Maclaren said, "Name is character so far as revealed." To "hallow" something means to count it as holy. Literally, it means "to make holy." Since it is related to God in this text, we know that it carries the force here of regarding or acknowledging something as holy. There is no way that the name of God can be made holy, for he is the eternal Holy One.

I. A petition for a revelation of God.

A. *The spirit of the petition.* While this first petition is voiced as a specific, urgent appeal, it has beneath it a confession. The only reason we would be moved to pray for God's name to be hallowed would be because it was not currently being done. Humankind is guilty of not regarding God as holy and of treating his name as a common, ordinary thing. We must confess that there are times when we show little regard for the name of God and times when we represent his name as a very common thing.

B. *The burden of the petition.* It is primarily through this petition that God will make himself known, that God will confront people with the truth about himself. This is a petition that God will reveal himself to people as he revealed himself to Moses at the burning bush and to Isaiah in the temple.

The conviction behind this petition is that only such a knowledge of God can meet the deepest needs of humanity. This first petition is not that people may have the strength to do what is right, but rather that they may know God. The conviction is that if people can come to know God, all of these other needs will be cared for in their lives. Humankind's deepest problem is ignorance of God. Though the evidence for God is all about them and God desires to make himself known, people still live in ignorance. We see this priority in the prayers of Paul for himself and for others. He was moved to pray that "I may know him, and the power of his resurrection." He longed for a deeper and fuller knowledge of God in his life. He prayed for other

Christians that they might be "filled with all the fullness of God." This should also be the priority in our prayers for others.

II. A petition for a recognition of God.

This petition goes deeper than that people may know God as holy. They must not only know what Moses, Isaiah, and Peter knew; they must do what these men did. When they knew God as holy, they responded to him accordingly.

A. *A missionary petition.* As we look upon the world in its sin and ignorance, no prayer is more appropriate than a petition that God may be known and acknowledged by sinful humans. It should be the passion of every Christian heart to see God reverenced by the nations of the earth.

B. *A personal petition.* We must also pray, "Hallowed be thy name in my life." We will be powerless in seeing God's name hallowed in the earth until it is first hallowed in us. What does this involve?

Our lips should speak the name of God with a sense of awe and reverence. If we really know who he is, we should speak of him accordingly. The Old Testament people of God had such respect for the name of God, such an awareness of his holiness, that they would not write his name and were even reluctant to speak it. They often spoke of him simply as "the Name." This stands in sharp contrast to the irreverent familiarity that has crept into our lives. Some speak of God flippantly and even use his name blasphemously. Some constantly use God's name to call down curses on people and things when God does not act that way.

This petition also includes our personal thoughts of God. Irreverent speech begins with irreverent thoughts. The mouth can speak only what has been conceived in the heart. What are your thoughts of God? This would include those secret thoughts you would not openly express. Do you harbor resentment toward God? Do you resent his claims on your life? Do you resist his purposes for your life? Do you insist on having your own way rather than following his way? This petition is that God may be reverenced, acknowledged, and adored in your heart. It is a prayer that in your heart there will be nothing except submission, adoration, and praise toward God.

Furthermore, the petition "Hallowed be thy name" includes our personal conduct. The conduct of our daily lives can be a blasphemy of the Name just as our speech can. Paul leveled such a charge against the Israel of his day. What is your conduct saying about God to those who watch? Is it speaking to them of a God of love, kindness, truth, and honesty? Or is it suggesting that God means very little to you? Does your conduct say to the world that God is worth knowing?

Conclusion

Jesus felt that the petition "Hallowed be thy name" should always be the urgent appeal of his people. He knows our needs better than we could ever know them, and he said that our greatest need is to know God and to walk day by day with reverent awareness of him in everything we do. This can be so in your life if you give this petition proper priority in your prayers.

Wednesday Evening, September 13

Title: When Religion Gets Sick

Text: "When [Jesus] had made a scourge of small cords, he drove them all out of the temple, and the sheep, and the oxen; and poured out the changers' money, and overthrew the tables; and said unto them that sold doves, Take these things hence; make not my Father's house an house of merchandise" **(John 2:15–16)**.

Scripture Reading: John 2:13–25

Introduction

A famous preacher once asked, "What is worse than having no religion?" Then after a pause, he answered his own question, "Having no religion is bad, but having the wrong kind of religion is even worse." Wayne E. Oates, in a provocative book titled *When Religion Gets Sick*, proposed the possibility of allowing religion to get sick. He concluded that having a sick religion may be worse than having no religion at all.

Jesus was concerned with sick religion as indicated by his driving the money changers out of the temple. Much of Judaism had gotten sick, and the Great Physician had come to bring healing. What did Jesus see in the temple that caused such aggressive action?

I. The lost sense of awe and respect for God.

A. *The Jews had lost the profound sense of awe and respect for God.* Look carefully at what Jesus observed when he visited the temple. Many Jewish patrons were coming and going. They had little respect for what took place in the temple, namely, communion with God. They bought and sold animals, and they exchanged money as if the court of the Gentiles was a marketplace.

God had intended the temple to be a meeting place for human beings and himself. He had not intended the temple to be a den of thieves. He wanted it to be a place of prayer.

B. *Christians often lose their sense of awe and reverence for God.* As people go about the routine of Bible study and church attendance, they can lose reverence for God. The Lord, his church, and his Book become rather ordinary.

Jesus' anger was aroused when he saw a lost sense of awe and reverence for his Father. Religion can get sick when the sense of the wonder of God departs from a person or a group of people.

II. The lost sense of the cost of religion.

A. *The Jews had lost sight of the cost of serving the Lord.* The presentation of the animals in temple sacrifice represented a commitment on the part of worshipers. God wanted the Jews to present the best animals out of their flocks. This would mean that they gave their best to God.

When Jesus walked into the temple, he saw that religion had been made cheap. People were told, "Leave your animals at home and buy one in the temple." Purchasing animals from the temple merchants cheapened the sacrificial system. And this angered the Master.

B. *Modern Christians have lost sight of the cost of commitment.* Following Christ and belonging to a church have become cheap. Dietrich Bonhoeffer, renowned German pastor from World War II, said that when Jesus calls a man to follow him, he calls him to die to himself. Nothing short of total commitment will satisfy the Savior.

III. The lost sense of the outsider.

A. *The Jews had lost the sense of the Gentiles' need.* The place where the money changers and merchants did business was in the court of the Gentiles. This was a place within the temple precinct where Gentiles, outsiders, could come and learn of the Lord. Most of the Jews in Jesus' time were not concerned for the Gentiles. They were concerned for their rituals but not for the mission of being a blessing to the nations that God had given them.

B. *Modern Christians can lose the sense of the outsider.* The church can easily become an exclusive club with a preoccupation for its membership. Religion gets sick when people turn inward and do not look outward for the sinners.

Conclusion

How is the health of your Christian expression? If you do not mind, let's have a checkup. Is there a great thrill over the greatness and grandeur of God? Or are you taking shortcuts? Are you asking for the minimal requirements? Then what about your concern for others? Let's keep our religion healthy and growing.

SUNDAY MORNING, SEPTEMBER 17

Title: The Joy of Knowing Jesus Christ as Savior

Text: "For by grace you have been saved through faith; and this is not your own doing, it is the gift of God—not because of works, lest any man should boast" **(Eph. 2:8–9 RSV)**.

Scripture Reading: Ephesians 2:11–22

Hymns: "Great Redeemer, We Adore Thee," Harris
"Jesus Is All the World to Me," Thompson
"We Have Heard the Joyful Sound," Owens

Offertory Prayer: Heavenly Father, we come to you as the great Giver of your grace. We worship you because you are of supreme worth to us. We come today praying for the help of your Holy Spirit that we might give ourselves completely to you as we bring tithes and offerings for the advancement of your kingdom's work. Bless these gifts in a tangible way so that your Word can be preached and your truth taught. May your blessings be on the unfortunate who stand in need of ministries of mercy. In Jesus' name we pray. Amen.

Introduction

As Paul wrote his letter to the Ephesians, he was rejoicing over the blessings of God that had come upon them as a result of their faith in Jesus Christ as Savior. Ephesians 2 points out some of the new relationships that make indescribable joy possible in the heart of each one who receives Jesus Christ as Savior, Lord, Teacher, and Friend.

I. Through Jesus Christ we are made alive with a new kind of life (Eph. 2:1, 4–6).

A spiritual resurrection takes place when we receive Jesus Christ as Savior. Up to this moment, we are in spiritual death and darkness because of sin. We do not have the divine life of God. Physically nonbelievers are walking, living, spiritual corpses in need of a spiritual-life implant. This new life comes in the miracle of the new birth when we respond to Jesus Christ by faith. To be alive from the dead is a joyous experience for those who know Jesus Christ.

II. We are brought near to God and to others through the blood of Jesus Christ (Eph. 2:11–13).

Man in his natural state is alienated from God. Alienation from God results in alienation from other human beings. Sin not only separates a man from his better self and from his higher nature, but it also serves to separate him from his fellow humans. Paul spoke of Gentiles who were separated from Christ as being "alienated from the commonwealth of Israel . . . and strangers to the covenants of promise, having no hope and without God in the world" (v. 12 RSV).

Man is a lonely creature unless he has established a relationship that makes fellowship possible with other human beings. Paul was rejoicing over the fact that now those "who once were far off have been brought near in the blood of Christ" (v. 13 RSV).

III. Through Jesus Christ we experience the peace of God and peace with God (Eph. 2:14–15).

In repentance we yield to the rule and the will of the Creator God. By faith we put our trust in him and signify that we are no longer rebels. Following this response of faith, we experience the peace of God and peace with others. We are no longer the enemies of God. The child of God, through faith in Jesus Christ, can know an inward peace that passes all human understanding.

IV. Through Jesus Christ we now have access into the presence of God by the Holy Spirit (Eph. 2:18).

Until we come to know Jesus Christ as Savior, we are outsiders and do not feel close to God. We do not have access to the throne room of the Eternal, where it is possible to address God as "our Father." Paul rejoiced in this new relationship that he and all of us have through faith in Jesus Christ. This is one of the supreme joys of being a follower of Jesus Christ.

V. Through Jesus Christ we become citizens of the kingdom of God (Eph. 2:19).

The privilege of citizenship in a great country is not properly appreciated by those who live there. The same can be said concerning those who are no longer strangers and sojourners but are now fellow citizens with the saints in the kingdom of our dear Lord and Savior. Paul spoke of this transfer of citizenship in his letter to the Colossians. He praised God and said, "He has delivered us from the dominion of darkness and transferred us to the kingdom of his beloved son, in whom we have redemption, the forgiveness of sins" (1:13–14 RSV). The joy of citizenship is one of the joys that comes as a result of knowing Jesus Christ.

VI. Through Jesus Christ we become members of the family of God (Eph. 2:19).

Being a creature made in the image and likeness of God is marvelous. Yet it is even more spectacular to experience a spiritual birth that makes us the sons and daughters of God and brothers and sisters to each other through Jesus Christ.

Membership in God's family is a joyous experience around the world. You can meet total strangers who have something intensely wonderful in common with you. The joy of being a member of God's family comes to us through faith in Jesus Christ.

VII. Through Jesus Christ we become a part of the living temple of God (Eph. 2:22).

Salvation is something more than a legal relationship with God. It is a dynamic experience in which God himself comes to dwell within the heart of each believer individually and in all believers collectively. We become a living example in which God dwells. We become the meeting place where others can come to know God and where God comes to minister to a needy world.

Conclusion

Rich beyond words is the person who comes to know Jesus Christ as Savior. Joyous indeed is this privilege. If you have not yet opened the door of your heart to let Jesus Christ become your Savior, I would encourage you to do so without delay. There is great joy for you through knowing Jesus Christ.

Sunday Evening, September 17

Title: Thy Kingdom Come

Text: "Thy kingdom come. Thy will be done in earth, as it is in heaven" **(Matt. 6:10)**.

Scripture Reading: Romans 14:13–23

Introduction

The gospel of Matthew presents Jesus as the King of the Jews. It is truly the gospel of the kingdom. Jesus' whole Sermon on the Mount is to be seen in this relationship. In the midst of the sermon, our Lord gave his disciples a model prayer, the second petition of which is "Thy kingdom come."

"Thy" calls our attention to the nature of the kingdom—it is the kingdom that belongs to and comes from God. It is to the heavenly Father that we pray, "Thy kingdom come." The "kingdom" of God is the dynamic reign of God as King. Jesus spoke of the kingdom of God existing in both the present and the future. He affirmed to his disciples, "The kingdom of God is within [or among] you" (Luke 17:21). Whether you understand the preposition "within" to mean that the kingdom was present in their hearts or present in their midst in the person of the King of heaven makes little difference. Jesus surely taught that the kingdom of God had come to earth in his ministry. He pointed his critics to his miracles as a sign that the kingdom of God was near at hand. But Jesus also spoke of the kingdom of God as something future, as the coming kingdom. To which aspect of the kingdom then does this prayer relate? Surely it must include both aspects. Let us see how it might relate to our prayers.

I. A petition for the present rule of God in human hearts.

A. *A confession of need.* The petition "Thy kingdom come" makes an important admission to God. It can be understood as a confession that another ruler is in charge now. The world has never been without a ruler. Since the fatal act of man in the garden of Eden, man has been in the kingdom of darkness that has Satan as its prince. He is the active ruler in this kingdom. So this prayer is a petition for the replacement of the rule of Satan with the rule of God through his Son, the Lord Jesus Christ.

B. *A missionary appeal.* This petition has strong missionary implications. Those who accept Jesus Christ as Lord and Savior are removed from the kingdom of darkness and placed under the rule of the Lord Jesus Christ in God's kingdom. The kingdom of God is present in our hearts in a spiritual way. According to what Jesus told Nicodemus, a spiritual birth is necessary to be transferred from the kingdom of flesh into the kingdom of God. So a prayer for the coming of the kingdom of God can be understood as a prayer that the rule of God may be extended to other hearts through our heeding the gospel of God's dear Son through repentance and faith.

C. *The personal.* This prayer, "Thy kingdom come," also has some important personal implications as it relates to the present. When we receive Jesus Christ as Lord and begin to know his saving power, we gain further insight. We become progressively aware of the incompleteness of God's rule in our lives. We have acknowledged Jesus as Lord yet find ourselves struggling with the application of his lordship. We find a sinful inclination to withhold parts of our lives from his rule. We find a resistance to his rule. This prayer is personal acknowledgment of our struggle and a request that God's rule will be imposed in a more complete way in our hearts. It is a prayer of submission to his rule. "Thy kingdom come—in my heart, in my business, in my home, in all of my affairs."

II. A petition for the future rule of God in the affairs of the universe.

A. *The dethronement of evil.* Jesus never deceived his disciples. He never encouraged them to believe that they would ever successfully dethrone the alien ruler in the universe. He always made it clear that this would be done by God himself. The coming of the kingdom of God will involve an invasion by the sovereign King himself. This is the great theme of the last book in our New Testament. God is going to intervene in human affairs. The kingdom of evil over which Satan rules will be crushed by the mighty Son of God. So this is a prayer for him to act in that way. It is a prayer for the King to come and bind Satan and put him in the bottomless pit, to dethrone all enemies of God and to make them his footstool, and to close down every power that is opposed to God.

B. *The enthronement of Christ.* This kingdom's coming will also involve the enthronement of the Lord Jesus Christ and his people. He is to exercise rule over the earth with a rod of iron. He will truly be the crowned Prince of Peace!

If we could begin to comprehend what this means, we would make it our earnest appeal day after day. We would ever be praying,

"Thy kingdom come!" The coming of the kingdom is the hope of the whole creation. Paul wrote in his letter to the Romans that the whole creation is groaning like a woman in childbirth in anticipation of that day! The coming kingdom will mean the removal of the curse and the restoration of the earth. It will be a beautiful experience of redemption and healing for the earth.

C. *Our hope.* This coming of the kingdom is the hope of the nations of the earth. Nations will continue to be troubled with wars and rumors of wars until God's kingdom comes. But under the rule of Jesus Christ, they will turn their destructive weapons into instruments for humankind's welfare, and the earth will know war no more. Peace will reign in God's kingdom.

This coming of God's kingdom is the hope of individual Christians. Until that kingdom comes in the glorious person of the King, our personal struggles will continue. Sickness and death will continue to hold sway over our families. Corruption will continue to be expressed in myriad forms. Our struggles with the flesh will continue until we see the King face-to-face. But then we shall reign with him.

Conclusion

Are you ready to pray this petition—"Thy kingdom come"? Are you ready to pray it for your personal life? Are you ready for Jesus to be the rightful, fully crowned King over all of the affairs of your life right now? Are you ready to pray this as a missionary prayer? Are you ready to make this your prayer for the coming of the kingdom in its ultimate expression? May God give us a heart for the coming of the King.

WEDNESDAY EVENING, SEPTEMBER 20

Title: Passport to the Kingdom

Text: "Jesus answered, Verily, verily, I say unto thee, Except a man be born of water and of the Spirit, he cannot enter into the kingdom of God" **(John 3:5)**.

Scripture Reading: John 3:1–21

Introduction

To travel from one country to another, every person—no matter how notable—must have a passport. Likewise, the new birth can be considered a sort of passport into the kingdom of God.

Jesus was visited by Nicodemus, a leading Pharisee of his day, who wanted to know more about Jesus' concept of the kingdom of God. The Lord clearly taught Nicodemus that new birth was the prerequisite for entering the kingdom of God.

People who desire God's kind of life need to be born again just as Jesus taught Nicodemus. Let us examine some facets of the new birth.

I. The new birth is a mandate.

A. *Look at the person who came to Jesus.* "There was a man of the Pharisees, named Nicodemus, a ruler of the Jews" (John 3:1). Nicodemus had many commendable qualities.

1. He was a Pharisee. Pharisees were the religious people of Jesus' day who worked meticulously at interpreting and keeping God's laws. Their religion was mainly one of external rules, but they were moral, upright people.
2. Nicodemus was a ruler of the Jews. Probably this meant that he was a member of the Sanhedrin. This was a group of seventy outstanding religious leaders.
3. Nicodemus acknowledged that Jesus had unusual powers from God. "Rabbi, we know that thou art a teacher come from God: for no man can do these miracles that thou doest, except God be with him" (v. 2).

Thus this person who came to see Jesus had a lot of commendable virtues—Pharisee, religious ruler, and one who acknowledged that Jesus possessed a gift from God.

B. *Look at Jesus' words to Nicodemus.* Jesus went abruptly to the need of Nicodemus. Without being impressed with his credentials or his compliments, Jesus said, "Verily, verily, I say unto thee, Except a man be born again, he cannot see the kingdom of God" (John 3:5). Jesus gave a mandate to Nicodemus: "Marvel not that I said unto thee, Ye must be born again" (v. 7). There is no other way to enter the kingdom.

II. The new birth is a miracle.

A. *Think about what Nicodemus thought.* When Jesus mentioned the expression "born again," Nicodemus thought of a physical birth. He questioned, "How can a man be born when he is old? Can he enter the second time into his mother's womb, and be born?" (John 3:4). Nicodemus acknowledged the mandate, but he confused the new birth with physical birth. To go through physical birth again would be an impossibility.

B. *Think about what Jesus meant.* The Lord was not talking about a physical birth. He was talking about the miracle of new beginning. To be born again means to allow God to come into your life and change you. That is a miracle indeed!

III. The new birth has a means.

A. *Listen to Nicodemus's questions.* Twice the Pharisee asked, "How?" (cf. John 3:4, 9). Without a doubt, Nicodemus wanted to know how he might have the new birth.

B. *Listen to Jesus' answers.* Jesus answered Nicodemus's question. He taught him that the means of experiencing the new birth was faith. "As Moses lifted up the serpent in the wilderness, even so must the Son of man be lifted up: That whosoever believeth in him should not perish, but have eternal life" (John 3:14–15). To believe means to open one's life to God. When one opens his or her life to God, the new birth occurs.

IV. The new birth has manifestations.

A. *Nicodemus was asked to observe the wind.* Jesus used an illustration about the wind: "The wind bloweth where it listeth, and thou heareth the sound thereof, but canst not tell whence it cometh, and whither it goeth; so is every one that is born of the Spirit" (John 3:8). The results of the wind blowing can be seen. Likewise, when the Lord comes into a life, changes are evident.

B. *Jesus wants people to observe the result of the new birth.* Human beings change when they open their lives to God. Attitudes and actions change. People become children of God.

Conclusion

Do you want to enter the kingdom of God? The only means of entrance is the new birth. Open your life to Christ, and he will change you.

SUNDAY MORNING, SEPTEMBER 24

Title: Salvation in the Present Tense

Text: "Work out your own salvation with fear and trembling; for God is at work in you, both to will and to work for his good pleasure" **(Phil. 2:12–13 RSV)**.

Scripture Reading: Philippians 2:12–13

Hymns: "O Worship the King," Grant
"More Like Jesus Would I Be," Crosby
"Since Jesus Came into My Heart," McDaniel

Offertory Prayer: Thank you, Father, for the gift of your love revealed in Jesus Christ. Thank you for sending the gift of your Holy Spirit to dwell in our hearts as your church. Thank you for the promise of our Lord to come and be with us today as we meet together in his name. We come bringing tithes and offerings that we may honor you and show you our love and gratitude. Accept these gifts and bless them to the end that others will come to experience your love and know Jesus Christ as Lord and Savior. In his name we pray. Amen.

Introduction

There are three days on everybody's calendar: yesterday, today, and tomorrow. Many people miss today because they are living in yesterday. Others miss the present because they are worried about tomorrow. Let's look at salvation in the past and future and then concentrate on salvation in the present.

I. Jesus Christ came to save us from the past.

As the Lamb of God, Jesus Christ came to take away the sin of the world (John 1:29). Jesus came and lived and loved and served and suffered on a cross that he might die in our place under the penalty of our sins (1 Peter 1:18–19; 2:24; 3:18). Many passages of Scripture confront us with the glorious truth that Jesus Christ died for our sins that he might save us from all we have done in the past or are doing in the present or will do in the future (1 Cor. 15:3–4). Through faith in Jesus Christ, we gain a position of acceptance with the holy God (Rom. 5:1). Through faith in Jesus Christ, we pass from under the wages of sin and receive the gift of eternal life (Rom. 6:23).

As we look at the great redemptive acts of Jesus Christ and our new relationship with God on the basis of faith in Christ, we need to beware lest we think in terms of salvation only in the past tense.

II. Jesus Christ came to save us in the future.

One of the main motives people have for trusting Jesus Christ is that they might be prepared for the future. The Scriptures tell us and observation verifies that it is appointed for all people to die (Heb. 9:27). This passage also informs us that after death occurs we all will meet God in judgment. The following verse informs us that Jesus Christ, who has already borne the penalty of our sins, will appear the second and final time, not to deal with our sin, but to save us from the very presence of sin. Paul wrote to the Philippians that the day will come when we will be raised from the dead and be fashioned after the likeness of our glorified and risen Lord (Phil. 3:20–21). Jesus encourages his people not to be anxious about the future, because he will not only go to prepare a place for them, but he will return to receive them unto himself. In Revelation we find a brief description of the house not made with human hands, eternal in the heavens, which God is preparing for those who love him (21:3–5).

III. The present salvation experience through Jesus Christ.

Jesus the Savior came into this world to do more than just save us from the sins we committed in the past. And he came to do more than save us from the presence of sin in the future. He came to save us from the power and practice and downward pull of sin as a present-day experience. Our text gives us the gospel of our present tense salvation: "God is at work in you, both to will and to work for his good pleasure" (Phil. 2:13 RSV). Jesus Christ died on the cross under the penalty of our sin. He conquered death and arose triumphant and victorious that he might deliver us from the power and practice of sin in the present.

In the conversion experience, we invite the living Christ to dwell within us in the person of the Holy Spirit. He dwells within each of us in order that we might experience a great salvation in the present. He teaches us how to relate to God and to our fellow humans.

A. *Our Lord would save us in the present from hate and hostility toward other human beings (Matt. 5:43–48).* By teaching us about Christian love, our Lord wants to deliver us from destructive relationships with others.
B. *Our Lord would save us in the present from anxiety about the necessities of life by encouraging us to have a great faith in our Father God (6:25–33).* Our Lord encourages us to seek first and foremost the rule of God in all of our relationships and to trust the Father to provide for us the necessities of life.
C. *Our Lord has bestowed on each of us the gift of his Holy Spirit so that we might be enabled to live a Christlike life in the present (Gal. 4:6–7; 5:22–23).*

Conclusion

The great salvation that Jesus Christ brings to us relates to the past and to the future but also very much to the present. It is not his will that you live in weakness and defeat. If you will come to him and trust him, not only for the gift of forgiveness but for victory in the present, you can be sure that he will assist you. He is not a Savior who is limited to the past. He is not a Savior whose power is to be revealed only in the future. Jesus Christ wants to give you victory over evil in the present.

SUNDAY EVENING, SEPTEMBER 24

Title: Thy Will Be Done

Text: "Thy will be done in earth, as it is in heaven" **(Matt. 6:10)**.

Scripture Reading: Luke 22:39–46

Introduction

"It is God's will." These words are used often to interpret the tragedies of life. In legal language, "an act of God" is used to explain the great catastrophes that bring so much suffering and ruin. Yet Jesus instructed us to pray, "Thy will be done." Does this mean that we are praying for catastrophes and tragedies to befall us?

Such tragic events are not what we find associated with God's will in the Bible. God wills to create a world, to create humans, to send his Son, to redeem humans. These things are an expression of God's eternal purpose and will be accomplished, so there is really no need for us to pray for the accomplishment of them. But God's will also includes his commands and his plan for our day-to-day lives. Thus we need to pray that his will might be done in our lives and in the lives of others.

The concern of this particular petition is how we are to do God's will. Since his will is to be done "on earth as it is in heaven," we are to look to heaven for our pattern of response. Even though we do not know as much about heaven as we would like to know, we do know enough to give us some helpful instruction at this point.

I. Submissively.

There is only one Lord in heaven. Every creature there bows before him in worship, adoration, and submission. In Isaiah 6 Isaiah records that he saw angelic beings with six wings. Two of their wings were used to fly with speed to carry out God's every wish, and two were used to cover their faces as an act of reverence in his presence. In the end-time revelation of Jesus Christ, John saw the saints bowing before God and casting their crowns at his feet. John described the saints as those who "serve him day and night." He is absolute Lord over everything there, and everyone is completely submissive to his will.

Sometimes we obey without actually being submissive. One little fellow expressed this thought eloquently to his mother when she made him sit in the corner as a form of discipline. He didn't like it, so he tried to stand up. But she was firm and insisted that he be seated. As he took his seat, he replied, "I may be sitting on the outside, but I am still standing on the inside." She could make him respond physically, but she could not make him submissive in spirit. Some of us respond to God's will in this way. We give in to the insistence of God, but we do not really submit to him as Lord. Thus the petition "Thy will be done on earth as it is in heaven" is a plea that we would have the very spirit of heaven as we approach God's will. Our attitude in doing God's will is just as important as the act itself.

II. Completely.

A. *Completely—not selectively.* In heaven God's will is done completely. The angels are not selective in their obedience to God's will. Whatever God says, they do. Those who refused to give the Lord God complete obedience and chose to exercise their own will in opposition to his will have been excluded from heaven. They are no longer privileged to enter into God's presence.

Jesus teaches us to pray that God's will may be done in our lives and in our world. We have a tendency to be selective in our response to God's will. We pick which of his precepts will guide us. For example, a man may choose to follow the Lord's will in attending public worship, but he may choose to ignore God's will when it comes to tithing. Another man may be very careful to follow the Lord's will for stewardship. He may be more careful than a Pharisee when it comes to calculating his tithes and offerings, but he may ignore the Lord's will for his marriage and instead follow the lust of the flesh. In heaven it is never so! There God's will is done completely.

B. *Completely—not partially.* We may also be partial in our obedience. We may reserve the right to determine exactly how far we will go in our response to God's will. But partial obedience is actually disobedience. Whatever God says, we must do.

III. Joyfully.

A. *Like the angels.* Joy is one of the most obvious marks of the heavenly response. Scripture tells us that the angels sing as they do the will of the Father in heaven.

B. *Like the Son.* In a great messianic psalm, we read, "I delight to do thy will, O my God: yea, thy law is within my heart" (Ps. 40:8). Jesus did not do the Father's will out of a sense of duty, but rather with great delight. In John 4:34 Jesus said, "My food is to do the will of him who sent me and to finish his work" (NIV). He found real joy in doing the will of his Father. It was food for his spirit.

Our response to the will of God will be one of our first concerns when we bow before him. We need to be concerned that we know his will fully and do it joyfully.

IV. Constantly.

We have no record of there ever being a need for a revival in heaven. No angel ever wavers in his devotion to God's will. No angel ever withdraws his support from the Lord's program. Day after day he does whatever God commands. Millennia pass by and angels still obey with the same joy and delight, doing whatever task God assigns.

Our Lord Jesus also provides us with a beautiful example. He allowed nothing to turn him from doing the Father's will. With a willing heart and delight in his God, he went all the way to the cross.

Conclusion

Are you giving consideration to God's will in your life? It should be one of your first considerations when you come to pray. It is more important that you know and do God's will than that you have daily bread. God makes this a matter of first concern. Will you?

Wednesday Evening, September 27

Title: A Meeting with the Master

Text: "Now Jacob's well was there. Jesus therefore, being wearied with his journey, sat thus on the well: and it was about the sixth hour. There cometh a woman of Samaria to draw water: Jesus saith unto her, Give me to drink" **(John 4:6–7)**.

Scripture Reading: John 4:1–42

Introduction

One of the significant features of Jesus' ministry was his meetings with people. Leonard Griffith examined many of these encounters in his book *Encounters with Christ: The Personal Ministry of Jesus.* Griffith emphasized Jesus' interest in individuals. The Lord was not so preoccupied with the multitudes that he lost concern for individuals.

Jesus met with many people. One of his most significant meetings was with a sinful woman at Jacob's well. Let us examine some fascinating facets of this famous interview.

I. The perplexing problems.

Jesus' meeting with the woman of Samaria was full of problems. To understand the difficulties, one must understand some geography and history of Israel. The pious Jew would not go through the land of Samaria. Following the northern kingdom of Israel's captivity in 722 BC by the Assyrians, the land was inhabited by Israelites and foreigners. They intermarried, which was repulsive to pious Jews, and therefore the pious Jews avoided Samaria. Regarding Jesus, John said, "He had to go through Samaria" (John 4:4 NIV). Various barriers existed for Jesus and the woman.

A. *An ethnic barrier.* Jews were somewhat tolerant of other races, but the Samaritans were contemptible to the Jews. When the woman met the Lord, she emphasized this barrier: "How is it that thou, being a Jew, asketh drink of me . . . a woman of Samaria?" (John 4:9).
B. *The gender barrier.* Rabbis were forbidden to greet a woman in public, but Jesus crossed this barrier. Not only did the Lord cross this barrier, but he chose to talk with a notoriously immoral woman.
C. *The religious barrier.* There was a wide religious gap between the Jews and Samaritans. The Samaritans worshiped at Mount Ebal, and the Jews worshiped at Mount Gerizim.

II. The Master's proposal.

Jesus had the interpersonal skills to overcome these barriers. Let us follow the strategy of the Master in how he made the meeting with the woman meaningful.

Jesus asked for a common necessity (John 4:7–9). When the woman came to the well, he asked for a drink. Jesus was thirsty, and the woman was thirsty. Even though the two were different in race, gender, and religion, they had a common need to drink.

A. *Jesus aroused the woman 's curiosity (John 4:10–15).* After he talked about his and her physical thirst, he mentioned something about "living water." Immediately the woman began to ask questions. "From whence then hast thou that living water?" (v. 11). The woman realized that Jesus was speaking of another type of water.
B. *Jesus awakened the woman's conscience (John 4:16–25).* The woman did not grasp everything about the living water, so Jesus appealed to her conscience. "Go, call thy husband, and come hither" (v. 16). Jesus wanted the woman to see that he knew the errors of her life. With her conscience awakened, the woman wanted to talk about her relationship with God. "Sir, I perceive that thou art a prophet. Our fathers worshipped in this mountain; and ye say, that in Jerusalem is the place . . . to worship" (vv. 19–20).
C. *Jesus acknowledged himself as the Messiah (John 4:26).* Skillfully and masterfully, Jesus led the woman to the fact that he was the Messiah. At the appropriate moment, he made the messianic disclosure, "I who speak to you am he" (RSV).

III. The woman's proclamation.

After the interview with Jesus, the woman left for the city of Samaria. She told the people about the Lord. "Come, see a man, which told me all things that ever I did: is not this the Christ?" (John 4:29).

The woman had been changed because of her encounter with Christ. A careful study of her attitude and actions reflects a radical change in character. The woman also had a new concern for her life. She left the water pots and went into the city. Her primary concerns had been the sensual things of life. After her life-transforming experience, she was concerned for the spiritual condition of an entire village.

Conclusion

Why don't you have a meeting with the Master? Let him tell you about his character and his ability to change people.

SUGGESTED PREACHING PROGRAM FOR THE MONTH OF OCTOBER

■ Sunday Mornings

"Recognizing and Responding to God's Gift of the Holy Spirit" is the theme for the October morning sermons.

■ Sunday Evenings

Complete the series based on the Lord's Prayer using the theme "The Master's Recipe for Effective Praying." On the last Sunday of the month, begin the series "The Church as the Body of Christ." These messages are primarily based on texts from Paul's letter to the Ephesians.

■ Wednesday Evenings

Continue the series of devotional sermons using the theme "The Christ of John's Gospel."

SUNDAY MORNING, OCTOBER 1

Title: The Gift of the Holy Spirit

Text: "'I will pray the Father, and he will give you another Counselor, to be with you for ever, even the Spirit of truth, whom the world cannot receive, because it neither sees him nor knows him; you know him, for he dwells with you, and will be in you'" **(John 14:16–17 RSV)**.

Scripture Reading: John 14:15–19

Hymns: "God, Our Father, We Adore Thee," Frazer
" 'Tis So Sweet to Trust in Jesus," Stead
"Holy Ghost, with Light Divine," Reed

Offertory Prayer: Heavenly Father, thank you for granting to us the privilege of coming to your house to meet with other members of your family that we might rejoice together in your love and that we might commit ourselves more completely to your purposes for us. Today we thank you for the gift of your Holy Word. We thank you for the gift of eternal life that causes us to love you and to love others. We come thanking you for the privilege of worshiping you with our substance, and so we bring tithes and offerings. Accept these gifts, and bless them to the good of our community and our world and to your glory, we pray. In Jesus' name. Amen.

Introduction

We all like to receive gifts. Parents enjoy receiving gifts from their children, and children enjoy receiving gifts from their parents. Husbands enjoy receiving gifts from their wives, and wives enjoy receiving gifts from their husbands. People enjoy receiving gifts from their friends. Employers occasionally receive gifts from their employees, and employees enjoy receiving gifts from their employers. There are times when we give gifts to strangers, and there are times when we receive gifts from strangers. But God is the greatest giver of gifts. James declared, "Every good and perfect gift is from above, coming down from the Father of the heavenly lights, who does not change like shifting shadows" (1:17 NIV).

Our Lord contrasted the good gifts of God with the ability of fallen man to give good gifts to his children: "If you then, who are evil, know how to give good gifts to your children, how much more will your Father who is in heaven give good things to those who ask him!" (Matt. 7:11 RSV). The only gifts that God bestows are good gifts.

I. God always gives his good gifts with the right motive.

All of us have received a gift that did not come with the highest motives. When God gives a good gift, it is always with the proper motive.

A. *God's gifts come as an expression of his love.* God's gifts are not substitutes for his love. They never come as a payment or bribe.

B. *God's gifts are an indication of his hope for us.* We should recognize his gifts as an affirmation of our worth. His gifts come to us as an expression of his divine confidence in us.

C. *God 's gifts to us are always chosen by his wisdom.*

   1. God's gifts are practical.
   2. God's gifts are good.
   3. God's gifts are helpful.

II. God's good gifts are always appropriate.

Someone remarked concerning a gift of money, which came in the form of greenbacks, "The color of the gift is always appropriate."

God's gift of the Holy Spirit to each believer as an indwelling presence is a gift. It is unmerited, and it does not come as an expression of gratitude or as a payment for service rendered.

A. *The Holy Spirit is a gift of unknown value to the recipient at first.* The value of this gift to the new believer is far beyond anything he or she could possibly evaluate.

B. *The Holy Spirit is a gift of unsuspected value to everyone.* Not a single person who receives this gift from God has any idea before receiving it of its significance to them.

C. *The Holy Spirit is a gift of undiscovered value to most believers.* Have you ever received a gift without understanding its value or recognizing its significance? This is true in every instance concerning the gift of the Holy Spirit.

D. *The Holy Spirit is a gift of unappreciated value to most of us.* How long has it been since you have expressed sincere gratitude and thanksgiving to God for his gift of the living presence of his Holy Spirit?
   1. This gift has great practical value.
   2. This gift can have great sentimental value.
   3. This gift can have great emotional value.
   4. This gift can have great spiritual value.
   5. This gift has great teaching value.
   6. This gift has great permanent value.

III. We need to recognize and appreciate God's gift of the Holy Spirit.

A. *The Holy Spirit is God's gift.*
   1. The Holy Spirit is not a reward for hard work.
   2. The Holy Spirit is not a prize to be won.
   3. The Holy Spirit is not a property to be purchased.
   4. The Holy Spirit is not a treasure to be stolen.

B. *The Holy Spirit is a gift from God to each of his children.*
   1. The Holy Spirit is a present gift.
   2. The Holy Spirit is a purposeful gift.
   3. The Holy Spirit is a powerful gift.
   4. The Holy Spirit is a precious gift
   5. The Holy Spirit is a personal gift.

C. *It is interesting to note how the promise of the gift of the Holy Spirit is translated in modern versions of the Bible.* The variety in the manner in which this verse, John 14:16, has been translated provides us with a key to the significance of this great gift that God has given to us. The Holy Spirit is called a "comforter" (KJV), "counselor" (RSV), "Helper" (NKJV), and "advocate" (NIV). The Holy Spirit is all of these.

Conclusion

God gave the gift of his Son, who came to die for us. He has also given us the gift of his Spirit to live within us to work the works of God so that we might be delivered from the power of sin.

If you are not yet a believer in Jesus Christ, the Holy Spirit invites you to come to him today that you might receive the gift of forgiveness and the gift of eternal life.

If you have already received Jesus Christ as Savior, the Holy Spirit is a gift you should recognize, appreciate, and respond to fully.

SUNDAY EVENING, OCTOBER 1

Title: Our Daily Bread

Text: "Give us this day our daily bread" **(Matt. 6:11)**.

Scripture Reading: Psalm 146

Introduction

Prayer begins with Godward concerns, but it does not end there. The first three petitions of the Lord's Prayer make petitions for the name, kingdom, and will of God. These must be the first concerns in our prayer life. But then Jesus gave us four petitions to cover our personal needs.

The last four petitions are inclusive. "Give us this day our daily bread" touches on the needs of the body. "Forgive us our debts" includes the needs of the soul. "Lead us not into temptation, but deliver us from evil" speaks to the spiritual needs of the person. This reminds us that we can take whatever concerns us to the heavenly Father in prayer.

"Give us . . . our daily bread" would seem to be a simple statement of need, yet many different interpretations have been set forth. Some have drawn back from thinking of it as a simple request for "daily bread." They have changed it to mean spiritual bread from the Word of God or Christ, the Bread of Life; and some have even referred to it as the bread of the Lord's Table. There is no need for such spiritualization of the request. Our God is just as concerned that the basic necessities of life be supplied as he is that we have spiritual bread for the spirit. Our God is concerned about the total person. What can we learn here?

I. The petition for daily bread acknowledges God as the source of bread.

A. *The explanation.* What does the petition for "bread" include? The word should be understood as including all of our material needs, whatever is necessary to sustain our physical life in the world. We are to come to God with our petitions for those necessities as an acknowledgment that we rely on God, the giver of every perfect gift, to provide for us. Later in this same chapter, Jesus rebuked worldly anxiety over the necessities of life. He declared that we deny God when we become anxious over what we will eat or what we will wear or where we will live. He affirmed that God knows that we need all these things.

B. *An example.* God gave his people a lesson on this truth early in their national history. Their food supply ran out soon after they left the land of Egypt, and no other supplies were available in the desert. They became very anxious about the situation and began to murmur loudly about it, but God graciously began to supply all the food they needed. They learned that the God of creation and redemption has an abundant supply of bread. He gave them a feast of angels' food, or manna, every day.

C. *The application.* Christians in America today are likely to forget the source of their bread—we simply pick up a loaf at the supermarket. And those who cannot afford it are provided bread by the government.

Jesus wants us to know, however, that the real source of bread is the God who never changes. He is behind every secondary source of supply. Without his sunshine and rain, without his creative presence in nature, we would have no food, shelter, or clothing.

Those of you who have always accepted responsibility for providing your own bread have not felt any need of asking God for his assistance. You have had plenty to eat and plenty to wear without asking. Do not be deceived! The bread you have been eating and the clothing you have been wearing have come to you as gifts from God. God has been merciful to bestow them upon you even though you have neither asked for them nor acknowledged him. A little thoughtful consideration on your part will make it clear that ultimately God is your source.

II. The prayer for daily bread affirms God's method of supply.

A. *"This day."* In this simple petition there are some important lessons about how God supplies our needs. In "Give us this day our daily bread," "this day" points out that God's regular method is to supply our needs as they occur. Literally, it is a cry for bread for "today." We are not to be praying about bread for next year or in our old age, but for today. God's wisdom in this is clear. If he gave us all that we would ever need for life at the beginning of life, we would forget the Giver as we went about using up the gift. But since he is pleased to give it to us daily in response to our prayers, we have less opportunity to forget that we are dependent on him to meet every need in our lives.

B. *"Daily."* This word indicates more than the receipt of a daily supply. It is a petition for just what is necessary to meet your need. We must be careful about asking God for material things. We should ask him only for whatever is necessary to meet our basic needs. If God is pleased to give us more than enough to meet our basic needs, we should be grateful to him and generous to others. And if he gives us only enough to meet our basic needs, we should be content.

III. The petition for daily bread expresses concern for others.

A. *Explanation.* There is no place for selfishness when we come before the heavenly Father in prayer. The Model Prayer makes this clear by making the pronouns plural, for example, "Give us this day our daily bread." When we come before the Father, we must bear a concern for any in God's family who have material needs.

B. *Application.* Do your prayers reflect concern for others? Selfishness is a hindrance to effective prayer. God will not hear you if you are only concerned about bread for yourself. James wrote, "Ye ask, and receive not, because ye ask amiss, that ye might consume it upon your lusts" (James 4:3).

Conclusion

This petition for daily bread surely mandates a practice of daily prayer. God wants you to come before him daily with the concerns of your life. This petition surely mandates daily thanksgiving as well. If God faithfully supplies the necessities of our lives each day, it would be a crime not to express genuine thanksgiving to him. Replace your anxieties about daily needs with prayer and know that God will hear and answer.

Wednesday Evening, October 4

Title: Audience Response to the Preacher

Text: "From that time many of his disciples went back, and walked no more with him" **(John 6:66)**.

Scripture Reading: John 6:1–71

Introduction

Preaching plays an important role in the life of a church. Congregations demand helpful sermons. They also expect thorough preparation, effective delivery, and decisions from the sermon. In return the preacher expects a listening, responsive audience.

The hearing of an audience plays an important part in a sermon. Jesus told a parable about how people listened to and received the gospel message. He told of a sower who was sowing seed. Some seed fell by the wayside, some amid thorns, some on rocky soil, and still some on good ground. From this parable we could say that every sermon has a response of some kind.

Jesus was a masterful preacher. When he preached, people responded. Let us notice the different responses to his sermons.

I. The religious leaders: rejection.

A. *The Jews resented the Lord's message.* "The Jews then murmured at him, because he said, I am the bread . . . of life; he that cometh to me shall never hunger; and he that believeth on me shall never thirst" (John 6:35, 41). Jesus had referred to the experiences of the Israelites when God fed them with manna. God gave them life, for life was in the bread. Jesus then applied the bread to himself.

B. *The Jews rejected the messenger.* To resent the message is to reject the messenger. "And they said, 'Is not this Jesus, the son of Joseph, whose father and mother we know? how is it then that he saith, I came down from heaven?'" (John 6:42). The Jews regarded Jesus only as the son of Mary and Joseph. They judged the Lord by external standards.

God's greatest message and messenger came through a Galilean carpenter. The Jews denounced both his message and him. Within every audience there will be those who will resent God's message and reject his Son.

II. The crowds: dropouts.

A. *Jesus was popular with the crowd at the beginning of his ministry.* People were attracted to Jesus. They heard his unusual sermons and watched him perform many miracles. They enjoyed the benefits of his multiplying the loaves and fish.

B. *The crowds began to depart from Jesus.* "From that time many of his disciples went back, and walked no more with him" (John 6:66). Why did these people leave? They left because they found the way of Jesus to be too difficult. "Many therefore of his disciples, when they had heard this, said, This is an hard saying; who can hear it?" (v. 60). They didn't mean that it was hard to understand; rather, it was hard to accept and put into practice. The crowds knew the claims of Christ, and they were not willing to accept and follow them.

People have not changed. They continue to respond to Jesus by dropping out. Of course this does not destroy the idea of the security of the believer. It just discloses the reality or pretense of a person's faith.

III. The apostles: dedication.

A. *Jesus posed an important question to the disciples to test their dedication.* "Then said Jesus unto the twelve, Will ye also go away?" (John 6:67). The disciples had only two alternatives—they could go away or they could stay.

Disciples are always put to the test. The passing of time and various life situations will disclose the reality of commitment.

B. *Peter answered the Master with a demonstration of dedication.* He said, "Lord, to whom shall we go? thou hast the words of eternal life" (John 6:68). Peter affirmed that there was no one else to whom the disciples could turn for life. Only Jesus could satisfy their deepest longings.

Conclusion

The sermon is almost over. You will make a response to this sermon. Either you will say, "It was good' or "It was bad." But that is not your only response. Jesus has been presented. Various responses to Jesus have been cited: You can reject him, drop out, or dedicate your life to him. What will be your response?

SUNDAY MORNING, OCTOBER 8

Title: The Holy Spirit: A Living Gift

Text: "'Even the Spirit of truth, whom the world cannot receive, because it neither sees him nor knows him; you know him, for he dwells with you, and will be in you'" **(John 14:17 RSV)**.

Scripture Reading: John 14:15–20

Hymns: "Holy, Holy, Holy," Heber
"Serve the Lord with Gladness," McKinney
"Holy Spirit, Faithful Guide," Wells

Offertory Prayer: Father in heaven, thank you for being so wise and generous. Thank you for being so great and good. Thank you for offering to us so many spiritual blessings and opportunities. Today we come offering ourselves to you. Accept our tithes and offerings as indications of our love and as symbols of our desire to participate with you in your ministry of mercy and helpfulness to a needy world. In Jesus' name we pray. Amen.

Introduction

Many different options are available to someone who is eager to bestow a gift on someone he or she loves. Some gifts are inanimate in nature and last a long time. Others, like cut flowers, are perishable. There are also living gifts like puppies, kittens, and lovely growing plants. God our Father has seen fit to bestow a living gift of a different nature within the mind and heart of each of his children at the moment of their conversion—the gift of the Holy Spirit, who is the living presence of God himself.

I. The Holy Spirit is a living gift.

The Holy Spirit is not a mere influence that comes from God. The Holy Spirit is more than a force, like gravity or magnetism or electricity. Jesus uses the personal masculine pronoun in our text to describe this living gift from God.

A. *The Holy Spirit speaks as a communicator.* "He who has an ear, let him hear what the Spirit says to the churches. To him who conquers I will grant to eat of the tree of life" (Rev. 2:7 RSV).

B. *The Holy Spirit intercedes as a divine intercessor in the interest of those who have received Jesus Christ as Savior.* "The Spirit helps us in our weakness; for we do not know how to pray as we ought, but the Spirit himself intercedes for us with sighs too deep for words" (Rom. 8:26 RSV).

C. *The Holy Spirit testifies regarding Jesus Christ.* "The Spirit of truth, who proceeds from the Father, he will bear witness to me" (John 15:26 RSV).

D. *The Holy Spirit leads the servants of Christ in service; Philip is a classic illustration.* "The Spirit said to Philip, 'Go up and join the chariot'" (Acts 8:29 RSV).

In Paul's letter to the Romans, he described the leading of the Spirit. "For all who are led by the Spirit of God are sons of God" (8:14 RSV).

E. *The Holy Spirit functions as a guide into an understanding of divine truth.* "When the Spirit of truth comes, he will guide you into all the truth; for he will not speak on his own authority, but whatever he hears he will speak, and he will declare to you the things that are to come" (John 16:13 RSV).
F. *The Holy Spirit appoints spiritual leaders for the churches.* "The Holy Spirit has made you guardians, to feed the church of the Lord which he obtained with his own blood" (Acts 20:28 RSV). A pastor needs something besides a majority vote of a congregation to be an effective minister. He needs to be appointed simultaneously by the Holy Spirit.
G. *That the Holy Spirit is a living gift can be perceived by virtue of the fact that he can be grieved by improper conduct on the part of those who are within the body of Christ.* "Do not grieve the Holy Spirit of God, in whom you were sealed for the day of redemption" (Eph. 4:30 RSV).

II. The Holy Spirit is a divine person.

When God bestows the gift of the Holy Spirit within the heart of his child, he is bestowing a living gift who is at the same time a divine person. "And because you are sons, God has sent the Spirit of his Son into our hearts, crying, 'Abba! Father!'" (Gal. 4:6 RSV). God is Spirit. God is not localized in a body as man is. God in Spirit comes to dwell within the body of each believer as a living presence.

A. *This living gift of the divine presence comes into our lives to purify us and reproduce within us the character and the personality of the Lord Jesus Christ.* "How much more shall the blood of Christ, who through the eternal Spirit offered himself without blemish to God, purify your conscience from dead works to serve the living God" (Heb. 9:14 RSV).
B. *This living gift of the Holy Spirit is all-powerful.* This power was demonstrated in the miraculous conception of the Christ when the Holy Spirit came upon Mary in great power (Luke 1:35).
C. *This living gift of the Holy Spirit knows all of the things of God as well as the things of man.* "The Spirit searches everything, even the depths of God. For what person knows a man's thoughts except the spirit of man which is in him? So also no one comprehends the thoughts of God except the Spirit of God" (1 Cor. 2:10–11 RSV). This divine person who has come to dwell within us knows all about us and, at the same time, has perfect understanding of the mind of God. He seeks to lead us to think the thoughts of God.
D. *The Holy Spirit, which God has given to us as a living gift, is spoken of as God in the Scriptures.* For example, Peter asked Ananias, "Why has

Satan filled your heart to lie to the Holy Spirit and to keep back part of the proceeds of the land? . . . You have not lied to men but to God" (Acts 5:3–4 RSV).

That the Holy Spirit is God is also seen in Paul's statement to the Corinthians: "We all, with unveiled face, beholding the glory of the Lord, are being changed into his likeness from one degree of glory to another; for this comes from the Lord who is the Spirit" (2 Cor. 3:18 RSV).

Conclusion

The Holy Spirit of God invites each nonbeliever to put faith in Jesus Christ and to receive him as Lord and Savior. He uses the Bible, the church, your family, your friends, and the emptiness of your heart to communicate this. If you will receive Jesus Christ as Savior, the Holy Spirit will enter you to work God's good work within you. He will work for your eternal welfare.

"Therefore, as the Holy Spirit says, 'Today, when you hear his voice, do not harden your hearts as in the rebellion'" (Heb. 3:7–8).

SUNDAY EVENING, OCTOBER 8

Title: Forgive Us Our Debts

Text: "And forgive us our debts, as we forgive our debtors" **(Matt. 6:12)**.

Scripture Reading: Mark 11:20–26

Introduction

Jesus instructs us to make all of our needs a matter of prayer. The needs of our body are to be a matter of prayer, which is why we pray, "Give us this day our daily bread." But we are also to pray about the needs of our mind. A part of the human soul is the conscience. God placed within us a little voice that protests when we violate our sense of right and wrong. What do you do when you feel guilty? You should pray. You should not carry guilt through even one day. You should pray, "Forgive us our debts as we forgive our debtors."

The Lord's Prayer is a prayer for disciples. Some mistakenly teach that once you become a Christian, you never need to confess or seek forgiveness again. But Jesus taught his disciples to pray this prayer daily.

I. The petition makes a personal confession.

A. *The possibility of sin in the Christian.* "Forgive us our debts." As with some of the other petitions in the Lord's Prayer, this is a confession of a felt need in one's life. The person praying this petition is admitting to the heavenly Father that he or she is indebted to him. This brings before us an important question about the Christian life. Do we sin after becoming a Christian? Are we still responsible for our sins after we become a Christian? Both the Scriptures and the Christian experience answer the first question. Scripture assures us that it is God's will that we not sin but that God has made provision for forgiveness in case we do sin (1 John 2:1–2). Scripture warns us that if we deny that we have sinned, we are just playing games with ourselves and seeking in futility to deceive God (1:8, 10). We will ever be aware that we are falling short of the glory of God. In our honest moments, we will have to admit that we have not given to God and our fellow humans all that we owe them.

B. *The response to sin in the Christian.* This petition is a personal confession that grows out of a person's taking sin seriously in his or her personal life. This word *debts* is an interesting word. In the giving of the same prayer in the gospel of Luke, the word *sin* is used. *Sin* means "to miss the mark" or "to come short." The interchange of these words indicates that when we come short of God's ideal or God's purpose for our lives, we run up a debt with God. Each act of sin puts us into debt with God, and we have nothing with which to pay the debt. We owe God a life of complete love, service, worship, and devotion. When we fail to give it to him, we have a debt we cannot pay. The same is true in our relationship to our fellow humans. We owe them love, concern, and care. We are to be as concerned for their welfare as we are for our own. A failure to have this kind of ministering concern runs up a debt.

II. The petition expresses an urgent appeal.

The appeal "Forgive us" is expressed in the most urgent way. It assumes that God is a forgiving God. From all that Jesus taught and revealed about God, we know this to be true. The holy God who has been offended by our sins and to whom we have become deeply indebted is a generous, forgiving God.

A. *Because of the nature of sin.* The heart of this appeal is an acknowledgment of our inability to pay the debt we have run up on God's books. The essence of the appeal is that God will cancel out all that is on the book against us. The word *forgive* means to "cancel," "dismiss," "send away." When we make this kind of appeal, we know that we are unable to do anything about the debt we owe, so we ask God to cancel it. It is really an appeal for God to bear the cost himself. Although there is no mention of it here, we know that God is a forgiving God because he has been willing to pay the price. Christ died in our stead and thereby paid the price so that God could forgive.

B. *Because of the broken fellowship.* But how does this relate to the life of a Christian? Didn't forgiveness come when we received Christ as Lord and Savior? The answer is an obvious yes. But this is a family prayer.

Receiving Christ as the Lord of your life put you in God's family, but you can lose the joy of being in the family if you do not continue to practice this confession and make this appeal for forgiveness. While the sins in your life do not cause you to lose your place in the family, they do interrupt your fellowship with the Father. He cannot and will not have fellowship with you as long as you fail to confess the sin in your life. The conscious communion we experience with God flows out of a cleansed heart. This cleansing comes only as we ask God daily for forgiveness. So the urgency of this appeal comes out of the sense of sin and the burden of broken fellowship.

III. The petition includes a testimony.

A. *The inevitable wrongs.* The appeal "Forgive us our debts" is of no value unless it is accompanied by this testimony: "as we forgive our debtors." Behind this testimony is a helpful insight into life. Life is so constructed that we must anticipate that we will be wronged by others along the way. Sometimes the wrongs may be verbal. We may be falsely accused, or we may be the victim of misrepresentation, or our good name may be misused. The wrongs may be material. Sometimes we may be the victims of dishonesty or deceit. The wrongs may be legal. Injustice is a fact in our world. Or the wrongs may be emotional or psychological. When we come to God to ask him for forgiveness, we must be able to give testimony that we have forgiven those who have wronged us.

B. *Our exercising forgiveness toward someone else does not build up some merit on which we can base our appeal.* We are no more deserving of God's forgiveness after we forgive the other person than we were before. It is our duty to be a forgiving person. We are in no position to receive or experience God's forgiveness as long as we have unforgiveness in our hearts. Jesus emphasized this: "For if ye forgive men their trespasses, your heavenly Father will also forgive you. But if ye forgive not men their trespasses, neither will your Father forgive your trespasses" (Matt. 6:14). We are not truly repentant until we have come to the place where we can forgive. So this testimony gives evidence of a broken spirit and a contrite heart.

There is one other question we need to consider: Can I forgive a person before he or she seeks my forgiveness? The answer is no. God cannot forgive us until we seek his forgiveness, but God is always ready to forgive. God will take the initiative in bringing us to a place where we will ask forgiveness. He will keep showering us with evidences of his goodness even though he must withhold from us the joy of his fellowship until we repent. So just as God is ready to forgive, so must we be. We must not harbor an unforgiving and bitter spirit. Our testimony must be pure and genuine, for God knows our hearts.

Conclusion

Are you ready to pray? Do you have your confession ready? Is it specific? Are you ready to make your appeal—"Forgive me"? Are you ready with your testimony? Can you say to God, "I have forgiven those who have wronged me"? This must be the daily pattern of your prayer life.

WEDNESDAY EVENING, OCTOBER 11

Title: What Do You Think of Sin?

Text: "They say unto him, Master, this woman was taken in adultery, in the very act" **(John 8:4)**.

Scripture Reading: John 8:1–11

Introduction

Psychiatrist Karl Menninger wrote a book several years ago titled *Whatever Became of Sin?* Menninger sounded like a preacher when he said that the word *sin* had virtually disappeared from the American vocabulary and had been replaced by crime and sickness. Menninger called for a new emphasis on sin with the idea of responsibility, guilt, and even punishment.

Jesus had a lot to say about sin. One example from his ministry that we can study is his encounter with a sinful woman. Some scribes and Pharisees were going to stone her because she had been caught in the act of adultery. But just before they were about to stone her, Jesus stooped and wrote on the ground. His words and action convicted the woman's accusers, and they left. John writes, "When Jesus had lifted up himself, and saw none but the woman, he said unto her, Woman, where are thine accusers? hath no man condemned thee? She said, No man, Lord. And Jesus said to her, Neither do I condemn thee: go, and sin no more" (John 8:10–11). From this episode we may learn much about sin.

I. Sin is a universal problem.

"He that is without sin among you, let him first cast a stone at her" (John 8:7).

A. *Some people are guilty of sensual sins.* No one could deny that this woman was a sinner, for she had been caught in the act of adultery. The world is filled with people who express their sin with the sins of the flesh. Murder, adultery, stealing, and countless other sensual sins abound. But this is not the only kind of sinner.

B. *Other people are guilty of sins of the spirit or temperament.* Although the scribes and Pharisees were not guilty of adultery, they were sinners too. They were guilty of self-righteousness. The world is filled with people who express their sin with sins of the temperament. If we are not careful, we will overlook these sins and point only to the sensual sins. Jesus taught the universality of sin, which is expressed in many ways.

II. Sin is to be condemned.

A. *Jesus condemned all types of sin.* With skill he made the Pharisees look at their own lives instead of at the sins of the woman. Yet Jesus was not light on sin when he spoke to the woman. He said, "Woman, where are they? Has no one condemned you?"

"No one, sir," she said.

"Then neither do I condemn you," Jesus declared. "Go now and leave your life of sin" (John 8:10–11).

In the cases of both the Pharisees and the woman, Jesus condemned the sins, not the persons. The Lord dislikes sin, and he condemns its presence and action in every person.

B. *Jesus condemns sin because continuing in its downward course destroys a person's potential and also fills that person's life with guilt.* Nothing is more debilitating than self-condemnation. Guilt was destroying the life of the woman who had been committing adultery, and sin had been destroying the lives of the Pharisees as well, but they were blinded to its effects.

III. Sin can be forgiven.

A. *Forgiveness is possible for everyone.* Sin need not destroy either the promiscuous woman or the religious leaders, for Jesus offered forgiveness to all people who acknowledged their sin. And no person need remain in the condition of sinfulness today, for forgiveness is available to anyone who repents.

B. *Forgiveness opens the door for new possibilities.* When Jesus forgave the adulterous woman, new and wonderful possibilities were open to her. Think of just a few benefits: she was not condemned; she was challenged to a new lifestyle; she could have a new beginning in her life. People today are burdened with unforgiven sin. A newness of life will come to those who repent and experience God's forgiveness.

Conclusion

The text does not record whether the woman caught in adultery accepted God's forgiveness. I hope she did. I hope you will accept his forgiveness too.

Sunday Morning, October 15

Title: Using the Gifts of the Holy Spirit

Text: "As each has received a gift, employ it for one another, as good stewards of God's varied grace" **(1 Peter 4:10 RSV)**.

Scripture Reading: 1 Peter 4:7–11

Hymns: "All Hail the Power of Jesus' Name," Perronet
"Holy Spirit, Faithful Guide," Wells
"Make Me a Channel of Blessing," Smyth

Offertory Prayer: Holy Father, thank you for the gift of your Son to us that we might know you and experience your salvation. Thank you for the gift of your Holy Spirit to dwell within us as Teacher, Guide, Counselor, and Helper. Thank you for the gifts that the Holy Spirit has imparted to us that we might minister effectively in the name of Christ for your glory in and through the church. Bless us now as we come bringing gifts to you to be used in the advancement of your kingdom's work. We pray in Jesus' name. Amen.

Introduction

God is the great giver. He has given us his Son, Jesus Christ, to be our Savior, Teacher, Friend, Lord, and Helper. God has also given us the Holy Spirit to dwell within us and enable us to do God's work. The Holy Spirit was given on the day of Pentecost to accomplish a number of significant purposes. He came to identify Jesus Christ as the risen, living Lord and Messiah. He was given to unite the followers of Christ into a living body in which Christ could dwell and continue his work of redemption in the world. The Holy Spirit was given to identify the church to the Jewish people as the new Israel through whom God would carry forward his eternal redemptive purpose. He was given to enable and to empower the church to succeed in preaching the gospel to the ends of the earth. He was given to impart and to plant the confession "Jesus Christ is Lord" at the very center of every person's being. The Holy Spirit was given to produce within each believer the nature and character and personality of Jesus Christ.

While the Holy Spirit is the great gift of God to each believer, the Scriptures teach us that the Holy Spirit imparts spiritual gifts to every member of the church that each one might fulfill the function God has for him.

I. The gifts of the Holy Spirit.

References to the variety of gifts of the Holy Spirit for ministering in the church and through the church to the world are listed in several different books of the New Testament.

A. *Paul listed some of the gifts of the Spirit in his letter to the church at Rome (12:3–8).*

B. *One of the major sections on the gifts of the Spirit is chapters 12–14 of Paul's first letter to the Corinthians.* In this passage, Paul was dealing with a problem that was dividing the church, an exaggerated emphasis on the value and use of the gift of speaking in tongues and a lack of emphasis on love as the supreme gift of the Spirit.

C. *In the letter to the Ephesians, Paul listed more gifts of the Spirit (4:11–12).*

II. The nature of the gifts of the Spirit.

A. *The gifts of the Spirit are all "grace gifts."* They are bestowed by the Holy Spirit, rather than merited or earned for outstanding service. They may take the form of talents, but in reality they are gifts from the Holy Spirit.

B. *The gifts of the Holy Spirit are his sovereign gifts.* "All these are the work of one and the same Spirit, and he distributes them to each one, just as he determines" (1 Cor. 12:11 NIV).

C. *The gifts of the Holy Spirit are functional gifts.* The gifts of the Spirit are not like decorative ornaments to be worn or boxes of candy to be enjoyed. Rather, they enable believers to minister as the body of Christ and are intended to produce harmony and effectiveness in service (14:5).

D. *The gifts of the Holy Spirit are primarily for the congregation, that is, for the good of the church (v. 12).* This is not to imply that the individual is not edified or built up by receiving a gift from the Holy Spirit.

E. *To every believer there is given a gift from the Holy Spirit.* "We have different gifts, according to the grace given to each of us" (Rom. 12:6 NIV). As far as we can observe, the Scriptures teach that each believer has received at least one gift from the Holy Spirit.

III. Discovering and using your spiritual gift.

How are we to be certain concerning our spiritual gifts? Is there a way by which we can discover them?

A. *We should study the scriptural lists of the gifts of the Spirit and then examine ourselves sincerely and honestly to see if we have some talent, gift, or inclination that would indicate that God has placed upon us the blessing and the burden of a particular gift.*

B. *We should experiment with acts of faith as we feel led, trusting the Spirit for guidance.* We can do this by identifying needs about us that we believe we can meet and then do what we can to meet those needs. We may discover that we have the gift after we have met a particular need.

C. *We should examine our spiritual satisfactions.* If we get a particular joy out of doing a certain type of Christian service, it could be that we are working in the area in which the Holy Spirit has given us a gift.

D. *We should evaluate our effectiveness in service.* Certainly it would follow that if we cannot carry a tune, we do not have the gift of singing solos or being a part of a singing group. The gifts of the Spirit are for the building up of the church. If what we attempt to do does not build up the church, then it probably follows that it is not an area in which we have a gift.

E. *We should recognize the affirmations of other believers.* Many times others who are more mature in the faith will recognize your gifts before you do. When others commend you for a service that is rendered, they may be giving you a clue concerning what your gift is.

Conclusion

God has given to humankind the gift of his Son. Have you received this gift in your heart? Have you let him become your Savior, Teacher, Friend, and Helper?

If you have received his Son, Jesus Christ, as your Savior, you have also received the gift of his Holy Spirit. When we become the children of God, God sends the Spirit of his Son into our hearts (Gal. 4:6).

If you have received God's Son and Spirit, then there is a gift or gifts that the Holy Spirit has given to you in order that you might be a living, vital, functioning part of the body of Christ. May God bless you and use you greatly as you recognize and respond to the gift or gifts the Holy Spirit has given you for ministering in the world.

SUNDAY EVENING, OCTOBER 15

Title: Lead Us Not into Temptation

Text: "And lead us not into temptation, but deliver us from evil" **(Matt. 6:13)**.

Scripture Reading: James 1:1–14

Introduction

The battle with temptation is a continuing battle in all of life and is what prompted our petition for today: "Lead us not into temptation."

Doubtlessly, the Teacher intended for each of these petitions to be repeated daily. Even one day of relaxation during the battle with temptation can be spiritually fatal. While Jesus did not experience the need voiced in the second of the petitions, "Forgive us," he did experience this one. That is, since he never succumbed to any temptation, he never had to request forgiveness. You may question whether Jesus really knew the power of temptation. The truth is that the only person who ever knows the full power of temptation is the person who resists it. Jesus knew more about the power of temptation than any of us.

This petition lends itself to deeper meditation.

I. This petition affirms the sovereignty of God.

We must not forget that all of the Lord's Prayer is addressed to "Our Father which art in heaven." We begin the prayer by addressing God as the sovereign, almighty Father in heaven. In a sense, each petition affirms this of him in some way, but this one does so in a special way.

In the petition "Lead us not into temptation," "lead us" translates the Greek word that is commonly translated "bring us." It is usually used with reference to a person's moving something from one place to another. It probably even expresses the Hebrew idea of causing something to be brought or led. So this petition affirms that God is in a position to cause things to happen, to bring us or lead us, as it may please him. He is affirmed to be Sovereign.

A. *Over circumstances.* Since temptation can come from finding oneself in the wrong circumstance, this petition affirms that God has control over circumstances. It addresses him as the one who orders the steps of his people. Do you believe that God can actually order the circumstances of your life to protect you from the allurements of evil?

B. *Over spiritual forces.* Since temptation forces usually come from spiritual forces outside of our lives, this petition affirms that God has ultimate and sovereign control over all of the spiritual forces in our world. Satan and his agents do not move outside the realm of God's control. While God does not cause them to do the things they do, he does still have them under his sovereignty.

C. *Over us.* Since many temptations are of our own making, this petition affirms that God has sovereignty over our lives. "Lead us, bring us!" It personalizes the sovereignty of God. It is so easy to see God as having control over everything except our lives. It is easy to slip into an attitude that sees all of life as being out of control, but this petition affirms that God is in control.

II. This petition acknowledges the significance of temptation.

You may be confused about the source of temptation. The Bible teaches that the devil tempts people but God only tests people. James 1:13 says, "When tempted, no one should say, 'God is tempting me.' For God cannot be tempted by evil, nor does he tempt anyone; but each one is tempted when they are dragged away by their own evil desire and enticed. Then, after desire has conceived, it gives birth to sin; and sin, when it is full-grown, gives birth to death" (NIV). God himself cannot commit sin, nor can he tempt anyone to commit sin. Therefore it is always a mistake to blame God for our temptation to do something that is wrong. God is in no way responsible for the temptation.

A. *Testing of character.* The Bible speaks of God's "testing" a person, for example, Abraham when God instructed him to offer Isaac as a sacrifice (Gen. 22:1). God was not tempting Abraham to do something sinful, but he was testing the depth of his commitment and the strength of his faith. Whenever God puts a person to the test, it is to give him the opportunity to prove himself. Of course, there is always the possibility of failure, but the test will not create the weakness of commitment—it will only reveal it.

B. *Temptation as allurement to sin.* Whenever the word *temptation* is used in connection with sin, another besides God is responsible. Ultimately Satan himself must bear the responsibility, but obviously he will work through our own evil nature, through others, and through circumstances. It is this type of temptation that is referred to in this petition. It is a prayer that we may escape a confrontation with a temptation to sin. Only fools flirt with temptation; there is always the possibility that they will succumb to the allurement of evil.

What can I expect if I pray this prayer? Can I expect that God will protect me from the influence of the tempter? Can I expect immunity from temptation? No! Even our Lord himself, who surely knew how to pray this prayer, did not totally escape confrontations with temptation. We can, however, expect that we will not be stumbling into temptation unprepared. We can expect that God's provisions to resist temptation will always be available and adequate. First Corinthians 10:13 says, "No temptation has overtaken you except what is common to mankind. And God is faithful; he will not let you be tempted beyond what you can bear. But when you are tempted, he will also provide a way out so that you can endure it" (NIV).

III. This petition announces the surrender of life.

"Lead us not into temptation" is a prayer of personal surrender to the lordship and leadership of God in one's life. It is a renunciation of the lordship and leadership of self.

A. *The desire to avoid sin.* This petition expresses a desire to avoid sin. The location of this petition in the prayer—after the petition for forgiveness—is significant. Whenever we experience release from guilt through forgiveness, we are left with a desire never to sin again.

B. *The depth of the surrender.* We are to give God complete control. Consider what this will involve. Since temptation occurs in certain circumstances, we have to agree to stay away from places and circumstances in which we are tempted. We must surrender to the Lord our free and recreational time and allow him to choose the places we go and the things we do. This includes the books we read and the television shows and movies we watch. Temptation occurs when we spend time with certain friends, so we even have to surrender the right to choose our own friends to the Lord. By praying this petition, we are asking the Lord to give us only friends who will help us avoid sin. Temptation also occurs when riches or poverty come to a person, so we must surrender even our finances to the Lord. We must be ready for him to determine how much of this world's wealth we will enjoy. Only when we surrender everything to the Lord can he protect us from temptation.

Conclusion

For the petition "Lead us not into temptation" to be part of your daily prayer, it must become the desire of your heart. You cannot pray this petition unless you consider personal sin to be a serious matter. As long as you take sin lightly, this will never be your earnest prayer. Praying this petition could lead to new freedom and a new walk with God in your life. Why not try it?

Wednesday Evening, October 18

Title: Christ and Time

Text: "Jesus said unto them, Verily, verily, I say unto you, Before Abraham was, I am" **(John 8:58)**.

Scripture Reading: John 8:48–59

Introduction

Once I gave a sermon titled "Jesus Was the Greatest" to my secretary for typing. She responded, "Preacher, I think you have the wrong verb tense in the title." I looked at it again and said, "Mrs. Givan, that is grammatically correct." "It's not the grammar but the doctrine," she said. Looking at the title again, I reworded it to read, "Jesus Is the Greatest." Thank God for wise secretaries!

Getting the verb tenses correct about Jesus is a difficult task. You can say, "He was," for he lived in history. You can say, "He is," for he lives today. You can also say, "He will be," for he will always exist. Jesus is the eternal contemporary.

Think of the bewilderment of the Jews when Jesus said, "Before Abraham was, I am." He used a striking contrast in verb tenses—was and am. This "I am" saying gives us insight into Christ and time.

I. Jesus is before time.

The Jews looked to the greatness of Abraham and boasted of their kinship with him. But Jesus claimed to be superior to Abraham. Over against Abraham's fleeting span of life, Jesus placed his timelessness. Jesus lived before Abraham and before creation. "In the beginning was the Word, and the Word was with God, and the Word was God. The same was in the beginning with God" (John 1:1–2). Jesus enjoyed fellowship with the Father before the sand went through the hourglass. Jesus was God in human flesh.

II. Jesus is in time.

The Jews would not grasp the fact that God entered into time and space. They could not accept that a baby born in Bethlehem and reared by Jewish peasants could be the promised Messiah.

When Jesus entered into time, he did not cease to be God. He did not divest himself of divinity. He entered into a new mode of being—human flesh. Thus, when Jesus entered into time, he identified with our plight. He subjected himself to life's trials and temptations. "For we have not an high priest which cannot be touched with the feeling of our infirmities; but was in all points tempted like as we are, yet without sin" (Heb. 4:15).

III. Jesus is supreme over time.

Jesus' words, "Before Abraham was, I am," describe Jesus' lordship over time. Oscar Cullman, in the book *Christus und die Zeit* (Christ and Time), builds the idea that time finds its central thrust in Jesus Christ. Jesus started the phenomenon of time. Because he created it and ordained it as a part of life, he is Lord over it. And in the future, Jesus will stop time. When he returns, he will usher in a timeless, glorified kingdom.

Conclusion

Jesus is the greatest person. He was before time. He was in time. He will be after time ceases. He is!

SUNDAY MORNING, OCTOBER 22

Title: Obeying the Command of the Holy Spirit

Text: "And the Spirit said to Philip, 'Go up and join this chariot'" **(Acts 8:29 RSV)**.

Scripture Reading: Acts 8:26–40

Hymns: "Rejoice, Ye Pure in Heart," Plumptre
"Guide Me, Thou Great Jehovah," Williams
"Jesus, Savior, Pilot Me," Hopper

Offertory Prayer: Holy, Father, thank you for the blessings of the past. Thank you for the blessed privilege of being alive today and being with your people. We rejoice in your grace and mercy. We thank you for the privilege of serving you and others. Accept our tithes and offerings as symbols of our desire to be totally at your disposal. In Jesus' name. Amen.

Introduction

Some people believe they are obeying the Great Commission when they attend Sunday school and worship services. Some believe they are obeying the Great Commission when they sing in the choir or teach a Sunday school class. Some believe they are obeying the Great Commission when they give a tithe of their income plus offerings or when they pray for missionaries. All of these are but partial responses to the Great Commission of our Lord. Philip provides us with a dramatic demonstration of how we are to obey the Great Commission on a one-to-one basis in our personal lives.

I. Philip was sensitive to the Holy Spirit's indwelling presence.

Many of us never respond to the Holy Spirit because we do not recognize that he is within us and that he is seeking to do the work of God in us, to us, and through us.

II. Philip was listening to the voice of the Holy Spirit.

A. *"An angel of the Lord said to Philip, 'Rise and go toward the south'" (Acts 8:26).* The remarkable thing is that Philip arose and went (v. 27). He was obedient to the messenger of God.

B. *"And the Spirit said to Philip, 'Go up and join this chariot'" (v. 29).* The Scripture then reads that Philip ran to him. Philip received an impulse from the Holy Spirit and had the wisdom to be responsive.

III. God's love was active in this whole experience.

A. *God loves all people.*
B. *God guides his people who will obey him to witnessing opportunities.*
C. *God supplies obedient witnesses with interested seekers.*
D. *God gave Philip a proper approach to share the good news with this needy man.*
E. *God gave Philip a message—the good news of God's grace.*
F. *God brought about conviction of sin and conversion.*
G. *God won a great victory.*

When God seeks a sinner and a sinner seeks God, they get together—particularly when one of God's children is listening and obedient to the Spirit.

IV. Philip had a heart surrendered to God.

A. *Philip believed that God is love and that you can trust him without fear.*
B. *Philip had a sensitive spirit that was open to God.*
C. *Philip had his spiritual receiving set turned on.*
D. *Philip had a heart that was obedient because of love.*
E. *Philip shared the good news.*

V. The Ethiopian official became spiritually rich.

A. *As the representative of his queen, he was:*
   1. Privileged.
   2. Powerful.
   3. Popular.
B. *As a human being, the Ethiopian official had:*
   1. An empty heart.
   2. A hungry heart.
   3. A needy heart.
   4. An open heart.
C. *The Ethiopian official responded with a believing heart and experienced happiness and joy through faith in Jesus Christ.*

Conclusion

A loving God and a needy heart got together because one of God's children was sensitive to the presence of the Holy Spirit and responsive as the Holy Spirit moved him to witness.

What if Philip had been too busy? What if he had been spiritually lazy? What if Philip had been untrusting and consequently too fearful? What if Philip had been spiritually dull and disobedient? God would have missed the privilege of saving a man, and a man would have missed the privilege of coming to know Jesus Christ.

Sunday Evening, October 22

Title: Deliver Us from Evil

Text: "And lead us not into temptation, but deliver us from evil; for thine is the kingdom, and the power, and the glory, for ever. Amen" **(Matt. 6:13)**.

Scripture Reading: Matthew 6:1–15

Introduction

Seven is the number for completeness in the Bible. It is of special interest that the Master of prayer gave us just seven petitions in the Model Prayer. This could indicate that he felt that the seven petitions covered every need that people might bring to God.

"Deliver us from evil" is the last of the petitions. It voices a cry that comes from the heart of the children of God as they live in this world. It is a cry expressing great urgency. Surely it is appropriate as we assemble for worship in the midst of a troubled world. Consider with me some important implications set forth by this simple petition. And let us recognize the urgent need for us to be taking this petition to our heavenly Father daily.

I. The reality of evil.

Translators do not agree on how this petition is to be translated. The Greek text has the definite article before "evil." How then is the noun to be translated? Is it to be translated as a neuter as in the King James Version? If so, then we would understand it to mean all of the evil things that are in the world and all of the evil things that happen to people. Or should it be translated as a masculine as in the New International Version? If so, then it is to be understood as a reference to the evil one, Satan. Bible scholars have been divided quite evenly over the translation. I realize a choice must be made in the translation, but does it really make that much difference in the interpretation? My honest feeling is that it does not, for the petition is surely a cry for rescue from all evil—evil persons and evil things.

A. *The presence of evil.* The reality of evil in the world is one of the issues that has occupied theologians and philosophers of all persuasions. Our Lord did not hide his face from the reality of evil in the world, nor did he deny the reality of a supreme evil being. Rather, he spoke often about his power over that evil being, Satan. Around the beginning of the twentieth century, learned men had just about excluded the idea of a supreme evil being from their thinking. They attributed all such ideas to superstition and ignorance. But the events of the twentieth century forced people to reconsider. How could the senseless injustice and violence in our world be explained apart from some kind of demonic influence?

B. *The experience with evil.* The petition "Deliver us from evil" comes out of a life that has been personally confronted with the presence and the power of evil. This is not the prayer of a proud and arrogant man who sees himself as the captain of his own ship, the master of his own fate. It is rather the prayer of a broken man who has had his eyes opened to the nature of the world in which he lives and has seen how powerful evil can be. He has beheld the shame, sorrow, and suffering that are present in the world and has been made to drink of the cup himself.

II. The responsibility for evil.

A. *God is not responsible.* This petition clearly assigns the responsibility for evil. Who is responsible for evil in the world? Clearly God is not! If God were responsible for the evil in the world, this would be a petition for God to deliver us from his own creation. While it is wonderfully true that God makes the evil in the world serve his ultimate purpose, it is a serious mistake to assign responsibility for the evil in the world to God. Whatever evil you may encounter may be used of God to perfect holiness in your life, but God does not accept ultimate responsibility for it.

B. *Satan is responsible.* If God is not responsible, then who is? The Bible assigns responsibility to Satan for the evil in the world. While man shares the responsibility with him because of his joining him in Genesis 3, Satan is still presented as the great adversary of God and enemy of man. He is the ultimate source of evil. So this prayer to God is ultimately a prayer against Satan.

Can we lay the ultimate blame on Satan? Yes! Ultimately, he is to blame for all of the physical evil in the world. All of the famines, earthquakes, tornadoes, plagues, diseases, and the like are ultimately the responsibility of the evil one. The world God originally created did not include these. They came only after the evil design of the enemy prevailed over man.

The same is also true of moral evil. While man is a sinner who creates his own shame, sorrow, and sadness, Satan is ultimately responsible. Murder, robbery, drug abuse, divorce, rape, and adultery are his idea. All of the moral evils that beset man on every side come from the evil one. Praying "Deliver us from evil" will keep you from blaming God and your fellow humans and will help you to lay the blame where it belongs—on the shoulders of the mastermind of evil who forsook his God-appointed place to lead an open rebellion against God's rule and thereby brought evil into being.

III. The rescue from evil.

Deliver is a strong word. It means to save, rescue, preserve. This petition is a request that God will do what only God can do. It is an acknowledgment that we cannot keep or preserve ourselves from the presence, power, and person of evil. Only God can do so.

A. *The present rescue.* It is a prayer that God will daily deliver us from the design that the evil one may have on our lives. It is a prayer that we might escape the shame and sorrow that he would impose on us through sin. It is renunciation of evil in every form and a genuine petition to be kept by God from every form of evil. This petition looks to the heavenly Father for his daily protection and intervention on our behalf. Only he can save us from evil.

B. *The future rescue.* However, it may well be that the primary thrust of this petition is for the future, ultimate, final, complete deliverance from evil. It is a prayer for the new heaven and the new earth. It is a prayer for the final binding of Satan and the coming of the day when God shall wipe away all tears and establish a world in which there will be no more sickness, sorrow, or pain. It is a prayer for God's final act of salvation, which will be inaugurated by the second coming of our Lord Jesus Christ.

Conclusion

Have you become too content with our world as it is? Have worldly pleasures so sedated you that you no longer feel the weight of the evil that is in the world? If you are spiritually in touch with the Lord and his world, surely you must be moved to pray, "Deliver us from evil!" The need of the hour is for a company of saints who will pray until deliverance comes.

WEDNESDAY EVENING, OCTOBER 25

Title: Distinctives of Discipleship

Text: "Then said Jesus to those Jews which believed on him, If ye continue in my word, then are ye my disciples indeed" **(John 8:31)**.

Scripture Reading: John 8:30–59

Introduction

What does it really mean to follow Jesus? Somehow in the early part of the twenty-first century, people have lost sight of what it means to follow Jesus. Discipleship is linked to external observance of religion rather than a relational experience with Jesus Christ.

During Jesus' life and ministry on earth, many people sought to follow him. "As he spoke, many believed in him" (John 8:30 NIV). Many motives moved people to associate with Jesus Christ. Some were infatuated with his miracles and teachings. Others were just curious. Jesus did not want people to follow him outside the motive of a genuine commitment. To distinguish the authentic followers, Jesus gave the distinctives of a true disciple.

I. A true disciple has continuance (John 8:31–33).

Jesus realized that some people made an impulsive decision to follow him. At times in Jesus' ministry, large crowds followed him. He knew they followed mainly to see his miracles or just to be a part of the crowd. He knew that many would decide not to follow him. After Jesus taught the crowds that he was the Bread of Life, "many of his disciples drew back and no longer went about with him" (John 6:66 RSV).

Jesus pointed out that perseverance would be the sign of a true disciple. "If ye continue in my word, then are ye my disciples indeed," he said (8:31). Discipleship is not the excitement of one moment. It is a patient continuance in the footsteps of Jesus Christ.

Renowned pianist and composer Ignacy Jan Paderewski started playing the piano at the age of three. He developed slowly, but he determined to become a master of the piano. He practiced six hours almost every day of his life. By discipline and determination, he reached his goal.

To a crowd of potential followers, Jesus gave a sure sign of a disciple. A disciple is one who follows Jesus continuously. The genuine evidence is in the sustained effort.

II. A true disciple has freedom (John 8:34–38).

A. *Jesus taught of a freedom that led to bondage.* "Jesus answered them, Verily, verily, I say unto you, Whosoever committeth sin is the servant of sin" (v. 34). Jesus taught a group of potential disciples about how sin leads to bondage. Going through life with self-will, self-trust, and self-assertion leads to a detrimental bondage. No one who follows Jesus can be a master to himself.

B. *Jesus spoke of a bondage that leads to freedom.* A true disciple is one who has renounced his or her way to follow the way of Christ. Bondage to the Lord leads to authentic freedom. Jesus said, "If the Son therefore shall make you free, ye shall be free indeed" (v. 36). The true disciple of Jesus lives to please only one person—Jesus Christ. A disciple of Jesus is not a slave to sin but is a slave to the Master.

III. A true disciple has Christlike behavior (John 8:39–47).

The Jews claimed to be Abraham's children. By physical lineage this was true. However, many Jews lived contrary to Abraham's example. They sought to kill Jesus (v. 40) and slandered his name (v. 41). Jesus said they were not God's children, for they did not reflect God's character. Rather, he said, "Ye are of your father the devil" (v. 44).

God's children behave like his children. "If God were your Father, ye would love me" (v. 42), Jesus said. And he added, "He that is of God heareth God's words" (v. 47). Nature will be true to itself. If one is born of God, then he or she will live in accordance with Christ's character.

IV. A true disciple honors Christ (John 8:48–59).

Many claimed to be disciples of Jesus, but they did not honor him. In fact, they accused him of being demon-possessed. Jesus said, "I have not a devil; but I honour my Father, and ye do dishonor me" (v. 49). They could not be authentic followers and dishonor the Lord in this way. True disciples honor and adore and obey Christ.

Conclusion

Are you a true disciple of Jesus Christ? The proof is a continuing commitment to him, freedom from sin, Christlike behavior, and a Christ-honoring life.

SUNDAY MORNING, OCTOBER 29

Title: The Holy Spirit Invites You

Text: "The Spirit and the Bride say, 'Come.' And let him who hears say, 'Come.' And let him who is thirsty come, let him who desires take the water of life without price" **(Rev. 22:17 RSV).**

Scripture Reading: Hebrews 3:7–11

Hymns: "God, Our Father, We Adore Thee," Frazer
"Christ Receiveth Sinful Men," Neumeister
"Softly and Tenderly," Thompson

Offertory Prayer: Heavenly Father, thank you for offering us the gift of eternal life through Jesus Christ. Thank you for offering us the gift of your living presence in the Holy Spirit. Thank you for the gift of membership in your family through the church. Thank you for the opportunity you give us to serve you and to minister in your name in our world. Bless these tithes and offerings that they might be used to exalt your name and minister to the needs of a needy world. In Jesus' name we pray. Amen.

Introduction

Humankind's greatest need is to know God through faith in Jesus Christ. Because our deepest need is spiritual, God sent his Son to die on a cross to show his love for us and to conquer death that he might demonstrate to us the reality of eternal life.

Following this great redemptive activity accomplished by Jesus Christ, God sent his Holy Spirit into the church and into the world to invite all nonbelievers to come to Jesus Christ through faith that they might receive the gift of eternal life and become the children and servants of God. If you are still a nonbeliever, you may be shocked to learn that the Holy Spirit of God is in the world today that he might invite you to become a believer in Jesus Christ. The words of our text declare that the purpose of the church and of the Holy Spirit is to invite you to come to Jesus Christ, who is the fountain of living waters. He alone can quench the thirst of your soul. Our Scripture reading urges us to listen attentively and responsively as the Holy Spirit of God speaks to our innermost being.

Jesus, in the closing days of his ministry, detailed some of the activities of the Holy Spirit who would come on the day of Pentecost. One of the primary functions of the Holy Spirit was to bear testimony to people's consciences regarding who Jesus Christ is and what he came to do (cf. John 14:26; 15:26; 16:7–11).

I. Listen to the Holy Spirit because of his divine person.

The Holy Spirit is more than just an influence. The Holy Spirit is more than just a power like magnetism or electricity or gravity. The Holy Spirit is the divine person of God. He uses various means of communicating with you.

A. *The Holy Spirit uses the Scriptures.*
B. *The Holy Spirit uses the church as a communicator.*
C. *The Holy Spirit uses individual believers as his spokespersons.*
D. *The Holy Spirit uses the events of life to interrupt your thoughts and to speak to you if you have ears to listen.*

II. Listen to the Holy Spirit because of his divine purpose for speaking.

A. *He speaks to those of you who are unsaved.* He comes to convince you that the sin of unbelief is the sin that separates a man from God (John 16:7–11). The Holy Spirit alone can convince a person of his sinfulness and of his need to cease rejecting God's love and his claims.

The Holy Spirit does not come to convict you and convince you of your unsaved and lost condition merely to make you feel negative about yourself and experience inward misery and depression. He comes to convert you from unbelief to belief and from rejection to acceptance. Only the Holy Spirit can take an X-ray of your heart and soul and reveal to you your lost condition. He does this that he might attract and persuade you to receive Jesus Christ as Lord and Savior.

B. *He speaks to those of you who are saved.* The Holy Spirit speaks words of comfort and assurance to the new convert (Rom. 8:15–16). It is the plan of the Father God to communicate the new relationship that follows faith to each believer.

The Holy Spirit comes to speak words of encouragement and to provide assistance for living the Christian life when one becomes a believer. God does not want us to attempt to live the Christian life in human strength alone. The Holy Spirit provides the power that is needed to overcome evil and to reap the harvest of the Spirit (Gal. 5:16–23).

The Holy Spirit will also speak to the saved about the needs of those who do not yet know Christ as Savior. He will seek to enlist us in leading people to become believers in Christ.

III. Listen to the Holy Spirit because of his divine power.

A. *Only the Holy Spirit of God has the power to produce the miracle of the new birth in the believer (Titus 3:3–7).*

B. *The Holy Spirit has the divine power to enable us to develop a Christian disposition and character.* He begins his good work within us at the moment of conversion and will continue this work of seeking to produce within us the very character of Jesus Christ throughout our lives (Gal. 5:22–23; Phil. 1:6).

C. *The Holy Spirit has been given to us to assure us of our victory over death and the grave (2 Cor. 5:5).* The indwelling gift of the Holy Spirit is God's guarantee that one day we will have complete victory over death and the grave.

Conclusion

Listen to the Holy Spirit now. He invites you to receive Jesus Christ today. Nowhere in all of God's Word do you find an encouragement to believe in Christ for the forgiveness of sin and the gift of new life *tomorrow.*

Today is the day of salvation (2 Cor. 6:2). Today is the day God wants to forgive your sins. Today is the day God wants you to become his child. Today is the day Christ wants to give you the gift of eternal life. Today is the day the peace of God can be yours. The Holy Spirit invites you. Come to him now while you have time and opportunity.

SUNDAY EVENING, OCTOBER 29

Title: The Church—the Body of Christ

Text: "Now you are the body of Christ, and each one of you is a part of it" **(1 Cor. 12:27 NIV).**

Scripture Reading: 1 Corinthians 12:12–31

Introduction

Centuries ago the psalmist said, "I will praise thee; for I am fearfully and wonderfully made" (Ps. 139:14). The human body is a marvelous example of unity in diversity. Dozens of organs perform different functions yet work in such harmony that we must make a deliberate effort to think of the human body in any way except as a unity.

In the church at Corinth, some had gifts the others did not have, and as a result, they thought of themselves more highly than they should have. This provoked the less gifted to jealousy. The result was discord and strife among the members. In substance Paul was saying to them, "You do not realize your relationship to one another and to Christ. You are joined to one another and dependent on one another just as the members of the body are joined to one another and dependent on one another. You are the physical expression and instrument of Christ in this world just as the body is the physical expression and instrument of the mind."

"Now you are the body of Christ, and each one of you is a part of it" (1 Cor. 12:27 RSV). Several practical suggestions about the church are called out by this text.

I. Each member of the church is different from every other member.

The church has the unity of a living organism. No two parts are alike, and each part discharges a different function for the good of the whole. Some inescapable, practical implications follow.

A. *Every member of Christ's church has some place of service cut out for him or her.* Sometimes we wonder about the function of the appendix or tonsils, but all in all, there are no useless members or organs of the body. They each have a function to perform, and unless they do it, the whole body suffers. Likewise, no two members of the church have equal abilities. But every member has a function to perform for the common good. Under the leadership of the Spirit, each person has a privilege and duty to discover what that place is and to fill it.

B. *Each member of Christ's church must perform his or her own function in the church.* As Paul said, "The eye cannot say to the hand, 'I don't need you!' And the head cannot say to the feet, 'I don't need you!' On the contrary, those parts of the body that seem to be weaker are indispensable" (vv. 21–22 NIV). Every pastor has had members of his church say to him, "All I can do is just go to church and sit there." The majority of those who say this could do more if they would. If every member of every church would only fill his or her place of service, what a difference it would make!

C. *No place of service is so low as to be despised or looked down on, and no place is so high that it justifies conceit on the part of the one filling it.* Some members at Corinth were discouraged. Their attitude was, *We don't amount to much in the church.* Paul said to them, "If the foot should say, 'Because I am not a hand, I do not belong to the body,' it would not for that reason stop being part of the body" (v. 15 NIV). Some at Corinth had too high an estimate of their worth. To them Paul said, "The eye cannot say to the hand, 'I don't need you!'" (v. 21 NIV). To the Romans, Paul was even more specific, "Do not think of yourself more highly than you ought, but rather think of yourself with sober judgment, in accordance with the faith God has distributed to each of you. For just as each of us has one body with many members, and these members do not all have the same function, so in Christ we, though many, form one body, and each member belongs to all the others. We have different gifts, according to the grace given to each of us" (12:3–6 NIV).

II. Each member of the church is to be devoted to the best interests of every other member.

Someone has said, "In brute creation, it is the stomach that rules the world." Selfishness rules. The law of the jungle is "Every man for himself and the devil take the hindmost." But in Christ's church the ultimate aim is the well-being of one's fellow members and therefore of the whole church. Since the church is a living organism, each member is to be devoted to the highest good of every other member.

Paul told the Corinthians, "There should be no division in the body, but . . . its parts should have equal concern for each other" (1 Cor. 12:25 NIV). He gave two reasons for this:

A. *"If one part suffers, every part suffers with it"* (v. 26 NIV). When one member is the victim of half-truths or untruths, when any member is the prey of cheap gossip, the church is the loser. When one member falls into sin, all suffer. Sinning on the part of one member of the church is like putting poison in the public reservoir. Sooner or later all the members are the worse for it.

B. *"If one part is honored, every part rejoices with it"* (v. 26 NIV). Since the church is a body, what is for the good of one is for the good of all. Paul urged the Romans, "Be devoted to one another in love. Honor one another above yourselves" (12:10 NIV). The members of a church are to be devoted to one another to the building up of the body in love. If only we followed that ideal, how different things would be in our churches.

III. Each member of the church is dependent on every other member.

The human body is dependent on the functioning of each individual organ. When one organ is diseased and unable to perform its function properly, the whole body is sick. The proper use of the hands and feet is dependent on the health of the nervous system. The welfare of the nervous system is dependent on proper circulation. No part of the body is independent of any other part.

In like manner, no member of the church is independent of any other member in the worship and service of Christ. And no member is the whole of himself; his fellow members complete him. If the church is to grow and move forward, every member must fill his place and perform his function, because every other member is dependent on him.

Conclusion

Consider a sober question: What is the function of the whole body, each member performing his or her individual part? "You are the body of Christ," our text says. What the physical body is to the mind and soul, the church is to Christ—the physical instrument by which he works his will in the world.

SUGGESTED PREACHING PROGRAM FOR THE MONTH OF NOVEMBER

■ Sunday Mornings

Leading up to Thanksgiving, focus on God's benevolent provision with a series titled "Thanksgiving to God and Thanksliving for God." On the last Sunday of the month, begin a series for Advent called "God's Affirmative Action Program."

■ Sunday Evenings

Complete the series "The Church as the Body of Christ."

■ Wednesday Evenings

Continue the series of devotional studies using the theme "The Christ of John's Gospel."

WEDNESDAY EVENING, NOVEMBER 1

Title: A Conversation about Suffering

Text: "[Jesus'] disciples asked him, saying, Master, who did sin, this man, or his parents, that he was born blind?" **(John 9:2)**.

Scripture Reading: John 9:1–12

Introduction

When Robert Louis Stevenson first saw the twisted and diseased bodies of those who suffered from leprosy, he almost became an atheist. Later he saw compassion in the leper colony in Malokai. Then his faith emerged triumphant. He wrote in the guest book at Malokai these words:

> To see the infinite pity of this place,
> The mangled limb, the devastated face,
> The innocent suffered smiling at the nod—
> A fool were tempted to deny his God.
> He sees, he shrinks. But if he gaze again,
> Lo, beauty springing from the breast of pain!
> He marks the sisters on the mournful shores:
> And even a fool is silent and adores.

Suffering is a fact of life. Its presence is always a mystery. Once the disciples of Jesus became perplexed over the suffering of a blind man. "And as Jesus passed by, he saw a man which was blind from his birth. And his disciples asked him, saying, Master, who did sin, this man, or his parents, that he was born blind?" (John 9:1–2). From this episode, we get various insights into suffering.

I. Suffering provokes questions.

A. *The disciples wanted to know the cause of the blind man's suffering.* The traditional idea that prevailed in Jesus' day was that suffering was caused by some specific sin. The disciples could see many sufferers, and they could say that the cause was sin. But the blind man was a special case—he had been blind from birth.

B. *Suffering continues to provoke questions.* When people observe other innocent people suffering, they want to know the reason. Some suffering can be explained. Moral and physical laws have been violated, and the results are predictable. Yet other suffering cannot be explained. Natural calamities, people with birth defects, illnesses, handicaps, and other maladies cannot be evaluated so easily. The questions continue, "Why? Why? Why?"

II. Suffering provides opportunities.

A. *Suffering provides an opportunity to find God.* The blind man had the opportunity to have an encounter with Jesus Christ. Some people never stop to think about God until they experience suffering.

B. *Suffering provides an opportunity to live for God.* Being blind and then being healed gave the man the opportunity to testify to what God can do. Numerous sufferers have used their misfortunes to testify to what God is doing to help them cope with their problems.

C. *Suffering provides an opportunity to help.* Jesus was not interested in explaining the reason for the man's blindness. The man's condition provided Jesus with an opportunity to help him. Sufferers in life provide numerous opportunities for others to help and minister.

III. Suffering produces benefits.

A. *Suffering gives a perspective on value.* Have you considered what was important to this blind man? Was it cash and clothes? I think not. It was his sight. During times of suffering, we have the unique adventure of finding out what really matters.

B. *Suffering builds character.* The blind man's character had been built through stress. The time of trials not only demonstrates faith, but it is a time for faith to be developed.

C. *Suffering increases compassion.* The blind man was healed. After his healing, he probably demonstrated compassion to other blind people. When one suffers, compassion for other sufferers increases.

D. *Suffering drives us to God.* During the time of his blindness, the man must have called on God. He could not depend on himself. Jane Merchant, famed invalid poet of Knoxville, Tennessee, wrote:

Full half a hundred times I've sobbed,
I can't go on, I can't go on.
And yet, full half a hundred times
I've hushed my sobs and gone.
My answer, if you asked me how,
May seem presumptuously odd.
But I think, what kept me on
When I could not, was God.

Conclusion

Storms of suffering will come into every life. Maybe the storm rages now. Jesus said a lot about suffering. Listen to his conversation and commit your life to him.

Sunday Morning, November 5

Title: Give What You Have to God

Text: "What is that in thine hand?" **(Ex. 4:2)**.

Scripture Reading: Exodus 4:1–8

Hymns: "Hark, the Voice of Jesus Calling," March
"I'll Go Where You Want Me to Go," Brown, Pryor
"Ready," Anonymous

Offertory Prayer: Our Father, you have proved yourself to be the "giver of every good and perfect gift" in many ways, but most of all in the sending of your Son. The world needs to hear the message of a crucified and risen Savior. Part of the money that we give this morning will go to tell people in other lands about the Savior. Some of it will be used here at home to preach the gospel, and some of it will be used in our own church program. Bless each gift that is given. We magnify your name through our stewardship of resources, and we thank you for the privilege of giving. Bless this part of the service and make it both worshipful and meaningful. We pray in Jesus' name. Amen.

Introduction

What a comedown Moses suffered! At one time, he enjoyed the possibility of sitting on the throne of Egypt. In our Scripture reading, he was looking after sheep in the desert, far removed from civilization.

What had caused his circumstances? He had tried to run ahead of God. Can you picture the mother of Moses, during those formative years, whispering to him that he should remember he was a Hebrew and someday God would raise up someone to deliver the Hebrews from bondage? As the years passed, Moses felt the deepening impression that he was the one whom God had chosen to do the job. The mistake he made was that one day when he saw an Egyptian oppressing a Hebrew, he killed him and buried his body in the sand. Later, fearing discovery, he fled the land. What a terrible price we often pay for our impatience and hotheadedness!

God had not forgotten Moses, however; and here before the burning bush he was ready at last to thrust Moses into the service he had planned for him. God works all things together for good to those who love him, and even the forty years' discipline in the desert served as a great school for the man who would later lead his fellow Hebrews throughout this very area.

I. God needs people to do his work.

Of course, God could have reached down with his strong hand and rescued his chosen people any way he desired. There is no limit to what God can do! Likewise, God could send angels to herald his message of salvation through the sky if he wished. But he doesn't want to do it that way! God uses people to do his work. Aren't you glad?

An old tale tells how, when Jesus returned to heaven, all of the hosts turned out to greet him. He explained to them the plan of salvation, how he had died and had risen from the grave, and that now salvation was possible for all the world. They were all rejoicing until one angel said, "But, Jesus, how will the world know what you've done?" He replied, "I told my friends to tell others. Then they will tell still others, and the message will be told around the world." The angel asked once more, "But suppose they don't do it? Suppose they are too busy or too careless—what then? How will the world know about you?" Jesus paused a moment, looked down, then raised his eyes and said, "They're my friends. They won't disappoint me. I have no other plan!"

Stewardship is humankind's acceptance of the responsibility to do with our lives what God has planned for us. Of course, it involves material possessions. We cannot do everything that needs to be done ourselves. We can, however, give our money so that those who can give full-time service may be able to devote themselves completely to the Lord's work. This does not exempt us from volunteer work, but it does enable us to have a share in the full-time work of those whom God has chosen for this ministry.

II. God supplies answers for our excuses.

Most of us are much like Moses. We hold back from accepting responsibility. Notice the excuses Moses set forth and how God answered them. When the call first came, Moses seems to have had an identity crisis. He asked, "Who am I, that I should go unto Pharaoh, and that I should bring forth the children of Israel out of Egypt?" (Ex. 3:11). God did not tell him who he was but rather promised to be with him and guide him. Likewise, we will never discover the full truth about ourselves until we commit to the Lord the abilities we possess.

Next Moses wanted to be assured of authority for his work. God gave him a new revelation of himself (3:14), insisting this was all of the credentials he needed. When Moses insisted further that the people would not believe him or listen to his voice, God worked two miracles for him. Let us learn a lesson about miracles at this point. God will provide the miracle if we need it, but he will only do for us what we cannot do for ourselves. When Moses pled his lack of eloquence, God promised to be with him, which he had already assured him he would do in a previous statement.

Moses' final plea was that God send somebody else. At this point, Aaron suddenly appeared. An interesting, almost amusing, scene took place. God promised Moses that Aaron would be his spokesman. The curtain of charity is drawn over the rest of the scene. One wonders if perhaps Moses suddenly realized that if he did not accept God's call, God might turn to Aaron. This is not stated in the text, of course, but it may have crossed Moses' mind. At any rate, Moses was now ready for the task.

Excuses are seldom, if ever, the real reasons why we hold back and refuse to accept God's will for our lives. The chief problem involved with stewardship is that it means we accept responsibility, and few people are eager to do it.

III. What is in your hand?

Moses' rod has become a symbol. Like David's small sling, what we have, little though it may be or seem, can be used tremendously if we will give it unreservedly to the Lord. The small boy had only five loaves and two fish, but he gave them to the Master. Someone has suggested that the boy went home and told his mother of the miraculous feeding. When he had finished, he said, "Mother, I wonder if he could do the same if I gave him everything I have." Of course, God can do with us far more than we can ever do ourselves.

Conclusion

What motivated Moses to a life commitment? Two things seem to have merged. First, he saw the need. Second, he knew that, in God, he had resources available. These two things will likewise lead us to discharge our stewardship. God will take care of us if we are faithful in doing our duty, whether it be the bringing of financial gifts for God's work to be carried on or by laying ourselves on the altar for service—or both.

Sunday Evening, November 5

Title: Walking Worthily as a Church Member

Text: "I therefore, the prisoner in the Lord, beseech you to walk worthily of the calling wherewith ye were called" **(Eph. 4:1 ASV)**.

Scripture Reading: Ephesians 4:1–6

Introduction

Walking is often used in the Bible as a figure of speech to describe a certain manner of life. This is true of the seven occurrences in Paul's letter to the Ephesians where he contrasts the walk of the believer with that of the unbeliever.

In chapters 1–3 of Ephesians, Paul described the height and depth, the glory and wonder of the Christian calling. Being a Christian is a glorious privilege. In chapters 4–6 he urged Christians to walk worthily of such a privilege. Paul was urgent: "As a prisoner for the Lord, then, I urge you to live a life worthy of the calling you have received" (4:1 NIV). Paul was saying, "You are representatives of Christ in this world. Let your manner of life be such that it will not be a reproach to your Master."

Three things about this worthy walk, all hinging on our text, are suggested in Ephesians.

I. The manner of the worthy walk.

Paul said, "With all lowliness and meekness, with longsuffering, [forbear] one another in love; [give] diligence to keep the unity of the Spirit in the bond of peace" (4:2–3 ASV). Let us measure ourselves by these two verses of Scripture. How far short we fall!

A. *First, Paul said, "with all lowliness and meekness."* More exactly, this reads, "with all modesty and humility of spirit." We need these qualities. The weeds of pharisaism spring up quickly in our hearts. How easily we feel ourselves to be spiritually superior to other Christians, but we are not to do so. This is not the worthy walk.

B. *Again Paul said, "with longsuffering."* Freely rendered, this reads, "enduring with unruffled temper." Sometimes we hear a person say, "I can endure what they say about me if it's true, but if it's not, I just can't stand it." That is not in imitation of Christ. That is not his spirit. Peter said of our Lord, "who did no sin, neither was guile found in his mouth: who, when he was reviled, reviled not again; when he suffered, he threatened not" (1 Peter 2:22–23). James exhorted, "Let every man be swift to hear, slow to speak, slow to wrath" (James 1:19). How often we turn these around. If we were to "endure with unruffled temper," what a difference it would make. As Christian men and women growing in Christ, we ought not to be easily offended.

C. *Again Paul said, "forbearing one another in love."* Freely rendered, he was saying, "Putting up with one another in a spirit of love." But what if some person in the church can't "endure with unruffled temper"? Paul said, "Put up with that person. Bear with him." As long as people are human, there will be a need for Christian forbearance. Why are we short on Christian forbearance? Perhaps it is because we are short on Christian love.

We practice forbearance in our homes. Ask any man about his wife or any wife about her husband. Our patience wears thin, but most of the time we forbear each other because we love each other. In like manner, we are to love one another as members of Christ's church.

D. *Still again, Paul said, "giving diligence to keep the unity of the Spirit in the bond of peace."* No member of any church is to do or say anything to mar or destroy the fellowship of the church. To be guilty of such a thing is a grievous sin with which few can compare, and the penalty is terrible (1 Cor. 3:17). But this is not a negative command. It is positive, something we are to do. We are to work diligently at keeping "the unity of the Spirit in the bond of peace."

II. The direction of the worthy walk.

We do not become worthy, mature Christians in a moment. We do not grow "unto a full-grown man, unto the measure of the stature of the fulness of Christ" (Eph. 4:13 ASV) in the twinkling of an eye. We must walk in that direction.

A. *We must walk in the direction that leads out of death into life.* "And you did he make alive," Paul said in chapter 2 of this epistle, "when ye were dead through your trespasses and sins" (v. 1 ASV). A Christian is a person who is now alive to God.

Thousands of people in the world are alive to worldly ambitions, pleasures, business, politics, and to all of the world's interests and demands; but they are dead toward God, "dead in trespasses and sins." As Christians we can remember when we had no interest in the things of the Spirit because we were dead to them. But if we are walking in the direction that leads out of death into life, we ought to be growing away from the fleshpots of the world and into the things of Christ. John pointed out that we cannot love things that are at opposite poles (1 John 2:15). We cannot walk in two directions at the same time.

B. *We must walk in the direction that leads from sin to holiness.* In Ephesians 4 Paul also said, "This I say therefore, and testify in the Lord, that ye no longer walk as the Gentiles also walk, in the vanity of their mind" (v. 17 ASV). Paul described the Gentile walk in the verses that follow (vv. 18–19). "That is the way you were," Paul was saying, "but there is to be a difference now. 'Ye did not so learn Christ'" (v. 20). It is tragic to see those who profess to be Christians but in whose lives you can tell no difference from the lives of unbelievers. They go to the same places, do the same things, and desire the same things; apparently they are the same.

If we are walking in the direction that leads from sin to holiness, we ought to reach the point in our pilgrimage where we no longer relish our old sins but rather the things of God.

C. *We must walk in the direction that leads from darkness to light.* In Ephesians 5 Paul said, "Ye were once darkness, but are now light in the Lord: walk as children of light" (v. 8 ASV). What a powerful figure! Christ is the Light of the World (John 8:12), and we are to walk toward him.

Two people walking in opposite directions may be at the same spot for just an instance, but their destinations are different. If we walk toward the darkness of sin, the darkness grows darker and darker. If we walk toward the light, our way grows brighter and brighter. "If we walk in the light, as he is in the light, we have fellowship one with another, and the blood of Jesus his Son cleanseth us from all sin" (1 John 1:7).

III. The results of the worthy walk.

A. *The result of good works.* In Ephesians 2 Paul said, "For we are his workmanship, created in Christ Jesus for good works, which God afore prepared that we should walk in them" (v. 10 ASV). Good works are the crown, the result, the proof, the test, the product of a Christian life; but they do not produce it.

B. *The result of growth in God's love.* Paul wrote in Ephesians 5: "Be ye therefore imitators of God, as beloved children; and walk in love, even as Christ also loved you, and gave himself up for us" (vv. 1–2 ASV). "Walk in love." That is what we need to do. Walk in the love of God, realizing more and more the constraining power of the greatest force in the world (2 Cor. 5:14).

C. *The result of maturity as a Christian.* Paul said we need to continue to mature "till we all attain unto the unity of the faith, and of the knowledge of the Son of God, unto a full-grown man, unto the measure of the stature of the fullness of Christ" (4:13 ASV). That is the destination of the Christian walk. He goes on to say that our purpose for growing is "that we may be no longer children, tossed to and fro and carried about with every wind of doctrine, by the sleight of men, in craftiness, after the wiles of error; but speaking truth in love, may grow up in all things unto him, who is the head, even Christ" (4:14–15 ASV).

Conclusion

As we apply this teaching of Paul to our lives, we find both a caution and an injunction. The caution is this: Let no man sit in judgment on his brother. Let no man attempt to judge whether someone else is walking worthily or not. The injunction is this: Let every man ask himself, "Am I walking worthily or unworthily of the calling with which I was called?"

Wednesday Evening, November 8

Title: The Door

Text: "I am the door: by me if any man enter in, he shall be saved, and shall go in and out, and find pasture" **(John 10:9)**.

Scripture Reading: John 10:1–9

Introduction

Going through the wrong door can be an embarrassing and frustrating experience. One time my family and I dined in a Mexican restaurant. One of my sons went through a door labeled "*Señoritas*" instead of "*Señores.*" Needless to say, he was embarrassed over his mistake.

People go through wrong doors seeking the meaning and significance of life. Their pursuits end in frustration. But Jesus said, "I am the door: by me if any man enter in, he shall be saved, and shall go in and out, and find pasture" (John 10:9). Jesus claims to be the access into genuine personhood. Let us notice the ways that Jesus is the Door.

I. Jesus is the Door to salvation.

Jesus opens the way to God. He introduces us to God in a unique manner. Jesus is the only Door to salvation. Many doors are marked "the Way to God," but Jesus is the right Door.

Jesus opens the door of possibilities. The term "saved" in John 10:9 presents two ideas. First, it means a rescue from danger. Second, it means healing of a disease. Only Jesus can rescue and heal.

II. Jesus is the Door of security.

Having gone through the door to salvation, the Christian can feel secure. Sheep feel secure because of a faithful, reliable shepherd. We, too, can feel secure because of the presence of our Shepherd. Trials, tribulations, and threats will come our way, but our security lies in the continual presence of the Good Shepherd. We can feel secure because of the fidelity of the Shepherd. Jesus is not fickle with his feelings. He seeks the highest good for his sheep.

III. Jesus is the Door to satisfaction.

Jesus said, "I have come that they may have life, and have it to the full" (John 10:10 NIV). Others promise satisfaction but fail to bring it. Jesus brings genuine satisfaction.

Jesus brings the essence of life. Real life comes with the spiritual birth. Paul said, "For me, to live is Christ and to die is gain" (Phil. 1:21 NIV).

Jesus also brings the exuberance of life. Christians not only have real life, but they have the superabundance of life.

Conclusion

Jesus is the Door. When we open our lives to him, we understand ourselves, and we are able to relate to others.

SUNDAY MORNING, NOVEMBER 12

Title: Such as I Have

Text: "Silver and gold have I none; but such as I have give I thee" **(Acts 3:6)**.

Scripture Reading: Acts 3:1–16

Hymns: "Something for Thee," Phelps
"All Things Are Thine," Whittier
"Trust, Try, and Prove Me," Leech

Offertory Prayer: Our Father, how vast is your creation! When we think of the birds of the air, the fish of the sea, and every creeping thing on the earth, we sing again, "How great Thou art!" We thank you for loving us as we are, men and women who are sinful, and we praise you for providing redemption through Jesus Christ. Help us to be still and know that you are God. Send your Spirit to arouse us from dullness and coldness. Help us to keep afresh in our spirit the thrilling thought of your unspeakable love for us. Make us diligent in your work, and use these gifts this morning to further the glorious work of spreading the gospel. We pray in Jesus' name. Amen.

Introduction

The book of Acts takes up the story of Christianity where the Gospels leave off. After Jesus ascended to heaven, the Holy Spirit came in a unique way, and the apostles moved forward dynamically and daringly to tell the story of the risen Christ.

Of course, the book of Acts tells only a few of the many wonderful events that must have occurred. The Holy Spirit led Luke to record the visit of Peter and John to the temple, where they healed a man who had been lame from birth. How strange Peter's words must have sounded when he said, "Silver and gold have I none; but such as I have give I thee"; but how exciting Peter's deed when he took the man by the right hand, lifted him up, and through the power of the Holy Spirit healed him. A double miracle occurred that day! The man learned to walk and leap at the very moment he was healed.

A great stewardship lesson is present in this story. We are to do "what we can with what we have where we are for Jesus' sake today" and never wait for a greater opportunity nor for a time when we have greater abilities and resources.

I. Money isn't everything.

Too often when we speak of stewardship, we think of money. How thrilling to see a story where money is not set forth as the most important thing. In fact,

Peter even came close to minimizing it. He said plainly, "Silver and gold have I none" and then proceeded to work the miracle.

Does the time ever come in the life of a church or a religious organization when money can actually be a stumbling block? Thomas Aquinas, an outstanding religious leader of another generation, once visited the pope and was shown all the treasures of the Roman Church. The pope said to Thomas, "Well, Thomas, no longer can the church say, 'Silver and gold have I none.'" Thomas replied, "Yes, Holy Father, but have you ever thought that the church is in danger of also not being able to say, 'In the name of Jesus Christ of Nazareth rise up and walk'?" We must be careful in our day not to evaluate our local churches and mission boards in terms of budgets alone. Pastors and missionaries of other days were not nearly as concerned about a "cost of living" raise as they were a "cost of loving" raise. Let us be careful, very careful, to keep our priorities correct!

II. But money is important.

The preceding paragraph is true, but something else is true also. It takes money—cold, hard cash—to carry on God's work in today's world.

God's Word says much about the stewardship of possessions, the giving of money. In Paul's second letter to the church at Corinth, two chapters (8 and 9) are devoted to the matter of giving. He said, "Therefore, as ye abound in everything, in faith, and utterance, and knowledge, and in all diligence, and in your love to us, see that ye abound in this grace also" (2 Cor. 8:7). He pointed out that our supreme example in giving is the Lord Jesus Christ who, though rich, became poor that through his poverty we might become rich.

God has given to some people the ability to make "big money." Their duty is to set aside an even larger part of that money for the work of the gospel. In Old Testament days, the tenth was the minimum. Certainly a Christian would not want to give less to spread the Christian faith than the Old Testament Jew gave for his faith. In fact, counting all of the special offerings and supplementary tithes, the Old Testament saint was commanded to give far more than a tithe.

Money is important! We live in a world far different from that of Peter, John, and Paul. There was, of course, a monetary system in that day, but money is far more essential as a means of exchange than it has ever been before in the world. And more than ever before, the importance of propagating our faith is clear. We must lead people to Christ, and soon, or our way of life as we know it is in serious jeopardy.

III. What do you have?

Whether we use the terms *talents and abilities* or *gifts* when we speak of what we have to offer God in service, we must answer the question "What do I have to offer my Lord?" And another question follows closely: "Am I willing to give myself—including my talents, abilities, and gifts—to be used anyway God sees fit?"

When General John Pershing landed in France with the American Expeditionary Force in World War I, he presented himself and his army to General Ferdinand Foch, commander of the Allied Forces, and said, "Our men, our equipment, our resources—all that we have are yours. Use them as you see fit." God is certainly waiting to hear every Christian say, in essence, the same thing. Stewardship is giving "such as we have" to our Master unreservedly for use in the service of his kingdom.

Conclusion

Everyone who believes in Christ and is dedicated to him has great possessions. They are, however, spiritual resources. We should find our greatest joy in sharing the gospel with others by lip and by life. This, however, does not relieve us from the responsibility of supporting God's work financially. We cannot evade our responsibility in financial things by rationalizing that we are "spiritual" and therefore are not required to bring financial gifts. In the Old Testament, even the Levites gave tithes of the tithes. On the other hand, giving money does not release us from the duty of serving in other ways. Stewardship involves both finances and lifestyle. It is not a case of "either/or." We are obligated to the "both/and" principle. Time, talent, tithe, influence—all that we have belongs to God!

SUNDAY EVENING, NOVEMBER 12

Title: The Goal of the Church

Text: "Till we all attain unto the unity of the faith, and of the knowledge of the Son of God, unto a full-grown man, unto the measure of the stature of the fulness of Christ" **(Eph. 4:13 ASV)**.

Scripture Reading: Ephesians 4:7–16

Introduction

The total impression of this passage from Ephesians 4 is that Christ has a goal, a supreme standard for his church, and that goal is so high, so exalted that it taxes the imagination to comprehend it. Nonetheless, here and now, in the body of this flesh, we are to strive to attain it.

Specifically, this passage leaves three impressions on the mind and heart: (1) Christ has given us the grace whereby we may reach the goal. (2) The means of growth for reaching the goal are at hand. (3) We must not stop nor be satisfied short of the goal, no matter how high the standard nor how great the difficulties in the way.

I. Grace for reaching the goal Christ has for his church.

We must never take our eyes away from the grace of God. We are always to remember that we are not Christians because we deserve to be. We have not been brought "out of death into life" (1 John 3:14) because of any merit of our own. The whole Christian transaction, whereby we cease to live unto sin and begin to live unto God, is all of grace—God's grace.

Two things strike us about this grace, this free gift of Christ toward those who are his own.

A. *First, there is its impartiality (Eph. 4:7).* "But unto each one of us was the grace given"—not to just a few out of the church, not just to the pastor or the leaders, "but unto each one of us." Although "according to the measure of the gift of Christ," the capacity of one member might exceed that of another, no member of his church is left completely dispossessed. His gifts are measured not by any favoritism on God's part, for his love is everywhere and toward all the same. God's grace is impartial.

B. *But second, there is its individuality (v. 11).* God's gifts are specifically fitted to the capacity of each individual to receive them. It follows, therefore, that each person in the church has a task cut out for that person "according to the measure of the gift of Christ" in equipping him or her to do that task. Paul said, "And he gave some to be apostles; and some, prophets; and some, evangelists; and some, pastors and teachers" (v. 11 ASV). And this is not a complete list.

That Christ's churches are not challenging our sin-sodden society and moving this needy world toward God is not his fault. He has given his people the grace to move toward the goal of "the measure of the stature of Christ."

II. Growth toward the goal Christ has for his church.

Paul said in this passage that we "may grow up in all things into him, who is the head, even Christ" (v. 15 ASV). Paul called some in the church at Corinth who had not grown "babes in Christ" (1 Cor. 3:1). He was saying to them, "You haven't grown a bit as Christians since the day you were converted. You are baby Christians, wholly immature."

How may Christian growth be attained? What are the means? Paul gave several suggestions.

A. *We grow by stability of Christian convictions (Eph. 4:14).* In typical fashion, Paul mixed his metaphors here to describe the instability of immature Christians, picturing them as infants being tossed by the waves like an unanchored ship driven about in a turbulent sea.

Instability of Christian convictions is one sure sign of immaturity of Christian character, while stability is a sure means of growth. There is such a thing as Christian certitude—as "the rock of ages" (Isa. 26:4) for our feet; as a standard in religion, God's Word; as an anchor and stay for our faith. Apart from certainty of faith and stability of convictions, we don't grow very much.

B. *We grow by sincerity of Christian love (Eph. 4:15).* "But speaking truth in love" (ASV). The marginal reading says, "But dealing truly in love." The problem is that we have no verb for truth in English, while the Greek does. Literally Paul said, "But truthing in love." The import of his words is that our manner of life is to be sincere and true, thinking truly, speaking truly, dealing truly, and all in a spirit of genuine love, without diversions to divide our allegiance, without hypocrisy to deny our witness, without divisions to hinder our purpose in him. "Truthing" in love—love for Christ, for one another, for those who are lost.

C. *We grow by the solidarity of the Christian community (Eph. 4:15–16).* Again Paul used the figure of the human body, "from whom all the body fitly framed and knit together through that which every joint supplieth" (v. 16). All the members of the church are knit and joined together. Every member is joined to every other member. What is for the good of one is for the good of all, and what causes the hurt of one is for the injury of all. Where there is no solidarity of purpose and unity of spirit in the church, there can be no growth.

III. The greatness of the goal Christ has for his church.

How great and how high is Christ's goal for his church? Paul took his readers step-by-step to the top. After naming the gifts that Christ through grace gives to individuals in the church (v. 11), he told why:

A. *"For the perfecting of the saints" (v. 12).* The word translated "perfecting" means "mending," the same word that is used where we are told of fishermen "mending their nets." When members of the church are quick-tempered, gossips, busybodies, and empty-headed, Paul said we must "mend these things." Why?

B. *"Unto the work of ministering, unto the building up of the body of Christ" (v. 12).* This is to the end that Christ might have a fit and usable instrument through which he can nurture his saints, grow his children, and save the lost.

C. *He goes on, "Till we all attain" (v. 13).* Christ's ideal for his church is not for just a few choice souls who excel, not for just a few who reach the top, but for every member of his church, all of his own.

D. *But Paul moved higher yet, "Till we all attain unto the unity of the faith, and of the knowledge of the Son of God, unto a full-grown man" (v. 13).* Paul was saying, "Till we all attain to his standard of unity and maturity, full-grown and united—no differences of opinion in the Lord, no divergences of conviction, no divisions of spirit." We say, "Surely that is the top! We could come no nearer to perfection than that." But Paul wasn't finished! The goal is one step higher. Listen to the grand and soaring height of the goal:

E. *"Unto the measure of the stature of the fulness of Christ" (v. 13).* Humans can move no nearer God's likeness than that: thinking like Christ in our minds, loving like Christ in our hearts, resembling Christ in our lives, giving ourselves to the purposes of God as he gave himself, reminding people of God because we are fashioned in the likeness of his Son.

Conclusion

Do you see the point of this great passage? Paul laid tremendous emphasis on the church, the body of believers, not on its size but on its soul quality. He had a burning desire to win souls, but he believed with all his heart that exalted Christian character within the church was the surest means of doing this.

This comes home to us, and we cannot avoid it. We emphasize quantity but not quality. We glory in reports, but we do not demand repentance. We have width and breadth but neither height nor depth. Our churches grow in size, but our members do not grow spiritually. It is useless to add members who do not grow in Christ. We are cursed with a low ideal. We are plagued with an unworthy contentment. We are satisfied far short of the goal. Let us pray over this passage until a blaze is kindled in our hearts.

Wednesday Evening, November 15

Title: The Good Shepherd

Text: "I am the good shepherd: the good shepherd giveth his life for the sheep" (**John 10:11**).

Scripture Reading: John 10:1–18

Introduction

Jesus used ordinary figures to describe his role. On one occasion, he said, "I am the good shepherd." The pastoral figure was familiar, and it communicated many wonderful truths about the Master. Jesus used the word *good* with *shepherd.* The word means "winsome," "attractive," or "virtuous." Although there were many shepherds, only Jesus deserved the name "good shepherd." Let's see why he deserved this name.

I. Jesus knows in a unique manner.

Shepherds of ancient Palestine knew their sheep, and the sheep also knew their own shepherd. Jesus, too, knows people in a unique manner.

Jesus knows the name of every person. Once two young men agreed to read the Bible to a blind man. They began with the New Testament and immediately encountered a long list of names in a genealogy in Matthew. They wanted to skip it, but the old man insisted that they read each name. He said, "God knew every one of those fellers by name, and he knows me!"

Yes, God knows us, and he knows our needs. He knows which sheep have peculiar proclivities to sensual temptations. He knows those susceptible to discouragement. People's needs vary, but Jesus relates to each need.

II. Jesus cares in a sacrificial way.

Shepherds often faced danger for the sake of their flock. They protected them from wild animals and sheep stealers. The Good Shepherd also put his life on the line for his sheep. John 10:11 says, "The good shepherd giveth his life for the sheep." Jesus gave his life sacrificially on the cross. He died so that others might live.

III. Jesus leads his flock in the right paths.

The shepherds of ancient Palestine led their sheep away from danger and toward green pastures and refreshing waters. Jesus does the same. He leads us in the right moral paths. And when we obey his will, we go in the right direction. Jesus leads us in the varied pilgrimages of life, but he also leads to a final destination.

Conclusion

Jesus is the Good Shepherd. No one compares to him.

SUNDAY MORNING, NOVEMBER 19

Title: Give Yourself in Service

Text: "I beseech you therefore, brethren, by the mercies of God, that ye present your bodies a living sacrifice, holy, acceptable unto God, which is your reasonable service" **(Rom. 12:1)**.

Scripture Reading: Romans 12:1–9

Hymns: "Serve the Lord with Gladness," McKinney
"Our Best," Kirk
"To the Work," Crosby

Offertory Prayer: Our Father, soothe the anxieties of your children. Bring calm where there is disorder and buoyancy where there is burden. Send peace for our distractions. Touch, guide, encourage, and empower us that we may commit ourselves afresh to living the Christian life in a world where there is so much opposition to your purposes. Give us the strength to bear the pettiness of people and to resolve the misunderstandings of incompatible natures. We know that the spirit is willing but the flesh is often weak. Rescue us from ourselves and from our sins. Keep us unspotted from the world. As we bring our offerings this morning, may it be not only a duty to be discharged but a privilege to be utilized and enjoyed as we invest in the spreading of God's Word to the world. We pray for Jesus' sake. Amen.

Introduction

When we come to chapter 12 in Romans, we are standing at the watershed of this great letter. There is, in Canada, a place where one can see the Great Divide, where one is on the "roof of the world"—from it water flows in opposite directions. Our text for today is like that. When Paul said, "Therefore," he looked back at the first eleven chapters of his letter, where he had stressed a systematic theology that presents all of the essential facts about man's relationship to God from a doctrinal standpoint.

When Paul said, "I beseech you . . . that ye present your bodies a living sacrifice," he looked at the practical side of religion, the true test of one's orthodoxy. Not what we say we believe, but what we do proves the genuineness of what we say we believe. Unless we put into practice in daily living what we profess to believe, we do not truly believe it.

I. How is your doctrine?

Paul began the Roman letter by clearly outlining man's depraved condition before God. After a few introductory words about himself, the Roman church's reputation, his thwarted plans to come to them, and the nature of the gospel he preached, he tackled the sin problem.

In the latter part of chapter 1, he dealt with the gentile world. Although they did not have the Mosaic law, they had a law within their own hearts, which they had violated, failing to live up to the truth they possessed. For that reason, the Gentiles stood as sinners before God. In chapter 2 Paul dealt with the Jewish people who had religious privileges but failed to realize their possibilities, violating God's law and refusing to live up to the light that had been revealed to them. Paul tied all the strings together in chapter 3, climaxing with the great statement that "all have sinned and come short of the glory of God" (v. 23).

Chapter 4 deals with salvation by faith. Man has always been saved by faith, even in Old Testament days—it was Abraham's faith that God counted for righteousness. In chapter 5 the glorious results of faith are outlined; and in chapter 6 Paul made clear the obligations of one who has been justified by faith, concluding with the timeless declaration that "the wages of sin is death; but the gift of God is eternal life through Jesus Christ our Lord" (v. 23). Chapter 7 pictures the struggle between the old man and the new man in the life of the believer. Chapter 8 shows the victory that comes to those who are in Christ and the security they enjoy because of his constant presence and unfailing power. Paul concluded chapter 8 with a glorious statement that nothing is able "to separate us from the love of God, which is in Christ Jesus our Lord" (v. 39).

Chapters 9 through 11 deal with the Jewish people and are, in a sense, a transition between the doctrinal section and the practical section. We should note, however, that God loves Israel and stands ready to receive the Jewish people unto himself when they come to Jesus Christ for salvation.

II. How is your dedication?

Notice the expression "a living sacrifice," which Paul used to express his concept of dedication. The people to whom he was writing—Jewish Christians who had accepted Christ on the day of Pentecost probably made up most of the group—were steeped in the Old Testament Scriptures. They understood the sacrificial system whereby an animal was slain as an offering to God. Paul suggested that Christians do not bring dead sacrifices to the altar but rather bring themselves as "living" sacrifices.

Most people despise the word *sacrifice.* To them it suggests asceticism, negativism, and narrowness. Paul, however, put the word *living* in front of it and thus removed the stigma of Jewish law and set forth an innovation. Someone translated it, "Put your bodies at God's disposal as a living thank offering." Our bodies are to be made available for God's service. He alone knows best how to use them to his glory and to our growth. In this context, the word *body* means the total person. Our hearts, minds, and physical energies should be brought to God for him to use as he sees fit to accomplish his redemptive purpose in the world.

III. How is your devotion?

We will never be any more dedicated to God than the measure of our love for him. Whether we wish it, seek it, or realize it, God loves us. Even when we devote our minds, hearts, and bodies to selfish ends, he still cares deeply for us and makes his sun shine on the just and unjust. When we refuse to love God, we are cowardly and selfish. No shame is equal to that of refusing to love the one who loves us so greatly.

Stewardship is more than the giving of money. It involves a proper attitude toward our material resources and giving a proper share to God. A person can give without loving; however, a person can never love without giving. What a revolution would take place in Christian work if God's people would, first of all, love him and then support God's work in this world.

When Paul said that the presenting of ourselves to God is our "reasonable" service, he used a word that can best be translated "spiritual." Of course, supporting God is reasonable and rational, but Paul meant even more. We serve God because our spirits are in tune with his Spirit. Even as God's Spirit bears witness with our spirit that we are the children of God (8:16), so our spirit testifies by our devotion and dedication that we have been transformed by the Holy Spirit of God.

Conclusion

The work of the Lord waits on two things—men and money, persons and purses! It takes both to do the Lord's work—someone to go and someone to "hold the ropes" while the other serves. How we serve, however, goes back to what we believe about Christ, about sin, about salvation, and consequently about service. Paul wrote later in this same chapter about the church being one body in Christ and everyone being a member of the others. He pointed out that since we have gifts differing according to the grace that is given to us, we should exercise those gifts in harmony with God's will. How is your doctrine? How is your dedication? How is your devotion? Each of the three is important! Each one builds on the other; but the climax, the top rung of the ladder, is our devotion to God based on our love for him.

Sunday Evening, November 19

Title: Christ—the Head of the Church

Text: "He is the head of the body, the church" **(Col. 1:18 RSV)**.

Scripture Reading: Colossians 1:9–23

Introduction

Paul was concerned about making clear the relationship of Christ with his people. Sometimes his emphasis was on Christ's people—his church—as his body. At other times, Paul's emphasis was on Christ as the head, or Lord, of his church. The latter emphasis is true of our text: "He is the head of the body, the church." This simple but profound text has three down-to-earth meanings for us.

I. The absolute primacy of Christ in his church.

Christ's people must understand this, subscribe to it, and glory in it. His interests are supreme; his cause comes first; his will is primary. To the world the church is a convenient group of respectable people to be used, when the occasion arises, to serve the interests of the world. Actually, the church is to serve only the interests, purposes, and will of Christ, to put him first.

A. *When in the church we put our own interests ahead of the interests of Christ, we dishonor him as head.* The question we need to ask ourselves is not "How will this affect me?" but "What will be the result for Christ's cause? Will this promote or injure? Will this serve his best interests or defeat them?"

B. *When in the church we put human sentiment ahead of the interests of Christ, we dishonor him as head.* Sometimes services are conducted that have little to do with the gospel but make a powerful appeal to sentiment. People respond to these appeals with enthusiasm that shames our response to the simple appeal of the gospel. When we let human sentiment become a more powerful force in our church life than our love for and loyalty to Christ, we are not putting Christ first; we are not letting him be the head of his church.

C. *When in the church we put the interests and claims of the world ahead of Christ, we dishonor him as head.* The world's interests do have some claim on us but not first claim (Matt. 6:33). Christ's claims are first always. Yet the cry of the majority of our church members is, "Don't you know I've got to make a living?" What they are really saying is, "I am only in this world on a business trip. If I can find a little time to spare, I'll use it to serve the Lord." To a man who put a worldly claim first, Jesus said, "No man, having put his hand to the plough, and looking back, is fit for the kingdom of God" (Luke 9:62).

D. *When in the church we put the desire to please people ahead of the desire to please Christ, we dishonor him as head.* Genuine harmony in a church is a vital necessity. Paul told the Thessalonians, "Be at peace among yourselves" (1 Thess. 5:13). Yet there is a spurious, superficial sort of harmony in the church, bought at the expense of pleasing people instead of Christ, that doesn't mean a thing except the defeat of the highest purposes of the gospel. Some in the church are childish emotionally. Their feelings will be hurt anyway. In Christ's church, we are not to be slappers of backs and dispensers of sugar cubes. We are to serve the interests of Christ.

II. The absolute authority of Christ over his church.

Christ is the supreme ruler of his church on earth. No one else is nor could be. Since his authority is supreme, since his church is answerable only to him, three inescapable implications follow.

A. *A New Testament church must be a pure democracy, a democratic body.* This is inescapable. Answerable only to Christ, who is the head, every member must be equal in rank, privilege, and power with every other member. Jesus said, "You have one Teacher, and you are all brothers" (Matt. 23:8 NIV). There are to be no ruling officials in the church.

B. *A New Testament church must be independent and self-sufficient.* Since Christ is the head of the church, the doctrine of the autonomy of the local church not only makes sense; it is necessary. Since churches owe their supreme and undivided allegiance to Christ, they must not accept rule from one another or any other kind of earthly rule. If Christ is the head of his church, no one else can be. This teaching denies all ecclesiastical systems that would substitute the rule of man for the rule of Christ. It also mandates that the church should not be subservient to or united in any way with the state. The sphere of the church is entirely spiritual and answerable only to Christ.

C. *New Testament churches, though independent of one another, must cooperate with one another in Christ's program.* Since Christ is head of the church, he is head of every local New Testament church. He has a program, and he can direct churches in that program. Churches working together under the leadership of Christ, the head, do not surrender their sovereign rights in cooperating with one another;

they exercise them. The whole program, therefore, both within and among the churches ought to be characterized by harmony, unity, and purpose.

III. The absolute dependence of Christ's church on Christ.

Just as the human body is helpless and lifeless apart from the head, so the church is helpless and lifeless apart from Christ. On the night before his crucifixion, Jesus gently warned his disciples, "Apart from me ye can do nothing" (John 15:5 ASV).

Do we not devise and promote and try to carry on programs that are of men and not of Christ? In our modern day we speak of "the program of the church." But apart from Christ, the church has no program and no power to conceive or to execute a program. The church is completely dependent on him.

Conclusion

"He is the head of the body, the church." How can we as individuals apply this text to our lives? Since the body is composed of members, Christ must be the head of every member of the body. Let each one of us ask, "Are his interests primary in my life? Is his rule over me complete? Is my faith in him implicit?"

WEDNESDAY EVENING, NOVEMBER 22

Title: You Are in Good Hands with God

Text: "I give unto them eternal life; and they shall never perish, neither shall any man pluck them out of my hand" **(John 10:28)**.

Scripture Reading: John 10:27–30

Introduction

The Allstate Insurance Company has a captivating slogan. In their advertisements they claim, "You're in good hands with Allstate." This statement attracts people, for there is within every human being the need and desire for security. People want their houses, cars, and especially their lives to be protected.

Jesus made a security claim for believers: "I give them [my sheep] eternal life, and they shall never perish; no one will snatch them out of my hand. My Father, who has given them to me, is greater than all; no one can snatch them out of my Father's hand" (John 10:28–29 NIV). The Lord gave a graphic illustration of security when he pictured the believer resting in the hands of the heavenly Father. Yet a person is "in the hands of God" for more reasons than just security. Jesus' words suggest other implications of being in God's hands. Let's look at them.

I. God makes a person.

A. *There was a time when we were not in God's hands.* Those who refuse to submit to the Good Shepherd stand outside the fold of safety. People want to take over their own lives and live as they please rather than as God wants them to live. Like rebellious sheep, people have looked to the mirage of greener pastures and have strayed only to find that they are alienated from God, abandoned to the wrong cause, and have abused every gift God gave.

B. *When we respond in faith to Jesus Christ, God begins a great work within us.* "I am the door; if any one enters by me, he will be saved, and will go in and out and find pasture" (v. 9 RSV). Two words in the verse help to describe God's work in believers. "Saved" refers to a rescue operation, and "find pasture" describes God's daily care. Not only does God rescue us, but he also provides nourishment and growth.

Paul said, "For I am confident of this very thing, that he who began a good work in you will perfect it until the day of Christ Jesus" (Phil. 1:6 ASV). When a person trusts the Lord, God begins a good work. The Lord will continue this work until the day of Jesus Christ.

II. God uses a person.

A. *God does not put a person in his hands just to save; he intends to use that person.* We do not enter into a relationship with God to sit and wait for the Judgment Day. No, God desires that the saved work in his service. We can see an illustration of service in an account from Elisha's ministry. Elisha told a young man to put out his hand and "take . . . up" the lost ax-head. It was not just to be rescued from a watery grave; it was to be restored to useful service again.

B. *We may be weak instruments, but in God's hands we may be used to do much.* Amazingly, God chooses ordinary human beings and uses them in his service. "But God hath chosen the foolish things of the world to confound the wise; and God hath chosen the weak things of the world to confound the things which are mighty" (1 Cor. 1:27).

A golf club in my hands may mean a high score. But the same golf club in the hands of a professional golfer may mean a low score. The difference is the one who uses the club. When we put our lives into God's hands, he uses us for his service.

III. God keeps a person.

A. *The security of the believer depends on the nature and character of God.* After we open our lives to God in faith, our security depends on God, not on our power to hold on to God. Rather, it depends on God's power to hold on to us. "For I know whom I have believed, and am persuaded that he is able to keep that which I have committed unto him against that day" (2 Tim. 1:12).

B. *The security of the believer does not mean a license to sin.* If a person uses the concept of the security of the believer to practice sinful ways, then that person does not really comprehend the idea of being in God's hands. In God's hand a person gradually experiences change. The Lord changes a person, and that person moves away from practicing sin.

Charles Haddon Spurgeon was asked, "Do you believe in the perseverance of the saints?" He replied, "No, but I believe in the perseverance of the Savior."

Conclusion

Are you willing to put yourself in God's hands? A party of inexperienced mountain climbers were facing a yawning crevasse that had to be crossed if they would reach the top. Their guide went over nimbly. Reaching back, he asked each member of the climbing party to give him his hand. One man came repeatedly to the edge, and each time he retreated. Finally, the guide reached for the man's hand once more and said, "For thirty years I've been helping men and women across that gap, and I've never let one go yet." Will you reach out to the Lord? He has not let one go yet!

Sunday Morning, November 26

Title: What Is Your Life?

Text: "What is your life? You are a mist that appears for a little while and then vanishes" **(James 4:14 NIV)**.

Scripture Reading: James 4:13—17

Hymns: "We Give Thee but Thine Own," How
"Serve the Lord with Gladness," McKinney
"To the Work," Crosby

Offertory Prayer: Dear Jesus, you have told us that you are the Alpha and the Omega, the Beginning and the End. You have also promised to be with us always. As we bring our tithes and offerings to you today, help us to remember that you are indeed the beginning of life for us and the one who stays with us until the very end. Help us to beware of feeding our bank accounts and starving our souls. Help us to understand that when Jesus said, "It is better to give than to receive," he was expressing one of the most profound truths of life. Help us to realize we can be "labourers together with God" by sending people to preach the gospel where we cannot go ourselves. As we have received many generous gifts from you, we now count it a joy to bring you our very lives so that your work may be carried on. Help us, above everything else, to seek a fuller life with you and to attain a closer walk with the one who loved us and gave himself for us. We pray in Jesus' name. Amen.

Introduction

The book of James is probably the most practical writing of the New Testament. The author, a half brother of Jesus, stressed conduct and behavior as the true test of whether someone is a genuine Christian. Some people have called his book "the Proverbs of the New Testament," while others have pointed out its similarity to the Sermon on the Mount.

Writing to Christians who were scattered throughout the Roman Empire, James emphasized the necessity for patience, especially as related to the tongue, warning that one of the worst sins Christians can commit is that of failing to carefully watch their words. In this particular section of Scripture, James emphasized the uncertainty of the future, which was certainly a relevant fact in the lives of the Christians who lived in a world that was hostile to the members of the new faith.

I. A worldly goal.

People have always sought to further their own interests. First, of course, is self-preservation, but most of us pursue an added security sufficient to protect us from possible setbacks. Of course, we too often think of security only in material terms. When we adopt this philosophy, we are never quite certain that we have enough financial resources to protect us from the hidden dangers in our capitalist society. James pictured a man as planning a business, confident that he could secure enough gain from it to immunize himself from any misfortune.

Such an attitude begins with materialism but leads to a complete Epicurean approach to life. Self-indulgence becomes the order of the day, and all goals are based on enjoying the things of life that appeal to the lower nature. The materialist heaps up gains for security and at the same time begins to indulge in things opposed to the Spirit. This may sound contradictory at first, since people are supposed to provide for themselves and their families, but this lifestyle usually emerges in those who set their goals primarily in terms of things rather than deeper and more meaningful values.

II. A timely truth.

James flashed a warning much needed by all people and especially needed by those who make worldly goals their aim in life. He compared human existence with a mist, joining the many other figures of speech in the Scriptures that describe our pilgrimage on this earth. For instance, various writers refer to life as a handbreadth, a thread cut by the weaver, a dream, a shadow, water spilled on the ground, and wind. All of these indicate the idea of brevity. When David complained to Jonathan that "there is only a step between me and death" (1 Sam. 20:3 NIV), he expressed a truth that applies to all of us, even though an evil king is not chasing after us with intent to kill. Life has been called "a little gleam of time between two eternities" and "scarce the twinkle of a star in God's eternal day."

III. What is life all about?

Since no one can be completely sure of the purpose of our stay on earth, those who are wise will endeavor to make the most of their days. The old cliché "The best use of life is to invest it in something that will outlast it" contains tremendous truth. Those who live for self alone will come to the end of their way with few friends. Those who dawdle through life, shifting from one goal to another, will end up with no accomplishments because they had no real purpose in living. Those who continually try to exploit others will become cynical and distrust everyone else because they have unconsciously transferred their own character to the ambitions of others.

The best approach to life is to live it with what the old-timers called "an eye single to God's glory," which means exactly what James said: "You ought to say, 'If it is the Lord's will, we will live and do this or that'" (4:15 NIV). In days when the emperors were crowned at Constantinople, a royal mason came to the new ruler and set before him a number of marble slabs. The emperor was asked at that time to choose one for his tombstone. Those who have already selected cemetery plots and made prearrangements for their funerals testify that that is an unsettling experience. Yet we each need to keep before us the fact that our time is in God's hands.

Stewardship steps in at this point and says, "All that you have comes from God. To rejoice in your own boastings is evil. If you know to do a good thing and refuse, it becomes sin." Whether in the realm of material possessions or other investments of life, we daily face the matter of how we will use our resources. Setting goals can be a dangerous thing, because most of us will probably come close to reaching them. Therefore, we should be certain they are worth the effort. The only aims in life that are worthwhile are those related to the advancement of God's work in this world.

Conclusion

When we come to the end of our way, will we be glad about how we have lived? Have we used our possessions for more than our own self-interests? Have we despised nothing in the world except falsehood and wickedness? Have we feared nothing except cowardice? Have we been governed by our admirations rather than our disgusts? Have we coveted nothing that belongs to our neighbors except their kind hearts, gentle manners, and compassionate attitudes? Have we sought to spend much of our time in personal communion with the Lord but never forgetting the practical world that needs our help?

Life is for living! True living, however, means service, which has been called the "rent we pay for living on this earth." When we live our lives in harmony with God's principles, we can find a little heaven here on this earth.

SUNDAY EVENING, NOVEMBER 26

Title: The Peace of the Church

Text: "Be at peace among yourselves" **(1 Thess. 5:13)**.

Scripture Reading: 1 Thessalonians 5:1–13

Introduction

In 1946 a pastor-evangelist was holding a series of meetings in a small, rural Kentucky community, where he was a guest in the home of one of the oldest families in that area. To his delight, he discovered that some member of that family had been the clerk of that church for more than one hundred years. Moreover, the book containing the minutes of all items of business back to 1839, when the church was organized, was in their care. For the visiting pastor, that book was interesting reading. In the minutes of almost every business conference, this entry appeared: "The peace of the church was called for."

The visitor was told that the moderator of the conference would ask, "Brethren, are we at peace?" No one knew what might follow. No doubt their business meetings were interesting and well attended, because almost any kind of gathering would have been hard-put to match these sessions in human interest, emotion-packed drama, and sometimes even comedy. But whatever might have been the shortcomings of these people, in whatever respects they may have failed, they sincerely tried to carry out the literal words of our text. They meant to have peace if they had to fight with one another to obtain it. If these people were too strict in the matter of church discipline, perhaps our churches today are too lax.

Three preliminary considerations should be noted concerning today's text:

1. The spirit of this text cannot be enforced by force. No peace of any sort can be either secured or maintained by force. Those who try to enforce "the peace of the church" cause strife and wound as many saints as they convert sinners.
2. This text presupposes an autonomous, independent, democratic body. The words "be at peace among yourselves" addressed to any other group would make no sense. Who else besides a plain, simple, New Testament church, where every member is equal in rank and privilege with every other member, a pure democracy, would even have the privilege of being at war among themselves?
3. The status of peace, the degree of fellowship within a church, is difficult to analyze. Sometimes a church is like a shallow, clear mountain stream where every ripple may be seen. At other times, a church may be like a deep, muddy river, calm and placid on the surface but torn by dangerous undercurrents.

"Be at peace among yourselves." This text provokes three pertinent questions.

I. What does this text mean?

The answer should be considered both negatively and positively.

A. *Negatively.*

1. Peace is not the painlessness of inertia and lifelessness. A church may appear to be at peace when in reality it is dead. Peace is a living thing—positive and dynamic, fruitful and productive.
2. Peace is not the stupor of indifference and unconcern. To have the spiritual senses stupefied is not to be at peace.
3. Peace is not the negative spirit of leaving an issue alone. (The French have a word for it, *laissez-faire*—"let it drift.") In every church, there are those who retreat to the safety of a judicial position, refusing either to be quoted or to get involved. But a cowardly retreat is not peace.

B. *Positively.*

1. The text implies the peace of a good conscience, resulting from a faithful and consistent walk before God as a Christian. Paul enjoined this in his epistles (e.g., Gal. 5:16; Eph. 4:1, 17; 5:8). John demonstrated the connection between a worthy walk and peace: "If we walk in the light, as he is in the light, we have fellowship one with another" (1 John 1:7). But if we walk after the manner of carnal people in jealousy and strife (1 Cor. 3:3), we violate "the peace of the church." If a Christian doesn't have the peace of a good conscience, what else matters?
2. The text implies the peace of an undivided heart. Jesus said, "Blessed are the pure in heart" (Matt. 5:8). *Pure* means being undivided, entire, without alloy. "Blessed are the undivided in heart."
3. The text implies the peace of a contented mind resulting from the knowledge of having done one's best for Christ while serving him in his church. People who work together get together and stay together. They have to because even a mule cannot kick when it is pulling nor pull when it is kicking.

II. Why is this text so necessary to a church?

"Be at peace among yourselves." Any other state of affairs in a church is a terrible blow, both to the church as a body and to the individual members. Why?

A. *For the sake of our growth in the grace and knowledge of Christ.* We are commanded to grow (2 Peter 3:18). We do not grow while on a spiritual hunger strike. The first thing a pouting child does is leave the table. Several years ago in India, Gandhi led his nation in their struggle for independence from Great Britain. His weapon was the hunger strike. The British could not persuade him to eat. They dared not let him die. He won. Some in the church try this weapon on God. He is not impressed, and they hurt only themselves.

B. *For the sake of our witness as a church before the world.* It is unthinkable that a child of God should have no resemblance to his Father. Paul said, "For God is not a God of confusion, but of peace" (1 Cor. 14:33 ASV). Jesus taught, "Blessed are the peacemakers: for they shall be called sons of God" (Matt. 5:9 ASV). True peacemakers are "sons of God" and are recognized as such. For peacemakers not to be at peace among themselves is an unthinkable contradiction.

C. *For the sake of the effectiveness of the church as a soul-winning agency.* To whom did Christ give his Great Commission? His church. To whom did our Lord commit the task of winning people to him? His church, and only to his church. Paul asked the Corinthians, "For if the trumpet give an uncertain sound, who shall prepare himself to the battle?" (1 Cor. 14:8). How less likely is the world to hear and understand if the notes are discord?

III. How can we apply this text to our lives?

How can we be at peace among ourselves in the church?

A. *We can be at peace with God within ourselves as members of the church.* In the church at Philippi there were two women—Euodia, meaning "fragrant," and Syntyche, meaning "fortunate"—who had some sort of disagreement, and this seems to have been more than a personal matter. Paul was impartial. He said simply, "I exhort Euodia, and I exhort Syntyche, to be of the same mind in the Lord" (Phil. 4:2 ASV). This was necessary for the peace of the church because these women had been active members (v. 3).

B. *We can have a consciousness of Christian love that will rule out strife by putting others first.* Jesus said, "One is your teacher, and all ye are brethren" (Matt. 23:8 ASV). Paul's admonition to the Philippians that they "be of the same mind, having the same love, being of one accord, of one mind" (2:2 ASV) would bring peace to any church anywhere. "We know that we have passed out of death into life," John said, "because we love the brethren" (1 John 3:14 ASV).

C. *We can be at peace through a common loyalty to the supreme head, Christ (Col. 1:18).* Jesus said, "For one is your master, even the Christ" (Matt. 23:10). Christ is the only true touchstone of fellowship. If we walk with him, we will be at peace (1 John 1:7).

Conclusion

If our fathers were too concerned about "the peace of the church" and how to maintain it, we are too unconcerned. Paul's injunction still applies. This text is as relevant and important as it ever was.

Wednesday Evening, November 29

Title: The Grave Robber

Text: "Jesus said unto her, I am the resurrection, and the life: he that believeth in me, though he were dead, yet shall he live" **(John 11:25)**.

Scripture Reading: John 11:1–53

Introduction

Crimes take diverse directions. This is especially true with robbery. Thieves steal a variety of items with different techniques. One of the most unusual kinds of burglaries is grave robbery, during which intruders go inside a cemetery and steal valuable jewelry from graves.

Jesus stole bodies from graves. He commanded some people to return from the dead. One of these persons was Lazarus. At the graveside of Lazarus, Jesus claimed to be the Prince of life itself. He said, "I am the resurrection, and the life: he that believeth in me, though he were dead, yet shall he live" (John 11:25). This is another great "I am" saying of the Bible. Let us notice why Jesus claimed to be the Prince of life.

I. Jesus is the beginning of life.

Jesus is the only one capable of creating physical life. He is responsible for the beginning of physical life. Jesus is also responsible for the initiating of spiritual life. When we open our lives to Jesus Christ, we begin to live.

II. Jesus is the fullness of life.

Jesus often spoke of living an abundant life. By this he meant that he brings full life. When we accept Jesus, we can have victory over the sins of life and live each day in the power of the indwelling Holy Spirit. And we can have deliverance from the fears and frustrations of life. Jesus brings meaning to life. He brings a better life—life in the fullest!

III. Jesus is the future of life.

Many people today are talking about life after death, and many popular books have been written on the subject. Trust in Jesus Christ results in life beyond the grave because Jesus opens the door of death for the continuation of life.

Conclusion

Jesus assured us not only of life after death but of a full life here on earth when we trust him as Savior and Lord. Have you invited him into your life? If not, do so today and find out what real living is all about!

SUGGESTED PREACHING PROGRAM FOR THE MONTH OF

DECEMBER

■ Sunday Mornings

Continue with the theme "God's Affirmative Action Program," as the church celebrates the coming of God in human flesh. End the year with a message on the joy of living as you look to the new year.

■ Sunday Evenings

"Go Tell It on the Mountain" is the theme for four sermons that emphasize the need for modern-day followers of Christ to broadcast the good news that was proclaimed so dramatically at the time of his birth. On New Year's Eve, close out the year with a message on finding joy in Jesus for the new year.

■ Wednesday Evenings

Complete the series "The Christ of John's Gospel."

SUNDAY MORNING, DECEMBER 3

Title: God's Affirmative Action Program: The Reason

Text: "In him was life, and that life was the light of all mankind. The light shines in the darkness, and the darkness has not overcome it" **(John 1:4–5 NIV)**.

Scripture Reading: John 1:1–5

Hymns: "Come, Thou Almighty King," Anonymous
"Joy to the World!" Watts
"Go Tell It on the Mountain," Work

Offertory Prayer: Our Father, as we enter the season in which we celebrate the birth of Jesus Christ, your Son, help us not to lose sight of him in the trappings of Christmas. Help us in our many activities to be attentive to the main event of the Christmas season.

The Christmas season makes us think of giving. As you have given so much for us, notably your Son who came to earth and died on the cross for us, may we not slight you in the giving of our gifts. Make us generous to your causes as you have been generous to us and our needs. Accept our gratitude for your generous mercy to us. Accept and bless our gifts as we give them to you. And forgive us our sins, we pray. In Jesus' name. Amen.

Introduction

In 1965 the federal government of the United States initiated affirmative action programs to see that businesses right some wrongs, balance some imbalances, correct some faults—ultimately, to bring reconciliation. God also had an affirmative action program designed to bring reconciliation—reconciliation between God and man. On these Sundays leading up to Christmas, we will examine God's affirmative action program as expressed in the prologue to John's gospel, John 1:1–18.

The first matter to consider is the reason for God's affirmative action program. Why did God need one?

Because humans had sinned against their Creator and broken fellowship with him, God had to make a way for them to come back into right relationship with him. He showed his love for humankind by initiating a plan to restore them to a position of right standing. Just as we say, "I love you," with words and actions, that is how God communicated his love to us. He sent his Son, the living Word, to earth. John 1:1, with words reminiscent of Genesis 1:1, says, "In the beginning was the Word."

I. God had a word for us.

A. *This Word of God is communicative.* When the writer of the fourth gospel wanted to tell us of God's Word to us, he chose a concept that would communicate to all people who would receive this gospel. The concept was "Word." To Jews, Greeks, Christians, and the world at large, this was a concept that would communicate what God had done in Christ Jesus.

1. Power. To the Jews the Word of God meant power. God spoke a word and the world came into being (Gen. 1). The Word of God could burn like fire or shatter like a hammer (Jer. 23:29). The Word of God could accomplish the divine purpose (Isa. 55:11). The Hebrews who would read this gospel would immediately understand the power of God when they understood that the Word was in the beginning with God and was God.
2. Principle. But to the Greek reader "the Word" would mean a rational principle. It had to do more with philosophical thought than personal power. The Jewish apologist Philo had adopted this Greek philosophical concept to refer to the projected thought of the transcendent God, the clue to the meaning and purpose of life.
3. Proclamation. The early Christian church viewed the preaching of the gospel as a "ministry of the word" (Acts 6:4). The entire event of Christ's life was a divine declaration, a redemptive proclamation. We are told in Revelation, "His name is the Word of God" (Rev. 19:13 NIV). In preaching the Word, the early Christians were proclaiming the redemptive message of Jesus Christ.

4. Person. The unique conviction of the prologue to John's gospel is that the Word of God is a person. The Word is not Jesus' power or principle or proclamation but his person. When truth becomes personal, it becomes meaningful to us.

   God had a word for us, a word that communicates to us in a personal way that we can be made right with God.

B. *The Word of God is comprehensive.*

1. The Word relates to God. The Word is not just identified with God; he is identical with God. When you want to see God and know what God is like, you look to Jesus Christ. He is related to God in being. He gives us an accurate communication of God.
2. The Word relates to the world. The Word of God relates to the world in that God was the agent of creation. He is revealed and known by his creative activity. John and Paul both wanted to make sure that we understood that creation was as much the work of Christ as was redemption. God relates to the world in creativity.
3. The Word relates to humankind. But the comprehensive Word that God spoke also relates to all of humankind. It is expressed in two terms: *life* and *light.* These translate to redemption. Jesus Christ is related to humankind redemptively.

   So the reason for God's affirmative action program is that God had a Word for us, a Word that was both communicative and comprehensive. By this Word, God spoke the last Word to us. Listen to the opening words of the book of Hebrews: "In many and various ways God spoke of old to our fathers by the prophets; but in these last days he has spoken to us by a Son, whom he appointed the heir of all things, through whom also he created the world" (Heb. 1:1–2 RSV).

II. God had a witness to us.

If the Word God has spoken to us shows us that Christ, the Word, *is,* it also shows us what Christ *does.* Through this Word that had become flesh, God gave a witness to himself in this world. Christ came into the world to reveal God and to redeem persons. That witness is expressed in two keywords in John's gospel: *life* and *light.*

A. *Life.* In Christ there is life. One thing Jesus did was to impart life to persons who lived with no hope of eternal life.

For all the hopeless, helpless, wondering, wandering people in the world, Jesus gives the promise that there is life—life with worth and meaning. Jacobo Timerman was a Jewish newspaper publisher in Argentina. In 1977 he was taken prisoner by the revolutionary government because of his writing and was placed in a prison and subjected to torture. He told his story in a book titled *Prisoner without a Name, Cell without a Number.* One night the guard failed to close the peephole in his door. When he looked out the peephole, he saw that the peephole in the door facing his was also open. Then he saw an eye behind it. Looking through the peephole was forbidden. Thinking it was a trap, he stepped back, waited, then returned to the peephole. The eye on the other side of the hall did the same. Through that night they looked through the peephole at one another. They never knew who the other was. But that blinking, that flutter of a movement proved to Timmerman that he was not the last human survivor amid that universe of torturing custodians. They invented games that night, moving away, then returning, creating movement in their confined world. And there was the blink, the acknowledgment that there was life. That night in the solitude he knew there was life (condensed in *Reader's Digest*, November 1981, 233–34).

In the Word, God has a witness to us that there is life.

B. *Light.* This life is also described as light. Christ brings light into the world—light about our darkened ideas about sin, self, and salvation. The light of God's love shines about us in Jesus Christ. Twice in John's gospel, Jesus made the claim for himself, "I am the light of the world" (John 8:12; 9:5).

Notice something about this light: the darkness cannot put it out. The light of God's grace shines with such power that the depths of darkness cannot put it out. In fact, darkness cannot even dim it. God's light in Jesus Christ is brighter than all the accumulated darkness of the world's sin.

God's witness to us is that the Word has become flesh and lived among us. This gives witness to both what we can know about God and what we can experience with God—life and light.

Conclusion

When you have something to say, you use a word to express it. God expressed his love for us, his life in us, and his light to us in a Word—Jesus Christ. That Word became flesh and dwelt among us. Through it we see God and respond to his love in faith.

Sunday Evening, December 3

Title: Telling the Good News

Text: "But the angel said to them, 'Do not be afraid. I bring you good news that will cause great joy for all the people. Today in the town of David a Savior has been born to you; he is the Messiah, the Lord'" **(Luke 2:10–11 NIV).**

Scripture Reading: Luke 2:8–14

Introduction

In today's Scripture reading, we find the angelic choir announcing the birth of Jesus Christ to an astonished group of shepherds. It has been the privilege and joy of Christ's followers to sing and speak of his coming since that significant night. It is the privilege of Christians today to join that angelic choir and tell the good news with joyful sound. The early followers of Christ were "traveling" witnesses, and as they journeyed, they told the good news. Tonight let's consider where they shared this good news.

I. They shared the good news in the city of Jerusalem where Jesus had been crucified (Acts 2:5–8).

II. They shared the good news in the temple area, which was dedicated to worship (Acts 2:46).

III. They shared the good news from house to house (Acts 20:20).

IV. They shared the good news in the streets and marketplaces (Acts 5:15; 14:8–10).

V. They shared the good news in the synagogues (Acts 13:14).

VI. Philip shared the good news with an Ethiopian eunuch on a desert highway (Acts 8:26–38).

VII. Peter and others shared the good news in the house of Cornelius the Gentile (Acts 10:22–48).

VIII. Paul and Silas shared the good news while confined to a prison cell (Acts 16:25–32).

IX. Paul shared the good news while aboard a ship at sea (Acts 27:22–25).

X. Paul shared the good news before governors and kings (Acts 24:1–27; 26:1–32).

Conclusion

We can see that in all kinds of circumstances and in all kinds of places, the early disciples joined the angelic choir in communicating not only Christ's birth, but also his miraculous life, substitutionary death, and victorious resurrection.

May we follow their example and tell others the good news everywhere we go.

Go tell it on the mountain,
Over the hills and everywhere;
Go tell it on the mountain,
That Jesus Christ is Lord.

—*John W. Work Jr., "Go, Tell It on the Mountain"*

WEDNESDAY EVENING, DECEMBER 6

Title: The Eleventh Commandment

Text: "'A new command I give you: Love one another. As I have loved you, so you must love one another'" **(John 13:34 NIV)**.

Scripture Reading: John 13:31–35

Introduction

Charles Templeton, in his book *Life Looks Up*, said that the history of the world has been affected by two events that took place in two small rooms, separated by thousands of miles and thousands of years. One room is found in a drab flat over a dingy laundry in the Soho district of London. In this small room, Karl Marx wrote *Das Kapital*, a book that changed the face of communism. The other room was in Jerusalem. It was the place where Jesus ate the Passover with his disciples and gave them some meaningful instructions.

Just as Jesus was about to go to the cross, he bequeathed to his disciples a badge they would need to wear. It would be a sign that they were in fact his disciples. "A new command I give you: Love one another. As I have loved you, so you must love one another. By this all men will know that you are my disciples, if you love one another" (John 13:34–35 NIV). Jesus called his exhortation to love "a new command." We could label it "the eleventh commandment." Let's examine the various facets of this command.

I. The supreme place for love.

A. *Jesus gave love a supreme place in his teachings.* Love was the central theme of the Master's teaching. "You have heard that it was said, 'Love your neighbor and hate your enemy.' But I tell you: love your enemies and pray for those who persecute you, that you may be children of your Father in heaven. He causes his sun to rise on the evil and the good, and sends rain on the righteous and the unrighteous. If you love those who love you, what reward will you get? Are not even the tax collectors doing that? And if you greet only your own people, what are you doing more than others? Do not even pagans do that?" (Matt. 5:43–47 NIV).

B. *Jesus gave love a supreme place in his life's relationships.* Love is the basis of a relationship with God and with other human beings. "Love the Lord your God with all your heart and with all your soul and with all your strength and with all your mind" (Luke 10:27 NIV).

C. *Jesus gave love a supreme place with his actions.* The Lord loved without recommendations, without restrictions, and without reciprocation. He always sought the highest good of others.

D. *Jesus wants his followers to give love a supreme place.* "If I speak in the tongues of men or of angels, but have not love, I am only a resounding gong or a clanging cymbal. If I have the gift of prophecy and can fathom all mysteries and all knowledge, and if I have a faith that can move mountains, but do not have love, I am nothing. If I give all I possess to the poor and give over my body to hardship that I may boast, but do not have love, I gain nothing" (1 Cor. 13:1–3 NIV). Love must have precedence in our lives.

II. The unique pattern for love.

If love is so important, how are we to love? Jesus gave the pattern for love: "Love one another. As I have loved you, so you must love one another" (John 13:34 NIV). The pattern for love cannot be determined by our standard but only by the pattern of Jesus Christ.

A. *Jesus loved inclusively.* He included the entire human race in his love. He loved outsiders and insiders; he even loved tax collectors, prostitutes, and others who seemed unlovable. As a part of God's family, we are called to love everyone, even our enemies. We cannot obey the eleventh commandment if we exclude anyone from our love.

B. *Jesus loved indescribably.* There is no way in all the world to describe the depth of Jesus' love: "Greater love has no one than this: to lay down one's life for one's friends" (John 15:13 NIV). Jesus practiced sacrificial love and ultimately gave his life on a cross to save others.

C. *Jesus loved selflessly.* Jesus never loved anyone because of ulterior motives. He never thought about what he should get in return.

III. The distinct purpose of love.

A. *The purpose of love is to identify true disciples (John 13:35).* Loving as Jesus loved distinguishes disciples from the world. Our identity as Christians is not the creed we recite or the church we attend, but the love that we have for Jesus and other people.

B. *The purpose of love is to attract lost people.* In a classic song, we are reminded that "what the world needs now is love, sweet love." The world is attracted to people who love.

Henry Drummond, in his classic sermon *The Greatest Thing in the World,* suggests that by placing a small piece of iron in the presence of an electrified body, that piece of iron becomes electrified for a time. Placing our lives in the presence of Christ means that Christ's nature can be seen in our lives.

Conclusion

The world desperately needs love, but the only way they can know true love is by watching Christian love in action. Will we obey the eleventh commandment? Will we love one another?

SUNDAY MORNING, DECEMBER 10

Title: God's Affirmative Action Program: The Revelation

Text: "There was a man sent from God whose name was John. He came as a witness to testify concerning that light, so that through him all might believe. He himself was not the light; he came only as a witness to the light" **(John 1:6–8 NIV).**

Scripture Reading: John 1:6–8

Hymns: "Send the Light," McCabe
"Come, Thou Long Expected Jesus," Wesley
"Christ Is the World's True Light," Briggs

Offertory Prayer: Our Father, we thank you for this day, this life, and all the blessings you have given to us. Help us to know the light that your Son Jesus Christ can bring into our lives. Allow us to open all the dark places of our hearts and lives to the sunshine of the Savior's love. Into your hands we place our tithes and offerings. May we be just as free to place our lives into your hands. Please use our gifts and ourselves for your glory. In Jesus' name and for his sake we pray. Amen.

Introduction

Revelation is a word we use to describe the disclosure of the truth. The first chapter of the book of John presents a great revelation: "The Word became flesh and made his dwelling among us" (1:14 NIV). Unlike the other gospel writers, John did not start his book with scenes of Christ's birth. Instead, he started at the very beginning. "In the beginning was the Word, and the Word was with God, and the Word was God" (1:1 NIV).

As part of his affirmative action program, God became one of us. Through his Son, Jesus, God came into the world to fulfill his plan to bring people back to himself and provide all humankind with an equal opportunity for reconciliation with him. In our Scripture reading today, we learn that God chose John the Baptist to act as a witness to this great revelation.

I. John was the instrument of God's revelation.

A. *John's commission.* John was an instrument to reveal God's plan of reconciliation. John's birth was no accident. Notice how the gospel expresses it: "There was a man sent from God whose name was John" (1:6 NIV). John was under commission from God himself. John 1:8 tells us that John the Baptist was called to reveal the Promised One sent by God. God sent a man to tell us that he had sent his Son. This was John's commission.

B. *John's mission.* John was also a man on a mission. He was called to bear witness to the light that would shine in the world. Notice that the gospel makes a clear distinction between Jesus Christ, the Light of the World, and John the Baptist, who was sent to bear witness to the light. John's mission was to introduce people to the one whose light could lead them into life.

C. *John's submission.* John submitted to God's awesome plan for his life. "He came as a witness to testify concerning that light, so that through him all might believe" (v. 7 NIV). Through his witness, many people came to faith in Jesus Christ and accepted him as personal Savior. Like John, we, too, are called to be instruments of God and to bear witness to his Son.

II. Jesus was the Light of God's revelation.

John the Baptist was not the light that would illuminate the world. But he would bear witness to the true light that would illuminate the darkened lives of people everywhere. Have you ever stood in pitch blackness, trying to get your bearings, when suddenly a flash of light illuminated the area sufficiently for you to see where you were? God's light flashes into our lives in Jesus Christ. William Barclay has listed three areas where the light of Jesus Christ illuminates the shadows of life.

A. *Doubt.* Many people doubt that they can know God. God seems so unreal and so unknowable to them. But Christ's coming into the world has removed the shadow of doubt. We don't have to wonder if God is real or what he is like. We have Jesus Christ to show us the character of God. Since the Word was with God from the very beginning and the Word was God himself, then the Word is what God is. Any doubts we may have had about God are gone. We can know God.

B. *Despair.* The world into which Jesus came was filled with despair. But Jesus gave hope. With Christ we have forgiveness, strength, and help for living. Christ's light dispels despair. We no longer have to live in despair with no hope or help.

C. *Death.* The ancient world feared death. At best, death was annihilation. At worst, death was torture by whatever gods there were. People were afraid of these possibilities. But Jesus—through his coming, his life, his death, and his resurrection—revealed that death was only the way to a larger life. People did not have to fear death any longer. Christ defeated death, and we can live in that victory.

III. God's revelation is inclusive.

Notice how inclusive God's revelation is: "so that through him all might believe" (v. 7 NIV). The ancient world was rather exclusive. The Jews hated the

Gentiles and the Gentiles stayed away from the Jews. The Greeks were smug and narcissistic, considering themselves far superior in knowledge and intellect; they raised their noses in disdain at the boorishness of other cultures. The Roman world despised the other peoples whose language they did not understand and called them barbarians. But Christ's coming gave light to everyone.

Notice the implications of this fact.

A. *Witness.* John's witness was for all persons; he was to tell the world that Jesus Christ gave both life and light. God's love and forgiveness are for everyone.

B. *Missions.* No person or nation is outside the circle of God's love. The Christmas season is a perfect time to think about missions because Christ's coming into the world assures us that God's love and salvation are intended for all the world.

   A missions volunteer once testified that one of the things that sharpened her call to missions was observing a door with an electric eye in a department store while Christmas shopping. She noticed that the door opened for anyone who came to it. Any person who broke the beam of the electric eye could enter the store. Similarly, she realized, the doors to the kingdom of heaven open to any person who approaches them. God's love is for everyone. That is the basis for missions.

Conclusion

During the Christmas season, we remember God's affirmative action program. God took affirmative action in sending his Son, Jesus, into the world to make himself known to us and to die on the cross to redeem us from our sin. John the Baptist was a witness to this revelation. He revealed God's plan for humankind as he pointed to the Christ. How will we respond to this revelation?

Sunday Evening, December 10

Title: The Motive for Telling the Good News

Text: "Those who had been scattered preached the word wherever they went" **(Acts 8:4 NIV)**.

Scripture Reading: Acts 8:1–8

Introduction

The angels hung out over the battlements of heaven to announce the good news that Jesus Christ was born. It is interesting to study the book of Acts and discover the dynamic enthusiasm of the early followers of Christ as they gave testimony to him. Tonight let's consider the various incentives that motivated them to share the good news.

I. Persecution motivated them to share the good news.

At first the church was completely Jewish in its constituency. Jesus came to a group of people who were rather clannish and restricted in their worldview. They found it impossible to believe at first that God loved the whole world. Soon, however, the pain and shock of persecution thrust them out of the city of Jerusalem into areas beyond. Our text tells us that everywhere they journeyed, they announced the good news. The fact that they did not necessarily go because of a great love for a lost world may disillusion us. If anything, this fact should cause us to consider the motives behind our own efforts to share the good news.

II. The joy of being bearers of good news motivated them to share the good news (Acts 2:41–47; 5:42).

No one likes to be the bearer of sad news. No one likes to convey the information that someone has died or is terminally ill. But we love to be the bearers of good news! The gospel is not good advice; it is good news from God about the fulfillment of his plan for our salvation. This was such wonderful news that once the early church grasped its implications, they could not remain silent. They were motivated by their joy in the privilege of being communicators of the good news.

III. Their personal relationship to Christ motivated them to share the good news (Matt. 28:18–20).

The early followers of Christ shared the good news as a personal response to the authority of their crucified but risen and living Lord. The lordship of Jesus Christ was real to the early disciples.

A. *They recognized him as Lord over nature.*
B. *They recognized him as Lord over the demonic.*
C. *They recognized him as Lord over disease.*
D. *They recognized him as Lord over death.*
E. *They recognized him as Lord of their very lives.* To the early Christians, bearing witness to Christ was not optional; it was imperative.

IV. The leadership of the Holy Spirit motivated them to share the good news.

The book of Acts is a success story. It declares the success of these early followers of Christ as they shared the good news of Christ under the leadership of the Holy Spirit.

V. The exclusiveness of the gospel motivated them to share the good news.

The early Christians believed that all people away from Christ are lost from God and do not know the way home. Salvation is found in Christ alone (Acts 4:12).

Conclusion

With the dynamic enthusiasm of the early Christians, we also should share the good news with others. As Christians, one of our foremost desires should be to lead others to faith in Christ. "As it is written, 'How beautiful are the feet of those who bring good news!'" (Rom. 10:15 NIV). Because of compassion and the command of Christ, we should do with great joy as the chorus tells us:

> Go tell it on the mountain,
> Over the hills and everywhere;
> Go tell it on the mountain,
> That Jesus Christ is born.
>
> —*John W. Work Jr., "Go, Tell It on the Mountain"*

WEDNESDAY EVENING, DECEMBER 13

Title: Going in the Right Direction

Text: "Jesus answered, 'I am the way and the truth and the life. No one comes to the Father except through me'" **(John 14:6 NIV)**.

Scripture Reading: John 14:1–6

Introduction

Driving down a one-way street in the wrong direction is a frustrating experience. It happened to me during rush hour in a big city one day. Meeting irritated drivers and trying to turn around added to my misery. For the rest of the time I was in that city, I carefully noted each subsequent turn to see if I was going in the right direction.

Jesus talked about the direction of his life. It involved a cross. Yet he taught the disciples that the cross was the way of life for the world. Thomas was not sure he knew the right direction, so he asked, "Lord, we don't know where you are going, so how can we know the way?" (John 14:5 NIV). Jesus replied, "I am the way and the truth and the life" (v. 6 NIV).

Going the right direction through life is important. It is a joyful experience. Let's learn the instructions for how to travel the pilgrimage of life.

I. Take the only way.

Thomas knew of many other claims to be "the way." There have been many such claims throughout history. Philo called his philosophy "the Royal Way." Buddha claimed to have discovered "the right path." Confucius called his teaching "the Way."

Jesus' claim goes beyond any philosophy. He said, "I am the way." He points us in the right direction and walks with us. He guides us on the journey. He does not tell us about the way. He *is* the way.

II. Believe the truth.

If we want to go in the right direction, we must believe the truth. Jesus said, "I am the truth." This claim goes beyond the idea of a truth. Jesus did not just tell truths; he embodied the truth. Many truths can be conveyed with words only. Anyone can teach truths about love, forgiveness, and humility. But only Jesus embodies these truths.

When we open our lives to Jesus Christ, we can live the good life. He is the perfect pattern of what life should be. To be open to Jesus, the Truth, means we are going in the right direction.

III. Live the life.

Going in the right direction means more than mere existence. Many philosophies offer an existence style, not a real lifestyle. Only Jesus gives life. He gives more than the breath that animates our bodies. He makes existence worthwhile. He fills life with meaning.

People search desperately for what they hope will make their days purposeful and worth living. When they encounter Jesus Christ, they are introduced to God himself. Other philosophies offer temporary solutions to life's great riddles. Jesus offers permanent solutions.

Conclusion

You can go in the right direction. On your journey, Jesus is the Way. To know the Truth is to encounter Jesus. To experience the Life is to have real life.

SUNDAY MORNING, DECEMBER 17

Title: God's Affirmative Action Program: The Response

Text: "He came to that which was his own, but his own did not receive him. Yet to all who received him, to those who believed in his name, he gave the right to become children of God" **(John 1:11–12 NIV)**.

Scripture Reading: John 1:9–13

Hymns: "Hark! the Herald Angels Sing," Wesley
"Awake, My Soul, Awake," Reach
"What Wondrous Love Is This," American Folk Hymn

Offertory Prayer: Our Father, we stand truly amazed at your love for us. When we consider the message of the Christmas season, that Jesus Christ, your Son, was born into the world for the forgiveness of our sins, we are breathless. But help us, O Lord, that we will not be so breathless that we cannot give witness to this great event and its meaning to our own lives. And help us, O Lord, that we will be responsive to the great gift of grace as we offer our gifts to you in love this day. Please accept our gifts, forgive our sins, renew us through your Holy Spirit, and guide our lives. We pray in Jesus' name. Amen.

Introduction

When the Word that existed from the very beginning became flesh and came to earth to dwell among us—when the light that illuminated the life of everyone came to the world that he had created—he was not always well received. The response to the Word was not always favorable.

God's affirmative action program affirmed people's need for salvation. He sent his Son, referred to in John's gospel as the Word, to be born on earth for the dual purposes of revealing God and redeeming humankind, explained in John's prologue as life and light. After a brief account of the man who came to bear witness to the light, John the Baptist, and a disclaimer that John the Baptist was not the light himself but rather a witness to the light, the prologue returns to the description of the Word that became flesh.

This portion of the prologue, John 1:9–13, portrays the response that people gave to the light of God. The response was generally negative. Jesus came to his own earth and to his own people, yet he was rejected by them. But sometimes the response was positive. Some accepted him, and to them he gave the privilege of becoming the very children of God.

Today let's consider the response to God's affirmative action program in more detail. And consider carefully your own response to it.

I. The response involves particularity.

A. *Nothing is ever universal until it is first local.* The universal light that could light up the life of every person in the world became a particular person—Jesus of Nazareth. The one who existed from before the beginning of the world came into this world at a particular place on the globe and at a particular time in history.

It is one thing to talk about the great universals such as light and life, but they become real to us when those universals are made local. We best understand light and life only when we see them infuse a single life. God has always made the universal known by showing us the local and particular.

1. God loves all peoples and all races, but through a particular people—the Jews—God revealed himself.
2. God loves all families of the earth, but in a particular family—the family of Abraham, Isaac, and Jacob—God worked out his love.
3. God delivers all people from the bondage of sin, but in a particular event—the exodus—God demonstrated his power of deliverance.
4. God existed for all time, created the world, and desired to reconcile sinful humankind to himself; but in a particular person—Jesus Christ, the Word who became flesh—God made his plan for salvation known to all people.

B. *Nothing is ever known until it is first experienced.* What God had been trying to get across to all of humankind was experienced in Jesus

Christ. Then it became known to people. They could see the light that shone brightly in our world because of Christ's coming into the world. All people had the potential to have their own lives illuminated by that light. Everything that had been known intellectually about acceptance, forgiveness, and family could finally be experienced.

God's love for all humankind became evident when the light that was the Word entered the world he had created in the particular person of Jesus of Nazareth. This event is what we celebrate at Christmas.

II. The response involves personality.

A. *The personality shows continuity.* John was careful to show the continuity of the Word that existed from the very beginning and the personality that we know as Jesus of Nazareth. The Christ who was born into the world on that first Christmas was not different from the God who had existed always. He was that God. There was a continuity in his existence. He was in the world already; in fact, he had always been in the world. But in the birth of the baby in Bethlehem, the one who had always been in the world took on a particular personality that we could see and know.

B. *The personality shows creativity.* The same God who had always been in the world, who had in fact created the world, chose to enter his world as a baby. No wonder the angels sang! No wonder the star shone brightly! It was a time for joy and wonder: the Savior was born!

C. *The personality shows closeness.* The God who had always been in the world had not actually been introduced to the world. Through the birth of Christ, God became close to us. He could be seen by us. He could be touched by our hands. John wanted to emphasize this point. In his day, many people believed that matter was evil and that a good God could not have created a world composed of matter. So they invented the idea that through a series of emanations from God came one who was so far removed from God that he could dwell amid the evil of matter.

John, on the other hand, went to great lengths to clarify that the eternal God not only created matter, he took on human flesh; he became matter. When he had a body and a personality, he could be seen, touched, and really known. God was personified in Jesus when the Word became flesh.

III. The response involves practicality.

Because God took on human flesh and became a person in Jesus Christ, everyone is confronted with the Christ and forced to make a choice. The light that can illuminate every life in the world has to be received. God did not force himself into the world, nor does he force himself into human lives. People must choose to reject Jesus or to accept him.

A. *Rejection of Christ.* People can choose to turn away from the light. They can refuse the life that he offers through faith. This scenario is expressed in the prologue of John's gospel. Christ came into the world that he had created, but the world did not receive him. He came to the people whom he had made and to whom he had made himself known, but his own people did not receive him.

B. *Acceptance of Christ.* People can choose to turn toward the light. John said that those who accept Christ are given the right to become the children of God. Notice that those who become the children of God do so through the miraculous means of new birth, not by human will or effort. God's grace has made redemption possible. We become a part of God's family by grace through faith.

Conclusion

Each of us must respond to God's affirmative action program. Will we reject Christ and continue to live in darkness? Or will we accept Christ and step into the light?

SUNDAY EVENING, DECEMBER 17

Title: Sharing the Good News

Text: "'You will receive power when the Holy Spirit comes on you; and you will be my witnesses in Jerusalem, and in all Judea and Samaria, and to the ends of the earth'" **(Acts 1:8 NIV)**.

Scripture Reading: Acts 1:6–11

Introduction

Each of us is called to share the good news with others. Tonight let's consider the various ways we can follow these words of exhortation:

> Go tell it on the mountain,
> Over the hills and everywhere;
> Go tell it on the mountain,
> That Jesus Christ is born.
>
> —*John W. Work Jr., "Go, Tell It on the Mountain"*

I. Pastors can communicate the good news through their sermons.

Pastors should continually listen for God's voice in Bible study and prayer. Each time they stand in the pulpit, they should deliver a relevant, penetrating message from God for those who are listening.

II. We can communicate the good news through song.

Those who have a special talent for singing should use their talent to glorify God rather than to show off their musical ability. But all of us can participate in the song portion of our worship services. By doing so, we express our praise and thanks to God for who he is and for all he has done in our lives.

III. We can communicate the good news by teaching Sunday school or Bible study.

Sunday school teachers and Bible study leaders should see themselves as communicators of the good news. We should remember that the Bible is not just a history textbook. It is the living Word of God. We should study it diligently and draw life applications from its truths.

IV. We can communicate the good news by sharing our personal testimony.

If we are sensitive and alert, we will have frequent opportunities to tell others what Christ means to us. When we give our testimonies, we must rely on God to give us the right words, and we should never create the impression that we are overly pious.

V. We can communicate the good news in our personal conversations.

Colossians 4:6 says, "Let your conversation be always full of grace, seasoned with salt, so that you may know how to answer everyone" (NIV). And 1 Peter 3:15 says, "Always be prepared to give an answer to everyone who asks you to give the reason for the hope that you have" (NIV).

VI. We can communicate the good news over the telephone.

We can't always communicate with people in person, but we can usually get in touch with them by telephone. We can call Christian friends to encourage them in their walk with Christ, and we can call non-Christian friends to offer them support and indicate our hope for their spiritual welfare.

VII. We can communicate the good news in letters or Christmas cards.

God can use a written message as well as a spoken message to help lead someone to faith in Jesus Christ.

VIII. We can communicate the good news by purchasing Bibles or Christian books for others.

IX. We can communicate the good news by investing in the work of God.

X. We can communicate the good news through causes we support.

Conclusion

Many means are available for communicating the good news "that Jesus Christ is born." We need to share this good news thoughtfully, thankfully, and persistently.

Wednesday Evening, December 20

Title: The Promise of the Holy Spirit

Text: "'I will ask the Father, and he will give you another advocate to help you and be with you forever'" **(John 14:16 NIV)**.

Scripture Reading: John 14:15–31

Introduction

Saying goodbye can be difficult. People struggle with words when a friend or family member will be going away for a long period of time. Likewise, the disciples had a hard time bidding farewell to the Master. Jesus had prepared them for the fact of his death, but they were not willing to accept this reality. The closer the time came for Jesus' departure, the more they recognized the reality. The Lord and his disciples had a difficult time leaving each other.

Jesus told the disciples that his departure would be only for a short time. "Before long, the world will not see me anymore, but you will see me. Because I live, you also will live" (John 14:19 NIV). Jesus promised that he would be with his disciples in the power and presence of his Spirit. In other words, Jesus himself would be present with his disciples in another manner. Maybe believers need to examine the promise Jesus gave to his disciples about the Holy Spirit.

I. The Holy Spirit is a personal presence.

A. *The personal presence of Jesus meant much to the disciples.* Think of the numerous times they were bewildered and afraid when Jesus was not present. On one occasion the disciples were afraid when a storm arose quickly on the Sea of Galilee. Jesus was not with them. And think of their frustration as they tried to heal a man's son while Jesus was on a mountain with Peter, James, and John. Jesus' absence brought a sense of loneliness to the apostles. His presence was a blessing to their lives.

B. *The personal presence of Jesus is promised to future disciples.* "I will ask the Father, and he will give you another advocate to help you and be with you forever" (14:16 NIV). When Jesus said "another," he suggested another of the same kind. The Counselor would be none other than the actual presence of God. This means that the Holy Spirit is not some impersonal force or energy. The Holy Spirit is God's personal presence with his disciples.

II. The Holy Spirit is a helpful teacher.

A. *The earthly teaching ministry of Jesus meant much to the disciples.* In the solitude of Galilean and Judean hills, Jesus taught his chosen disciples. He taught them many truths about life, character, interpersonal relationships, and countless other issues.

B. *The continuing presence of the helpful Teacher is promised.* "But when he, the, Spirit of truth, comes, he will guide you into all truth. He will not speak on his own; he will speak only what he hears, and he will tell you what is yet to come" (16:13 NIV). Jesus had taught numerous truths during his earthly ministry, but the disciples failed to understand them.

The Holy Spirit leads into new understanding of truth. Think about how Peter did not understand the universal nature of the gospel. He had a prejudice against non-Jews. Jesus often rebuked this attitude in Peter, but Peter failed to grasp the universal scope of the mission of the Jews. The Holy Spirit guided Peter to this truth.

III. The Holy Spirit is an authoritative guide.

A. *The guidance of Jesus meant much to the disciples.* Jesus was an authoritative guide for the disciples. They had a hard time saying goodbye to him because they were bewildered about life's journey. Jesus had told them where to go, how to serve, what to say, and what to do. They felt Jesus' absence would leave them doubtful about which route to take in life.

B. *The guidance of God is promised with the Holy Spirit.* "But the Advocate, the Holy Spirit, whom the Father will send in my name, will teach you all things and will remind you of everything I have said to you" (14:26 NIV). Believers do not have to be confused about which way to go. The Holy Spirit lives within each Christian, and he guides in the right direction.

IV. The Holy Spirit is a dynamic resource.

A. *Jesus lived alongside the apostles as a dynamic resource.* Think of the numerous times Jesus walked alongside these men to encourage them. They were going to feel helpless when the Lord left.

B. *Jesus promises the continuous presence of a divine resource.* The Holy Spirit would be a counselor to the disciples. He would be their source of comfort and inspiration, their help in times of trouble.

Conclusion

We need not be discouraged because the physical presence of Jesus is not with us. He is present in the Holy Spirit. Celebrate his presence!

SUNDAY MORNING, DECEMBER 24

Title: God's Affirmative Action Program: The Reality

Text: "The Word became flesh and made his dwelling among us. We have seen his glory, the glory of the one and only Son, who came from the Father, full of grace and truth" **(John 1:14 NIV)**.

Scripture Reading: John 1:14–18

Hymns: "It Came upon a Midnight Clear," Sears
"Angels, from the Realms of Glory," Montgomery
"Silent Night, Holy Night," Mohr

Offertory Prayer: Our Father, on this day when we celebrate the birth of Jesus Christ, your Son and our Savior, into the world, give us the grace to truly celebrate. We celebrate your loving concern for us. We celebrate your willingness to share life with us. We celebrate your identification with us. And we celebrate your redemption of us. On this day when so much attention is focused on gifts, may we think primarily of the gift of your Son, of his sacrifice that gives us eternal life, and of your abiding presence through the Holy Spirit that gives us meaningful life. We offer our gifts to you. Please accept them, bless them, and strengthen each one of us with the gift of grace. In Jesus' name we pray. Amen.

Introduction

God's affirmative action program became a reality on a cold winter's night when Jesus was born in Bethlehem. At that time the eternal Word took on human flesh and came to dwell among us. From this point on, John no longer calls him "the Word" but lets us in on the secret and gives us his name—Jesus Christ.

God took affirmative action toward us. He came into our world through Jesus Christ. What people had hoped for and looked toward had become a reality.

I. The reality involves exaltation (John 1:14–15).

A. *Limitation comes before exaltation.* "The Word became flesh and made his dwelling among us" (v. 14 NIV). This verse indicates three ways in which the Word was limited through the incarnation.

1. The limitation of time. The eternal Word who had existed from the very beginning became a person who lived during a certain time in human history. He who transcended all time was born at a specific time.
2. The limitation of temperament. The Word became flesh. Jesus actually became a human being. He took on the full temperament of a person. Jesus' appearance in history was not a theophany but an incarnation. God's appearance to Moses at the burning bush was a theophany, a manifestation of God. God commandeered the burning bush for his purpose.

   Jesus' appearance, on the other hand, was an incarnation. He was not commandeered but surrendered his will to the Father's purpose. His human nature was not marginal but central to his mission. The biblical record tells us that the child Jesus developed and increased in wisdom. As any child grows physically and matures mentally, so did Jesus. To make him anything else makes him less than human.

3. The limitation of transience. Jesus' life on earth was temporary. He was limited to one life, and a brief life at that. Even though Jesus was fully God, he was also fully human. He experienced the limitations that all humans face.

B. *Beyond limitation is exaltation.*

1. Exaltation comes through his glory. *Glory* is a word used throughout Scripture, especially by John. As we go back to its Old Testament roots, we are reminded of the tabernacle. There the people could sense the glory of God. His glory was given the name *shekinah,* which means "that which dwells." The glory of God inhabited the tabernacle, so the glory of God really means the presence of God. In Christ there is exaltation because the very presence of God is there in all his glory.
2. Exaltation comes through his sonship. Jesus was called "the only begotten son of God." The word *begotten* literally means "the only one of a kind." Jesus is not simply another son of God; he is the one and only Son of God. He can be compared to no one else.
3. Exaltation comes through his character. Two significant aspects of Jesus' character are grace and truth (v. 14). Grace is the unmerited favor of God, his divine compulsion to give us more than we deserve. Truth shows us that God is determined to be predictable, consistent, trustworthy. In Christ we see truth that is thoroughly trustworthy. It is a truth that sets us free, that liberates us from the bondage and baggage of sin that has bound us.

II. The reality involves evaluation (John 1:16–17).

A. *Evaluation of the witness.*

1. A witness of presence. Because of Jesus' incarnation, we can know the fullness of God. We can know with confidence that God is not just something or someone "out there." He is right beside us and shares life with us fully. Ernest Shackleton said that on his thirty-six-hour march over ice to the South Pole with his two comrades, he sensed that often there were four of them rather than three. One of his companions said to him, "Boss, I had a curious feeling on the march that there was another person with us." The third companion confessed to the same idea (George A. Buttrick, ed., *Interpreter's Bible* [Nashville: Abingdon, 1978], 8:474). God is indeed always with us as we march through life.
2. A witness of purpose. "Out of his fullness we have all received grace in place of grace already given" (v. 16 NIV). We never exhaust the blessings of God. Instead, they come rolling upon us one after another.

B. *Evaluation of the winner.* "For the law was given through Moses; grace and truth came through Jesus Christ" (v. 17 NIV). To Jewish minds, Moses was the great hero of the faith. Moses had led them from captivity in Egypt. Moses had led them on the wilderness wanderings. Moses had led them to the promised land. Moses had given them the law of God that directed their lives and determined their relationship to him.

Moses gave the law, but Jesus gave grace and truth. In any evaluation, then, Jesus would be deemed superior. Through him came the realization of the grace of God and the reality of the truth of God.

III. The reality involves explanation (John 1:18).

A. *Jesus, the seen, explains the unseen.* "No one has ever seen God, but the one and only Son, who is himself God and is in closest relationship with the Father, has made him known" (v. 18 NIV). From the seen, Jesus Christ, we can know the unseen, God. Jesus Christ has made God known to us precisely and clearly. By Jesus' teachings and actions, we can know what God is like.

B. *Jesus explains the Father by the Son.* Jesus' life is the divine disclosure of God. When we want to know about God, we look to that Word who was from the very beginning with God, who was God himself. From the Son we can see the Father.

Conclusion

God's affirmative action program worked! Its reality is seen in the incarnation. The eternal Word took on temporal flesh and shared life with us. As we celebrate the birth of Christ this week, may we thank God for his unspeakably great mercy and love.

SUNDAY EVENING, DECEMBER 24

Title: The Content of Our Testimony

Text: "'I bring you good news that will cause great joy for all the people. Today in the town of David a Savior has been born to you; he is the Messiah, the Lord'" **(Luke 2:10–11 NIV)**.

Scripture Reading: Luke 2:1–20

Introduction

The angels rejoiced at the birth of the Savior. Now, more than two thousand years later, we still rejoice over Christ's birth. More than that, we rejoice over his death and resurrection and what they mean to us. Christmas is the time when we reflect on all the good things God has done in our lives throughout the year. It is also a time when we focus on reaching out to others.

Jesus put a song in our hearts; let's share that song with others! We have many reasons to tell others that Jesus Christ is indeed a wonderful Savior.

I. We can sing of the joy of forgiveness.

Jesus Christ came into this world to redeem us from our sins. He suffered the penalty of our sins on the cross. He paid the wages of our sins, which is death (Rom. 6:23).

Only through faith in him can we have forgiveness (Acts 10:43). If we have asked Jesus into our hearts, we no longer stand condemned before the Father God. This knowledge should bring great joy to our hearts—the joy of forgiveness.

II. We can sing of the joy of eternal life (John 3:16).

"For God did not send his Son into the world to condemn the world, but to save the world through him" (John 3:17 NIV). Jesus came into this world to give us eternal life (John 10:27–28). This eternal life is more qualitative than quantitative. It is something much more than mere existence. It is the very life of God. Eternal life is the life of the Eternal.

III. We can sing of the joy of friendship with Jesus Christ (John 15:15).

One of life's greatest treasures is a genuine friend. Jesus is the Friend we need. He is the best Friend any of us could ever have. Those of us who have come to know him not only as our Savior but also as our Friend have something to sing about.

IV. We can sing of the joy of the Holy Spirit's help.

The Holy Spirit came to be a counselor, a comforter, a helper (John 14:16; Acts 1:8). Those of us who have achieved some degree of spiritual maturity should testify to the blessings of allowing the Holy Spirit to indwell our lives and guide our ministry to others. By doing so, we can encourage others to trust Jesus Christ as Savior.

V. We can sing of the joy of our Lord's presence with us always (Matt. 28:20).

Our Lord has promised the blessing of his personal presence to those who trust and obey him. Those who have experienced the fulfillment of that promise have a joy to sing about.

Conclusion

We have many reasons to share the good news with others. It is not enough to sing about the birth of a baby. We need to tell others about the significance of this baby!

> Go tell it on the mountain,
> Over the hills and everywhere;

Go tell it on the mountain,
That Jesus Christ is born.
—*John W. Work Jr., "Go, Tell It on the Mountain"*

Tell it with joy. Tell it with expectancy. Tell it expecting God to bless and use your testimony for the good of others.

WEDNESDAY EVENING, DECEMBER 27

Title: Becoming a Christian

Text: "'Remain in me, as I also remain in you. No branch can bear fruit by itself; it must remain in the vine. Neither can you bear fruit unless you remain in me. I am the vine; you are the branches. If you remain in me and I in you, you will bear much fruit; apart from me you can do nothing'" **(John 15:4–5 NIV)**.

Scripture Reading: John 15:1–17

Introduction

Do you desire to be a better Christian? Most Christians sincerely want to be better. But how do we become better Christians? Some people say that reading the Bible or other Christian books will make you a good Christian. Other people say that doing a lot of good works will make you a better Christian. Actually, we don't *begin* the Christian life in faith and continue it merely through faithful study and good works. Genuine faith results in faithful study and good works.

Jesus used the illustration of the vine and the branches to describe the Christian life. Jesus referred to himself as the Vine and to his followers as the branches. Using this analogy, we can learn more about the Christian life.

I. A vital union with Christ.

A. *Many people have mistaken concepts about how to become a Christian.* The Jews considered themselves branches because of birth, nationality, and race. Yet they refused to have vital union with Jesus Christ.

People take many measures to be united with God. However, union with the Lord does not come by belonging to a church. Nor does union come by being born into a Christian home. Nor does it come by observing rules and regulations.

B. *Becoming a Christian means to be united with Christ.* How does a branch receive life? It receives life by being grafted into the vine. The life of the vine then flows into the branch.

How then do you become a Christian? You become a believer by opening your life to Jesus Christ. The Lord comes into your heart and gives you new life. Paul's favorite expression for a Christian was a person "in Christ."

II. A constant abiding in Christ.

A. *Abiding in Christ is essential to Christian growth.* "Remain in me, as I also remain in you" (John 15:4 NIV). A branch cannot bear fruit of itself. We can't be better Christian by our own power. As branches we must abide in the Vine. The word *abide* means to keep in constant contact.

B. *Abiding in Christ will result in Christlikeness.* "If you remain in me and I in you, you will bear much fruit; apart from me you can do nothing" (John 15:5 NIV). We bear fruit and become more like Christ as we depend on him to sustain us. No one attaches a branch of grapes to a vine and expects them to receive nourishment. A person who is not really attached to Jesus Christ will not bear fruit.

Abiding in Christ results in God's kind of character. "But the fruit of the Spirit is love, joy, peace, longsuffering, gentleness, goodness, faith, meekness, temperance" (Gal. 5:22–23).

III. A reaching out for Christ.

A. *Christians are chosen for a divine purpose.* The analogy of the vine and branches had been a significant symbol of the mission purpose for Israel. When Israel failed to fulfill God's intention, the prophets applied the analogy of the vine. Isaiah pictured Israel as a vineyard run wild (cf. 5:1–7). Jeremiah described Israel as a degenerate branch (2:21). Hosea called Israel an empty vine (10:1).

B. *Christians can reach out and bless the world.* Christian have been chosen for joy. "I have told you this so that my joy may be in you and that your joy may be complete" (John 15:11 NIV). Christians have been chosen for love. "My command is this: Love each other as I have loved you" (v. 12 NIV). Christians also have been chosen to be ambassadors. "You did not choose me, but I chose you and appointed you so that you might go and bear fruit—fruit that will last—so that whatever you ask in my name the Father will give you" (v. 16 NIV).

Once a German prince wished to possess a Cremona violin. He offered an enormous price. It was published at marketplaces throughout the region. For months he had no success. One day an old man appeared at the castle gate. The man was poorly dressed and had a worn violin case under his arm. The servants refused to admit him.

Finally, the old man insisted that the servants carry a message to the master. He asked them to say, "Heaven's music is waiting at your door." The prince ordered him to be admitted immediately. The old man took a perfect violin from the worn case. He made marvelous music and won the prince's praise.

"The violin must be mine. Name your price!" the prince said.

"I want no money," said the man. "The violin may be yours on the condition that I pass my life within your house and use the instrument every day." The prince accepted the old man's offer.

Conclusion

God wants to enter your life and abide within you through the person of, the Holy Spirit. If you allow him, he will abide in your heart and make your life meaningful.

SUNDAY MORNING, DECEMBER 31

Title: The Rich Rewards of Prayer

Text: "The prayer of a righteous man has great power in its effects" **(James 5:16 RSV)**.

Scripture Reading: James 5:13–18

Hymns: "Have Faith in God," McKinney
"Open My Eyes That I May See," Scott
"Teach Me to Pray," Reitz

Offertory Prayer: Holy and loving Father, thank you for giving us your love, grace, and mercy. Thank you for giving us the privilege of being your children and allowing us to come into the throne room to thank you, praise you, and petition you. Help us this day to give ourselves to you in body and mind and spirit so that our lives will praise you and be a blessing to others. Accept our tithes and offerings today as emblems of our desire to be in the center of your will. In Jesus' name we pray. Amen.

Introduction

Scripture teaches that those who have the habit of prayer experience rich spiritual blessings in their hearts and lives. Scripture and contemporary Christian history both testify that those who have served God significantly have been men and women with an earnest prayer life. Today let us look at some of the rich rewards that come to those who have faith in God that expresses itself in a life of prayer.

I. A vivid awareness of the nearness of God.

"Draw near to God and he will draw near to you" (James 4:8 RSV). When the grateful and humble child of God seeks to come into the throne room of the heavenly Father, one of the great benefits that will come to him is a vivid awareness of the nearness of God.

A. *Experiencing the nearness of God can be frightfully disturbing for one who has not experienced genuine repentance, sincere confession, and the joy of being cleansed from the pollution of sin (Isa. 6; Luke 5:8–10).*
B. *Experiencing the nearness of God can also be very comforting (Ps. 23:4).* He gives strength and help in times of difficulty.
C. *Experiencing the nearness of God can be very exciting (Phil. 4:13).* The assurance of the nearness of God can give great courage and joy as one faces the crises of life.

II. A vital experience of the dearness of God.

Jesus taught his disciples to approach the Creator God not on the basis of his being their Creator but in terms of his being "our Father who art in heaven" (Matt. 6:9). While he is the God who is in heaven, he is also the Father with whom we can have dialogue in the closet of prayer (v. 6). It is in the prayer experience that the Father communicates his nearness and his dearness to those who look to him in faith and trust.

III. An enlightening experience of the wisdom of God (James 1:5–8).

Throughout the length and breadth of Holy Scripture and in the experience of the saints, we have testimony after testimony of how, as they prayed, God stimulated their thinking and caused them to have new insight that helped them to cope with the strains and pressures of life.

We have instance after instance in which God recalled to the memory of his discouraged children his goodness in the past to help them face the pressures of the present.

IV. An enabling experience of the strength of God.

"He gives power to the faint, and to him who has no might he increases strength. Even youths shall faint and be weary, and young men shall fall exhausted; but they who wait for the LORD shall renew their strength, they shall mount up with wings like eagles, they shall run and not be weary, they shall walk and not faint" (Isa. 40:29–31 RSV). Time spent in God's presence fills the child of God with the strength that comes from heaven.

Many are familiar with the famous cartoon character Popeye. He faced many difficult and dangerous crises but was never adequate for these until he had eaten a can of spinach, which gave him superhuman powers. I have often thought of how time spent with the heavenly Father brings to his children strength comparable to that which the spinach brought to Popeye.

The apostle Paul prayed for the believers at Ephesus that they might be strengthened with might through God's Spirit in the inner man and that they might be filled with all of the fullness of God (Eph. 3:16,19). He encouraged them to trust in and depend on the God who was at work within them and who was able to do far more abundantly than anything they had previously asked for or even thought about (vv. 20–21).

V. A cleansing experience of the forgiveness of God (1 John 1:6—7).

God is eager to forgive his sinful children. He is eager to cleanse us and make us as white as snow. Our heavenly Father does not delight in our being guilty of or burdened by sin. He is eager that we forsake those ways and attitudes that are destructive and come to him for forgiveness and cleansing.

Scripture tells us that our God is a forgiving God who forgives fully and freely and forever when his children sit in judgment on their own sins and turn from the sin that disrupts their fellowship, destroys their influence, and deprives them of joy. Prayer is the divine gift by which we can come into God's presence, receive his forgiveness, and experience both the cleanness that follows and the joy of a restored fellowship.

Conclusion

Do not rob yourself by neglecting to pray. When you do not feel like praying, that is all the more reason you should pray. Prayer is not a process by which you make "brownie points" with God. Prayer is not a magical means by which something happens automatically. Prayer is meant to be an experience in which a spiritual transformation takes place. This is why we are commanded, "Rejoice always, pray constantly, give thanks in all circumstances; for this is the will of God in Christ Jesus for you" (1 Thess. 5:16–18 RSV).

Sunday Evening, December 31

Title: The Joy of Living

Text: "'I have told you this so that my joy may be in you and that your joy may be complete'" **(John 15:11 NIV)**.

Scripture Reading: John 15:11–17

Introduction

Talking about joy in today's world is a difficult task. John Steinbeck, in his book *Travels with Charlie,* told of traveling across the United States in his camper with his dog Charlie. Traveling incognito, not as a Pulitzer Prize–winning novelist, Steinbeck met many people. And almost all the people he met were unhappy with their vocations and the places where they lived.

Joy seems to have vanished from our world. Study the faces of people around you, and you will probably see many frowns. Listen to people's conversations, and you will probably hear complaints and bickering. What can bring joy to living?

Jesus wanted people to have joy. He said, "I have told you [to remain in me and obey my commands] so that my joy may be in you and that your joy may be complete" (John 15:11 NIV). What kind of joy was Jesus talking about?

I. It is an independent joy.

A. *Many people believe happiness depends on circumstances.* They think a new job or a new car or a new outfit would make them happy. They wish they had more money or more power; then they would be happy.

B. *Jesus gives a joy that does not depend on external circumstances.*

   1. At what point in Jesus' ministry did he speak the words of tonight's text? He was talking to his disciples about joy on the day before he was going to die. Even then Jesus could speak about joy.

2. The joy that Jesus gives is an inward joy. It does not depend on eternal circumstances. Regardless of circumstances, Jesus' joy makes a person happy.

II. It is a resultant joy.

A. *Many people make the pursuit of happiness the energy of their existence.* Happiness eludes us when we expend all our energy searching for it. True happiness is the result of a relationship with the Lord. Albert Schweitzer said, "One thing I know. The only ones among you who will be really happy are the ones who have sought and found how to serve."

B. *Jesus gives a joy that results from service to him.*

1. Jesus had joy because he obeyed the Father. "Let us . . . [fix] our eyes on Jesus, the pioneer and perfecter of faith. For the joy set before him he endured the cross, scorning its shame, and sat down at the right hand of the throne of God" (Heb. 12:1–2 NIV). To Jesus, joy was the result of accomplishing the Father's will. We have joy only when we obey God's will. Joy is a result of obedience.
2. Jesus had joy because he trusted the Father. Jesus believed that no matter what happened, the providence of God would prevail. God will never lose control. Joy results from a profound trust in the Lord.

III. It is an abiding joy.

A. *Many people search for short-lived happiness.* Many people experience temporary pleasure when they receive a salary increase or some other monetary gain. But the pleasure the world offers does not satisfy for long.

B. *Jesus gives a lasting joy. Nothing can destroy the joy Jesus brings.* The joy of the Lord will prevail through all kinds of crises.

IV. It is a full joy.

A. *Many people survive on a false happiness.* Abraham Maslow, a Jewish psychologist, identified several levels of human needs. The first two needs are survival and safety. People need food and shelter, and they need a feeling of security. Yet, according to Maslow, there are much deeper needs. A person could have the basic needs met and still be unhappy. Some people never move beyond basic physical needs to discover the joy of finding meaning for life.

B. *Jesus gives a joy that satisfies to the fullest.* He wanted his disciples to have "complete joy." This means a joy that lacks nothing. Jesus alone can provide a joy that fulfills every part of our existence.

Conclusion

You don't have to be miserable in the new year. Jesus wants to give you joy. Don't be fooled by the world's temporary joy. Abide in Jesus, obey his commands, and let him fill you with his everlasting joy.

MISCELLANEOUS HELPS

MESSAGES ON THE LORD'S SUPPER

Title: Making Ready

Text: "The disciples did as Jesus had appointed them; and they made ready the passover" **(Matt. 26:19)**.

Scripture Reading: Matthew 26:17–29

Introduction

In the early days of our country, the Quakers were scorned and considered strange because of the ways in which they quietly, in prayer and meditation, conducted their periods of worship. They sat silently until someone in the group felt moved by God to sing a hymn or deliver a message. This was their way of preparing themselves for an encounter with God, for an experience of worship. They understood and practiced the exhortation of the prophet: "The LORD is in his holy temple: let all the earth keep silence before him" (Hab. 2:20).

This is not the pattern most evangelical Christians follow today, however. We have confused frivolity with joy—and there is all the difference in the world. There is a time and a season for everything according to the writer of Ecclesiastes—a time to laugh and a time to cry, a time to keep silent and a time to speak. A "holy stillness" is a special time fraught with anticipation.

Today we have come to the Lord's Table. Probably nothing Jesus did with the disciples before his crucifixion was more deeply moving, more unforgettable, than his last supper in the upper room. And part of the reason for the impact it made on the disciples was that it was prepared for. Jesus had told his disciples to "make ready" for it, and they did. There are three basic preparations Christians ought to make before they come to the Lord's Table.

I. Physical preparation.

Jesus obviously had made previous arrangements privately for the Passover meal with the disciples. He told them that as they entered the city, they would see a man carrying a pitcher of water. They were to follow him to a house, and they were to go to a particular "upper room." Jesus took care that the proper physical preparations were made.

One of the cherished memories of my childhood is the preparations our family made on Sunday mornings to get everyone ready and off to church and

Sunday school on time. Our father helped to get the three of us children ready, while mother was busy with the major chores. It was a cooperative venture. My parents believed in the right kind of physical preparation on Sunday morning. Many times when tempers flared, Father would lecture us on the uselessness of going to God's house with a wrong attitude. I am grateful my parents taught me the importance of making the proper physical preparation for worship. Certainly it is especially important to be physically prepared for the sacred experience at the Lord's Table.

II. Mental preparation.

The prophet Isaiah gave us one of the most precious promises in the Bible in regard to one's relationship with the Lord: "Thou wilt keep him in perfect peace, whose mind is stayed on thee: because he trusteth in thee" (Isa. 26:3). What about mental preparation for worshiping God and for coming to the Lord's Table? Peter, in his first epistle, said that we are to have minds that are "alert and fully sober" (1 Peter 1:13 NIV). He meant for us to learn the art of concentration by allowing the Holy Spirit who indwells us to control our minds.

How often have you had the experience, before or during the worship hour, of having your thoughts wander into some areas of unusual sensitivity for you? Perhaps you have had a misunderstanding with a fellow worshiper, and you see that person sitting across the way. Immediately you begin to be uncomfortable. You start to remember certain things that have happened. Soon you are angry and upset and unable to enter into the spirit of worship.

How can we overcome such experiences? Isaiah told us. We must "stay our minds" on Jesus Christ. Open God's Word and let it speak to you. It is "sharper than a two-edged sword," and the Holy Spirit will empower it to excise those offending thoughts and prepare you mentally to worship God at his table.

III. Spiritual preparation.

In 1 Corinthians 11:26–34 Paul spoke about the Christian's conduct in regard to the Lord's Table. He dealt plainly with our spiritual preparation. He said that the ordinance of the Lord's Supper is not a meaningless, perfunctory "ritual" in the church. It should never be something we "tack on" to the end of a worship service.

So what do we do? Paul said that we should examine ourselves (1 Cor. 11:28). In the presence of God, in the light of his Word, we must examine ourselves to see whether we are spiritually prepared to come to the Lord's Table. First, we must see if we have confessed and repented of all known sin. No experience is as sublime and glorious as sensing forgiveness and full acceptance in the presence of God. With that certainty of spiritual well-being, we can come to the Lord's Table truly with "joy unspeakable." "If we confess our sins, he is faithful and just to forgive us our sins, and to cleanse us from all unrighteousness" (1 John 1:9).

Second, consistent Christian living is an essential part of proper spiritual preparation for the Lord's Table. If the Holy Spirit convicts us of wrongness in our hearts toward God or toward our fellow humans, then it must be righted. We cannot enjoy the Lord's Table when we have a wrong spirit within us. John plainly said that the proof that we are children of God is that we love one another.

Conclusion

The Lord's Supper ought to be a precious and unforgettable experience every time we come to God's table. Why? Because we are "showing forth the Lord's death till he comes." We must be clear reflectors, cleansed of all known sin. And to do this requires that we be physically prepared—our bodies, which are temples of the Holy Spirit, must be tuned physically for this worship experience. We must be mentally prepared—we must "stay our minds" on the Lord and ask him to help us, by his indwelling Spirit, to focus our thoughts on the Lord Jesus. Then we must, of all things, be spiritually prepared. When these basic preparations have been made, we can come with joy to the Lord's Table, and we will leave having truly experienced his presence.

Title: The Discipline of Discipleship

Text: "And he said to them all, If any man will come after me, let him deny himself, and take up his cross daily, and follow me" **(Luke 9:23)**.

Scripture Reading: Luke 9:23–27

Introduction

As we prepare to come to the Lord's Table for this high and holy experience of remembrance, I would like for us to consider two words: *discipline* and *discipleship*. Actually, *discipleship* means "discipline." The disciple is one who has been taught and trained by the Master. He or she has come with ignorance, superstition, and sin to find truth and forgiveness from the Savior. Without discipline we are not disciples, even though we profess Jesus' name.

Recent generations have resented and rebelled against discipline. Liberty and license have replaced law and order. Furthermore, permissiveness has become a lifestyle with most people—even Christians. This lack of discipline is the avowed enemy of faithfulness to God. It weakens compassion, for it places the first and primary emphasis on self.

But just what do we mean by *discipline*? One dictionary defines it as "training that corrects, molds, or perfects the mental faculties or moral character." Without difficulty, we can translate this definition into the spiritual realm. As growing, maturing, Christians, we will constantly be undergoing correction and molding, all leading to the ultimate perfection we will experience when we stand in Christ's presence.

I. Discipleship requires the discipline of conversion, wherein we recognize our rebellion against God and repent.

Conversion takes two forms in the Christian's life. First, it is the initial experience that occurs when we realize we are lost and without hope and, repenting of our sins, recognizes Jesus Christ as Savior. This is the most difficult discipline of all, for it is the death blow to pride, the parent sin spawned by Satan himself. It is never easy to humble ourselves to the point of admitting that we are sinners. But when this happens, the miracle of conversion takes place. It is all God's doing. It is "not by works of righteousness which we have done, but according to his mercy he saved us" (Titus 3:5).

But conversion takes yet another form in the Christian's life. We experience conversion experiences daily as we turn from sins and begin the difficult but glorious journey of Christian growth. As we walk with the Lord, we are daily being subjected to the discipline of change, or conversion, and are being "conformed to the image of God's own dear Son."

II. Discipleship also requires the discipline of cost.

Jesus said, "He that loveth father or mother more than me is not worthy of me: and he that loveth son or daughter more than me is not worthy of me" (Matt 10:37). And on a later occasion, he expanded that statement: "If any man come to me, and hate not his father, and mother, and wife, and children, and brethren, and sisters, yea, and his own life also, he cannot be my disciple" (Luke 14:26). What did Jesus mean by those statements? The quality and intensity of love we have for God, because of this great salvation through his Son, should be so superior to even our love for our closest kin that the comparison would be like "love versus hate"! Only one person is qualified to sit on the throne of our hearts—the Lord Jesus. We should abhor anything or anyone who would vie for that place.

It is always difficult to truly make Christ Lord of one's life and allow him to remain in that position. Total lordship of Christ in our lives is costly. It means that we have submitted every waking hour to him and that there has come to exist within a constant awareness of his presence.

III. Finally, discipleship requires the discipline of cross bearing.

Three things seem to be necessary for us each day: our daily food (for which we are told to pray, "Give us this day out daily bread"), our daily work (in which we are to be faithful, "if any would not work, neither should he eat"), and our daily cross. What is the cross we are to bear daily? It is not the cross of our Savior, who suffered for our sins upon the tree, for we can add nothing to the price of our redemption. Least of all is it the bearing of some burden, some inconvenience. Rather, it is the denial of oneself, in the deepest meaning of that word. It is full surrender to the will of God. It is saying no daily to the desires and demands of self and saying yes to the loving commands of Christ.

The cross is an instrument of death. There is no such thing as "sinless perfection" for the Christian in this life. Therefore, every day that we live, we must, in the power of the Spirit of Christ, deal a "death blow" to self. That is cross bearing. Furthermore, it is not a morbid, long-faced experience. No joy is as deep, as permeating, as that which comes to the Christian who has placed self under the control of God and has acquiesced to the lordship of Jesus Christ.

Conclusion

As we prepare to come to the Lord's Table to partake of these precious emblems, let us consider seriously this matter of discipline. Are we experiencing daily the discipline of conversion—are we letting God change us, correct us, mold us, perfect us? Have we dealt with the discipline of cost—are we willing to relinquish all in order that Christ might inhabit the throne of our heart? And what are we doing about the discipline of cross bearing? Are we letting God deal that death blow to the ugliness of self every day, thus becoming more and more like Jesus?

Title: A Labor of Love

Text: "I have glorified thee on the earth: I have finished the work which thou gavest me to do" (**John 17:4**).

Scripture Reading: John 17:1–11

Introduction

Today we will sit as a family of believers at our Lord's Table. These elements of which we will partake speak both simply and eloquently of the mission and purpose of our Lord on earth. One of the many facets of his life and ministry had to do with his own concept of his mission in regard to the will of his heavenly Father. When Jesus spoke the words recorded in our Scripture passage for today, he had come to a very lonely moment in his life. Peter, James, and John—the "inner circle" of his disciples—had gone to sleep in the garden of Gethsemane. They could not stay awake to watch and pray with him. But his heavenly Father was near, and in this great High Priestly Prayer, Jesus poured out his heart to him.

One statement in the prayer stands out in particular: "I have glorified thee on earth: I have finished the work which thou gavest me to do" (John 17:4). If Jesus had not accomplished what he implied here, all else would be lost.

I. Jesus glorified the Father by his teachings and by his miracles.

God is glorified before man when man comes to know what God is like—who he is. This was the first part of Jesus' mission on earth. When Jesus came, according to the apostle Paul, "in him dwelleth all the fulness of the Godhead bodily" (Col. 2:9). God dwelt in a perfect, sinless human body. With human emotion, understanding, and interaction, Jesus showed man God—and thus God was glorified in the person of his Son. His teachings brought to maturity, fulfillment, and perfection the word of the law.

In the Sermon on the Mount, Jesus laid down with unmistakable clarity how his people are to live. He set forth the most difficult spiritual obstacle course imaginable. In fact, the only way one can "live" the Sermon on the Mount is in the Spirit of Christ who indwells every believer. We yield to him as we die to self. This is the paradox of our faith: Life and victory come through death and defeat!

Jesus also glorified the Father through the miracles he performed. He overruled the known laws of nature and, with divine power, healed broken and diseased bodies. Yet Jesus never intended for his healing ministry to become an end in itself. Sometimes God chooses to use physical infirmity and adversity as a means of refining our faith. In such times of trial and testing, a Christian learns to concentrate on Christ more completely. We cannot always know the mind of God in these matters. When it is his will to exercise his miraculous healing power, we give him all the praise, for he does so always to glorify himself and not man.

II. Jesus also glorified the Father in that he finished the work God gave him to do.

Jesus said, "I have finished the work which thou gavest me to do." On the cross he cried, "It is finished!" The work of redemption he had come to do was complete. He had endured the cross because there was set before him the joy of a completed task.

Thus the Bible indicates that Jesus found joy in this work assigned to him. How could Jesus "enjoy" a mission or task so fraught with opposition and rejection, with misunderstanding and cruelty? He did so because, having been "one with the Father," he had experienced from before the beginning the divine thrill of the plan of salvation. Before God laid the foundations of the world, he knew humans would choose evil instead of righteousness. Because of that foreknowledge, he planned for humankind's salvation. Certainly it broke the heart of God when people acted out what God in his omniscience saw them do before they were even created.

This great plan of salvation had been conceived and incubated in the mind of God; it had been symbolized and typified in the Old Testament; and now it was actualized in the life, death, and resurrection of Jesus. Indeed, it was a "labor of love" when Jesus finished the work God gave him to do.

III. Christians can glorify the Father as they allow the risen Christ to shine forth from their lives.

The miracle of God's grace ought to constantly announce to the world that Christ lives in us. Jesus said to his disciples, "Ye are the light of the world." The flickering light of an inconsistent Christian testimony can be disastrously misleading to one who is trying to find the way. What a glorious anticipation to be able to say at the end of life's day, "Father, I have finished the work which thou gavest me to do." Paul was able to say it: "I have fought a good fight, I have finished my course, I have kept the faith" (2 Tim. 4:7). That should be our desire and goal.

Conclusion

As we partake of these blessed emblems today, let us remember that our Lord's life, from Bethlehem to Calvary, fulfilled the purpose of his heavenly Father. That purpose was "to glorify the Father" and to finish the work God gave him to do. That, to Jesus, was "a labor of love." Let us, during these sacred moments, commit ourselves anew to glorify our Lord and Savior through our lives.

Messages for Children and Young People

Title: The Poor Little Rich Man

Text: "When Jesus came to the place, he looked up, and saw him, and said unto him, Zacchaeus, make haste, and come down; for to day I must abide at thy house" **(Luke 19:5)**.

Scripture Reading: Luke 19:1–10

Introduction

Zacchaeus—could we call him "the poor little rich man"? Zacchaeus's name, ironically, means "pure." He was a man whose short physical stature has come to symbolize the littleness that characterized him in other ways. He was a cheat, a traitor, a turncoat to his own people. He was selfish and self-centered, greedy and totally uncaring toward others.

Yet, as has been true in so many other cases, Jesus saw something in Zacchaeus. Through all of those outside layers of ugliness and sin, Jesus saw potential—he saw what this man could become. Everybody else had long since given up on Zacchaeus—but not Jesus. This little man was one of the last persons Jesus gathered to himself before he went to the cross. For when he passed through Jericho this time, he was on his way to Jerusalem and to the cross.

I. The condition of Zacchaeus.

In one verse we have Luke's description of Zacchaeus: "Behold, there was a man named Zacchaeus, which was the chief among the publicans, and he was rich" (Luke 19:2). That sounds like a note you would put on a person's loan application! It tells us about his occupation—a lucrative one—and about his financial condition—he was "rich." His name, Zacchaeus, was Jewish, and as I said earlier, it means "pure." Perhaps when Zacchaeus was presented by his parents in the temple, they gave him that name to express their hope for him. If that was true, and if his parents were still living, I am quite sure they were heartbroken, for Zacchaeus had become anything but pure in his manner of living.

Luke tells us that Zacchaeus was a "chief publican," which means that he was appointed by the Roman government to supervise the collection of taxes from an entire district. The tax rate was fixed by Rome, and then the schedule of taxes was given to the chief publican. He was free to increase the amount of taxes he collected as much as he dared to pay himself and the tax collectors working under him. Thus Zacchaeus and his fellow tax collectors were hated by the Jews not only because they had betrayed their people by selling out to Rome, but also because the taxes they assessed were unbelievably high.

Consequently, in spite of his great wealth, Zacchaeus was banned from any social life with his people, and he was excommunicated from the temple and the synagogue. In a very real sense, he was "a man without a country."

II. The curiosity of Zacchaeus.

Listen again to Luke: "He wanted to see who Jesus was, but because he was short, he could not see over the crowd. So he ran ahead and climbed a sycamore-fig tree to see him, since Jesus was coming that way" (Luke 19:3–4 NIV).

How wonderful that Zacchaeus was curious! A healthy curiosity is always a hopeful sign about a person. Curiosity and the urge to investigate indicate that a person is in a state of good mental health. Zacchaeus "wanted to see who Jesus was." Some have thought that Zacchaeus was already convicted of his sins and was running to Jesus. They say that Zacchaeus had been waiting for Jesus to come and that he knew this was his "big moment." I doubt that. Rather, the situation was simply that a great crowd of people surged down this Jericho street, and Zacchaeus was overcome with curiosity to see what was going on.

Zacchaeus, being a short man, could not see easily over the heads of the people. So he found a sycamore tree with a low-hanging limb and boosted himself up among the leaves of the tree, right over the roadway where Jesus was to pass. The Holy Spirit often uses curiosity to bring people to an awareness of their lostness and their need for a Savior, and that is what he did with Zacchaeus.

III. The encounter Zacchaeus had with Jesus.

"When Jesus reached the spot, he looked up and said to him, 'Zacchaeus, come down immediately. I must stay at your house today.' So he came down at once and welcomed him gladly" (Luke 19:5–6 NIV).

Note the words "When Jesus reached the spot, he looked up." Most of us, walking along that street with hundreds of people crowding around us, would easily have missed a man looking down from the limb of a tree overhead, especially if he was hidden among the leaves! But Jesus looked up because he knew there was someone "lost" up in that tree, and he "came to seek and to save that which was lost"! Always the compassionate, loving eyes of Jesus were searching the crowds for those who were candidates for his kingdom.

There is no doubt that Jesus stopped when he came beneath that overhanging limb where Zacchaeus was perched. He called Zacchaeus by name. Could they have met before? Probably not. Because he was the Son of God, Jesus knew who Zacchaeus was before he ever saw him! So Jesus commanded Zacchaeus to come down and informed him that he would be a guest in his house that very day. Only one other time did Jesus ask for some gesture of hospitality—from the Samaritan woman at Jacob's well when he said to her, "Give me to drink." Isn't it strange that both of these persons were "outcasts" from the standpoint of their acceptance by others?

The people were aghast that Jesus would be seen in the company of Zacchaeus. Before Jesus' visit in Zacchaeus's home was over, a radical change had taken place in that tax collector's life. His sins were forgiven, and his heart was changed. Whereas once his life had been characterized by getting, he was now saying, "I give." That is the way of Christianity. Before he met Jesus, he was mastered by greed; afterward he was mastered by grace.

Conclusion

What then was the glorious ending to this story? Jesus said to Zacchaeus, "Today salvation has come to this house" (Luke 19:9 NIV). This was Jesus' mission. "For the Son of Man came to seek and to save the lost" (v. 10 NIV).

Title: The Man Who Wouldn't Give Up

Text: "And when he heard that it was Jesus of Nazareth, he began to cry out and say, Jesus, thou son of David, have mercy on me. And many charged him that he should hold his peace: but he cried the more a great deal, Thou son of David, have mercy on me" **(Mark 10:47-48)**.

Scripture Reading: Mark 10:46–52

Introduction

Clustered around the gate leading out of Jericho toward Jerusalem were the usual beggars. Among them was Bartimaeus, ever raising his sightless eyes in response to the sound of footsteps passing his way, begging for money to buy food. As Jesus and his disciples were leaving Jericho, they passed by these beggars. One of them seemed particularly interested in getting Jesus' attention.

I. The encounter between Jesus and this blind beggar by the Jericho roadside.

Apparently Bartimaeus and his father were well known in Jericho, for Mark is careful to name him and then to translate the name "son of Timaeus."

When I was growing up, there was such a character in my hometown. He was always downtown with his collection cup and the pencils he sold. All of the children knew and loved Jake because he was a kind and jovial man. He had been blind from birth. His face was covered with large warts, and until you got to know him, his appearance was a bit repulsive. He played a harmonica, and he played amazingly well. Children would gather around him, and he would play the "fun tunes" we liked so well. Everybody knew Jake, the blind man. Likewise, everybody in Jericho seemed to have known Bartimaeus and his father.

On this particular day in Jericho, the crowds were larger because great numbers of people were passing through on their way to Jerusalem for Passover. But there seemed to be something else going on, a sort of tension in the air. Immediately the sensitive Bartimaeus knew this. He may have grabbed the cloak of a passerby and asked him, "Man, will you tell me what is going on? Something is happening! Somebody unusual is in the crowd. Tell me, who is it? What is happening?" And apparently someone told Bartimaeus that it was "Jesus of Nazareth" who was causing all the commotion.

No doubt Bartimaeus had already heard about Jesus. Being a Jew, he was familiar with the words of the prophet Isaiah and others who had prophesied that a Savior would come, who would be of the line of David. Immediately the Holy Spirit helped Bartimaeus make this connection in his mind. For he cried out, "Jesus, thou son of David, have mercy on me!" The people who were talking with Jesus tried to hush Bartimaeus, "but he cried out the more a great deal." Maybe Bartimaeus felt that this was his last chance; we don't know. Anyway, ignoring the protests of the people, Bartimaeus kept on crying out to get Jesus' attention.

II. The conversation between Bartimaeus and Jesus.

"And Jesus stood still, and commanded him to be called. And they called the blind man, saying unto him, Be of good comfort, rise; he calleth thee" (Mark 10:49). It is significant that we read, "And Jesus stood still." Instantly, Jesus knew all about Bartimaeus. When Bartimaeus called out, "Jesus, thou son of David, have mercy on me," Jesus knew that the moment of transformation had come for that blind beggar. So Jesus "commanded him to be called." The people who had been trying to hinder Bartimaeus from getting Jesus' attention caught the urgency and felt the authority of Jesus' words. Quickly they did an about-face. "Be of good comfort, rise; he calleth thee," they said to the beggar. With no hesitation at all, Bartimaeus, "casting away his garment, rose, and came to Jesus."

Jesus asked him, "What wilt thou that I should do unto thee?" Certainly Jesus knew what the man wanted more than anything else in the world. He was blind; he wanted to see! But Bartimaeus needed to state his need before the Lord. God knows that we are sinners; but still he wants us to state that fact with our own mouths. So Bartimaeus said, "Lord, that I might receive my sight."

III. Jesus' accommodation of Bartimaeus.

The climax of the story is wonderful. Jesus accommodated the physical need of Bartimaeus; that is, he healed his blindness. Jesus said to him, "Go thy way; thy faith hath made thee whole" (Mark 10:52). But far more important is the fact Jesus added Bartimaeus to his spiritual family, for we read, "And immediately he received his sight, and followed Jesus in the way" (Mark 10:52). The greatest blessing that came to Bartimaeus that day was that he received salvation.

Conclusion

Bartimaeus became a traveling companion with Jesus and his disciples as they left Jericho and went to Jerusalem. Most probably Bartimaeus was in Jerusalem when Jesus was arrested, tried, and crucified. He may well have been among the 120 believers who were instructed by Jesus, after his resurrection, to wait in the upper room in Jerusalem until the Holy Spirit came.

The story of Bartimaeus is another in a long succession of miracles Jesus performed. And these miracles continue to this day, for whenever people, recognizing their spiritual blindness, call out, "God, have mercy on me!" Jesus stands still, bids them come, and changes their darkness into light.

Title: A Father and His Son

Text: "Straightway the father of the child cried out, and said with tears, Lord, I believe; help thou mine unbelief" **(Mark 9:24)**.

Scripture Reading: Mark 9:14–29

Introduction

Under normal circumstances, few human relationships are as special as that which exists when there is a strong bond between a father and his son. Yet, when the son is the helpless victim of an incurable disease and the parents must watch him suffer without being able to do anything to relieve his suffering, that is a scene that will break the hardest heart! Such is the case with this moving story Mark has recorded for us.

The setting in which this incident took place was one of breathtaking beauty. An artist could have a field day with this, for in the background there was the majestic and towering Mount Hermon, silent, snowcapped, and regal on the horizon. Somewhere on that mountain Jesus had just been transfigured before three of his disciples and had appeared before them, along with Moses and Elijah, in the stunning brilliance of his glorified body.

Therefore, as our story opens, we find it is:

I. A scene of extremes (vv. 14–19).

Let's imagine for a moment that we have been waiting with the other nine disciples down in the valley, somewhere at the base of Mount Hermon, for Jesus and Peter, James, and John to return. A serious problem had developed while they were away. A father, hearing that Jesus could cast out demons, had just brought his demon-possessed son to the nine disciples. Instead of detaining the father and son until Jesus could return to deal with the problem, they proceeded to deal with the matter themselves. They had watched Jesus perform many miracles, including the casting out of evil spirits. They had heard the words he had spoken, and they thought they "knew the formula."

There is every possibility the disciples could have thought within themselves, *Here's our chance! When Jesus is here, we are always in the background. No one ever pays any attention to us. Why don't we just cash in on a little of this glory for ourselves!* And how many times have you and I taken some matter into our own hands, foolishly thinking that we were capable of handling the situation in our own strength? We knew the "magic formula"; we could say all the right words. And we fell on our faces! Why? Because we forgot that we can do nothing effectively for God apart from the power of the indwelling Christ. The disciples failed miserably because they tried to heal the disturbed boy in their power and for their glory.

When Jesus appeared, the father of the demon-controlled boy related to Jesus what had happened. Jesus replied sadly, "O faithless generation, how long shall I be with you? How long shall I suffer you?" (Mark 9:19). When he said this, he was including not just the disciples who had failed but the scribes who also were there and this suffering father and his son. Jesus was saying that he lived in the midst of a faithless people.

Then, for a few moments, the situation grew worse. We have seen that it was a scene of extremes. Now we see it as:

II. A scene of tragedy.

"And they brought him unto [Jesus]: and when he saw him, straightway the spirit tare him; and he fell on the ground, and wallowed foaming" (Mark 9:20). Do you remember what happened when Jesus and the disciples approached a wild man who lived in the region of Gadara? He came screaming down the cliffside, begging Jesus to go away and not torment him "before his time." The demons knew what was about to take place. So it was with the boy in this story. For while Jesus and the boy's father were talking, the evil spirit in the boy seized him, and he lapsed into what may have been the worst convulsion he had ever had.

The father said to Jesus, "If thou canst do any thing, have compassion on us, and help us" (Mark 9:22). He might have been saying, "Lord, I came with my boy hoping that you could heal him. But you were not here, and your disciples were helpless. Does this mean that you cannot help us either? But still, Lord, if you can, please help us!" Jesus saw a tiny flicker of faith in what the father said, and he seized upon it and replied, "If thou canst believe, all things are possible to him that believeth" (v. 23). The father cried, "Lord, I believe; help thou mine unbelief" (v. 24).

III. A scene of victory.

And Jesus "rebuked the foul spirit, saying unto him, Thou dumb and deaf spirit, I charge thee, come out of him, and enter no more into him. And the spirit cried, and rent him sore, and came out of him: and he was as one dead; insomuch that many said, He is dead. But Jesus took him by the hand, and lifted him up; and he arose" (Mark 9:25-27). Realizing that it was about to be disembodied, the evil spirit made one last, violent attempt to hurt the boy. Then the boy lay "as one dead." The experience was so utterly exhausting, both physically and spiritually, that the boy appeared to have no life in him at all. Then Jesus took his hand and lifted him up. Luke, in his account of the incident, adds, "He gave him back to his father" (Luke 9:42).

Conclusion

Jesus' disciples were perplexed about why they had failed so miserably. As they were leaving the scene, they asked Jesus, "Why could not we cast him out?" (Mark 9:28). Jesus answered them plainly: "This kind can come forth by nothing, but by prayer and fasting" (v. 29). In effect, he was saying, just as he would say to you and me when we fail in our Christian witness and testimony, "You don't live close enough to God!" God's power was available for their use, but what activated that power was an intimate relationship with God.

Paul once said, "I can do all things"; and if he had stopped there, we would be justified in calling him an egotist. But he said, "I can do all things through Christ which strengtheneth me" (Phil. 4:13). That's the secret. Like the father in the story, we "believe," but our belief is often weak, unsupported by prayer and obedience to God. The disciples became overconfident, and they failed. May God help us to be certain that our confidence is always in him and not in ourselves.

Title: Pilate—a Man on Trial

Text: "Pilate saith unto him, What is truth? And when he had said this, he went out again unto the Jews, and saith unto them, I find in him no fault at all" **(John 18:38)**.

Scripture Reading: John 18:28–40

Introduction

Pontius Pilate—we know his name only because of his encounter with Jesus Christ. Had he never come in contact with the Son of God, history would have ignored him, passed him by. But what do we know about him?

Pilate was a man who had a haughty disposition. He loved his authority; he was cold and without compassion. His whole attitude toward Judea and toward the Jews was that of scorn and hatred. The only reason he made any attempt to quell uprisings and bloodshed was because of Caesar's insistence that the famed "Roman peace" be maintained in the empire.

Pilate was a contemptuous man. When the Jewish priests brought Jesus to him, the first question he asked was couched in satire and contempt. If Pilate had lived in our day and had spoken to them in the vernacular of our generation, he would likely have said, "Oh, it's you again! Now what?"

Yet, in all fairness, when we read between the lines of Pilate's story on the pages of the New Testament, we find that Pilate understood justice. He had a passion for the observance of the Roman law. He did everything he could except the one final thing he could have done to save Jesus. In fact, he probably would much rather have had Caiaphas crucified that day than Jesus!

But let's move a bit closer to this complicated and strange man and see if we can follow just what happened to him as he came under the influence of Jesus Christ.

I. Pilate annoyed.

First, Pilate was annoyed when the priests brought Jesus to him. "Then said Pilate unto them, Take ye him, and judge him according to your law" (John 18:31). Probably this was the first time Pilate had ever seen Jesus. He may not even have looked closely at Jesus at this first encounter, for this was not the first time these troublesome and hypocritical Jewish priests had brought prisoners to him for arraignment. Then perhaps he whirled around with a swish of his judicial Roman robes and said over his shoulder, "Don't bother me with your religious disputes! You have your law in these matters! Take him and judge him according to your laws. Now get out of here!"

But Pilate was stopped cold in his tracks when Jesus' accusers said, "But, Governor, our court is not permitted to put a man to death. You know that." In a moment, Pilate saw that these Jews were not seeking justice. They wanted blood! It was then that Pilate walked back to the center of the judgment hall and "called Jesus." This prisoner was not like the usual rabble-rouser they brought to him.

II. Pilate arrested.

So, in the progression we are following with Pilate, we find now that he was arrested by this prisoner, this Jesus, whom the Jews had brought to him. The first question Pilate asked Jesus as they stood aside in the Praetorium was, "Art thou the King of the Jews?" Jesus' answer was interesting: "Sayest thou this thing of thyself, or did others tell it thee of me?" Or, in other words, "Is this an original thought with you, or are you just repeating what you have heard others say?" This obviously was uncomfortable ground for Pilate, for he quickly changed the subject.

It is at this point that Pilate apparently abandoned his cat-and-mouse game. With obvious sincerity and judicial decorum, he asked Jesus, "What have you done? Why have they brought you here to me? Why do they want the death sentence?" Pilate was amazed all the more when he heard Jesus say, "My kingdom is not of this world; if my kingdom were of this world, then would my servants fight, that I should not be delivered to the Jews: but now is my kingdom not from hence" (John 18:36).

Then quietly, incredulously, Pilate asked Jesus, "Are you, then, really a king? Did I hear you correctly? You spoke of a 'kingdom.' Does that mean that you are a king?" And with no hesitation, Jesus answered Pilate: "Thou sayest that I am a king. To this end was I born, and for this cause came I into the world, that I should bear witness unto the truth. Every one that is of the truth heareth my voice" (John 18:37).

III. Pilate astounded.

Now the progression moved yet further along for Pilate: From annoyance to being arrested by this strange man, Pilate was now astounded by what he heard.

After Jesus had spoken, Pilate exclaimed, "What is truth?" In all of this, we can see how rapidly Pilate was being brought to the point of facing himself, of facing the God of truth, of making a decision about life and destiny. This is the same progression any individual follows when he or she is about to reach a point of decision. Before we can come to receive Jesus Christ as Savior, we must become thoroughly disenchanted with ourselves. We must realize that there is one source of truth, and it lies in God, expressed in his Son, the Lord Jesus Christ.

Then it was that Pilate went out and faced the Jews, saying to them, "I find in him no fault at all. But ye have a custom, that I should release unto you one at the passover: will ye therefore that I release unto you the King of the Jews?" (John 18:38–39). By this time, Pilate likely was the most confused man in Jerusalem. He did a cowardly thing. He submitted Jesus to the dreaded Roman scourge. He had Jesus beaten. After the beating and after the mocking soldiers had placed the crown of thorns on Jesus' brow and the mock robe about his bleeding shoulders, Pilate brought him forth before the mob: "What shall I do then with Jesus which is called Christ?" (Matt. 27:22).

IV. Pilate defeated.

There is one last, tragic, hopeless step in this progression with Pilate: we have seen him annoyed, arrested, and astounded; now we see Pilate defeated.

Pilate stalled for time. He called Jesus before him again, but Jesus would not answer him. Then, in spite of the accusations of his conscience, Pilate bowed to the evil wishes of the mob. And in the final analysis, it was not Jesus who was on trial, but Pilate! A choice was being forced upon him. Throughout that bleak day, there was one clear issue before him. And the same issue is before very person who is faced with the truth about God and his Son Jesus. "What shall I do then with Jesus which is called Christ?"

Conclusion

As to what ultimately happened to Pilate, we do not know. We do not know exactly what happens when a person violates his conscience and slams the door for the last time in the face of God. But we do know that today is the day of salvation. This moment is the acceptable time. It may be your time.

FUNERAL MEDITATIONS

Title: The Beauty of Death

Text: "O death, where is thy sting? O grave, where is thy victory? The sting of death is sin; and the strength of sin is the law. But thanks be to God, which giveth us the victory through our Lord Jesus Christ" **(1 Cor. 15:55–57)**.

Scripture Reading: Ecclesiastes 1:1–11; 1 Corinthians 15:51–58

Introduction

Sometimes, out of the darkness of our sorrow in the face of death, we find ourselves asking, "Is there anything logical about death? Why do we die? Is death just a tragic waste?" The apostle Paul explained that death is the means whereby we shed our bodies of corruption to receive bodies that are not subject to decay. When man sinned, his body became subject to disease, pain, and the ravages of time. God did not intend that man should live forever in such a body. Suppose man could not die but was fated to live forever in a body that grew ever older, weaker, and more painful, an eternal victim of corruption? So, while death is an enemy, God causes even this enemy to serve us for our good. In this sense, therefore, death is a blessed release, offering the anticipation of a resurrection body that is incorruptible and immortal.

The great problem with human life, for those of us who remain, is our ability to see only one side of it. In a sense, we see the "underside" of life. Truly, we "see through a glass darkly," and we "know in part." But in the midst of these human questions and doubts, we hear this promise buried in the ancient book of Ecclesiastes, "[God] hath made every thing beautiful in his time" (3:11).

I. In God's own time and in his own way, he gives us the perspective to see things as they truly are and as he intended them to be.

A. *This principle operates in nature.* Consider the seed as an example. A seed looks dry and ugly and dead—shriveled and lifeless. Could you imagine a person giving a packet of flower seeds in memory of a departed loved one or friend? Yet the seed contains within itself all the beauty of the flower. In the orderly processes of nature, the seed puts forth the shoot, the shoot becomes the plant, the plant bears the bud, and the bud breaks open into glorious blossom. "God makes all things beautiful in his time."

B. *Notice also the beauty in the cycle of our seasons.* We naturally enjoy the beauty of the springtime, as all nature seems to throb with returning life. In the summer, the fields are golden with their ripening grain. Then the season moves on to autumn. The trees turn to scarlet and gold, and we bow our heads in thanksgiving for the harvest of the earth. But then the winter comes, with the glistening magic of icicles and snow. Each part of the year has its own beauty—how can we compare them? We can only agree that "God makes all things beautiful in his time."

C. *The same principle can be seen in human life.* Which of the ages of humankind is most beautiful? We think of the dimpled smile of the tiny babe in its helplessness and innocence. Then there is the schoolgirl with her hair in pigtails and braces on her teeth running down the walk to meet her dad. Or the young man dressed in his academic cap and gown. Then time moves on to motherhood and fatherhood and to the busy years of building a home and family. Finally, the wrinkles of old age appear—the face is creased with lines drawn there by love. Every age seems to offer a greater beauty than the age before. "God makes all things beautiful in his time."

D. *But then, one day long ago, an ugly cross was raised on the outskirts of an ancient city.* Upon that instrument of torture was nailed the mangled body of a young Galilean prophet who had been stripped and beaten. A crown of thorny branches was crushed down upon his head and a sarcastic inscription placed above him: "This is the King of the Jews." Could anything change such a picture into a thing of beauty? Yet three days later his tomb was empty! God made him both Lord and Christ, this Jesus who was crucified. Today lives are devoted in loving service in the name of this same Jesus. Even his cross has become a thing of beauty to us. "God makes all things beautiful in his time."

II. In the face of what Christ has done, we can grasp something of the challenge of Paul's words: "O death, where is thy sting? O grave, where is thy victory?" (1 Cor. 15:55).

A. *Where is the sting of death?* It is the terror of the person who approaches God unforgiven of his sins. It is the fearful anticipation of an unknown and mysterious future.

B. *What is the victory of the grave?* It is the eternal claim on the soul unsurrendered to God—the hopeless, endless imprisonment in a Christless eternity. Apart from God, death is indeed a fearful state; there is an awesome finality about it.

C. *But, thank God, Paul does not leave us there.* To learn the secret of his courage and the courage and strength of every child of God, we must consider these words: "But thanks be to God, which giveth us the victory through our Lord Jesus Christ" (1 Cor. 15:57). Paul anticipated death—not with a morbid desire to escape from life, but realizing its inevitability (for the Scriptures declare that "it is appointed unto man once to die"—Heb. 9:27). Paul delighted in the fact that Christ had removed from death all the fearful and chilling aspects that once accompanied it. He came back from death not only to tell us that there is more beyond, but to promise us, "In my Father's house are many mansions: if it were not so, I would have told you. I go to prepare a place for you. And if I go and prepare a place for you, I will come again, and receive you unto myself; that where I am, there ye may be also" (John 14:2–3).

Conclusion

Certainly every living Christian anticipates the return of Christ. This is the abiding hope of the New Testament. But our human bodies grow tired and weak. Jesus comes for his children also in death. And there, in the presence of God, they no longer "see through a glass darkly," and they no longer "know in part." The mysteries of life that perplex us are revealed to them. If they could speak to us today, no doubt they would echo the words of Paul: "Therefore, my beloved brethren, be ye stedfast, unmoveable, always abounding in the work of the Lord, for as much as ye know that your labour is not in vain in the Lord" (1 Cor. 15:58).

Title: Ready!

Text: "For I am now ready to be offered, and the time of my departure is at hand. I have fought a good fight, I have finished my course, I have kept the faith: Henceforth there is laid up for me a crown of righteousness, which the Lord, the righteous judge, shall give me at that day: and not to me only, but unto all them also that love his appearing" **(2 Tim. 4:6–8)**.

Scripture Reading: Psalm 121; Romans 1:16

Introduction

In his farewell address to the United States Congress following his recall, General Douglas MacArthur quoted these lines, which have been made all the more immortal because of his dramatic use of them: "Old soldiers never die; they just fade away."

Whereas that may hold true for earthly soldiers, it is not true of soldiers of the cross. There is no "fading away" for those who have faithfully served the Captain of their salvation. Rather, a far more fitting epitaph for them would be the words of Paul as he anticipated his departure from this life (2 Tim. 4:6–8).

I. "I am ready."

Note first that the great apostle made a victorious declaration: "I am now ready to be offered, and the time of my departure is at hand" (2 Tim. 4:6).

"I am ready!" What a victorious, electrifying declaration! Yet it is a statement every member of God's family should be able to make at a moment's notice. It does not mean that every single thing in one's life that should have been done has been done, nor that every milestone of maturity in the faith which should have been passed has been passed. Rather, it describes the believer who has grown daily, steadily, consistently in the faith.

Then, to be ready means also to accept firmly and irrevocably the sovereign will of God. Committed Christians, though they may and should love this earthly life filled with opportunities to serve their Lord, see no conflict in saying, "I am ready" for the moment of homegoing. Certainly dedicated believers want to fill every minute that God allots them on this earth with "sixty seconds' worth of distance run" (Kipling). But still they believe that the "time of departure" for every person is imminent. Thus they see to it that their attitude is one of readiness.

II. "I have fought a good fight."

Then, after Paul made his thrilling declaration, he did a bit of reflecting: "I have fought a good fight, I have finished my course, I have kept the faith" (2 Tim. 4:7).

A. *"I have fought a good fight."* Paul did not mean that he had always fought at his best or that his ministry had always been at "peak performance." The word "good" does not describe the manner of "fighting," but the fight itself. The warfare in which God's people are engaged is a good one because victory is assured. No earthly general, however, convinced though he might be of the ability and proficiency of his troops, could ever say, "Go forth to battle, men; but have no fear, you have already won!" That would be the height of presumption. But this is what the Lord says to his soldiers, for on the cross the battle between good and evil was won for time and eternity. We are simply "attending to the details" here on earth according to the will and purpose of an all-wise and sovereign Lord.

B. *"I have finished my course."* Paul was not saying that he had done perfectly and without flaw every single thing that was included in God's will for his life and ministry. Though he was a giant among God's servants, Paul was still subject to the frailties of humanity, and he would have been the first to admit that fact. But what he was saying was that God has set out a course for his people, and his desire is to leave them here until they finish it. They will not perform it perfectly, but they will finish it.

C. *"I have kept the faith."* By this Paul meant that he had guarded the truth of God's Word. He had not let his emotions run away with his common sense and with the spiritual discernment God had given him to comprehend and to apply God's Word to his life. He had received his orders, and he had not tampered with them. He merely sought to carry them out in accord with the instructions God had given him. He was true to his calling.

III. "A crown of righteousness" awaits.

Finally, Paul stated with thrilling overtones a glorious fact: "Henceforth there is laid up for me a crown of righteousness, which the Lord, the righteous judge, shall give me at that day: and not to me only, but unto all them also that love his appearing" (2 Tim. 4:8). Whose righteousness? Paul's? No! The righteousness of Jesus Christ which had been given to him at the moment of his surrender to God in repentance and faith. Paul would have been the first to say that "in me there is no good thing." He would have agreed fully with the prophet who said, "All we like sheep have gone astray; we have turned every one to his own way; and the LORD hath laid on him the iniquity of us all" (Isa. 53:6).

Thus the "crown" the believer will receive in heaven is the crown of Christ's righteousness, which we will receive not because of our goodness but because of the unmerited grace of almighty God.

Conclusion

We can see that what Paul wrote to young Timothy about his anticipated homegoing is not so high and exalted a testimony that it should be reserved only for such spiritual giants as this illustrious apostle. Rather, Paul was describing the legacy every child of God should leave behind. Thus the believer, like a true soldier of the cross, is retired temporarily from the ranks. Yet, through that person's lingering testimony of faith, he or she continues to serve and praise God in "heavenly retirement."

Title: The Legacy of the Good Shepherd

Text: "The LORD is my shepherd; I shall not want" **(Ps. 23:1)**.

"I am the good shepherd, and know my sheep, and am known of mine. As the Father knoweth me, even so know I the Father: and I lay down my life for the sheep" **(John 10:14–15)**.

Scripture Reading: Psalm 23

Introduction

During our childhood years, we learn to quote this beautiful Shepherd Psalm. Then, in the middle years, when we grapple with the common problems of family and home and of our busy lives in general, we find ourselves returning to this psalm in moments of exasperation and frustration, finding a new sense of comfort and strength. We come to understand more about a Shepherd who will guide us through the difficult times. But then, as the years pass and the autumn and winter of life come upon us, the words of this lovely psalm become more meaningful than ever. Loved ones are taken away. The emptiness, the void that is left behind, is sometimes almost unbearable. Then we find ourselves quoting with an even deeper understanding, "Yea, though I walk through the valley of the shadow of death, I will fear no evil: for thou art with me" (Ps. 23:4).

There is little doubt that David wrote this psalm during the sunset years of his life. He was reflecting, thinking back on the countless ways in which the Lord was a shepherd to him.

I. The key to the psalm is found in the first verse: "The Lord is my shepherd; I shall not want."

Who is the Lord? Let us allow Jesus himself to answer for us with the words he spoke to those who listened to him one day long ago: "I am the good shepherd, and know my sheep, and am known of mine. As the Father knoweth me, even so know I the Father: and I lay down my life for the sheep" (John 10:14–15). Isn't this, in essence, what David was saying? Because the Lord was to him as a true shepherd is to his sheep, he would not be in want for the things his soul needed. When David walked through the dark valley of sorrow, he would not be without grace and strength to carry him through the long and weary days.

Furthermore, not only did the shepherd know his sheep, but the sheep also knew their shepherd; they would not follow a stranger. Jesus said it like this: "He that entereth in by the door is the shepherd of the sheep. To him the porter openeth; and the sheep hear his voice: and he calleth his own sheep by name, and leadeth them out. And when he putteth forth his own sheep, he goeth before them, and the sheep follow him: for they know his voice" (John 10:2–4). Indeed, "The LORD is my shepherd; I shall not want."

II. But that is not all: "He maketh me to lie down in green pastures: he leadeth me beside the still waters. He restoreth my soul" (Ps. 23:2–3).

Here, in essence, is the life story of a child of God. He begins life with the morning and the labor and toil of the day. But then come the resting periods, the times for communion with God, for getting in touch afresh with Heaven. "He maketh me to lie down." Could it be that this is what weariness, and perhaps even illness, is for? In the hustle and bustle of life, we sometimes forget how to relax, to have time to think, to enjoy the God who created us to serve him.

Then David said that God is able to transform the most difficult situation into "a green pasture" and the most violently tossing waves into "still waters." Green is the most restful of all colors and, at the same time, the most hopeful. The "green pasture" requires clouds and showers and then sunshine. Storm clouds are often necessary to bring the rain, but sunshine always follows.

Inevitably God leads us "in the paths of righteousness for his name's sake." By this, David meant "straight paths," paths with direction, leading somewhere. Life, when it is directed by God, is never without direction. It is always moving toward a goal. Likewise, when God calls one of his own to be with him, he is fulfilling his plan and completing his purpose in that person's life.

III. "Yea, though I walk through the valley of the shadow of death, I will fear no evil: for thou art with me; thy rod and thy staff they comfort me" (Ps. 23:4).

Note that the refreshing time beside the still waters and in the green pastures comes before the most difficult part of the journey with the Shepherd—the part that leads "through the valley of the shadow of death." Trials in life—the hard stretches on the road—do not often come in the morning years of our living. Rather, they come in the afternoon, after we have had time to become acquainted with our God as Friend and Lord, as well as Savior. We have had time to walk and talk with him and to hear him tell us that we are his own.

IV. The last two verses of this delightful psalm prepare us for the journey's end.

Here the imagery changes abruptly from that of a shepherd leading his sheep through the wilds of life's wilderness to that of a kind host providing lovingly and generously for his guests. The Good Shepherd has brought his flock home, and the idea of home is made all the more appropriate by the picture of the spread table and the lavish provisions made ready by a most fatherly Host. The sheep are safe in the fold; the enemies are outside, glaring but helpless. Truly one's "cup of joy" overflows at the prospect of our Good Shepherd's thoughtful and loving care for his sheep.

Conclusion

Not only is our Shepherd the one who leads and guides us and goes before us to smooth the rough path and lighten the dark way, but he also sees to the "rear guard." He takes care that we won't be "ambushed" from behind by evil, for his twin courtiers, "goodness" and "mercy," are following us all the days of our lives; and in the end, we are assured of "dwell[ing] in the house of the Lord for ever."

Weddings

Title: What God Hath Joined Together

Minister (as the bride and her father, or the person giving her away, stand before the minister): Dearly beloved, we are now about to hear the wedding vows of ______ (Bride) and ______ (Groom). May I ask who presents the bride?

Thank you, ______. You are to be commended for bringing your lovely daughter, ______, to the altar so that, before God, her marriage might be solemnized.

Let us pray. "Our Father, look down upon us with your smile of approval. May your Son and our Savior, the Lord Jesus Christ, be present to add his blessing. May the Holy Spirit attend and seal these vows in love. In our Savior's holy name we pray. Amen."

When God created man, he saw that it was not good for him to live alone. Thus he prepared for him a helpmeet, a beloved companion. He took not the woman from Adam's head, lest she should rule over him; nor from his feet, lest he should trample upon her; but from his side, that she should be equal with him. He took her from close to his heart, that he should love, cherish, and protect her.

Marriage was honored by the presence of Christ at the marriage feast in Cana of Galilee, and it was used by him as the emblem of that great day when he, the Bridegroom, adorned in all his glory, shall come for his church, whom he has purchased with his blood, and who shall be dressed in the spotless garment of his righteousness.

Marriage was commended by the apostle Paul, who, speaking under the inspiration of the Holy Spirit, declared that it was "honorable in all things." A marriage made in heaven is a union of two lives—two hearts that beat as one—so welded together that they walk together; they work and labor together; they bear each other's burdens; they share each other's joys.

I want to remind you both that you are to cultivate the habit of being congenial, loving, and tenderhearted. You must always receive each other, just as you are, in love, remembering that the vows you are about to take are as binding in adversity as they are in prosperity, and that these vows are to be broken only by death.

I will ask you now to join hands.

Groom's vow

Will you, ______, take ______ as your wedded wife, to live together after God's ordinance in the holy estate of matrimony? Will you promise to love her, comfort, honor, and keep her, and forsaking all others, remain only with her so long as you both shall live?

Answer: I will.

Bride's vow

Will you, ______, take ______ as your wedded husband, to live together after God's ordinance in the holy estate of matrimony? Will you promise to love him, honor and keep him, and forsaking all others, remain only with him until death parts you?

Answer: I will.

Vows to each other and ring ceremony

Minister addresses the couple together: Do you solemnly promise before God and in the presence of these witnesses to receive each other as husband and wife, pledging yourselves to love each other, and to make every reasonable exertion to promote each other's happiness until the union into which you are now entering is dissolved by death? (*They answer together:* "We do.")

I will ask you then to seal the vows which you have just made by the giving and receiving of rings. The circle is the emblem of eternity, and gold is the symbol of all that is pure and holy. Our prayer is that your love and your happiness will be as unending as these rings. They are tokens of remembrance, and in the years to come they will remind you of this happy hour. My prayer is that you will be as happy then as you are now.

Minister directs groom to place ring on the bride's finger, and then to repeat after him: With this ring I thee wed. I take thee, ______, to have and to hold, to love and to cherish, in sickness and in health, for richer or for poorer, for better or for worse, so long as we both shall live.

Minister directs bride to place ring on the groom's finger, and then to repeat after him: With this ring I thee wed. I take thee, ______, to have and to hold, to love and to cherish, in sickness and in health, for richer or for poorer, for better or for worse, so long as we both shall live.

Then the couple declare in unison: "Whither thou goest, I will go; and where thou lodgest, I will lodge; thy people shall be my people, and thy God, my God."

Minister: And now, according to the laws of this great country in which we live, and by my authority as a minister of the gospel, I pronounce you husband and wife, in the name of the Father, and of the Son, and of the Holy Spirit. What God has joined together, let not man put asunder.

Let us pray: "Our Father, send your blessings upon these your servants, this man and this woman whom we bless in your name. Help them always to keep the vows and the covenant they have made with each other today. May their lives be crowned always with the benediction of your love and grace, and may they share your peace, which passes all human understanding. Fill them with your grace. Through Jesus Christ our Lord we pray. Amen."

Recessional

Title: Marriage Ceremony

Procedure: Organ prelude
Lighting of the candles
Seating of the grandmothers and mothers
Processional
Solo (Father remains with bride before the minister)

Minister: There is no human relationship as high, as holy, or as beautifully rewarding as that which exists between a Christian man and woman in the bonds of marriage. Marriage is one of three carryovers from the garden of Eden. The Sabbath day of rest for the body, mind, and soul and the dignity of labor are the other two. Thus marriage is an experience that God intended to bear the primeval blessings of Eden upon it.

______ and ______ share already the highest possible relationship with each other because of their faith in Jesus Christ. They are a handmaiden and a servant of the Lord. When they are united in holy matrimony, the light of God in their lives will be fused into one light; the music in their hearts will blend into one beautiful symphony of love.

Who gives this woman to be married to this man? *(Father answers, "Her mother and I," and places the bride's hand on the groom's arm. He returns to be seated beside the bride's mother. Bride, groom, minister, maid of honor, and best man ascend steps to platform.)*

Minister: (Reads 1 Corinthians 13.) After God had made Adam in the garden of Eden and observed this solitary man attending to the task in the garden which had been assigned to him, God said: "It is not good that man should be alone; I will make an help meet for him." Then Moses, in recording the incomparably beautiful account of the creation, stated: "And the LORD God caused a deep sleep to fall upon Adam, and he slept: and he took one of his ribs, and closed up the flesh . . . thereof: and the rib, which the LORD God had taken from man, made he a woman, and brought her unto the man. And Adam said, This is now bone of my bones, and flesh of my flesh: she shall be called Woman, because she was taken out of Man. Therefore shall a man leave his father and his mother, and shall cleave unto his wife: and they shall be one flesh."

So we can see that the beautiful institution of marriage is a product of the garden of Eden. And further, the sanctity of the marriage vows was guarded in one of the Ten Commandments God gave to Moses and to the world on Mount Sinai.

I think it is far beyond the level of coincidence that our Lord's first miracle was performed not in the hallowed and sacred precincts of the temple or in a synagogue, but on the joyous occasion of a marriage feast in Cana of Galilee.

Thus we are assembled here to witness the pledges which ______ and ______ are now to make to each other, and to assure them of our prayers for their happiness and joy in this new and sacred relationship. What marriage was in the garden of Eden, it can be now. Marriage, as a holy institution, has never fallen. It is that part of paradise which still continues to soothe troubles and comfort sorrows. ______ and ______, it can, and will, be this to you, if you will guard it with your tender care, with your attention to little things, and most of all, with your patience and understanding toward each other and your continued devotion to God. These things I charge you here, in God's name, to remember.

The marriage vows

(Pastor addresses the groom.)

______, wilt thou have ______ to be thy wedded wife, to live together after God's ordinance in the holy estate of matrimony? Wilt thou love her, comfort her, honor and keep her, in sickness and in health, and forsaking all others, keep thee only unto her so long as you both shall live? (*Groom answers,* "I will.")

With what token do you wish to seal this vow? (*Groom takes ring from best man and, handing it to pastor, says,* "With this ring.")

The ring is a symbol of eternity. In its perfect roundness, it has neither beginning nor ending. It is made of gold, which is a symbol of purity. Our prayer for you, ______ and ______, is that your love for each other may be symbolized in these rings, which you shall wear as tokens of your love for each other—that it will be lasting and will grow deeper and deeper as long as you both shall live on this earth.

______, will you take this ring and place it on ______'s finger as a token of the vow you have made to her and before God and all of us—and hold it in place as you repeat to her the following vow:

"I, ______, take thee, ______, to be my wedded wife; to have and to hold from this day forward; for better, for worse; for richer, for poorer; in sickness and in health; to love and to cherish till death do us part. With this ring I thee wed, and with all my worldly goods I thee endow. In the name of the Father, and of the Son, and of the Holy Spirit."

(Pastor then addresses the bride.)

______, wilt thou have ______ to be thy wedded husband, to live together after God's ordinance in the holy estate of matrimony? And wilt thou love, honor, and keep him, in sickness and in health, and forsaking all others, keep thyself only unto him, so long as you both shall live? (Bride answers, "I will.")

With what token do you wish to seal this vow? (*Bride takes ring from maid of honor and says,* "With this ring," *and gives it to the pastor.*)

Then, ______, as ______ has placed on your finger this token of his love for you, will you do likewise for him? Now, will you hold the ring, as you repeat after me the following vow: "I, ______, take thee, ______, to be my wedded husband; to have and to hold from this day forward; for better, for worse; for richer, for poorer; in sickness and in health; to love and to cherish till death do us part. With this ring I thee wed, and with all my worldly goods I thee endow. In the name of the Father, and of the Son, and of the Holy Spirit."

"And Ruth said, Entreat me not to leave thee, or to return from following after thee: for whither thou goest, I will go: and where thou lodgest, I will lodge: thy people shall be my people, and thy God my God. Where thou diest, will I die, and there will I be buried. The LORD do so to me, and more also, if ought but death part thee and me."

For as much as ______ and ______ have consented together in holy wedlock, and have witnessed this committal before God and all of us, having pledged and sealed their vows with these rings, I pronounce that they are husband and wife, in the name of the Father, and of the Son, and of the Holy Spirit. What God hath joined together, let not man put asunder.

Prayer

God the Father, the Son, and the Holy Spirit bless, preserve, and keep you; the Lord graciously and with his favor look upon you and fill you with all spiritual blessings and love. May he cause his face to shine upon you and grant you the peace that passes all understanding. In the name of his Son and our Savior, the Lord Jesus Christ, we pray. Amen.

Recessional

Sentence Sermonettes

Love is the golden thread that ties the heart of all the world.

The visions of God are seen only through the lens of a pure heart.

The conversion of a soul is the miracle of a moment.

Love does not dominate; love cultivates.

Those who bring sunshine to the lives of others cannot keep it from themselves.

Never hold on to the failures of yesterday.

Worrying is like a rocking chair. It will give you something to do but will get you nowhere.

Fear can be used as a springboard.

You cannot get anywhere today if you are still mired down in yesterday. Defeat must be faced, but it need not be final.

Lord, help me remember that nothing is going to happen to me today that you and I can't handle.

Tomorrows are only todays waiting to happen.

Happy hearts make happy homes.

Patience endures today while it works for tomorrow.

A house is built by human hands; a home is built by human hearts.

God helps the helpless.

When you are hemmed in, the only way to look is up.

We must nourish the roots of faith before we can expect the fruits of action. The impossible is often the untried.

Worry never robs tomorrow of its sorrow; it only robs today of its strength. So live that those who know the most about you have the greatest confidence in you.

The Lord gives us talents, but we have to develop them.

There is no better exercise for the heart than reaching down and lifting someone up.

God's assurance gives us endurance.

God does not love you because you are important. You are important because God loves you.

Don't be weakened by too much weekend!

Good friends are sunshine on a rainy day.

We can measure our likeness to Christ by our sensitivity to the pain, trials, and loneliness of others.

Prayer is the key, but faith turns the knob that opens the door to heaven's blessings.

Walking with the Lord is the best exercise to build a healthy soul.

Success is not measured by heights attained but by obstacles overcome. Every day brings a child of God one day nearer home.

The safest hiding place in the world is in the center of God's will.

There is only one place in which success comes before work—that is in the dictionary.

You can never do a kindness too soon, because you never know when it will be too late.

God still speaks to those who take time to listen.

Kind words never die.

You will live as long as God lives—either in heaven or in hell.

Fear and faith travel the river of life, but only faith should be allowed to anchor.

Worry pulls tomorrow's clouds over today's sunshine.

When God gives burdens, he also gives shoulders.

He is no fool who gives away that which he cannot keep in order to gain that which he cannot lose.

When troubles assail you, turn to God—he will never fail you.

When praying, do you give instructions or report for duty?

Formula for living: Keep your chin up and your knees down.

There is nothing so kingly as kindness and nothing so royal as truth.

Love is the master key that opens the gates of happiness.

A world without a Sabbath would be like a man without a smile or like a summer without flowers.

Regret and fear are twin thieves who would rob us of today.

God in our heart can mean the difference between despair and victory.

The true measure of love is loving without measure.

Subject Index

Index of Scripture Texts